WITHDRAWN

Active Living in Older Adulthood:

Principles and Practices of Activity Programs

Active Living in Older Adulthood:

Principles and Practices of Activity Programs

by

Barbara A. Hawkins

Venture Publishing, Inc.

Production Manager: Richard Yocum
Manuscript Editing: Richard Yocum, George Lauer
Cover Painting by Barbara A. Hawkins

Library of Congress Catalogue Card Number: 2009935591
ISBN-10: 1-892132-86-9
ISBN-13: 978-1-892132-86-4

Dedication

to my husband Bob

and our children—Priscilla and Garrett—

for all their love and support throughout my career

Table of Contents

Preface

This revised edition of *Therapeutic Activity Intervention with the Elderly: Foundations and Practices* (1996) has undergone significant changes from the original text. The book has been broadened beyond a narrow focus on therapeutic intervention to embrace principles and practices that are applicable to professional activity specialists who serve older adults in a wide range of settings. This revised edition has been renamed, *Active Living in Older Adulthood: Principles and Practices of Activity Programs* to reflect the broader focus.

In the years that have ensued since 1996, the older adult population has changed considerably, as also has the field of gerontology. The population has grown in size and diversity as it will continue to do throughout the first half of the 21st century. With the aging of the 76 million Baby Boomers, activity specialists should be ready for significant changes in the needs, interests, and preferences of the older adults to whom they provide services. Health, longevity, educational achievement, and other cohort attributes will challenge the activity specialist to be more nimble in their expectations of what their clientele will want and what might be unpalatable to them. Other forces such as medical advances, technological change, and an unsteady political economy will undoubtedly challenge the ways that activity services are available, sought, and delivered. These are unpredictable and shifting times.

This text has attempted to reach the following important goals:

1. To update and add important foundations, principles, and practices that pertain to human aging including the needs, problems, and concerns of older adults in the early 21st century. We are at the beginning of the long Baby Boom generation's entry into older adulthood. This large and diverse cohort will continue to re-shape and challenge the activity service sector throughout the first half of the century. They bring to the table a much different profile than previous generations of older adults. This book addresses these differences and expectations.

2. To redirect attention away from labels, myths, and stereotypes that engender unfavorable views toward older adults (such as the term "elderly"). This goal is intended to promote more fluid and positive views of people as they age across the adult life course. Viewing people as people first and a specific age as secondary may be far more palatable and appropriate for Baby Boomers, especially those who see themselves as vibrant, vital, and living life to its fullest through engagement in active life-styles across their entire lives.

3. To incorporate current concepts and terms that promote active aging such as successful aging, aging well, productive aging, and health aging. These concepts again reflect positive approaches to living long, active, and healthy lives no matter what age a person is. They shift the focus away from disablement and infirmity and toward a more positive view of what it means to grow older.

4. To celebrate the role and importance of activities throughout one's entire life course. It is well understood that having a passion, that is an activity that centers and focuses the meaning of one's daily life, is a central key to a long, healthy, and happy life.

Activity professionals from a wide array of disciplines should find this book to be useful in providing basic information about older adults as well as practical details in the design and delivery of activity programs and services for older adults. Also course instructors will find the book applicable for general courses for certified nurse assistants and day activity providers to college courses in recreation therapy, occupational therapy, and other related therapies (e.g., music, art, dance, horticulture, animal-assisted therapies).

In preparing this edition I have been helped enormously by the many students who have taken my courses as well as the many doctoral students who have work on research projects with me. I thank each of them for their enthusiasm, ideas, and challenging discussions for it is my students who keep my curiosity alive and well. I am also grateful to Venture Publishing for their patience regarding this complete revision of the original text. Readers should pay particular attention to the renaming of this text. My intent is to encourage all who read and use this text to acknowledge the richness in living long and living well. It is truly a gift of our time in history that we have the opportunity to experience tremendous longevity filled with active living through engagement our most passionate activities. With that thought in mind, I am off to the ski slope in winter and the high mountain hike in the summer.

Live long and age well,

Barbara A. Hawkins
2009

The people in this photo are "living well and aging well" because they have passions that they pursue each and every day of their lives. High in the Rocky Mountains are, left to right: Emily Bartsen (64), Gene Bartsen (55), Jacquie Hawkins (55), Marilyn Repsher Raymond (67), Doc (4 years old and top dog for long hikes), Jody Enderlin (50), and Dave Raymond (70). Photo by James R. Hawkins.

UNIT I

Introduction

The provision of activity programs and services for older adults requires a thorough knowledge of the needs and desires of individuals who are aging into the later stages of the life course. This textbook provides principles and practices for understanding human aging within an adult development framework. The reader will develop a basic understanding about the needs of older adults who engage in activity programs for health, well-being, and rehabilitation purposes. The book introduces professionals, caregivers, and students to basic concepts dealing with the normal aging process, age-related functional changes, illnesses, and diseases that are responsive to activities as an appropriate and productive health promotion and/or treatment strategy. In this text, the focus is on a conceptualization of activity that is broad and encompassing.

Unit I chapters introduce the reader to trends and issues related with population aging. Of particular interest are issues related to increasing diversity within an aging population, national health trends that affect the health of older persons, and changes within the human services professions that impact access to activity programs and services by aging adults. Chapter 1 begins with background information about the older adult population including demographic characteristics and population diversity considerations. Chapter 2 provides an overview of the need for health care services by older adults. The chapter distinguishes between chronic and acute diseases as well as describes the process of impairment that leads to disablement among older persons. The chapter concludes with information pertaining to current trends that are influencing health care and activity intervention to older adults.

• CHAPTER 1 •

Population Aging:
Impact and Implications of Demographic Change

Learning Objectives

1. Describe general characteristics of the older adult population including distribution by age, gender, marital status, educational status, living arrangements, income, employment status, poverty, and geographic location.

2. Discuss common misconceptions and stereotypes concerning older adults.

3. Discuss age discrimination and the impact of ageism on the health and well-being of older adults.

4. Describe the growth trends in the size of the aging and older adult population.

5. Identify demographic trends as they relate to gender, ethnicity, and health conditions.

6. Define the term feminization of poverty and describe how it relates to older women.

7. Explain the differences among biological age, functional age, and chronological age.

8. Discuss how demographic characteristics, age differences, national health trends, and diversity affect the utilization of formal services.

9. Describe factors that influence life expectancy and life span.

Key Terms

- Age Cohort
- Ageism
- Aging Well
- Baby Boomers
- Blue Zones
- Biological Age
- Centenarians
- Chronological Age
- Dependency Ratio
- Diversity
- Feminization of Poverty
- Functional Age
- Heterogeneity
- Life Expectancy
- Life Span
- Livable Communities
- Older Adults
- Population Aging
- Super Centenarians

Introduction

This chapter will familiarize the reader with one of the most dramatic demographic changes in the history of the United States and the world–*population aging*. Population aging is a term that is used to describe the continued and sustained increase in the proportion of the population that is represented by older adults. The older population is a diverse group in many ways and understanding this diversity is a focus of the chapter. Current trends are described in relation to racial and ethnic diversity, geographic distribution, living arrangements, income, poverty, employment, and education. Further, diversity is discussed in terms of differences across age cohorts, gender, race, and ethnicity. Frequently, older adults are referred to as a single demographic group; however, there are distinct differences in the functional abilities of aging adults within different age groups, which also will be highlighted in the chapter.

The chapter concludes with a discussion of factors that contribute positively to individual aging. *Blue Zones* and *aging well* are contemporary ideas that hold important implications for personal well-being in older adulthood. *Ageism* is a practice that undermines the possibilities for living long, living well, and having a high quality of life in older adulthood. The chapter closes with a brief discussion of the future of population aging and the delivery of services to older adults. A number of difficult challenges and important issues will face American society in the near future as healthcare and social service systems prepare to serve an ever enlarging older adult population.

Population Aging

One of the most important trends of the 21st century is the aging of the population. The ever increasing number of older adults in our population has become the focus of media attention, healthcare industry, and academic community. The United States and countries around the globe are experiencing population aging. According to an Administration on Aging Fact Sheet (Challenges of Global Aging, October, 12, 2007), population aging on a global scale is a result of dramatic decreases in diseases and mortality, as well as improved nutrition, medical advancements, science, technology, and education. Population aging affects all people worldwide. Population aging is unprecedented in the history of the human race and it is a trend that will continue to challenge policymakers, healthcare systems, families, communities, and individuals throughout the first half of the 21st century. On a global scale,

the number of people age 60 and older in 2000 was estimated to be 605 million and that number is projected to be nearly 2 billion by the year 2050. By that time there will be more older people than children 14 years old and younger (Kinsella & Velkoff, 2001). No longer are we in awe over the number of *centenarians* (people who live to be 100) who live in our communities; we now have a new group at which to marvel: the super centenarians (people who live to be 110 years or older). The aging of society goes beyond our national borders, which is an important point to keep in mind while considering national demographic change. What happens at a global level will likely also impact national policies and services for the growing older population within the United States.

The Federal Interagency Forum on Aging-Related Statistics (2008) reported that there were 37 million U.S. citizens who were 65 years of age or older in 2006. As the Baby Boomers continue to age into this group, growth of the over-65 population will increase even faster through 2030 and continue its rapid pace as the Baby Boomers move into the age 85 year old age group. The first of the Baby Boomers will turn 65 in 2011. Just imagine the profound nature of this change in the nation's demographic profile. In 1900, the percentage of people over age 65 in the population was 4.1%; by 2006, this percentage had grown to 12.6%. By the year 2030, the number of people age 65 and older is projected to be more than 71.5 million people, or 20% of the total U.S. population (Federal Interagency Forum on Aging-Related Statistics, 2008).

The increase in the older population since 1900 has been truly remarkable. Even more impressive is the growth in the subgroup of people age 85 and older. By 2006, there were 5.3 million people 85+ and this number is projected to be 8.9 million by 2030 (Administration on Aging, 2006). The 85+ segment of the older population has increased at the highest rate. Even more remarkable is the increasing number of adults who are 100 years and older. There is little doubt that Americans are living longer in greater numbers than ever before in the history of the country, and this trend extends to the rest of the world. Population aging is not just a domestic trend, it is a global event.

Life expectancy, or the average number of years a person can expect to live "at a given age if death rates were to remain constant," has improved dramatically, thus contributing substantially to the growth of the over-65 age group (Federal Interagency Forum on Aging-Related Statistics, 2008, p. 24). Several factors account for improvements in life expectancy, including lower infant and maternal mortality rates, medical advances that produced vaccines or cures for infectious diseases, access to nutrition, treatment for chronic conditions, lifestyle changes, and improved public sanitation (Federal Interagency Forum on Aging-Related Statistics, 2008). According to the Federal Interagency Forum on Aging-Related Statistics, survival to age 65 years will add an extra 18.7 years; for people who reach 85, men can expect to live, on average, another 6.1 years and women an additional 7.2 years.

It is important to understand the difference between *life expectancy* and *life span*. *Life span* is considered to be the maximum potential age that the human species could survive to if all diseases and illnesses were avoided or successfully treated. At present, the life span for humans is thought to be around 124 years (Tepper, 2004). It may be possible in the near future extend human life span through genetic engineering, which could even more dramatically impact population aging nationally and worldwide.

Life expectancy is different across racial groups and gender. On average, women outlive men (Federal Interagency Forum on Aging-Related Statistics, 2008). Women born in 1990 can expect to live to near 79 years of age. The life expectancy for men born in 1990, however, is approximately 72 years of age. In the over age 65 population in 2006, there are about 21.6 women to every 15.7 men (Administration on Aging, 2006). Life expectancy is greater for whites and Asian Americans compared with Hispanics and African Americans (Satarino, 2006). It also varies across geographic regions. Taken as a whole, population aging is an undeniable and startling trend that is here to stay throughout the 21st century.

Heterogeneity and Diversity in the Older Population

Although the older population is often stereotyped as a homogeneous group, nothing could be further from the truth. Older adults vary greatly from one another in their biopsychosocial functioning. Functional abilities and personality vary from one older adult to another more than differences among individuals in any other younger age group. One way to think about this characteristic of older adulthood is to recognize that, as we age, we become more individualized, more like our "true selves." As babies, we are more like each other, or homogenous, but as older adults, we are more individualized. Thus, the older adult population is the most heterogeneous group in the population.

Based on wide ranging differences in the older population, many service providers and researchers tend to divide the older population into subgroups based on chronological age. The 65 to 74 years of age group is frequently referred to as the *young old*. The *old old* are those who fall into the group who are 75 to 84 years of age. Individuals who are above 85 years of age are referred to as the *oldest old*. The United States Census Bureau (Population Division, released May 1, 2008) estimated that as of July 2007, older adults between the ages of 75 and 84 accounted for 11.5 million people or 4.7% of the nation's population. Citizens over the age of 85, number 4.9 million or 2.02% of the population.

Even more remarkable is the sustained growth in the number of centenarians. As predicted by the Administration on Aging (2005), by 2025, one in 26 persons in the U.S. can expect to survive to 100 years of age. This figure represents a dramatic change from the year 2000 when one in 500 people could expect to live to be 100. According to mid-range population projections by the U.S. Census Bureau (Day, 1996), by 2010 it is expected that there will be 131,000 centenarians in the U.S., which is a figure that is expected to increase to 324,000 by 2030. In 2000, there were more than 50,000 people who had reached 100 years of age or older.

The over-85 age group is in greatest need of health and social services. As the size of this group continues to grow, they will become a primary concern to healthcare providers and social policy planners. Professionals who work with the oldest old understand that longevity and good health do not always go hand-in-hand. Chronic conditions lead to functional limitations and disability with much greater frequency in the oldest old population. Based on a three-year average for national data from 2004–2006 (Federal Interagency Forum on Aging-Related Statistics, 2008), for all people 65 and older, 74% self-rated their health as very good to excellent. Among different subgroups of older adults, the percentages who rated health as good to excellent were as follows: 60.3% of African Americans, 62.9% of Hispanics or Latino, and 76.3% of whites. Also, on positive note, the majority or 67.4% of the oldest old (85 and older) assessed their health status as good to excellent. In addition to health concerns, the oldest old are also more likely to live alone and in poverty, more likely to be female, and less likely to be married.

The presence of pronounced differences in the ability to function independently among older adults has created the need for a method to define the age of an individual in more useful ways than just in years or chronologically. *Functional* age is determined by the individual's ability to carry out activities of daily living (ADLs) and live independently. Consequently, an individual whose chronological age is 80 may be functionally younger than someone who is age 65, if he or she requires less assistance with basic activities. It is also possible that a person who is 65 years of age could have limitations in functioning that are far greater than an optimally healthy 85 year old. Disparities in functional age are largely due to lifestyle and health factors that the individual exhibited throughout his or her entire life. We might think of functional age as the accumulated effects of either a healthy or unhealthy lifestyle. One's lifestyle throughout adulthood is a major contributor to the presence or absence of chronic disease, which has a significant impact on the ability of one to continue to function independently in older adulthood. Among Medicare enrollees age 65 and older in 2005, 57.9% reported no limitations in Instrumental Activities of Daily Living (IADLs) and Activities of Daily Living (ADLs) while 12.3% experienced limitations in IADLs only, 18.3% had limitations in 1 to 2 ADLs, and 7.2% experience limitations with 3 to 6 ADLs (Federal Interagency Forum on Aging-Related Statistics, 2008). Chronic conditions that are common among adult over age 65 include "hypertension (48%), diagnosed arthritis (47%), all types of heart disease (29%), any cancer (20%), diabetes (16%), and sinusitis (14%)" (AoA, 2008b, p. 2). Chapters 2 and 5 further discuss the importance of functional age in regard to the healthcare and health status of older adults.

Race and Ethnic Differences

According to U.S. Census Bureau statistical estimates for 2006, about 8.4% of all citizens over age 65 were African Americans, 6.4% were Hispanic or Latino, and 3.2% were Asians (U.S. Census Bureau, Population Division, 2008). The over 65 group, as a whole, was estimated by the Census Bureau to reach nearly 13% of the total population in 2007. As the first half of the 21st century unfolds, the proportion of the older population that is composed of African Americans, Hispanics, and Asian Americans is expected to grow at a faster rate than that of the white Americans.

The *double jeopardy hypothesis* has been used to describe differences in the patterns of health and longevity that are attributable to race and ethnicity (Satarino, 2006). This hypothesis suggests that additional challenges and burdens for specific racial and ethnic subgroups have a greater impact on the health, survival, and well-being of individuals in these groups. Whether or not an empirical test of the double jeopardy hypothesis can substantiate claims based on it, the fact remains that differences between older adults with different racial/ethnic backgrounds do exist. Character-

istics of older adults in each major racial/ethnic group in the population are briefly highlighted in the sections that follow.

African Americans

Among African Americans, 29.7% are under age 18 while only 8.4% are over age 65. The young outnumber the old among African Americans in a greater percentage than in the general population primarily because of the higher fertility of African American women and higher mortality at mid-life (Hooyman & Kiyak, 2008). In general, the life expectancy at birth for African Americans is a little over five years less than it is for white Americans (Federal Interagency Forum on Aging-Related Statistics, 2008).

Black women live longer than black men but they tend to have a lower socioeconomic status (Grundy, 2006). Traditionally, the older black woman was viewed as the backbone of the family. Grandmothers frequently assumed at least partial child care responsibilities. Older black women were more likely than women of other ethnic groups to have children, grandchildren, and other relatives living in their homes (Yee, 1990). In 2006, 23% of older African American women lived with husbands while 41% lived alone and another 34% lived with other relatives (Administration on Aging, 2008). According to 2006 data, 50% of older African Americans live in the following states: New York, Florida, California, Georgia, Illinois, North Carolina, and Virginia. In addition, the poverty rate among older African Americans (23%) was more than twice the rate compared with all older adults (9.4%) in 2006; however, this rate is dramatically lower than it was in 1965 (65%).

Disabled older African Americans are more likely to be cared for at home as opposed to an institution. Older African Americans are institutionalized at only 50% to 75% the rate of older white Americans. A number of factors have been suggested that may influence this trend including limited financial resources, lowered access to care, cultural values, and the tendency for extended families to live together in the African American community (Belgrave, Wykle, & Choi, 1993).

Older African American women's status in the family may be due to their history of independence (Yee, 1990). Since times of slavery, black women have worked independently and not relied on the resources of men. Older black women today have long histories of employment, which frequently began in childhood as field workers and domestic servants (Allen & Chin-Sang, 1990). Unfortunately, history of employment is not enough to help older black women stay out of poverty. Median income for African American women ($11,062) continued to lag behind all older women

($13,603) in 2006 (AoA, 2008a). Allen and Chin-Sang (1990) described the status of older women as that of "quadruple jeopardy" (old, poor, female, and of minority status).

Native Americans

Older Native Americans represent 8% of their population according to U.S. Census Bureau estimates for 2007. Youth under age 18 remain a significantly larger (27%) segment than adults over age 65 in the Native American population. Native Americans are continually improving in their life expectancy, which is due to better living conditions and overall better health. Native American life expectancy is difficult to ascertain due to inaccurate information that is reported on death certificates (Hayward & Heron, 1999). Median age among Native Americans was reported to 31 years compared with that of 36.6 years for the population as a whole (U.S. Census Bureau estimates for 2007, released May 2008). Many older Native Americans, however, can expect to live into their 80s and 90s as community service delivery systems continue to improve for this population group.

Using U.S. Census Bureau Estimates for 2007, approximately 53.52% of all older Native Americans live in the following states: Alaska (3.53%), Arizona (10.12%), California (14.4%), New Mexico (6.34%), Oklahoma (9.73%), Texas (5.81%), and Washington (3.59%). Native Americans mostly live in rural areas without much access to healthcare and social services. The older Native American has traditionally been viewed as a revered member of the extended family. Older adults provide spiritual guidance and share cultural heritage to younger family members. It is also common for older women to assume major child care responsibilities (Yee, 1990).

The lack of resources and social support provided to this population is evident through widespread poverty, discrimination, inadequate education, poor housing, isolation, and unemployment (Hooyman & Kiyak, 2008; Indian Health Service, 2006). Older Native Americans are more susceptible to a number of healthcare problems due to reduced access to healthcare; however, initiatives in recent years have attempted to address problems associated with health (Indian Health Service). Alcoholism is a major health concern for many older Native Americans, as are tuberculosis, diabetes, homicide, and suicide. Rates for these health problems are significantly higher than other Americans. Greater support through better healthcare, opportunities for education, and employment is needed to improve the quality of life for older Native Americans (Yee, 1990).

Asian Americans

The Asian, Hawaiian, and Pacific Island older population in the United States is extremely diverse in terms of both cultural heritage and language. In fact, they represent at least 30 different cultures and more than 100 languages (Hooyman & Kiyak, 2008). This population group represents diverse histories, values, religions, lifestyles, and immigration patterns. Some members of the population, such as Japanese Americans, have become highly Westernized. Other members who have immigrated more recently, however, still hold more traditional values. It is nearly impossible to provide a single characterization for this group, and it would be inappropriate to do so.

Most Asian American cultures traditionally place a strong emphasis on prescribed gender roles. Older adults within these cultures are highly valued and respected for their wisdom and cultural knowledge. Interdependence between generations is strong. As younger Asian American become accustomed to Western culture, however, they have begun to lose their reverence toward the older adults in their population group and the lines between gender roles also have become less well-defined. Consequently, today generational differences are growing more apparent.

In 2007, older Asian Americans represented 9.24% of all Asian Americans and 3.73% of the total population of adults over age 65 (U.S. Census Bureau estimate, May 2008). Most older Asian Americans (60%) live in California, New York, and Hawaii (AoA, 2008b). Texas, Washington, New Jersey, and Illinois also have significant numbers of older Asian American residents. More older Asian American men (84%) were living with their wives in 2007 than were women (47%) living with their spouses.

Among older Asian Americans, median household income in 2006 was $43,035, which is higher than the median income for all older persons ($39,649). The median income of older Asian women, however, lags behind the median income of all older women ($13,603). Poverty is higher among older Asian Americans, 12% compared to general older population rate of 9.4% in 2006 (AoA, 2008b).

Hispanic Americans

Older Hispanic or Latino Americans are the fastest growing group in the U.S. and is projected to be larger than the older African American group by 2030 (Hooyman & Kiyak, 2008). In spite of sharing a common language, the older Hispanic American population is culturally diverse. Mexican Americans represent the largest percentage (50%) of the Hispanic American population followed by South/Central Americans (23%), Cuban Americans (16%), and Puerto Rican Americans (11%). Many Mexican Americans are not first generation residents of the United States and have become acculturated to the "American way of life." Intergenerational differences are evident in this population, as younger Mexican Americans are especially likely to reject traditional roles. Other Hispanic Americans, such as those originating from Puerto Rico and Cuba, are mostly first generation Americans and may be more accepting of traditional roles (Yee, 1990). In general, the Hispanic population is youthful due to higher fertility and lower life expectancy. This population group also experiences higher than average rates of poverty and health problems.

Traditional Hispanic culture has held strong with approximately one-third of older Hispanics speaking only their native language (Hooyman & Kiyak, 2008). Older adults in this group tend to have very low educational attainment, many having never graduated high school. It follows, therefore, that earning capacity is also lower in this group. Access to services may be difficult for those who entered the country illegally, which is another problem specific to this population. Lower education, socioeconomic status, and employment may culminate in greater risk for health problems, including depression, by older Hispanics (Angel, 2003; Chiriboga, Black, Aranda, & Markides, 2002; Munet-Vilaro, 2004).

The extended family is an important element in Hispanic culture (Hooyman & Kiyak, 2008). There is a strong sense of family within Hispanic groups wherein older adults are more likely to live with family, to turn to family when in need, and to hold strong beliefs about the importance of family. Intergenerational exchange is common with older adults providing valuable cultural history and assistance with child rearing. Within the Hispanic older population there is a higher ratio of men to women than in the white older population (Hooyman & Kiyak). Aging is accepted in the Hispanic culture and elders are viewed with respect (Yee, 1990).

Older Hispanic Americans represent less than 5% of the population due to high fertility rates, immigration, and repatriation of some older and middle age adults (Hooyman & Kiyak, 2008). The majority of older Hispanic Americans live in urban areas. The population is especially concentrated in the southwestern states (Mexican Americans), Florida (Cuban Americans), and eastern states (Puerto Ricans).

Geographic Distribution, Livable Communities, and Living Arrangements

The number of people over the age of 65 represents approximately 13% of the total U.S. population, but this percentage varies considerably across states (Federal Interagency Forum on Aging-Related Statistics, 2008). Based on 2006 population estimates, in eight states the percentage of the population over age 65 was 14% or greater: Florida (16.8%), West Virginia (15.3%), Pennsylvania (15.2%), Iowa (14.6%) North Dakota (14.6%), Maine (14.6%, South Dakota (14.2%), and Hawaii (14.0%). The following states had the lowest proportion of their population who were age 65 and older: Alaska (6.8%), Utah (8.8%), Georgia (9.7%), and Texas (9.9%). Based on U.S. Census Bureau estimates for 2007 (release May 2008), the majority of older adults live in the most heavily populated states: California, Florida, New York, Texas, Pennsylvania, Illinois, Ohio, and Michigan. California leads all states with over 4.5 million older adults. Nearly 3.5 million older adults reside in Florida, the state with the highest percentage of older adults. Pennsylvania, Texas, and New York each claim over 2 million older persons.

The majority of older adults live in metropolitan areas but the density of elders in rural areas is higher than it is in urban areas. More than 75% of adults age 65 and older live in urban and suburban areas (Hooyman & Kiyak, 2008). Older adults of ethnic minority groups are especially likely to live in inner cities. Unfortunately, the older adults in the central cities carry the greatest burden in terms of poverty, crime, lack of adequate housing, and other social problems.

Older adults in rural areas, especially African Americans, generally have lower incomes and poorer health than do those in urban areas. This situation may be due, in part, to reduced availability of social services, healthcare services, and transportation. Rural older adults are less likely to live close to their children. Evidence does indicate, however, that older adults in small communities interact more frequently with friends and neighbors (Hooyman & Kiyak, 2008).

In spite of the popular myth that portrays older adults as lonely people abandoned by their children, the majority of older adults have regular contact with family members and social networks. For older adults who are not in the geographic proximity of their children, interaction with friends and neighbors is important. Increasingly, older adults maintain regular contact through letters, phone calls, email, and visits to their children (Hooyman & Kiyak, 2008).

Recent national initiatives have focused on creating communities and living environments that are responsive to the needs of aging and older adults. Based on the results from a number of surveys, community development officials and leaders are increasing their attention to creating *livable communities*. Livable communities reflect urban designs that enhance transportation, housing, neighborhood services, and access to social and health-related services (AARP, 2003; Hooyman & Kiyak, 2008). Safety, affordability, access, and opportunities are important to older adults, especially those who are frail. The livable community concept is consistent with creating environments that fit the full range of capabilities and needs of older adults, thus enhancing community-based living rather than institutionalization for old, older, and the oldest adults in the community.

The majority of older adult men (78%) live with a spouse or other family members; however, this percentage varies comparing older men (78%) with older women (59%) (Federal Interagency Forum on Aging-Related Statistics, 2008). Considerably more older women (39%) than men (19%) live alone. Among women over the age of 75, 50% live alone. These statistics also vary by race/ethnicity wherein older Asian men and women have exceptionally high rates of living with a spouse or other family relative. Older persons living alone are more likely to be in poverty, thus increasing their vulnerability to a lower health status. Less than 5% of adults age 65 and older reside in nursing homes or other long-term care facilities; however, the percentage of the population who live in nursing homes increases dramatically with age. For example, among people age 85 and older, 15.4% reside in nursing facilities (AoA, 2008b; Federal Interagency Forum on Aging-Related Statistics, 2008; Hooyman & Kiyak, 2008).

Income, Poverty, and Employment

In 2006, 35% of older people were in the combined "low income" plus "poverty" group (Federal Interagency Forum on Aging-Related Statistics, 2008). A steady decline in the number of older adults living in poverty accounts for the lower rate of 9% for this group. This rate is a dramatic improvement from 1959 when 35% of older adults lived below the poverty level. Its important to note that poverty rates vary by age, gender, and race/ethnicity. In general, older women are more

vulnerable to living in poverty. Older Hispanics and African Americans are also more likely to be living in poverty compared with whites.

About 36% of older adults are in the middle income group and over time, the high income group has grown to represent 29% by 2006. Median income has steadily improved over time; in 2006, median household income was $27,798. Although the income of older adults is lower than the national population median, it is important to keep in mind that older adults frequently have fewer expenses than younger adults (Crispell & Frey, 1993). Mortgages, child care, college tuition, and similar major expenses typically are not present in older households. As the need for healthcare increases in these households, however, lower income may certainly become a problem for many older adults. The average older adult head of household spends 13% of annual expenditures on health including services, medications, insurance, and supplies (Federal Interagency Forum on Aging-Related Statistics, 2008). More recently, issues related to a crisis in costs for healthcare tend to be driven by increasing numbers of individuals who do not have health insurance (Hooyman & Kiyak, 2008). Because older adults have the highest expenditures for healthcare, more than four times that the expenditures of people under age 65, there is concern that government sponsored health programs will not be able to keep up with the needs of an enlarging older adult population.

Poverty affects older adults slightly more than it does younger adults. Approximately 9% of the older population is living under the poverty level set by the federal government (Federal Interagency Forum on Aging-Related Statistics, 2008). Poverty rates should be viewed with skepticism, however, since they do not indicate the high percentage of older adults whose incomes are only slightly higher than the poverty level. These individuals are often referred to as the *near poor*.

Feminization of Poverty

Women continue to represent one of poorest population groups in the U.S. (Hooyman & Kiyak, 2008). The *feminization of poverty* is a term used by sociologists to describe how society locks many women into poverty through social institutions and economic structure. Single women who are over age 85, frail, and living in rural areas, and especially women of color, are at high risk of living in poverty. Most older women have not worked enough consecutive years or with high enough pay to receive substantial pension or social security benefits (Heinz, Lewis & Hounsell, 2006; Herd, 2006). Many women are not eligible for any pension benefits of their own. Widow's benefits from most pensions typically are reduced to as much as 50% of what the husband was receiving (Hartman, 1990).

Employment

Approximately 14% of older adults were involved in the labor force in 2004 (Hooyman & Kiyak, 2008). Labor force participation among adults over age 65 varies by race with about 16.2% of whites, 14% of African Americans, 17% of Asian Americans, and 16% of Hispanics participating in work in 2007 (Rix, 2008). While labor force participation has increased from 2005 to 2007, in 2008 an increase in unemployment began. In 2007, nearly 63% of people in the 55 to 64 age group were in the labor force, only 28.3% of people ranging in age from 65 to 69 were working. This rate drops to around 16% in the 70 to 74 age group and to 6.4% in the 75+ age group. The number of older adults who are seeking employment, however, is expected to continue to increase (Hooyman & Kiyak, 2008). Factors contributing to this trend include smaller numbers of younger workers coupled with healthier older cohorts, many of whom are accustomed to careers and lifestyle expectations that depend upon discretionary income.

There also are barriers to employment for older adults. Some older adults who have been in lifelong careers may have lower skills at job hunting. Others may feel that in a high-tech age, their skills are not as competitive, especially those skills associated with information technology (Hooyman & Kiyak, 2008). Finally, age discrimination continues to be a problem for many older workers. Many employers and younger workers believe that older workers are (a) less productive than their younger counterparts, (b) unable to change, (c) slow to perform and train, and (d) diminished in their abilities to perform mentally and physically (Hardy, 2006; Hayslip & Panek, 1993). Subtle forms of discrimination also exist; for example, negative stereotypes about older people and issues of attractiveness. In order to combat age discrimination, the Age Discrimination Employment Act was passed in 1967. This legislation includes measures that restrict employers from (a) failing to hire a person because of age, (b) discharging an employee because of age, or (c) discriminating in pay because of age. While this legislation may have helped to reduce "blatant forms of age discrimination," it has been "less effective in promoting the hiring of older workers" (Hooyman & Kiyak, 2008, p. 490).

Education

Educational attainment has steadily improved among older adults and education plays an important role in the health and well-being of older adults (Federal Interagency Forum on Aging-Related Statistics, 2008). Among adults age 65 and older in 2007, more than 75% had earned a high school degree and 19% had attained a bachelor's degree or more. The gap between men and women in educational attainment continues to shrink. Differences among racial and ethnic groups, however, persist. Among older adult whites, 81% had obtained high school degrees as compared with 72% of older Asians, 58% of older African Americans, and 42% of older Hispanics (Federal Interagency Forum on Aging-Related Statistics).

Adult education programs provide important opportunities for older adults to continue to grow intellectually. Many colleges and universities offer reduced or free tuition. Local recreation and park departments offer adult education programs. Lifelong Learning Institutes (LLI) are opening up around the country. One of the most widely known and well-established programs that promotes lifelong learning is Elderhostel. Elderhostel programs where adults engage in learning adventures take place all around the world on campuses and affiliated locations (Hooyman & Kiyak, 2008). Adult education is likely to continue to grow as the Baby Boomers enter the senior marketplace seeking lifelong learning and adventure.

The Future of an Aging Population

There are many exciting trends and new initiatives that will influence future generations of older adults in the U.S. In this section, the following are briefly presented: *Blue Zones*, *aging well*, and *ageism*. Each of these topics represents important issues and emerging ideas for those professionals who will provide services to the aging adult population. The section is completed with a continued discussion of the implications associated with *population aging*.

Blue Zones

Some very interesting and exciting work has been done by Dan Buettner regarding concentrated groups of people who live exceptionally long and healthy lives (Buettner, 2008). Buettner's research was supported by the National Geographic Society and the National Institutes of Health as well as a number of other organizations and groups. His focus was to identify areas of the world where people live longer and in better health, and he named these concentrations *Blue Zones*. Not surprising, Buettner identified the island of Sardinia off the coast of Italy as having more male centenarians than any other location on earth. Another Blue Zone described by Buettner was a Seventh Day Adventist community in Loma Linda, California. People in this community were found to have a life expectancy of 9–11 years longer than that of the American population in general. Okinawans were another Blue Zone population where the survival rate to age 100 is three times that of Americans. People in Okinawa tend to live about seven years longer, on average, than Americans, and in considerably better health. Buettner's quest in studying Blue Zones was to identify the major factors that contribute to long and healthy life in the Blue Zone populations. The factors that he identified include living in an environment that encourages a lifestyle that keeps people physically active, especially with everyday tasks, rather than a focus on what Buettner called "pumping iron." Another interesting finding was that people who ate nuts on a regular basis tended to live 2–3 years longer than others who did not. An important factor that has been long recognized as important is that of having a central purpose or reason to get up each day and to be engaged in life (Poon, Johnson, Davey, Dawson, Sigler & Martin, 2000). People who have a reason and motivation for living will live longer and healthier lives in general. Finally, who we spend our time with will also help us to live longer and in better health. Surrounding one's self with people who eat well, live active and engaged lives, and hold values and beliefs that are congruous with healthy lifestyles are important factors for personal well-being in older adulthood.

Aging Well

Buettner's work on Blue Zones is reflective of the steady growth in the public's interest in how to promote well-being and health in older adulthood (Hawkins, 2003). Length and quality of healthy life is also noted as a primary health goal in the United States (cf. Healthy People 2010). While significant gains have been made in addressing national health objectives, the interactive relationships among environmental factors, individual behaviors, and mediators (such as age, gender, education, culture) as determinants of health are not fully understood from a scientific perspective. There is growing interest in studying healthy aging including such ideas as successful aging, productive aging, and aging well. Research on these concepts has been motivated by the

quest to identify and produce useful information regarding the promotion of optimal health and well-being in the older adult population; a worthy goal given the projected increases in the older adult cohorts throughout the first half of the 21st century.

Aging well is a concept that is of particular relevance in the provision of activities and services to older adults (Hawkins, 2003). *Aging well* seeks to counterbalance negative images of older people as a burden to society with newer images that convey positive expectations for living long and living well. The ideal of *aging well*, as opposed to experiencing a difficult old age, reflects a number of similarities with the concept of *successful aging* (Rowe & Kahn, 1997; Valliant, 2002). Both concepts–*aging well* and *successful aging*, reject one-sided, negative, ageist ideas about older people (Scharf, van der Meer, Thissen & Melchiorre, 2003).

Aging well is understood as a blend of personal behavior in interaction with the social and physical environment, and individual life circumstances (Hawkins, 2003). To achieve a quality of life that produces individual *aging well*, in part, requires a vision of the desirable future (Fontane, 1996) as well as the ability to exercise personal adaptation when circumstances are less than optimal (Johnson, 1995). For individuals, *aging well* depends upon personal, social, and physical environments that provide supports and opportunities to reach that vision. In a robust sense, *aging well* conveys a positive person-centered process in which the promotion and protection of physical, mental, social, economic, and daily lifestyles are paramount for achieving a sense of satisfaction, health, dignity, and well-being in old age. To age well is dependent upon both the ability to adapt to aging coupled with living in a positive environment. Five areas of individual functioning are affected: physical health and functional status, mental efficacy, social resources and social support, daily life activity, and material security.

Social and health services, public policies, and local agencies increasingly are responding to the call for an aging well society. This trend can be seen both within the United States as well as around the world in international initiatives. It is most important to keep in mind that older adulthood is not a sentence to illness, disability, destitution, or deterioration; rather, it is a call to live long and live well.

Ageism

As the well-known scholar and advocate of the longevity revolution Robert Butler so aptly noted, we, in the United States, suffer from ageism. That is, we fear getting old and we hold untrue and unreasonable stereotypes about older people (Butler, 2008). "The young dread aging, and the old envy youth" according to Butler (pp. 43–44). Butler noted that ageism in the U.S. is probably the result of an unreasonable worship of youth. "Denial [of growing older] is a close cousin of ageism; in effect, it eliminates aging from consciousness" (Butler, p. 44).

It is curious that we spend so much effort in avoiding aging. If it were possible to alter the nation's consciousness toward the idea of aging well, of a good old age, would we succeed in replacing ageism with a profound respect for living long, healthy, and wise lives? These are questions and ideas that interest today's social gerontologists, those scholars and scientists who study the social and psychological aspects of growing older in today's world. These are the questions that the reader will continue to grapple with while reading this text and having discussions with fellow students and teachers. If we all knew that we could age well, would we embrace our adult years with zest and yearning for a very long life?

Future Implications of Population Aging

The rate of growth of the older population has serious implications for healthcare and social policy planners. A greater number of older people will rely on Medicare, Social Security, and other social programs without a substantial increase in the number of working taxpayers. The *dependency ratio* is a useful numerical indicator for understanding the economic burden associated with the number of workers who are supporting the number of nonworkers in a population (Moody, 2006). This ratio can be calculated for that part of the population that is represented by children, and it can be calculated for the number of older adults who are not in the workforce. As the first half of the 21st century unfolds, the dependency ratio for older adults may grow considerably while it will continue to decline for children due to the trend in smaller family sizes. While there will be more older adults who are dependent upon wage earners' contributions to programs like Social Security, growth in the overall dependency ratio that includes both children and older adults will probably not be excessive (Moody). In any event, as this ratio changes in response to a larger older adult population, government will need to address issues associated with entitlement to social benefits and programs by older people. Specifically, decisions will need to be made regarding whether or not all older adults will continue to be entitled to the current level of support from Social Security, Medicare, and other social programs regardless of their ability pay for services. Innovative ways to continue to finance these programs will become the work of public policymakers and policy analysts.

The prospect of greater demands on the healthcare system by older adults in the future is real but not a given. At the heart of the matter are issues related to identifying who are the most vulnerable members of the older adult population as well as who are the least advantaged (Moody, 2006). Chronic conditions requiring expensive, long-term care are projected to continue as the primary health concern of older adults. A growing debate already exists regarding the medical profession's obligation to preserve life and initiate treatment versus the right to refuse care and die peacefully without unwanted medical intervention when the quality of life becomes so low that the patient wishes to no longer live. What obligations does society have in providing medical care to the dying elderly? Because the majority of medical expenses are incurred during the last month of life, should the healthcare system initiate and government pay for expensive treatments that will only prolong the inevitability of death for only a short time? Should these economic questions drive healthcare policy? These are tough questions that currently face society and the professionals who serve older adults.

The need for long-term care for the oldest old is a topic of growing interest as the size of this population segment expands. Traditionally, daughters, wives, and daughters-in-law have provided the majority of care to disabled older adults. Lower fertility rates, high rates of divorce, and increased female commitment to lifetime careers may reduce the number of women who are able to take on primary care responsibilities. In spite of this trend, family members and older patients will probably continue to prefer home-based care as opposed to institutionalization. The demand for home-based care services and increased levels of reimbursement from Medicare and private insurance companies are likely to grow.

The growing ethnic diversity among the older population can be expected to influence the delivery of services to older adults. Service providers will need to understand cultural difference to better serve a diverse older population. Traditional methods of reaching older adults to inform them of services will not be as effective for all members of this diverse population. New links between service providers and key members of ethnic communities with access to their older population must be established and trust must be gained. The healthcare and social service systems need to be viewed not as symbols of majority bureaucracy, but as systems open to all members of the population.

Future implications for the healthcare system are not all negative. The current population of older adults is better educated, has greater access to healthcare services, and is more aware of living a healthy lifestyle than any previous generation. These are trends that will continue as the population ages. It is reasonable to expect that the majority of older adults can and will continue to remain independent throughout their lives. The percentage of the younger old requiring formal services may potentially decrease in the next few decades.

A growing healthy older population also will demand expanded service delivery. Adult education, community recreation, arts, exercise, and travel programs are examples of the types of services that new cohorts of older adults may as they move through their retirement years. These older adults also may seek opportunities to remain productive members of the community through volunteer work, part-time employment, or even whole new careers. Much enthusiasm for new opportunities and a healthy life in older adulthood comes with the aging of the Baby Boomers. The story of "population aging in the United States" is just beginning to unfold.

Summary

The older population grew remarkably during the 20th century and will continue to do so throughout the first half of the 21st century. This growth can be attributed to lifestyle and medical changes that have greatly increased the life expectancy of the average adult. The population of older adults is concentrated in those states with the largest populations. However, the states with the largest percentages of older adults are located in the rural south and midwest. Most older adults live with a spouse or other family member, although the number of older adults living alone has grown recently. The majority of older adults are not in poverty and they can support themselves without financial assistance. Single women, some ethnic groups, and the oldest old are more likely to be living in poverty than other older adults. The majority of older adults are not employed full-time and their income typically comes from one or more of the following sources: Social Security, pension funds, part-time work, and earnings from assets. The current population of older adults is more highly educated than any generation to come before them. Most have completed a high school education. Older adults generally are productive and independent individuals who do not utilize formal services and seek assistance with care until very late in life.

The older population can be characterized as diverse. Differences in functional ability are evident in the older population more so than any other age group. There are marked demographic differences between age groups within the older population. Gerontologists frequently refer to older adults as the young old, the old, and the oldest old; however, there are still problems associated with these categories. Chronological age is not always a good indicator of functional ability. It may be more useful to refer to an individual's functional age rather than his or her chronological age. Diversity also is evident in terms of clear and distinct cultural differences between ethnic groups. It may be helpful for service providers to understand various cultures and to subsequently offer services with a sensitivity to cultural differences.

As the older population continues to expand in the first half of the 21st century, service providers will be faced with a variety of economic challenges and ethical decisions regarding the types of services that can be offered to older adults who are frail, disabled, or vulnerable. The number of healthy older adults also will continue to grow in size, thus increasing the demand for leisure, travel, and other related services. As activity professionals, it will be our challenge and opportunity to be responsive to population aging while being innovative in ways to meet the needs of aging individuals.

Comprehension Questions

The reader can check for comprehension of the material presented in this chapter by answering the following questions:

1. Select three general characteristics of the older population and describe them in regard to recent trends.

2. Name two common misconceptions about older adults.

3. What does the *feminization of poverty* mean and describe the impact that this phenomena has on older women.

4. What impact does cultural diversity have on the older adult population, now and into the future?

5. What did Buettner discover about older adults who live in "Blue Zones?"

6. What does *aging well* mean and what areas of individual functioning are affected by an aging well lifestyle?

7. What does the future hold for older persons regarding health and social service programs?

References

Administration on Aging. (2007). Fact Sheet—Challenges of Global Aging. Washington, DC: U.S. Department of Health and Human Services, Administration on Aging.

Administration on Aging. (2008a). Fact Sheet—A Statistical Profile of Black Older Americans Aged 65+. Washington, DC: U.S. Department of Health and Human Services, Administration on Aging.

Administration on Aging. (2008b). Fact Sheet—A Statistical Profile of Asian Older Americans Aged 65+. Washington, DC: U.S. Department of Health and Human Services, Administration on Aging.

Administration on Aging. (2005). Profile of Older Americans: 2005. Washington, DC: U.S. Department of Health and Human Services, Administration on Aging.

Allen, K. R. & Chin-Sang. V. (1990). A lifetime of work: The context and meaning of leisure for aging black women. *The Gerontologist, 30*(6), 734–740.

American Association of Retired Persons & Administration on Aging. (1992). A profile of older Americans. Washington, DC: Author.

Angel, J. (2003). Devolution and the social welfare of elderly immigrants: Who will bear the burden? *Public Administration Review, 63*, 79–89.

Aronson, J. (1992). Women's sense of responsibility for the care of old people: "But who else is going to do it?" *Gender and Society, 6*(1), 8–29.

Belgrave, L. L., Wykle, M. L. & Choi, J. M. (1993). Health, double jeopardy, and culture: The use of institutionalization by African-Americans. *The Gerontologist, 33*(3), 379–385.

Buettner, D. (2008). The Blue Zone–Lessons for living longer from the people who've live the longest._ Washington, DC: National Geographic Society.

Butler, R. N. (2008). *The longevity revolution: The benefits and challenges of living a long life*. New York, NY: PublicAffairs, Perseus Books Group.

Chiriboga, D., Black, S., Aranda, M. & Markides, K. (2002). Stress and depressive symptoms among Mexican American elderly. *Journals of Gerontology, 57B*, P559–P568.

Crispell, D. & Frey, W. H. (1993, March). American maturity. *American Demographics*, 31–42.

Day, J. C. (1996). Population projections of the United States by age, sex, race, and Hispanic origin: 1995 to 2050. Washington, DC: U.S. Bureau of the Census, Current Population Reports, P25-1130, U.S. Government Printing Office.

Ferrini, A. F. & Ferrini, R. L. (2008). *Health in the later years*. (4th ed.). Boston, MA: McGraw Hill.

Federal Interagency Forum on Aging-Related Statistics. (2008, March). Older Americans 2008: Key Indicators of Well-Being. Federal Interagency Forum on Aging-Related Statistics. Washington, DC: U.S. Government Printing Office.

Fontane, P. E. (1996). Exercise, fitness, and feeling well. *American Behavioral Scientist, 39*(3), 288–305.

Gibson, M. J., Freiman, M., Gregory, S., Kassner, E., Kochera, A., Mullen, F., Pandya, S., Redfoot, D. L., Straight, A. & Wright, B. (2003, April). Beyond 50.03: A report to the nation on independent living and disability. Washington, DC: AARP Public Policy Institute.

Grundy, E. (2006). Chapter 11. Gender and healthy aging. In Z. Yi, E. M. Crimmins, Y. Carriere, and J-M. Robine, Longer life and healthy aging (pp. 173–199). Dordrecht, The Netherlands: Springer.

Hardy, M. (2006). Older workers. In R. Binstock and L. George (Eds.), *Handbook of aging and the social sciences* (6th ed.). New York, NY: Academic Press.

Hartman, A. (1990). Aging as a feminist issue. Social Work, 35(5), 387–388.

Hawkins, B. A. (2003). Aging well: Construct genesis and ideology. Global Aging Initiative Newsletter, Spring 2003. Bloomington, IN: Indiana University Center on Aging and Aged.

Hayslip, B. H. & Panek, P. E. (1993). *Adult development and aging*. New York, NY: HarperCollins College Publishers.

Hayward, M. D. & Heron, M. (1999). Racial inequality in active life among adult Americans. *Demography, 36*(1), 77–91.

Heinz, T., Lewis, J. & Hounsell, C. (2006). Women and pensions: An overview. Washington, DC: Women's Institute for a Secure Retirement (WISER).

Herd, P. (2006). Crediting care or marriage: Reforming Social Security family benefits. *Journals of Gerontology, 61B*, S24–S34.

Hooyman, N. R. & Kiyak, H. A. (2008). *Social gerontology: A multidisciplinary perspective*. (8th ed.). Boston, MA: Allyn and Bacon.

Indian Health Service. (2006, January). HIS Fact Sheets—Indian Health Disparities. Retrieved June 13, 2008, from http://www.info.ihs.gov/Disparities.asp.

Johnson, T. F. (1995). Aging well in contemporary society: Introduction. *American Behavioral Scientist, 39*(2), 120–130.

Kinsella, K. & Velkoff, V. A. (2001). An aging world: 2001. Washington, DC: U.S. Census Bureau, Series P95/01-1, Government Printing Office.

Moody, H. R. (2006). *Aging – Concepts and controversies* (5th ed.). Thousand Oaks, CA: Pine Forge Press.

Munet-Vilaro, F. (2004). Health promotion for older adults: Latino elders. Seattle, WA: University of Washington, Northwest Geriatric Education Center.

Neugarten, B. L. & Neugarten, D. A. (1991). Policy issues in an aging society. In M. Storandt and G. R. VandenBos (Eds.), *The adult years: Continuity and change* (147–167). Washington, DC: American Psychological Association.

Pol, L. G., May, M. G. & Hartranft, F. R. (1992, August). Eight stages of aging. American Demographics, 54–57.

Poon, L. W., Johnson, M. A., Davey, A., Dawson, D. V., Sigler, I. C. & Martin, P. (2000). Psychological predictors of survival among centenarians. In P. Martin, A. Rott, B. Hagberg & K. Morgan (Eds.), *Centenarians*. New York, NY: Springer.

Renzetti, C. M., & Curran, D. J. (1992). *Women, men and society.* Boston, MA: Allyn and Bacon.

Rix, S. (2008, May). Fact Sheet—Update on the aged 55+ worker: 2007. Washington, DC: AARP Public Policy Institute, Fact Sheet # 142.

Rowe, J. W. & Kahn, R. L. (1997). The Forum—Successful aging. *The Gerontologist, 37*(4), 433–440.

Satariano, W. A. (2006). Epidemiology of aging: An ecological approach. Sudbury, MA: Jones and Bartlett Publishers.

Scharf, T., van der Meer, M., Thissen, F., & Melchiorre, M. G. (2003/4). Contextualising adult wellbeing in Europe: Report on sociocultural differences in ESAW nations. University of Wales, Bangor, UK: ESAW Project Report.

Sommers, T. (1985). Caregiving: A woman's issue. *Generations, 10*(11), 9–13.

Yee, B. W. K. (1990). Gender and family issues in minority groups. *Generations, 15,* 39–42.

Tepper, L. M. (2004). Chapter 1—Aging in America. In L. M. Tepper, and T. M. Cassidy (Eds.), *Multidisciplinary perspectives on aging,* (3–23) New York, NY: Springer.

U.S. Department of Health and Human Services. (2000). *Healthy people 2010: Understanding and improving health* (2nd ed.). Washington, DC: U.S. Government Printing Office, Stock Number 017-001-00-550-9.

Vaillant, G. E. (2002). *Aging well: Surprising guideposts to a happier life from the landmark study of adult development.* Boston, MA: Little, Brown, and Co.

Additional Resources

A premiere source of information and data on trends on the aging population can be found at www.aging-stats.gov. This website contains statistical files, reports, and PowerPoint presentations produced by the Federal Interagency Forum on Aging-Related Statistics. The mission of the forum is to provide high quality data through collaborative and cooperative efforts among Federal agencies. The Forum can be contacted at the following email address: agingforum@cdc.gov, or telephone (301) 458-4460.

• CHAPTER 2 •

Overview of Healthcare and the Elderly

Learning Objectives

1. Describe functional status and healthcare needs as they pertain to older adults.

2. Define the concepts of *pathology, frailty, impairment, functional limitation*, and *disability*.

3. Describe the difference between chronic and acute disease.

4. Discuss how functional impairment and the need for healthcare are served in different settings.

5. Explain the difference between *preventive intervention* and *rehabilitative intervention*.

6. Discuss the importance of personal control, adaption, and independence in the provision of intervention services to older persons.

7. Discuss current trends that are influencing healthcare and intervention services to older adults.

Key Terms

- Acute Disease
- Adult Day Services (ADS)
- Adults Day Health Service (ADHS)
- Chronic Disease
- Comorbidity
- Compression of Morbidity
- Continuing Care Retirement Community
- Disability
- Frailty
- Frail Older Adults
- Functional Competence
- Functional Limitation
- Health Promotion
- Home-Bound
- Impairment
- In-Home Care
- Lifecare Community
- Long-term Care
- Morbidity
- Nursing Home Care
- Pathology
- Prevention
- Quality of Life
- Rehabilitation
- Skilled Nursing Facility

Introduction

This chapter provides an overview of the need for health-care services by older adults based on the processes by which health conditions and frailty lead to impairment, functional limitation, and disability. Disability is described as an outcome that is not only related to level of impairment and functional limitation, but also as influenced by the social and physical environment in which the individual lives. Functional status of older persons is described as it relates to pathology, impairment, functional limitation, and disability. Each of these terms are defined and distinguished from one another.

Functional impairment and disability underlie the need for health-related services that are delivered on the basis of three levels of care (e.g., inpatient, outpatient, in-home) and across a variety of service settings. Services may be provided in institutions on an inpatient basis or for individuals who are not institutionalized within community-based or home-bound service settings by a range of service providers. Many service options exist on a continuum including adult day programs, in-home services, continuing care retirement centers, nursing homes, rehabilitation centers, and acute care hospitals. These service settings are described in this chapter.

Overviews of prevention and rehabilitation intervention services are provided in the chapter. Prevention strategies may be primary, secondary, or tertiary depending upon the functional status of the individual. Prevention services are aimed at preserving optimal health and well-being of the individual. When functional limitations and disability are present, rehabilitative interventions often are directed toward restoring or preserving the individual's health and functional capabilities at the highest possible level. Prevention and rehabilitation form the basis for therapeutic activity intervention with older adults.

Health and Functional Status

It is well-known that older persons are far greater consumers of healthcare services than any other age group (Federal Interagency Forum on Aging-Related Statistics, 2008). It is also of concern that healthcare costs vary by demographic characteristics and that among the oldest of the old, they are the highest. The Federal Interagency Form on Aging-Related Statistics reported that in 2004 healthcare costs were about $13,101 for whites compared with $14,989 for African Americans and $11,962 for Hispanic older adults. Also, lower income individuals tended to have higher costs than

white older adults taken as a whole. It is widely known that as age increases so does the incidence of frailty (Stoukides, Holzer, Ritzau & Burbank, 2006). Frail older adults consume more healthcare services than any other population group. Later in this chapter frailty and frail older adults are explored in greater detail.

As one would expect, healthcare costs also vary by the presence of chronic conditions. Comparing 2004 to 1992, healthcare costs had changed somewhat in the percentage spent for different types of services or goods (Federal Interagency Forum on Aging-Related Statistics, 2008). For example, in 1992, 32% of expenditures were for physician and outpatient hospital goods and services compared with 35% in 2004. There were decreases in the percentage of expenditures comparing the two years for inpatient hospital care (from 32% to 25%) and long-term care facility care (from 20% to 14%). Both of these declines reflect the trend toward more outpatient and home care. Also noteworthy was the increase from 4% to 15% in healthcare costs attributable to prescription drugs, thus reflecting the dramatic rise in the cost for medications among older adults. While healthcare has steadily improved, it remains a serious concern due to continually rising costs. The highest portion of healthcare expenditures among the older adult population is for hospital care, physician services, and long-term care (e.g., placement in a nursing home).

Among older adults, the configuration of healthcare services varies by age with healthcare costs significantly higher in the oldest age groups. For example, long-term care costs average $7,057 among adults age 85 and older (Federal Interagency Forum on Aging-Related Statistics, 2008). Among adults aged 65–74, however, average long-term care costs were only $431. One factor that has affected long-term care expenditures is the trend toward alternative care in one's home or new alternatives of care such as assisted living. There was a steady decline in the rate of nursing home admissions from 1985 through 2004 and this pattern is expected to continue. According to 2004 data reported by the Federal Interagency Forum, the rate of nursing home placement was less than 1% among older adults ages 65–74, 3.6% among people ages 75–84, and 13.9% among people age 85 and older. Over the years, the nursing home population changed to reflect older, frail, and more seriously impaired persons. As a result, the percentage of the older adult population who reside in nursing facilities increases with each age group. Despite a decline in the rate of long-term care or nursing home placement, and because the population size has steadily increased over time, the overall size of the population that resides in nursing homes has increased. The steady growth in the oldest of old cohorts who use a disproportionately higher share of health resources will continue to exacerbate the high cost of healthcare in the U.S. Estimating growth in the healthcare expenditures attributable to the older adult population is a challenging and daunting task (Goldman et al., 2004). One of the greatest challenges stems from the fact that people are living longer and in healthier states, thus compressing morbidity to a shorter time frame in late life. The compression of morbidity is the shortening of the amount of time that older adults live with disease, functional limitations, or disability. While the pattern of healthcare expenditures is high among the older adult cohorts, there is uncertainty about how future expenditures will unfold with new cohorts of Baby Boomers entering their older adult life stages.

Of equal importance, however, is the dramatic increase in alternative sources for healthcare services. The movement toward community-based care is intended to support older adults to maintain their independence. Avoiding institutionalization is the preference among older adults. Some of the more recent service alternatives include in-home care, assisted-living residential options, and other community-based housing with special healthcare services. In large measure, the kinds of services needed for frail or impaired adults are related to activities of daily life such as housekeeping, laundry services, and assistance with medications. As age increases, the need for help with activities like dressing, bathing, eating, and other activities of daily living (ADLs) becomes more common.

As previously noted in this chapter, the likelihood that older persons will need healthcare services and products increases with age. In spite of positive gains in life expectancy, the quality of very old age is still problematic for a significant number of people. As a consequence, the prevalence of impairment and disability continue to rise among certain groups of older persons such as (a) those who have lower socioeconomic status, (b) persons with less education, (c) ethnic minorities, or (d) very old females.

Another reason for the increase in disability and impairment among older adults is the steady increase in chronic diseases in the overall population. Chronic diseases are those that result from unhealthy lifestyles or behaviors that produce long-term impairment and disability. Chronic diseases are rarely, if ever, cured. The most common and costly of chronic conditions are heart disease, stroke, cancer, and diabetes (Federal Interagency Forum on Aging-Related Statistics, 2008). The quality of life is compromised considerably in the

presence of chronic disease, especially when two or more conditions are present. Recalling the discussion about *aging well* in Chapter 1, the presence of chronic disease undermines the possibility for *aging well* and can lead to a difficult old age if access to healthcare services and products is difficult or the individual lives in an unsupportive environment. According to the Federal Interagency Forum on Aging-Related Statistics, "Many chronic conditions can be prevented or modified with behavioral interventions" (2008, p. 27). The following chronic conditions are leading causes of death among the older population: heart disease, cancer, stroke, chronic respiratory diseases, influenza/pneumonia, and diabetes (Tepper, 2004). Two chronic conditions that are particularly problematic for older persons are heart disease and circulatory conditions (Ferrini & Ferrini, 2008; Pope & Tarlove, 1991). On the other hand, acute diseases, such as influenza, can be managed through immunization, nutrition, improved public health practices, and sanitation. Acute diseases do not pose the same degree of pressure on the healthcare system and healthcare dollar as do chronic conditions. Because older persons experience functional limitations due to impairment from health problems, it is useful to examine the process by which pathological conditions result in impairment and disability.

Functional Status and Disability

It is not uncommon for adults, as they age, to experience the onset of chronic health conditions, many of which may result in some level of impairment or functional limitation. Through the use of geriatric assessment, professionals and caregivers can evaluate the overall impact of a chronic condition on the individual's ability to perform daily tasks and activities, thus making it possible to determine the degree of impaired function. Not all chronic health conditions, however, will result in serious impairment or disability. Disability is a status that places the individual's functional limitations within a social and physical context that undermines independence. The degree of environmental demand and support that are present will determine whether the individual is seen as disabled or nondisabled. Individual functional competence, or ability of the person to perform everyday tasks and activities, is related, in part, to the degree of impairment, which may or may not result in disablement. Independent functioning is dependent upon environment factors (Hiatt, 2004). This is one reason why it is important for older adults to live in environments that are socially designed to support changes due to growing older with a chronic health condition, as well as environments that are physically designed to support functional losses that are present at higher levels in the older adult population.

It is important to recognize that whether a person can and does "perform a socially expected activity depends not simply on the characteristics of the person but also on the larger context of social and physical environments" (Hiatt, 2004; Pope & Tarlove, 1991, pp. 5–6). A complex process involving individual functional capabilities in interaction with the social and physical environment results in disablement (Hiatt). Four basic concepts can be used to better understand the process by which a health condition impairs the individual and when impairment becomes a disability. These concepts are: *pathology, impairment, functional limitation*, and *disability* (Ferrini & Ferrini, 2008; Pope & Tarlove, 1991).

Pathology is a direct result of changes in the tissues and cells of the human organism that are produced by injury, infection, disease, birth defects, or other agents (Ferrini & Ferrini, 2008; Pope & Tarlove, 1991). Pathological states in older persons involve either acute or chronic conditions. An acute condition is a bacterial or viral infection that results in immediate illness, which is usually confined to a set time period and then it resolves. Distinguishing characteristics of acute illnesses are: abrupt onset, usually caused by a virus or bacteria, treatable with medication and sometimes surgery, short term in duration, and usually involving a low cost for the cure (Ferrini & Ferrini, 2008). Common acute illnesses among the elderly stem from respiratory (e.g., common cold, influenza, pneumonia) and gastrointestinal infections (e.g., indigestion, abdominal pain, heartburn, gas, diarrhea, constipation).

Chronic illnesses, on the other hand, are characterized by (a) progressive onset, (b) multiple causes usually associated with lifestyle behaviors and environmental carcinogens, (c) the expectation that they will last a lifetime, (d) the fact that they often are irreversible even with treatment, (e) a progressive outlook, and (f) management through medical care and rehabilitation (Ferrini & Ferrini). Some of the common chronic conditions experienced by older persons include cardiovascular disease (e.g., high blood pressure, heart disease, stroke), cancer, respiratory disease, sensory disorders (e.g., hearing, vision), skeletal disorders (e.g., arthritis, osteoporosis), and diabetes. Most older adults will have one or more chronic health condition (Tepper, 2004). Chronic conditions affect quality of life and are long-term with the unlikelihood of a cure; however, they can be prevented or modified with changes in lifestyle behaviors (e.g., increased physical activity, healthy eating, and reduced health risk behavior). Often, serious chronic conditions may threaten the ability of the older adult to remain living independently in the community (Federal Interagency Forum on Aging-Related Statistics, 2008). The aforementioned and other acute and chronic conditions are covered in greater detail in Chapters 5 and 6.

Impairment occurs when there is a loss in mental or physical function that results from the specific condition of an organ or organ system. Impairment may be caused by more than one type of health problem and all health conditions will result in some level of impairment. Depending upon the degree of impairment, individuals may experience limitations in their ability to function independently with normal activities and tasks in everyday life such as being able to get up and out of bed, or being able to move about their homes doing typical activities like bathing and dressing (Ferrini & Ferrini, 2008; Pope & Tarlove, 1991).

A *functional limitation* describes the effects that are present in the person's capacity to perform as a whole, as well as independently or with some assistance. For example, older persons have functional limitations when they are unable to open kitchen cabinets and remove items for use. Older adults respond to impairment on an individual basis. For example, the same condition that is experienced by two individuals may manifest as different levels of impairment. One individual may experience limitations in overall functional capacity while the other may not, based upon other factors that are influencing the capacity of the individual. The manner in which all bodily systems work together to accomplish the demands of a specific activity has an impact upon the functional competence of the individual. For example, if two individuals experience the same degree of loss in visual acuity but one individual has been an active athlete throughout his or her life while the other has been sedentary resulting in low overall physical fitness, then it would not be unexpected that the first individual might experience less impairment in balance, spatial orientation, and mobility compared with the second person. As can be seen by this example, it is likely that impairments will result in functional limitations differentially across individuals. It is also true that "all functional limitations result from impairments" (Pope & Tarlove, 1991, p. 80).

Disability is an outcome that moves pathology, impairment, and functional limitation beyond of the individual into the context of the social and physical environment. Disability is a limitation in the individual's ability to perform roles and tasks that are socially defined and expected. "These roles and tasks are organized in spheres of life activities such as those of the family or other interpersonal relations; work, employment, and other economic pursuits; and education, recreation, and self-care" (Pope & Tarlove, 1991, pp. 81–82). It is important to recognize that not all impairments or functional limitations result in disability. Disability is largely determined by social and cultural expectations as well as environmental demands. Other factors that also contribute to disablement include (a) the individual's definition of the situation and reactions, which at times compound the limitations; (b) the definition of the situation by others, and their reactions and expectations—especially those who are significant in the lives of the person with the disabling condition (e.g., family members, friends and associates, employers and coworkers, and organizations and professions that provide services and benefits); and (c) characteristics of the environment and the degree to which it is free from, or encumbered with, physical and sociocultural barriers" (Pope & Tarlove, pp. 81–82).

A variety of determinants increase the risk of experiencing health-related conditions that can lead to impairment and disability. Primary sources of risk are (a) biological characteristics of the individual such as genetic predisposition to disease; (b) features of the social and physical environment such as unsanitary or unsafe living conditions; and (c) lifestyle habits or behaviors such as smoking, physical inactivity, and alcohol/drug abuse. The risk for experiencing one or more chronic diseases increases with age and is related to socioeconomic status, as well as level of education (Ferrini & Ferrini, 2008; Marge, 1988; Pope & Tarlove, 1991). Marge identified 16 specific causes that produce disability, and the following are relevant for older persons: genetic disorders, accidents and injuries, nutritional disorders, lack of proper sanitation, stress, alcohol and drug abuse, poor environmental quality, lack of access to adequate healthcare, poor education, use of tobacco, lack of physical fitness, deleterious family or cultural beliefs, violence, and acute and chronic illness.

Hiatt (2004) described other factors that are believed to affect physical and mental functioning including:

1. Daily schedules that are more appropriate to older adults and individual preferences.

2. Environments and programs that involve smaller groups rather than larger groups.

3. Ensuring that time is occupied with meaningful activities.

4. Promoting environments that have natural qualities.

5. Creating environments that embody familiar routines and care such as familiar foods, familiar patterns, and preferred choices.

6. Stressing collaborative activities in which the focus is not caregiving but rather engagement in mutual activities and the recognition that time is precious.

One can conclude that circumstances and situations that do not embody these factors may also promote functional limitations, impairment, and disability in older adults.

In general, as age increases the risk of experiencing one or more chronic conditions also rises, therefore elevating the possibility of disablement. The prevalence of having a chronic condition or comorbidity (having more than one chronic condition at a time) differs among men and women, and by race/ethnicity (Federal Interagency Forum on Aging-Related Statistics, 2008). For example, as reported by the Federal Interagency Forum, "Women report higher levels of arthritis than men. Men report higher levels of heart disease and cancer" (p. 45). The need for assistance, which is directly related to the presence of functional limitation, also increases with age. Poverty, lack of education, and social isolation also contribute to increased risk. Among older adults who are age 65 to 74, 63% who have limitations with daily activities receive personal assistance; the percentage increases to 67% among people 75 to 84 and 74% among people age 85 and older (Federal Interagency Forum on Aging-Related Statistics).

In summary, the profile of the older adult population in terms of the need for health-related services and products is complex. The continuing shift in the population age structure coupled with the emergence of chronic disease as a leading cause of functional limitation impairment, and disability have resulted in heightened national efforts to develop strategies for promoting health and functional independence across the life span. Health promotion and preventive health services are popular approaches for impacting the health and quality of life of older adults. As the number of choices for service settings and levels of care continue to improve, new intervention strategies and activity programs will arise in an effort to meet the demands of the diverse and growing older adult population. It also is expected that healthcare technology and life expectancy will continue to improve, and that the older adult segment of the population will be a growing service sector. These factors, as well as others, combine to make health-related services an important and challenging area—now and throughout the 21st century.

Service Settings and Scope of Care

Older persons who are in need of health-related services may seek different levels of care from a variety of service settings. Health-related therapeutic intervention may be provided on an inpatient, outpatient, or in-home basis. Inpatient care is given in settings where the older individual is a resident such as acute care hospitals, rehabilitation facilities, assisted living facilities, and long-term care facilities (Ruzicka, 2007). For individuals who remain living in their own homes or in the homes of family members or others, community-based services provide an alternative to inpatient care. Finally, for individuals who are unable to leave their homes to obtain needed health services, in-home care may be an option. Broad levels of care (inpatient, outpatient, in-home) form a continuum that spans service settings ranging from residential institutions to noninstitutional programs and services. Figure 2.1 portrays this continuum of care with associated service settings.

Noninstitutional Care

Noninstitutional care is provided in various settings depending upon whether the older person is living at home on a fully independent basis, living with others, or living in a retirement community (see Figure 2.1). One model of a highly successful community-based service setting is the *adult day care center*. The adult day care movement has been very beneficial for a growing number of older adults, especially those who

choose to remain in their own homes or with family members/friends, and who have needs that can be served by increasing the availability of community-based medical, social, health, and psychological support service providers. Since the early 1970s when there were fewer than 25 adult day programs nationwide, adult day care has grown to more than 3,500 centers (Mankoff, 1984; MetLife Mature Market Institute, 2008; Pegels, 1988; Von Behren, 1986). There is a wide range in the character and scope of adult day care programs, all of which are responsive to the desire by older adults to remain at home and age in place. As a constellation of activities and services, adult day care is designed to assist functionally impaired individuals who would otherwise be at risk of institutionalization to remain at home while receiving social, health, and therapeutic activities. While programs may vary in terms of specific features, most centers offer social activity, personal care, meals and snacks, transportation, and therapeutic activities (MetLife Mature Market Institute, 2008). According to a national study of adult day services (National Adult Day Services Association, 2006), almost 78% of centers are nonprofit or publicly supported with the remaining centers (22%) are private, for-profit operations. Two broad foci characterize adult day care: adult day health service (ADHS) and adult day services (ADS).

Adult day health service programs focus on providing health and rehabilitative services much like those that are available in assisted living facilities, hospitals, and nursing homes. The individuals who attend adult day healthcare programs may either be experiencing increasing levels of impairment or disability as a result of a chronic health problem, or may have been recently discharged from a hospital or rehabilitation center. The primary purposes of adult day healthcare are to prevent further decline in health status, to provide rehabilitation services that restore the individual

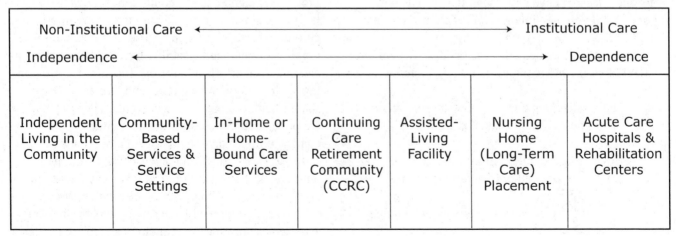

Non-Institutional Care ⟷						Institutional Care
Independence ⟷						Dependence
Independent Living in the Community	Community-Based Services & Service Settings	In-Home or Home-Bound Care Services	Continuing Care Retirement Community (CCRC)	Assisted-Living Facility	Nursing Home (Long-Term Care) Placement	Acute Care Hospitals & Rehabilitation Centers

Figure 2.1 Continuum of Care and Service Settings

to her or his previous level of functioning, and to provide caregiver respite. "Most adult day health service programs provide: health assessments, nursing supervision, and nursing assessments; medication administration and assistance with toileting, bathing, and other Activities of Daily Living (ADLs); therapeutic recreation, socialization, and group activities; and nutrition assessment, case management/care coordination, and transportation" (Lucas, Rosato, Lee & Howell-White, 2002, p. viii). Regulation of adult day health programs varies by state with most states providing for certification, standards of practice, general guidelines of operation, and licensure.

Adult day services programs, on the other hand, are more social-oriented day care (Lucas, Rosato, Lee & Howell-White, 2002). Activities are structured to provide maximum social, emotional, and physical stimulation, thus preventing loss and/or decline that is associated with a chronic and degenerative disease. Individuals in adult day services programs typically do not need ongoing medical assistance or supervision. They usually need activity involvement and benefit from the social support that characterizes these programs. Their family members or caregivers also benefit by being able to maintain their own work activity, enjoy some respite from caregiving, and have some time to take care of personal matters.

The cost of adult day care varies based on the type of care (medical vs. social) and the range of services provided (social/ recreational activities to skilled nursing care). Basic adult day care services include: client assessment and case management; meals (1–3 plus snacks); personal care assistance (e.g., eating, grooming, going to the bathroom); ancillary services (e.g., occupational therapy, physical therapy, nutritional/ dietary counseling, nursing, social work); therapeutic recreation and socialization; and education (Pegels, 1988). In general, costs vary by facility and state with little standardization for this type of service (Lucas, Rosato, Lee & Howell-White, 2002).

Other community-based service models, in addition to adult day care, include outreach services, multipurpose senior centers, area agencies on aging, and a plethora of voluntary organizations and agencies (e.g., religious, civic, social groups). These community-based efforts provide a wide range of services including (a) volunteer opportunities such as the Retired Senior Volunteer Program (RSVP), (b) friendly visitor services, (c) handyman or homemaker assistance, (d) health screening services, (e) fitness programs, (g) transportation assistance, (g) recreational activities, and (h) educational programs. Often, the challenge

confronted by older adults and their caregivers is just finding out what is available in their community and how to access these services and programs. Many community-based services and programs are essential for maintaining optimal health and the ability to engage in everyday functional activities in aging persons, especially as they reach very old age and the risks increase for the need for assistance.

For many older adults, functional limitations coupled with other circumstances may mean that they are unable to use community-based services, yet their overall need does not require residential care in a *long-term care facility* (nursing home). In some cases, the individual may prefer to stay in his or her home or with family caregivers rather than be placed in a congregate care facility. In either or both cases, if the degree of impairment has resulted in disablement such that ongoing care is needed then home healthcare may be an appropriate alternative.

There are many factors that support the choice for *in-home* or *home-bound* healthcare. The most prevalent reason given by older adults is to avoid institutionalization. Placement in long-term care results in a loss in individual autonomy and independence that is not preferred by most adults. According to research findings, receiving services on a home-bound basis as opposed to nursing home or other congregate care setting, is the alternative of choice by most older adults and their primary caregivers (Jett, 2008b). Also, with the continued growth of the older population coupled with skyrocketing healthcare costs, in-home care is one possible means for containing healthcare expenditures if, and only if, the individual's need is not as great as what it would cost to provide services in a long-term care facility. Therefore, *in-home healthcare* is another alternative on the continuum of care settings.

In-home services are a priority area of the aging services network and refer to a range of services including "home health aid, family respite services, visiting and telephone reassurance and chore maintenance which enable older persons to remain in their homes for as long as possible" (Ficke, 1985, p. 104). In-home services can be grouped by categories such as (a) home health including "nursing care, medical social services, home health aid care, nutritional and dietary services, medical supplies and equipment, occupational therapy, speech therapy, and other specialized services"; (b) social support including "housekeeping/chore services, personal care, transportation, pastoral services, telephone reassurance, friendly visiting, shopping, and laundry services"; (c) channeling or case management programs including "screening of clients, assessment of service needs, prescription of services, acquisition and coordination of services, monitoring of services, and reassessment" (Pegels, 1988, p. 95). In summary, in-home healthcare is a constellation of services that includes assessment and diagnosis, rehabilitation and treatment, monitoring, and support services for maintaining noninstitutionalized living. "It is a wholistic concept of care that strives to restore, maintain, and enhance the quality of life" for both the elderly individual and their caregiver(s) despite "illness, infirmity, or even impending death. The term 'home care' is preferred within the industry because home care includes social and other human services, not health services alone" (Nassif, 1986, p. 6; 1985).

Retirement community living is a growing enterprise and many residential retirement complexes also include a variety of health and social support services (Jett, 2008b). Within the planned retirement community, village, or complex, residents may be leading fully independent lifestyles or be receiving some level of assistance with health and social needs. In 2007, approximately 2240 licensed continuing care community facilities were in operation compared with 16,100 nursing homes, 21,203 licensed senior housing facilities, and 39,500 assisted living facilities (Jett, 2008b). The residential populations of these facilities were 1.4 million people in nursing homes, 900,000 in assisted living facilities, and 745,000 in licensed continuing care communities. These statistics continue to demonstrate the large nursing home population, which resides in a comparatively fewer number of facilities. All too often, the choice of residence is shaped by the economic capacity of the older person, with the cost of those housing options that promote greater independence (e.g., retirement community living) being largely borne by the consumer.

While many retirement communities are established with the concept of providing housing units and social services for older adults who are primarily healthy, a growing number of organizations are developing *Continuing Care Retirement Communities* (CCRCs), which are retirement communities that also offer long-term care units on site. Some elderly persons find the concept of a CCRC or *lifecare community* very appealing when making the decision to sell or move out of their home. The idea that they will be able to receive in-home assistance and social support, as well as be assured of short-term and long-term nursing care in a CCRC-based health pavilion, provides a sense of comfort and reassurance of stability throughout the remaining years of life. The CCRC may be thought of as self-contained community-based living

with the same range of services one finds in a larger community such as in-home care, adult day assistance, and long-term care. CCRCs offer the older adult the opportunity to *age in place*, which means that he or she will never need to move again throughout the remainder of his or her life. While financing for CCRCs is costly, thus restricting enrollment to more financially capable individuals, the current enrollment demand exceeds the available space.

Institutional Care

Inpatient service settings typically represent institutional care and fall into the following types: nursing homes or long-term care facilities, assisted living facilities, acute care hospitals, and residential rehabilitation centers (see Figure 2.1). Healthcare provided in hospitals or residential rehabilitation facilities is typically for a short period of time and ends in a transfer to some other level of care, either long-term, community-based, or home-bound care. In nursing facilities, a range of health and social services may be provided depending upon the needs of the individual and the type of nursing facility. The term *nursing facility* is a general term for facilities that provide long-term residential care for frail, infirm, and disabled individuals. As Jett pointed out, however, residential facilities that provide care are "known by more than 30 different names across the country, including *adult congregate living facilities, foster care homes, personal care homes, homes for the elderly, domiciliary care homes, board and care homes, rest homes, family care homes, retirement homes, and assisted-living facilities*" (2008b, p. 439). These other types of care facilities are the fastest growing housing option for older adults and are considered more cost-effective and preferred compared with nursing homes. The aim is to preserve a home-like environment while ensuring that the healthcare needs of the older adult are delivered.

Some nursing homes are primarily concerned with providing a protective environment and assistance with basic daily living skills. These basic skills include being able to get out of bed, feed oneself, dress, bathe, and go to the bathroom. These facilities are known as Intermediate Care Facilities (ICFs) or in some states, as Health Related Facilities (HRFs). Other nursing homes offer more intense medical care and usually individuals who are critically ill reside in these facilities. They are referred to as Skilled Nursing Facilities (SNFs) and are more like traditional hospital care. Older individuals typically reside in nursing homes for two main reasons: (a) their level of functional impairment is so disabling as to require ongoing round-the-clock supervision and medical care; and (b) the individual does not have the psychological capability, social support, and/or economic means to deal with his or her needs outside of institutional care (Jett, 2008b; Pegels, 1988). The nursing home industry is largely supported by public funds and therefore, it is also closely regulated by laws in order to protect the residents' quality of care and safety.

The population in nursing homes was around 1.9 million people in 2007 and is expected to continue to rise due to the growth in the over age 65 population (Jett, 2008b). Residents of nursing homes are typically older women (over age 85). Somewhere between 4–5% of the over age 65 population reside in nursing facilities at any one time and about 15% of people over age 85 are institutionalized (Ferrini & Ferrini, 2008). These figures underscore the fact that the risk for institutionalization increases with age. Older women who are poor and white are the dominant residents in long-term care facilities. The typical nursing home resident may suffer from heart disease, mental disorders, or from some type of physical impairment. Multiple conditions are common and thus, the need for several kinds of assistance is not unusual (Ferrini & Ferrini). Among older people who are living in long-term care facilities, 12% have limitations *only* in instrumental activities of daily living (IADLs), 18% have limitations in activities of daily living (ADLs), and 64% have limitations in 3 or more ADLs (Federal Interagency Forum on Aging-Related Statistics, 2008). Because nursing home care is costly and the expenditure of public funds for acute as well as long-term care will continue to grow, other alternatives to long-term care are increasingly more desirable, such as community-based and in-home care.

Acute care hospitals and rehabilitation facilities are the most expensive alternative and deliver the most extensive level of medical services of all healthcare settings (Jettt, 2008b; Ferrini & Ferrini, 2008). To be admitted to these facilities, an older person must be experiencing an acute health problem that is in need of the full range of diagnostic and treatment services. A comprehensive assessment must be completed and admission requirements must be met. The level of care in this type of facility is the most costly alternative to the individual and to society. New medical technology has further exacerbated the problem of rising healthcare costs associated with acute care. For example, advancements in medical technology have greatly impacted the number of older patients who are receiving kidney dialysis, cancer treatment, organ transplants, and open heart surgery in acute care settings today (Jett, 2008b).

Because of the high costs associated with acute and long-term care, coupled with the rising incidence in chronic healthcare problems among the older adult population, the utilization of preventive healthcare is an important service delivery modality. The next section deals with the overall goals and purposes of intervention with the elderly in order to influence overall health status and quality of life.

Intervention through Prevention

The values and vision of today's society are exemplified by a life that is abundant with good health and good fortune. The nation, however, is experiencing several trends that are placing strains on these values and vision. The growing size of the older adult population, the continuing rise in healthcare costs, the emergence of chronic disease as a major source of impairment and disability, a severe downturn in the economy, and sustained advancements in medical technology are collectively creating significant challenges for the service delivery system. Consequently, public policy advocates and professionals are looking for new ways to protect, as well as promote, the health, well-being, and quality of life for all older Americans. Health professionals, activity staff, caregivers, public officials, and citizens are focused on the rights of older persons to live with dignity and respect, and enjoy an acceptable quality of life. Activities, programs, and services are increasingly attending to the goals of improving, maintaining, and enhancing access to high quality care for all older citizens. Efforts have broadened to include optimal health through active lifestyles that emphasize physical fitness, intellectual stimulation, and social inclusion in the mainstream of community life.

Service delivery to promote health and well-being is guided by several levels of care that when done well provide continuity of care but when done poorly result in "a tangled mass of knots and loose ends" (Ruzicka, 2007, p. 827). *Prevention* services fall into three levels— *primary*, *secondary*, and *tertiary* care (Ruzicka, 2007).

The goal of *primary prevention* is to prevent illness, impairment, functional limitation, and/or disability. Primary prevention services are often provided in physicians' offices and public health settings. Typical approaches to primary prevention include educational programs, basic immunizations, and information distribution. The purposes of these activities are to prevent accidents, promote health, prevent illness and disease, and inform older persons of risks that may result in morbidity and mortality. Classes, seminars, written materials, preventive health services, and audiovisual information all can be used productively in primary prevention. For example, videotaped adult fitness programs can be designed and marketed to help elders achieve optimal physical and mental functioning, as well as prevent acute and chronic diseases. Nutritional counseling, prescription education, primary immunizations, and accident prevention programs are other examples of primary prevention strategies to enhance optimal health and well-being of older persons. Essential immunizations include influenza, pneumonia, hepatitis B, and tetanus booster (Touhy, 2008).

Primary prevention programs can be found in many places in the community. Primary prevention emphasizes more than just the prevention of illness; it also includes a focus on positive well-being and growth. Primary prevention through health promotion expands healthcare beyond the medical technologies of surgery, medications, and palliative care to include the *quality of life* dimension of the individual's health status.

An example of primary prevention through health promotion can be seen in the Healthy Older People project initiated by the U.S. Department of Health and Human Services in 1985. This project was a national effort to promote healthy lifestyles among older citizens. The Healthy Older People project embraced six areas of concern: nutrition, safe use of medications, smoking cessation, exercise and fitness, injury control, and preventive and mental health. A variety of activities aimed at some or all of these targeted areas were carried out by state and local aging agencies under this program. All activities were intended to address the overall goal of preventing illness and disablement among older persons. These and other prevention goals have continued as national health targets through the Healthy People 2000 and Healthy People 2010 objectives for adults age 65 and older (Touhy, 2008).

Secondary prevention targets the minimization of the impact of an illness or disease through screening, early detection, and treatment in order to contain or ameliorate the condition (Ruzicka, 2007). Secondary prevention maintains the individual at a minimal level of health compromise, and/or restores the individual to a former level of health and functional capacity based on early detection. Typical services in the secondary prevention area include high blood pressure screening, cholesterol screening, osteoporosis screening, pelvic exam and screening for cervical cancer, stool screening and colonoscopy (sigmoidoscopy) for colon cancer, prostate exam, diabetes screening, mammography, vision and hearing screening (Touhy, 2008).

Tertiary prevention occurs after a pathological condition is present and has become serious (Ruzicka, 2007). This level of prevention is aimed at limiting the level of functional impairment and managing the process by which impairment becomes a disability. It is not unlike the restorative functions of rehabilitation. Tertiary prevention will often focus on reducing the risks of additional impairment based on the diffusion of the health condition to other areas of functioning. For example, a diagnosis of terminal cancer of the liver and lymphatic system will influence overall physical functioning and stamina. Added consequences of the disease may involve an emotional response by the individual to the diagnosis of a life threatening disease. Therefore, tertiary prevention may involve mental health counseling to (a) assist the patient with his or her adjustment to a terminal disease, (b) make plans for promoting a quality of life for the remaining time, and (c) help the person work through his or her disease with family members or friends. Another example of tertiary prevention programs are cardiac rehabilitation services following a heart attack for the purpose of preventing another heart attack (Ruzicka, 2007). Tertiary prevention is useful in recognizing the wholistic nature of the human organism and that illness in one area of functioning will usually influence the person in other areas of functioning.

Some of the barriers to effective prevention include provider attitudes, personal characteristics, and lack of knowledge as well as inadequate or poorly organized medical records (Ruzicka, 2007). Older persons also may be unaware of services and benefits, or may be afraid of discomfort or the ability of the medical practitioner's ability to meet their needs. In some cases, older persons are not highly motivated to make changes in their behaviors that would affect their health status. Finally, the health system continues to present barriers to obtaining preventive services due to an inadequate availability of geriatric healthcare professionals, poor insurance and reimbursement systems, and inadequate information systems. Thus, even though it is well understood that prevention is essential to good health and well-being in older adulthood, the delivery of prevention services is remains problematic.

Intervention through Rehabilitation

For older individuals who are living with functional limitations that are producing disablement, learning to live with dignity and control is a fundamental goal (Jett, 2008a). The underlying philosophy of rehabilitation intervention services is best reflected in the statement, "What can I help my patients do for themselves?" (Dominquez, 1988, p. 65). The purpose of rehabilitative intervention is to facilitate, cause, or maintain the individual's control over his or her physical, cognitive, emotional, and social capacities within the environment where they are living (Robinson, 1989). The goal is to facilitate the highest level of functioning within the individual's strengths and needs (Jett, 2008a). Activities that are applied in rehabilitation intervention are selected and implemented because they promote the maximum functioning and satisfaction within the individual. A sense of control through independence and autonomy are integral aspects of activity design and are used in meeting rehabilitation goals. The individual's quality of life is dependent upon personal control over care and treatment in the process of promoting functional competence through activities of daily living, mobility, socialization, communication, and mental health. Rehabilitation services more often take place in an acute care hospital or rehabilitation hospital and in long-term care facilities (nursing homes) but more recently, are expanding to other service settings. Sometimes, rehabilitative care will be provided at home where the focus is usually on restorative care whereas in the latter instances, the focus is typically upon maintenance (Jett, 2008a).

Rehabilitation intervention often is achieved through a coordinated program of services that involves a team of professionals. Rehabilitative intervention involves an activity program where the emphasis is on the development or reacquisition of skills, or the maintenance of abilities. Therapies, including activity therapy, are engaged to assist the individual in regaining functional capacity in one or more areas such as walking, getting out of bed, reaching, dressing, bathing, using community services, home care, and memory skills. For individuals whose skills are at the highest possible functional level, given the nature of their impairment and disability, a program of maintenance and prevention of further loss may be appropriately implemented. *Maintenance rehabilitation intervention* programs are integrated into the individual's everyday routines such as wheelchair exercises throughout each day for the purpose of preventing further losses in physical stamina due to excessive inactivity imposed by the necessary and constant use of a wheelchair. Maintenance rehabilitation programs are essential in order to prevent further declines when disability is permanent (Jett, 2008a; Robinson, 1989).

Rehabilitation teams often include several professionals who represent a variety of areas of care including medicine (e.g., nursing), social work, psychology

and psychiatry, pastoral/spiritual, legal, and various therapies. Rehabilitation intervention programs often involve several types of therapies including occupational therapy, physical therapy, mental health counseling, recreation activity therapy, and speech therapy. Understanding the whole individual is important in a successful rehabilitation program and therefore, teamwork and communication among all professionals is important. Creating a match between optimal functioning, individual control, and professional service delivery lies at the heart of an effective rehabilitation program.

Summary

This chapter provides the reader with an overview of health status and the health-related needs of older adults as they are addressed through intervention services. The process by which an illness becomes a disability is instrumental to understanding the levels of need for healthcare services. Older persons may seek a variety of services on an inpatient, outpatient, or home-bound basis. Typical services and programs represent a continuum from noninstitutional to institutional care. Prevention and rehabilitation intervention are basic approaches to therapeutic care with older persons. Based on an understanding of the material presented in Chapters 1 and 2, the reader is now prepared to explore the process of normal aging as well as common illnesses and diseases of the elderly, which are covered in greater detail in Unit II of the text.

Comprehension Questions

The reader can check for comprehension of the material presented in this chapter by answering the following questions:

1. Describe health and functional status as they pertain to the older adult population.

2. By what process does impaired functioning become disablement?

3. What are three differences between a chronic condition and an acute illness?

4. What is personal control important in the rehabilitation process?

5. Describe the continuum of care and service settings for the delivery of healthcare services to older persons.

References

Dominquez, S. E. (1988). Rehabilitation: A nurse's viewpoint. In R. D. Sine, S. E. Liss, R. E. Roush, J. D. Holcomb, & G. B. Wilson (Eds.), *Basic rehabilitation techniques: A self-instructional guide* (3rd edition)(pp. 65–68). Rockville, MD: Aspen Publishers.

Federal Interagency Forum on Aging-Related Statistics. (2008, March). Older Americans 2008: Key Indicators of Well-Being. Federal Interagency Forum on Aging-Related Statistics. Washington, DC: U.S. Government Printing Office.

Ferrini, A. F. & Ferrini, R. L. (2008). *Health in the later years*. (4th ed.). Boston, MA: McGraw Hill.

Ficke, S. C. (Ed.). (1985). *An orientation to the Older Americans Act* (Revised Edition). Washington, DC: National Association of State Units on Aging.

Goldman, D. P., Shekelle, P. G., Bhattacharya, J., Hurd, M., Joyce, G. F., Lakdawalla, D. N., Matsui, D. H. Newberry, S. J., Panis, C. W. A. & Shang, B. (2004). Health status and medical treatment of the future elderly. Final report. Pittsburgh, PA: RAND Corporation.

Hiatt, L. G. (2004). Chapter 4. Environmental design in evoking the capacities of older people. In L. M. Tepper & T. M. Cassidy (Eds.), *Multidisciplinary perspectives on aging* (63–87). New York, NY: Springer.

Jett, K. (2008a). Chapter 10. Chronic disease in late life. In P. Ebersole, P. Hess, T. A. Touhy, K. Jett, & A. S. Luggen (Eds.), *Toward health aging: Human needs & nursing response* (222–268). St. Louis, MO: Elsevier/Mosby.

Jett, K. (2008b). Chapter 17. Economics, residential, and legal issues. In P. Ebersole, P. Hess, T. A. Touhy, K. Jett, & A. S. Luggen (Eds.), *Toward health aging: Human needs & nursing response* (428–447). St. Louis, MO: Elsevier/Mosby.

Lucas, J. A., Rosato, N. S., Lee, J. A., & Howell-White, S. (2002). *Adult day health services, A review of the literature*. New Brunswick, NJ: Rutgers Center for State Health Policy, The Institute for Health, Health Care Policy, and Aging Research, Rutgers University.

Mankoff, L. S. (January 1984). Adult day care—A promoter of independent living. *American Health Care Association Journal, 10*(1), 19–21.

Marge, M. (1988). Health promotion for people with disabilities: Moving beyond rehabilitation. *American Journal of Health Promotion, 2*(4), 29–44.

MetLife Mature Market Institute. (2008). *The MetLife market survey of adult day services & home care costs*. Westport, CT: MetLife Mature Market Institute.

Nassif, J. Z. (1985). *The home health care solution*. NY: Harper and Row.

Nassif, J. Z. (1986). There's no place like home. *Generations, 11*(2), 5–8.

National Adult Day Services Association. (2006). *Adult day centers: The facts*. Seattle, WA: National Adult Day Services Association.

Pegels, C. C. (1988). *Health care and the older citizen—Economic, demographic, and financial aspects*. Rockville, MD: Aspen Publishers.

Pope, A. M., & Tarlove, A. R. (Eds.). (1991). *Disability in America—Toward a national agenda for prevention*. Washington, DC: National Academy Press

Robinson, K. M. (1989). Rehabilitation medicine— Module 2.B. In B. A. Hawkins, S. J. Eklund & R. Gaetani (Eds.), *Aging and developmental disabilities: A training inservice package*. Bloomington, IN: Indiana University—Institute for the Study of Developmental Disabilities.

Ruzicka, S. A. (2007). Chapter 29. The geriatric continuum of care. In A. D. Linton & H. W. Lach (Eds.), *Matteson & McConnell's gerontological nursing: Concepts and practices* (3rd ed.) (827–849). St. Louis, MO: Elsevier/Saunders.

Stoukides, J., Holzer, C., Ritzau, J. & Burbank, P. (2006). Health issues of frail older adults. In P. M. Burbank (Ed.), *Vulnerable older adults: Health care needs and interventions*. New York, NY: Springer.

Tepper, L. M. (2004). Chapter 1. Aging in America. In L. M. Tepper & T. M. Cassidy (Eds.), *Multidisciplinary perspectives on aging* (3–23). New York, NY: Springer.

Touhy, T. A. (2008). Chapter 3. Health and wellness. In P. Ebersole, P. Hess, T. A. Touhy, K. Jett & A. S. Luggen (Eds.), *Toward health aging: Human needs & nursing response* (43–64). St. Louis, MO: Elsevier/Mosby.

Von Behren, R. (1986). *Adult day care in America: Summary of a national survey*. Washington, DC: The National Council on the Aging, Inc.

UNIT II

The Aging Process

The provision of care and activity programs to older adults requires a foundation of knowledge about the aging process as well as diseases and illnesses that affect older adults. Normal human aging is explored from various perspectives including a theoretical view of the biology of aging as well as systematic description of changes that occur in humans as the bodily systems age. In addition to gaining an understanding of the physical processes of human aging, caregivers and activity specialists need a background understanding of the social and psychological changes that take place in adults as they age. Based upon this information, we can then distinguish pathological states from normal processes of aging. This distinction is particularly useful when activity programs are intended to remediate, prevent, or rehabilitate in the case of an illness or diseased state.

Four chapters comprise Unit II of this text. Chapters 3 and 4 cover the normal aging process across the major domains of human functioning: physical, cognitive, and psychosocial. Following this background on normal aging, Chapters 5 and 6 introduce the reader to common physical diseases, illness, and disabilities (Chapter 5), and typical psychological illnesses and psychiatric disorders (Chapter 6) among older adults. Based upon the foundations provided in Units I and II, the reader will be prepared to approach the more practice-oriented information contained in the remaining chapters of the text.

• CHAPTER 3 •
Overview of Normal Aging

Learning Objectives

1. Define gerontology, social gerontology, and geriatrics.

2. Identify three broad areas that are studied in gerontology.

3. Describe the aging process and factors that influence normal aging.

4. Describe biological theories of aging.

5. Describe how the process of normal aging influences physical functioning in humans.

6. Describe how normal aging affects psychological functioning in humans.

7. Discuss how lifestyle can influence the process of normal aging.

Key Terms

- Ageism
- Cardiovascular System
- Endocrine System
- Gastrointestinal System
- Genetic Theories of Aging
- Geriatrics
- Gerontology
- Integument System
- Intelligence
- Learning
- Life Expectancy
- Life Span
- Lifestyle
- Lymphatic System
- Memory
- Musculoskeletal System
- Nervous System
- Reproductive System
- Respiratory System
- Senescence
- Sensory System
- Social Gerontology
- Stochastic Theories of Aging
- Urinary System

Introduction

In this chapter, the reader is introduced to the normal processes of human aging. The concept of *ageism* is described in order to alert the reader to common and inappropriate stereotypes and myths about older persons. These *ageist* views often result in lowered expectations of older adults by others and society. By systematically studying aging (e.g., gerontology and geriatrics) readers are helped to recognize and dispel these myths and false ideas about older people and the aging process.

In this chapter the process of aging is described, including a cursory overview of biological theories of aging. Physical changes associated with normal human aging are described according to the following key systems: sensory, integument, musculoskeletal, cardiovascular and respiratory, gastrointestinal and urinary, lymphatic, nervous, endocrine, and reproductive. Cognitive changes in intelligence, learning, and memory are then presented. The chapter concludes with a section on lifestyle and how it influences the aging process.

Why Study Aging?

The significance of human life, whether it be your own or that of someone close to you, is something that you will eventually think about from time to time as you move through your own adult years. Each occasion that you stop to reflect upon life, you might take notice of how you have changed. This growth reflects your own human development as you move through your life; in other words, as you age.

In the time that it takes for you to read this book, you will have *aged*. While perhaps only small, almost imperceptible changes in you will have occurred, it is through the passage of time that you will grow, develop, and change, and thus, experience *human aging*. One of the most compelling reasons for each of us to study aging is to gain a personal perspective of our own lives so that we might anticipate what it will be like as we grow older, what we can do to influence our own aging process, and how we can be involved in shaping the best possible future for ourselves. Most people want to know about aging so that they can better understand themselves and their own destiny.

By building an understanding of the aging process, you will be better informed about one of the most significant changes taking place in our nation today—the graying of the population—or, as we learned in Chapter 1, population aging. Not only will you be empowered to manage your own life as you age, but you will have the knowledge that you need to take care of aging family members and loved ones. Finally, if you happen to accept employment in a setting where you provide services for older adults, it is essential that you have a solid understanding of the aging process. One of the most unfortunate situations that can happen is when false stereotypes, myths, and inaccurate information form the basis upon which professionals give care to and interact with older persons.

Negative stereotypes and false information about the aging process often lead to prejudice and discrimination toward older adults. Robert Butler (2008), a well-known gerontologist, developed the term *ageism* to describe what happens when inaccurate views of the aging process influence the manner in which society as well as individuals treat older adults. Ageism is a set of attitudes and behaviors that arise when society assigns certain characteristics (most of which are negative) to all older persons based solely on the one shared attribute, chronological age (Butler; Hooyman & Kiyak, 2008).

Societal expectations of older persons, in general, are shaped by several factors, of which chronological age is unfortunately the dominant force. As people grow older, society assigns certain expectations in terms of social roles, responsibilities, characteristics, and behaviors. For example, as individuals reach their 60s, society expects that they will retire from full-time work and subsequently, that they will disengage from the social responsibilities typically associated with work. However, this view is changing because aging Baby Boomers are likely to want to continue to engage in some kind of paid work and they will resist being "put out to pasture," as the saying goes. Likewise, when older persons reach very old age (e.g., in their 80s, 90s, or 100s), the ageist stereotype implies that they will be frail, not very vigorous, and also helpless to some degree. Again, this stereotype is likely to be unpalatable to aging Baby Boomers who will resist such negative views and many of whom will likely continue to engage in vibrant lifestyles well into very old age. Other inappropriate stereotypic views of older persons include rigid, senile, feeble, sexually inactive, crabby, and unattractive, none of which are true in terms of general characteristics of all older adults. Based on what is known about the aging process and older persons, these descriptors are inaccurate, inappropriate, unacceptable, and patently untrue (Butler, 2008).

An important reason for studying aging, then, is to dispel *ageism* from society, especially as increasing numbers of individuals, especially the anti-aging Baby

Boomers, enter the older adult life stages. Distinguishing the normal changes that occur in the aging individual by learning about the aging process also will enhance society's understanding and approach to service provision for older adults. The concern for promoting an accurate understanding of the aging process has given rise to two broad fields of education and professionalism: *gerontology* and *geriatrics* (Lach, 2007).

Gerontology is a multidisciplinary field in which the biological, psychological, and social aspects of the normal aging process are studied (Lach, 2007). The field involves researchers, educators, and practitioners from the behavioral, biological, and social sciences including biology, psychology, epidemiology, anthropology, sociology, nursing, medicine, pharmacology, biochemistry, social work, economics, nutrition/dietetics, rehabilitation sciences, recreation and leisure studies, education, political science, and many other disciplines. The main concern of gerontologists from these disciplines is how to improve the quality of life for older adults, as well as providing accurate information about the aging process from a biopsychosocial perspective. Gerontologists in these disciplines conduct applied science as opposed to basic science (Lach). The biopsychosocial model of aging encompasses the total view of the aging process as it involves the following main areas of human functioning: (a) biological aging, which is concerned with the changes in physiology and physical functioning as the individual becomes older; (b) psychological aging, which includes mental, sensory, and perceptual functioning; and (c) social aging, which focuses on changing social roles and contexts with advancing age (Ferrini & Ferrini, 2008; Hooyman & Kiyak, 2008; Lach).

An area of particular interest to professionals who provide activity programs to older adults is *social gerontology*. Social gerontology can be distinguished as a specific focus within the field of gerontology that is mainly concerned with how social and cultural conditions impact the aging process and social consequences (Hooyman & Kiyak, 2008). Of special interest to social gerontologists are the social and cultural factors that influence older adults, as well as how an aging population impacts upon society. Some of the diverse issues that are studied today in the area of social gerontology are the result of the aging of the Baby Boomers, changes in work and retirement, housing and community design, income and poverty, national health trends and healthcare, leisure and lifelong learning services, care for frail or infirm older adults, racial and ethnic diversity, growth in the size of the older adult population, and public policy concerns like

Social Security and medical financing programs (e.g., Medicare).

Geriatrics, on the other hand, primarily refers to the medical care and management of disease in older persons (Lach, 2007). Geriatric medicine involves physicians, nurses, and other medical practitioners who are concerned with the changes that take place in older persons as a result of illnesses or diseases, and which are not primarily caused by growing older. The medical and health problems of older people are the central focus of geriatrics (Ferrini & Ferrini, 2008; Hooyman & Kiyak, 2008; Lach).

With sustained growth in the older adult population expected throughout the 21st century, gerontologists and geriatricians will continue to be concerned with the issues of older adults and conditions that affect them. Accompanying the sustained growth in the older adult segment of the population will be new cohorts of Baby Boomers who may be more politically active, have higher levels of education, hold new and perhaps different ideas about their own older adult years, and have greater financial resources with which to pursue the resolution of their concerns. They can be expected to advocate for the development of appropriate health and social programs, as well as public policies that benefit older adult population. Thus, the knowledge that is gained from studying the aging process, thereby preparing professionals to work with older adults, is vitally important for improving the quality of life and health status of all aging adults and their families.

The Aging Process

While early growth and development in humans is generally described in terms of increasing size and the development of complexity in structure and function, the same general description does not apply to the aging process when the individual reaches adulthood. According to Moody, aging, or senescence, is a "time-dependent biological process that, although not itself a disease, involves functional loss and susceptibility to disease and death" (2006, p. 29). The changes that occur after reaching maturity are differentiated from early development in several important ways. The rate of change slows and the rate is not uniform across all areas of human functioning (e.g., physical, cognitive, and social); nor does change occur the same across all individuals. There is a great diversity among individuals in how "aging-related change" is manifest and how each person adapts to the aging process. Older adults are the most heterogeneous of any age group in the population with each individual having his or her own personal trajectory in the aging process. If we typically think of older adulthood as a period of time that can span 20, 30, 40 or more years, it would be meaningless to try to characterize all older adults as the same or as a homogeneous group (Lach, 2007). Also, it is extremely important to distinguish between normal aging change and the disease process. While the incidence of illness and disease increases among older persons compared to younger persons, not all older persons will automatically become ill or have a disease with advancing age. Aging and the normal changes associated with growing older, however, do happen to every human organism (Ferrini & Ferrini, 2008; Lach, 2007; Moody, 2006; Shock et al., 1984).

While there is no uniform course to aging for all individuals, six patterns can be used to characterize the overall process (Shock et al., 1984). First, relative stability across the adult years can be expected. The process of change is gradual. The human organism will adapt and adjust in order to provide for relative stability in performance overall. Second, declines due to illnesses that are associated with age can be expected and third, in spite of good overall health, steady declines will occur for all individuals. A fourth pattern suggests that any changes that are precipitous (e.g., onset is rapid and acute) are associated with disease rather than aging-related change. A fifth pattern involves the human organism's tendency toward natural compensation for losses in order to maintain function. The sixth and final pattern relates to the influence that society and culture have on the aging process. The greater the understanding that a particular culture has about the aging process and the more progressive they are in promoting a conscious health milieu for elderly persons, the better the outcomes are for individuals as they move into their later years. For example, the movement to promote physical fitness and activity in adulthood in order to preserve functional capacities is one way in which the rate of loss in physical performance due to aging may be slowed.

In summary, the normal process of aging can be described as cumulative with all humans experiencing aging-related changes. The process continues from birth to death within each individual and will, ultimately, increase the likelihood of mortality for the individual. The next section provides a general overview of biological theories of aging.

Overview of Biological Theories of Aging

One fact is evident in the research literature, no one theory adequately serves to explain the biology of ag-

ing, or put another way, there is no universal theory to explain human aging (Arking, 1991; Butler, 2008; Finch, 1990; Finch & Ruvkun, 2001; Hooyman & Kiyak, 2008; Moody, 2006). The changes associated with aging are complex and multileveled. Biological aging is a "sum total of many independent causes, some operating at the level of individual molecules, others at the level of individual cells, and still others at the level of tissues, organs, and whole organisms" (Schneider, 1992, p. 7). Thus, several different theoretical perspectives are required in order to gain a clearer understanding of the biology of aging. Biological theories of aging fall into two broad categories: programmed or genetic theories, and stochastic theories (Schneider, 1992).

Programmed, or genetic theories, describe the influence of human genes on the cell division and replacement process as it causes systemic change across the life span. The average human being expects to live around 75–80 years and each individual's genetic endowment will contribute to the chances of meeting this expectation; however, there is a relatively small variance in the actual length of life in the human species (Butler, 2008). There are about 200 genes that specifically influence the aging process (Schneider, 1992). The cells of the human organism, however, do not continue to divide and replace themselves indefinitely; they are regulated by these 200 "aging" genes. Researchers have discovered that genes will direct the cells to divide and replace themselves about 40–60 times, thus limiting the maximum life span potential of the human organism (Ferrini & Ferrini, 2008; Schneider, 1992).

Genetically programmed aging can be readily recognized by several obvious changes in humans such as graying of the hair, length of the reproductive cycle of females, and decline in immune system function after age 20 (Schneider, 1992). As cell division and replacement occurs, cell function declines partly due to loss in function and partly attributable to mutation. Often, the human organism dies before it reaches the maximum capacity for cell division as programmed genetically. Research findings about genetic endowment, and the limits of genetically controlled cell division and replacement, contribute greatly to our understanding of the biology of aging at both the cellular and the systemic level (Arking, 1991; Brookbank, 1990; Schneider, 1992).

Several stochastic theories of aging describe the influence of random or chance attacks on the body by accumulated external forces in the environment (e.g., toxins) and by internal factors (e.g., caloric restriction). One theory, the Metabolic Theory of Aging/Caloric Restriction, is based on the idea that the rate of metabolism is directly related to the length of life for the organism; that is, higher metabolism is related to shorter life and lower metabolism is related to longer life. Experiments with lowering caloric intake in animals have demonstrated this relationship. Similar experiments are needed with humans (Schneider, 1992).

The Autoimmune Theory of aging suggests that the body's immune system declines over time and is unable to maintain its effectiveness in fighting attacks from viruses and bacteria (Finch, 1990; Hooyman & Kiyak, 2008). Because the immune system is less effective with age, greater vulnerability to infection and disease results.

The Free Radical Theory describes changes in cell function that are the result of damage caused by attacks from internal and/or external factors (Finch, 1990). Free radicals are thought to be organic molecules that are a byproduct of the metabolism of oxygen and they are toxic and reactive when in contact with other cell structures (Ferrini & Ferrini, 2008; Moody, 2006). As free radicals attack cells, mutations and cell damage occur. Free radicals are caused by normal cellular functions, as well as from environmental factors (e.g., toxins from cigarette smoke, poor drinking water, chemical additives in food). Free radicals have a short life but can damage the cell or genetic material (Ferrini & Ferrini, 2008; Finch, 1990; Moody, 2006; Schneider, 1992). Accumulated damage over time from free radicals is known to occur. Some of the current thinking regarding free radicals is that by increasing the intake of antioxidants, more people may actually lengthen their survival toward reaching life expectancy (Hooyman & Kiyak, 2008). However, improving the chances of reaching life expectancy does not translate into lengthening the maximum life span of the human species. What is not yet established is whether free radical damage causes aging, per se.

Cross-Linkage Accumulation Theory of Aging suggests that as the human grows older, cell molecules connect themselves with other molecules to form cross-linkages as caused by free radicals (Ferrini & Ferrini, 2008; Gafni, 2001; Moody, 2006). It has been proposed that the accumulation of these cross-linkages causes aging (Ferrini & Ferrini, 2008; Schneider, 1992). The ability of the cells to repair does not keep pace with the damage and subsequently, the result is loss of cell function. Cross-linkage damage affects the collagen or connective tissues of the body, causing them to be more rigid and less elastic. The outcomes of this kind of damage can be seen in skin damage (e.g.,

wrinkling) and losses in other bodily functions (e.g., lung movement in respiration, blood vessels, the lens of the eye).

Other biological theories of aging have been described in the literature but are beyond the scope of the present chapter. The preceding information serves to distinguish between genetic and damage theories, and thus the reader is provided with a cursory orientation to biological theories of aging. For further or more detailed study of this topic, the reader is encouraged to consult the references at the end of the chapter.

The next two sections of this chapter provide a brief overview of the physical and cognitive changes that occur with normal aging. Social changes are covered elsewhere in the text (Chapter 4). Common illnesses or diseases of the body and in mental functioning also are covered separately in Chapters 5 and 6.

Physical Changes

The physical body is a complex system of organs and structural components, which are individually and interactively influenced by aging. As the human organism grows older, the body continues to change as a result of both cellular division and replacement, as well as the accumulated effects of environmental factors (Finch, 1990). Taken together, these forces manifest uniquely in each individual. The following general information focuses on the physical changes that occur in each of the major bodily systems. It is important to be mindful of the fact that individuals vary greatly in their rate of change and the expression of age-associated physical change. Readers who are interested in knowing more detail are encouraged to consult the reference list at the end of the chapter. It is stressed that this chapter provides only a general introduction to normal aging. In each section, an attempt is made to cover the composition, function, and aging-related changes that accompany the area under discussion.

The Sensory System

Changes in the senses are perhaps the most critical to the aging adult. It is through the senses that information is received and responses are made that govern our interactions with others and the environment. Changes in vision, hearing, touch, pain, temperature sensation, taste, smell, and equilibrium influence the quality of these interactions. If the losses are great enough in one or more of these senses, everyday functioning becomes impaired. In general, however, sensory losses are gradual and when they reach a level that impairs functioning, aids and environmental modifications may be implemented. The most common of the losses are experienced in visual and hearing acuity. Glasses and hearing aids can effectively offset losses in these areas provided that the older adult is motivated to use them.

Vision

The changes in vision are primarily in the forms of loss of acuity or seeing clearly at a distance, decreased ability to adjust to light and dark, decreased ability to tolerate glare, decreased peripheral vision, and decreased accommodation or ability to sharply focus on near images (Ferrini & Ferrini, 2008; Linton, 2007a). These changes are influenced by alterations in the structure of the eye and the loss of elasticity in the eye muscles. In general, the lens yellows, thickens, and clouds with age, thus impeding the amount of light that can pass through it. Also, the opening/closing of the pupil diminish in speed, regularity, and size. When the eye can no longer adjust the lens and pupil quickly, the older adult has difficulty focusing on near objects. This condition is called *presbyopia* (Ferrini & Ferrini, 2008). Changes in vision that create problems increase with age (Hooyman & Kiyak, 2008). Adults who are 85 or older may experience vision losses that make everyday activities more difficult, such as reading or adjusting to quick changes in lighting. Environmental design adaptations can help avoid accidents for very old adults who experience these vision losses.

The primary outcomes associated with vision changes include (a) the need for glasses to aid in focusing near objects with ease; (b) the need for greater light in order to see; (c) the need to be aware of a sensitivity to glare; and (d) the need to accommodate difficulty in discriminating certain colors, especially the blues, greens, and violets. Other age-related changes include the loss of facial muscle elasticity around the eye and the loss in fat around the eyeball. These changes can result in a drooping of the eyelid which affects facial appearance (Ferrini & Ferrini, 2008). The most important point to keep in mind is that environmental modification along with the use of glasses can make a dramatic difference to the older adult who is experiencing significant vision loss. Diseases of the eye are covered in Chapter 5.

Hearing

Hearing loss is more common in older adults than is the total loss of sight. Whereas vision usually begins to decline in the 40s, hearing losses can begin as early as in the 20s, gradually accumulating and becoming more pronounced by old age. Among adults over the age of 65, 31% have hearing loss and this percentage increases to nearly 50% of adults over age 75 (Linton, 2007a). Hearing losses are a result in changes in the ear structure and functioning (Ferrini & Ferrini, 2008; Linton, 2007a).

The ear is constructed so that sound enters through the outer ear and is received in the middle ear as impulses which are processed by the auditory nerve to the brain and interpreted as sound. The ear also contains the structures that support the sense of equilibrium. Balance relies on special cells in the semicircular inner ear canals that contain fluid. This vestibular system, working along with the visual system, helps the individual to maintain balance. As vision and hearing acuity decrease, problems with equilibrium may begin to occur, especially under certain circumstances such as at night when the eyes refocus more slowly or when the individual has a head cold.

In general, as the adult grows older there is a stiffening of the inner ear structures such that the ear is less able to perceive and transmit sound. The resulting hearing loss most often manifests in an inability to perceive high pitched tones and is called, *presbycusis*. Older adults who experience presbycusis will have difficulty in discerning the following high frequency sounds: *f, g, s, t, ch, sh,* and *z* (Ferrini & Ferrini, 2008).

Another common hearing difficulty with age is the inability to sort out background noise from foreground conversation in crowded, noisy environments such as, at a party, conference, or large gathering of people with background music. This phenomenon is called the "cocktail party effect" and older adults may remark that they are unable to hear the person who is talking to them in a room filled with background noise. This kind of hearing loss creates discomfort for many older adults in social situations where there are many competing noise sources.

Hearing loss can occur other than that which is caused by the natural aging of the human ear structures. For example, persistent high environmental noise (noise pollution) can hasten a decline in hearing acuity, as well as result in additional damage to inner ear structures such as the ear drum. Illnesses, diseases, and traumatic injuries also may impact hearing in later life. Some medications and dietary habits have known side effects on hearing (e.g., ringing in the ears). Finally, some individuals "choose" not to hear as a result of psychological disturbances in their lives.

Unacknowledged and untreated hearing losses often result in lowered mental states and a lack of enjoyment of social activities. Paranoid ideas and behaviors, suspiciousness, withdrawal, disorientation with regard to reality, and depression may be observed when hearing loss becomes acute or prolonged without intervention. Providing hearing aid support and good, preventive healthcare to the ear (e.g., ear wax removal) can be effective in diminishing the impact of aging-related changes in hearing in everyday life.

Taste and Smell

The senses of taste and smell are governed by approximately 9000 taste buds on the tongue and in the mouth, as well as smell receptor cells located high inside the nose (Linton, 2007a). Taste perception primarily involves sensing sweetness, sourness, saltiness, and bitterness. Taste buds are composed of 15–20 taste cells; taste cells have a life span of about 10–101 days (Linton, 2007a). Turnover of taste cells may be slower with age. Most changes in taste and smell are experienced on a highly individual basis. Often lifestyle habits, such as cigarette smoking or poor oral hygiene, are the cause for decreases in a sense of taste. A decreased sense of taste may be noticed in the 60s and more severe loss is often notice by people who are over age 70 (Linton, 2007a).

Smell is affected by receptor cells in the nasal cavity. Sense of smell peaks around the 30s or 40s, and then begins to decline such that by the 70s there may be a very noticeable loss in this sense. Both taste and smell can be affected by a range of factors including certain medical conditions (e.g., nutritional, endocrine, and other diseases, as well as allergies and infections), medications, and poor oral hygiene (Linton, 2007a).

Touch

Somatic receptors that are responsible for the sense of touch (pain, pressure, heat, cold, spatial relationship) are part the skin, as well as internal organ systems of the body. As the body ages, a decrease in sensitivity to heat, cold, and pain has been documented (Ferrini & Ferrini, 2008; Linton, 2007a). Environmental temperature management is important in supporting an appropriate and comfortable body temperature in older persons. Also, proper attention and responsiveness to pain in older adults is important.

The Integument System

The integument system is the largest bodily system comprising the skin and related structures of hair and nails. This system is, by far, the most visible to us in terms of aging-related changes. Functions of the skin include protection from environmental factors, temperature regulation, waste excretion, sense perception (e.g., touch, pain), and maintenance/balance of bodily fluids/electrolytes (Linton, 2007b).

The skin is composed of the epidermis, dermis, and subcutaneous layer. The outermost layer, epidermis, protects the body from sunlight exposure by producing melanin. Dead skin cells are constantly being replaced by new cells produced by the epidermis. The inner layers, the dermis and subcutaneous layer, are composed of blood vessels, nerves, hair follicles, glands, connective tissue, and fat. The dermis and subcutaneous layers provide the primary functions of the integument system, which are (a) protection from environmental elements, as well as from internal injury from bumps and falls; (b) retention of vital bodily fluids; (c) control of body temperature through sweating and shivering; (d) elimination of body salts and waste products; (e) sensation through touch or injury; (f) production of vitamin D from exposure to sunlight; (g) absorption of medication through patches; (h) cushioning for other internal organs; and (i) fat reserves for energy (Ferrini & Ferrini, 2008; Linton, 2007b).

Heredity, hormones, and lifestyle habits are the primary influencing factors affecting changes to the integument system. For example, exposure to sunlight is one of the leading causes of wrinkles and drying of the skin. Cigarette smoking also is very damaging to the skin. The major changes to the skin with age are the appearance of wrinkles, folds, grooves, mottling, drying, thinning, and loss of elasticity. Hair becomes gray and less dense, and may be coarser on certain areas of the body such as ear lobes and eyebrows for men, and the upper lip and chin among women. It is not uncommon for men to bald with age while balding is less common among women who will experience thinning hair, however (Ferrini & Ferrini, 2008; Linton, 2007b).

Nails will grow slower and may be thinner with age, as well as develop ridges. Some older adults have difficulty trimming their nails due to poor vision, arthritis, lack of flexibility or coordination, and obesity. The prevention of injury or disease associated with nail care is important to older adults and a podiatrist may often be sought for assistance with nail care.

When obvious changes in the integument system (e.g., wrinkles or gray hair) occur, many adults become aware for the first time that they are growing older. Changes in skin, hair color, and nail texture give each individual his or her own unique appearance with age (Jett, 2008). Fortunately, good skin care through protection against excess sunlight and exposure coupled with good nutrition and sleep can do much to prevent premature aging of this system.

The Musculoskeletal System

The musculoskeletal system provides the support structure for the human body. Composed of bones, muscles, ligaments, cartilage, and tendons, it protects the other major bodily organs. The health and structural integrity of the musculoskeletal system also provides support for body shape, movement, stability, posture, and as a mineral reservoir (Ferrini & Ferrini, 2008; Jett, 2008; Linton, 2007c).

The human skeleton consists of more than 200 bones that are held together by specialized connective tissues—ligaments, cartilage, tendons (Ferrini & Ferrini, 2008; Linton, 2007c). These connective tissues bind the musculoskeletal system together, bone to bone, muscle to bone, muscle to muscle. The elasticity of these connective tissues declines with age, which subsequently results in functional losses in the joints. As joints stiffen and range of motion becomes less, losses in flexibility and mobility result. The aging of joints begins before the skeletal system reaches full maturity; thus, the cumulative effects of joint degeneration are associated with old age (Ferrini & Ferrini, 2008; Linton, 2007c).

Bones are built as calcium and minerals are stored (Ferrini & Ferrini, 2008). Regular exercise will promote bone growth along with sufficient amounts of nutritional intake of calcium and essential minerals. Losses in bone strength and mass are hastened by poor diet and/or the lack of adequate exercise (Linton, 2007c). There is no question that sustained physical activity will slow the rate of bone and muscle loss throughout the adult years. The opposite is also true; among older adults who are sedentary, muscle and bone losses are faster.

Bone demineralization with age results in bones that are more porous; thus, bones are weaker and prone to being easily broken. Women experience greater bone loss than do men, with as much as 20-30% bone density loss over the average life span among women compared with only 10-15% in men (Ferrini & Ferrini, 2008). Loss in bone strength and mass over time will ultimately compromise physical function while increasing susceptibility to disease as well as elevating the risk for injury (Linton, 2007c). Changes in gait, stance, posture, height, and overall neuromotor performance occur with progressive losses in bone density, mass, and strength in old age.

There are over 700 muscles in the body that are grouped into three types: skeletal or striated, cardiac, and smooth. The skeletal muscles help to support the skeletal frame and provide the mechanisms for controlled movement, endurance, and reflexes (Jett, 2008; Linton, 2007c). The cardiac muscle, or the heart, maintains the heart pumping actions in support of the cardiovascular system. Smooth muscles, which are

muscles that are not consciously controlled, maintain internal functions such as the digestive system, the bladder, and the lungs. Smooth muscles function on a rhythmic, wave-like, sustained movement basis (Ferrini & Ferrini, 2008).

The muscles of the body atrophy at a fairly rapid rate when not regularly used. The decline with age in muscle mass and strength, therefore, may be greater or lesser depending upon exercise, as well as diet. The rate of loss in musculature is small until late in life (e.g., the 70s and 80s). Leg strength loss is greater than that of arm strength; however, all losses can be greatly influenced by whether the individual has a sedentary or active lifestyle. Overall, decreases in strength and endurance will vary greatly across individuals based on activity patterns.

The long-term impact of aging-related decreases in bone and musculature will affect several areas of human performance: (a) lowered strength, (b) restricted/reduced range of motion, (c) increased stiffness and pain, (d) gait changes; (e) diminished height, (f) postural change; (g) reduced movement (slower), (h) cramping, (i) declined motor performance, (j) increased susceptibility to injury and disease, and (k) restricted lifestyle (Ferrini & Ferrini, 2008; Jett, 2008; Linton, 2007c). One of the most important thoughts to keep in mind about aging and declines in the musculoskeletal system is the important influence that diet, exercise, and other lifestyle habits (e.g., cigarette smoking, alcohol use) have on the rate of decline.

The Cardiovascular and Respiratory Systems

The cardiovascular and respiratory systems are closely related systems that together provide major support for the transport of nutrients and oxygen to body. The respiratory system's major function is to provide oxygen from the air we breathe to the blood stream and to remove carbon dioxide from the blood transporting it back into the environment. The cardiovascular system is instrumental in transporting oxygen-rich blood throughout the body and returning carbon dioxide laden blood to the lungs for the exchange with fresh oxygen (Ferrini & Ferrini, 2008; House-Fancher & Lynch, 2007; Jett, 2008). The respiratory system depends upon the nervous system and cardiovascular system for full function (Jett, 2008).

The major structures of the respiratory system are the nose, oral cavity, pharynx, larynx (voice box), trachea (wind pipe), bronchi (bronchial tubes and bronchiole), and lungs. Air passes through these structures to tiny air sacs in the lungs called alveolus. In the lungs are close to a billion alveoli, which are covered with capillaries here the exchange of oxygen and carbon dioxide takes place. With each inspiration and expiration of air, the lungs expand and constrict thereby taking in oxygen-rich air and transporting out carbon dioxide. Breathing rate and depth are controlled by the brain according to oxygen and carbon dioxide levels in the blood (House-Fancher & Lynch, 2007; Jett, 2008).

Aging-related changes in the respiratory system are primarily in the loss of elasticity and thus, the hardening or stiffening of support tissues, airways, and diaphragmatic function. The bronchi degenerate with age, also. These changes result in a reduction in overall vital capacity (amount of air moved in and out of the lungs) so that the uptake and diffusion of oxygen is reduced. The chest wall and skeleton become more rigid and thus, influence breathing functions. Reserve capacity of the lungs declines with age. These changes are somewhat inevitable; however, aerobic exercise can be helpful in minimizing the functional effects. It is appropriate to recognize that environmental pollution is as much a hazard to respiratory decline and wellness as is any other single factor including advancing age and a lack of exercise. Older adults are generally less able to accommodate air pollution and therefore, are at greater risk for pulmonary conditions or death during times of high air pollution (Ferrini & Ferrini, 2008; House-Fancher & Lynch, 2007; Jett, 2008).

The heart and blood, along with a vast network of veins, arteries, and capillaries comprise the cardiovascular system. This system, while transporting oxygen to cells and carrying away carbon dioxide for removal through the lungs, also delivers other nutrients to body cells. Nutrients from the digestive track, antibodies from the immune system, and hormones from the endocrine system are provided to the body's cells via the circulatory system. Body wastes also are transported to the kidneys and lungs by this complex network. Finally, body temperature is regulated by the circulatory system (Ferrini & Ferrini, 2008; House-Fancher & Lynch, 2007; Jett, 2008).

The major pump for the circulatory system, the heart, is composed for four main chambers: two atria (upper chambers) and two ventricles (lower chambers). In the process of pumping about 170 gallons of blood each hour, the right chambers of the heart receive and distribute deoxygenated blood to the lungs while the left chambers receive the oxygen-rich blood from the lungs and distributes it to the rest of the body. Arteries transport the blood to the capillaries, which supply body cells. There are specialized arteries (coronary arteries) that supply the heart muscle cells. Veins carry the blood back to the heart for distribution to the lungs for oxygenation.

As the body ages, some structural changes occur to the cardiovascular system. Age-related declines in maximal function and efficiency can be expected. The heart muscles become less elastic with some calcification and degeneration of the internal valves to be expected. The walls of the heart thicken, which influences contractibility and oxygen consumption by the heart muscle cells. With gradual thickening, thus increasing weight of the heart, pumping force may increase as compensation. Increased pumping force contributes to an elevated blood pressure which can, if high enough, damage other bodily organs. It is well-known, however, that cardiovascular function is greatly influenced by physical activity. Thus, highly active older adults tend to have much higher cardiovascular function than do inactive elders (Ferrini & Ferrini, 2008; House-Fancher & Lynch, 2007; Jett, 2008).

Throughout the body, the arteries progressively become less elastic due to a process called arteriosclerosis; which is more commonly described as "hardening of the arteries" (Ferrini & Ferrini, 2008; House-Fancher & Lynch, 2007; Jett, 2008). Arteriosclerosis is a stiffening of the connective tissue and calcification in the arterial walls. This process will occur regardless of the level of activity that the older adult may exhibit. Lifestyle will not slow or alleviate arteriosclerosis. Along with this change to the body's arteries, blood flow to internal organs will decline with age. The general impact of cardiovascular changes on functioning can be summarized as follows: (a) diminished cardiac reserve; (b) reduced exercise capacity; (c) decreased blood flow to the coronary arteries; (d) decreased ability of the heart to use and distribute oxygen; (e) increased blood pressure; (f) lowered ability of the heart to recover, especially following exercise; and (g) lowered blood flow to other organs thus impacting upon their functioning (Ferrini & Ferrini, 2008; House-Fancher & Lynch, 2007; Jett, 2008).

The Gastrointestinal and Urinary Systems

The digestive (gastrointestinal) system consists of the mouth and salivary glands, pharynx, esophagus, stomach, liver, pancreas, gallbladder, small intestine, large intestine, rectum, and anus. This modified muscular tube is responsible for receiving and processing food for the usable nutrients that maintain the human body. As food passes through this system, it is broken down into and moved along by rhythmic, wave-like motions to that portion of the intestine where nutrients are absorbed and waste products are passed on for elimination via the bowels. It is the least likely system to be overly affected by aging-related change; however, common age-related health problems (e.g., poor oral hygiene, poor eating habits) can greatly affect this system. Because the cells of the digestive system are replaced often and there is a large capacity in reserve, serious decrements need to accrue before functional losses are noticed (Ferrini & Ferrini, 1993; Jett, 2008; Linton, 2007d).

Aging-related changes in the stomach and small intestine are manifest as decreases in the enzyme content necessary for food digestion. In addition, the production of saliva may decrease along with a generalized slowing in the swallowing reflex. These changes coupled with muscle fiber changes in the digestive tract result in a slowing of digestive capacity and the absorption of nutrients. Liver weight and functions decline between age 60 and 90 which results in a lessened capacity for the metabolism of hormones and drugs. It is known that some drugs take much longer to be absorbed and utilized in elderly persons, which has serious implications for the medical management of diseases and illnesses (Ferrini & Ferrini, 1993; Jett, 2008; Linton, 2007d).

If older persons are healthy, then the changes that do occur to the digestive system will be minimally noticed with age. Other disturbances that are of concern to older adults tend to be induced by poor diet or dental hygiene. Although teeth will wear down with age, normal diets and good care of the teeth will minimize the effects. Receding gums and tooth loss are not normal consequences of aging (Linton, 2007d).

The urinary tract consists of the kidneys, ureters, bladder, and urethra. The primary function of the urinary system is to cleanse the blood of waste products produced by body cell use of nutrients. The blood transports waste and other toxic substances to the kidney where it is removed from the blood. Along with this cleansing, the urinary system controls body fluid composition and amount. Kidneys filter the waste and toxins from the blood which become urine which is then transported out of the body through the ureters, bladder, and urethra. The bladder is an expandable muscular sac which contains sensory receptors that signals the brain when the sac is about half full (Ferrini & Ferrini, 1993; Jett, 2008; Linton, 2007d).

Changes with age in the urinary tract system consist of decreases in weight and volume of the kidney thus influencing filtration. Decrease in size and function begin to accelerate after age 40; by age 80, the kidney is 20% to 30% smaller (Jett, 2008). A weakening in the bladder wall and lowered capacity with age influences the ability to completely empty the bladder. The result of age-related changes in bladder structure

and functioning are more frequent filling of the bladder, more frequent need to urinate, and increased incidence of incontinence. The combined changes in the kidneys and bladder produce the need to get up in the night to void, a common occurrence among older adults (Ferrini & Ferrini, 1993; Jett; Linton, 2007d).

The Lymphatic System

The lymphatic or immune system consists of the thymus and bone marrow as principal organs with the spleen and lymph nodes as secondary organs. The thymus is located in the upper chest and the spleen in the upper left part of the abdomen. Lymph nodes are located throughout the body in the following areas: the underarm, neck, inside the chest, abdomen, groin, and around joints. Bone marrow, of course, is located inside the bones. When the body is invaded by a virus, bacteria, fungi, or other foreign substance, the immune system goes into action. The first mechanism to mobilize is the immune system's ability to identify "self" from "non-self." When the invader is detected as "non-self," the immune system goes into action protecting the body from the invader. Thus, two important functions are performed by the immune system: (a) first, it is the body's military system against infections that would mean death if not destroyed; and (b) second, the immune system is responsible for the collection of excess fluids from around the body's cells (Ferrini & Ferrini, 1993; Jett, 2008).

Age-related changes in the immune system stem from the deterioration of the thymus beginning at sexual maturity. A subsequent decrease in the levels of thymic hormones occurs. There is evidence that supports a functional decline in the immune system with age, although the underlying causes are not completely known at this time (Ferrini & Ferrini, 1993; Jett, 2008).

The Nervous System

The nervous system consists of the brain, spinal cord, and peripheral components. All knowledge and information that we have about ourselves, as well as the automatic regulation of bodily functions are controlled by the brain and nervous system. The brain receives sensory input from nerves connecting the senses (eyes, nose, and ears) to it, and messages from the other bodily systems through the spinal cord. The brain receives, organizes, processes, and sends messages that govern all aspects of bodily function, as well as our personality and identity (Ferrini & Ferrini, 1993; Jett, 2008; Millsap, 2007).

A detailed discussion of the different regions of the brain, including the structure and functioning of each, is beyond the scope of the present chapter. The most predominant structural change to the brain is a gradual reduction in weight and size with age. Changes in the brain are not uniform across all older adults and the impact on functional capacities is also highly variable from one person to the next. The rate of loss is accelerated after age 60 (Ferrini & Ferrini, 1993; Jett, 2008; Millsap, 2007).

The brain is made up of billions of neurons, or nerve cells that conduct and store information. Nerve cells transmit information to other nerve cells by impulses which are chemically and electrically induced. With age, there is a gradual reduction of the number of neuron cells which results in some loss in function. A noticeable consequence of losses in neurons and neuron functioning is in reaction time. Nerve conduction velocity slows and it takes longer for an impulse to cross the synapse. Additionally, the number of synaptic interconnections declines (Ferrini & Ferrini, 1993; Jett, 2008; Millsap, 2007).

While it might take some older adults longer to learn new material or to react to stimuli, the loss in reaction speed has not been shown to influence memory function or intelligence. Also, many other factors may influence nervous system functioning and subsequently, have an impact on memory functioning. Changes in hormone levels, blood transmission of nutrients to the brain, as well as the influence of medications on brain functioning are as common as are the effects of structural changes. The brain and nervous system, while experiencing changes with age, function well into very old age in the absence of illness or a pathological condition such as dementia (Ferrini & Ferrini, 1993; Jett, 2008; Millsap, 2007). Cognition and functional changes in cognition with age are covered under a separate section later in this chapter. Diseases of the brain and nervous system are covered in Chapter 6.

Endocrine System

The endocrine system consists of a group of glands located in the brain and throughout the body that are responsible for the production and secretion of chemical messengers. These chemicals or hormones regulate a broad range of bodily functions. The pituitary, which is located at the base of the brain, produces a wide range of hormones that govern the other glands in the endocrine system. The thyroid is located in the central part of the neck in front of the trachea and regulates metabolism, as well as lowers calcium levels in the bloodstream. The parathyroid, located on the back of the thyroid, increases blood calcium levels, as needed. The adrenal glands, which are located above the kid-

neys, regulate the body in response to stress, maintain potassium and sodium balance, and supplement sex hormone production. The pancreas, located behind the stomach, provides glycogen that stimulates the liver to break down sugar and produces insulin that promotes the utilization of glucose. The thymus, which is located in the lower neck, produces certain white blood cells and the gland atrophies after puberty. The ovaries (in women) are located in the pelvic area and the testes (in men) within the scrotum behind the penis. These glands secrete hormones that govern the development and maintenance of sex characteristics and reproduction (Ferrini & Ferrini, 2008; Jett, 2008; Linton, Hooter & Elmers, 2007).

Aging-related changes in the production of hormones are complicated by changes in the nervous and circulatory systems (Linton, Hooter & Elmers, 2007). The most is known about the pancreas and changes associated with insulin in the break down and utilization of sugars. Hormones are released and then are used when they link with target cells. The response of target cells in the utilization of insulin may be slowed significantly with age and in some cases may result in non-insulin dependent diabetes, which is discussed in Chapter 5.

With the exception of the female reproductive hormones (e.g., estrogen), decreases in the amount of other hormones produced by the endocrine system is not consistent with advancing age. There may be a lowered sensitivity, however, in the stimuli that cause the glands to respond; thus, hormone deficiencies can occur with age. In the case of females, reproduction ceases with menopause when estrogen declines. However, other sex hormones (testosterone) continue to be produced after menopause, thus sexual interest is maintained. While testosterone levels in males decrease gradually, sexual activity is maintained well into very late in life (Ferrini & Ferrini, 2008; Linton, Hooter & Elmers, 2007).

Reproductive System

As can be seen by the information presented in each previous section, some aging-related change does occur in the functioning of each bodily system; however, no system will shut down completely with age in the absence of illness or disease. The one exception to this general statement is in the female reproductive system, which ceases to function typically sometime between age 45-55. It is wise, however, to separate reproduction from sexual activity, which does not cease with age (Linton, Hooter & Elmers, 2007).

The reproductive system is governed by hormones (from the hypothalamus, testes or ovaries, and pituitary) and the reproductive organs (in females: ovaries, uterus, vagina, and external reproductive organs; in males: testes, scrotum, penis, accessory ducts, and glands). Hormones control arousal and sexual activity, egg and sperm production, and the development of characteristics associated with gender (e.g., facial hair in men, and hip and buttock fat in women). Hormones also govern the bearing and nursing of children by women. In later life, hormones generally maintain sexual activity and sex characteristics (Ferrrini & Ferrini, 2008; Jett, 2008; Linton, Hooter & Elmers, 2007).

A major aging-related change in the reproductive system occurs in women at menopause (the cessation of reproduction). As women experience a reduction in the production of estrogen, other secondary sex characteristics may change somewhat. Hair pattern, skin texture, and a loss in breast mass may occur.

Men also experience a decline in fertility around the same time that women do: their 40s–50s. The main difference between men and women is that men are capable of fertilizing an egg well into late life, whereas women cease reproduction at menopause. Men do experience an enlargement of the prostate gland that may begin in the 40s and be fairly common among men in their 80s. Sexual activity will be unaffected by this enlargement but other bodily functions may be affected (e.g., urination frequency and urgency, urinary retention). Dysfunction in sexual activity or performance in older men is more often due to psychological reasons. For example, men who are aging may experience anxiety over performance, negative effects of medications, or declines in health. Any of these factors may influence male sexual activity in late life (Linton, Hooter & Elmers, 2007). The point is well-made that there is no physiological reason for a decrease in sexual activity for men and women, alike, in old age.

Cognitive Changes

Cognitive functioning consists of intelligence, learning, and memory, which collectively support normal psychological and social functioning in everyday life. Without normal cognitive functioning, many of life's tasks (e.g., family responsibilities, work roles, and leisure activities) are more challenging and this situation may present added stress for the individual. Much of the research on cognitive functioning throughout the life course, including in older people, suggests that abilities in this area do not decline with age (Carroll & Linton, 2007; Ferrini & Ferrini, 2008; Hooyman & Kiyak, 2008).

Intelligence, for example, is difficult to define, measure, and verify across the life span. Intelligence is, theoretically, the ability to deal with information, new situations, symbols, abstractions, and ideas. Intelligence can only be estimated rather than definitely known, and this estimate is easily influenced by environmental factors rather than actual abilities. IQ (intelligence quotient) is the measure used to estimate intelligence by evaluating performance in a number of areas such as reasoning, judgment, words and verbal meaning, etc., and then comparing performance with that of other people of the same age (Carroll & Linton, 2007; Hooyman & Kiyak, 2008).

Intelligence is composed of different dimensions and abilities in those dimensions. A theoretical model that is commonly used to understand intelligence and aging-related change in older adults describes two broad categories of ability: *fluid intelligence* and *crystallized intelligence* (Cattell, 1963; Horn, 1972, 1988; Horn & Cattell, 1966; Hooyman & Kiyak, 2008). *Fluid intelligence* is represented by skills that are biologically determined; that is, abilities or skills that are not learned through experience. *Crystallized intelligence*, however, represents accumulated knowledge or abilities that are learned (e.g., words, concepts). While research has been controversial regarding whether older people experience a decline in intelligence compared to younger persons, it is believed that fluid abilities do decline with age but crystallized abilities continue to show improvement throughout the life course.

The *Classic Aging Pattern*, used for describing cognitive performance in old age, has emerged from the results of much research in this area (Hooyman & Kiyak, 2008). The Classic Aging Pattern purports that verbal scores (e.g., measures of crystallized intelligence) will remain stable while performance scores (e.g., measures of fluid intelligence) will decline with age. Because performance related intelligence tasks require the use of other noncognitive functions (e.g., psycho-motor skills, perceptual abilities, and sensory abilities), aging-related declines in fluid intelligence may be a finding that is influenced by many factors that are difficult to separate. Other research in this area suggests that the speed of cognitive processing declines with age which will then result in slower performance in other cognitive performance measures. Verbal skills, however, remain stable across the life span. When and if declines are exhibited in the ability to recall verbal information, they are usually in persons who are very, very old.

Other factors also affect performance on intelligence-related tasks. Health status, sensory loss, hypertension, education, and occupation have been shown to influence performance on intelligence tests (Carroll

& Linton, 2007; Hooyman & Kiyak, 2008). Therefore, given that intelligence is a difficult concept to define and measure, a more definitive understanding of cognitive performance with age remains a topic of continuing research.

Learning and memory are cognitive processes that also must be considered when understanding aging and cognitive functioning. Learning involves the processing and storing of new information, while memory is the process of retrieving the learned information. Memory contains all the information that has been learned across the life course. Three types of memory have been identified: short-term memory, long-term memory, and sensory memory (Carroll & Linton, 2007; Hooyman & Kiyak, 2008).

When new information is received by the senses (sensory memory), it is passed along to either short-term or long-term memory. There are two primary types of sensory memory: visual (iconic) and auditory (echoic). Stimuli that we see and hear are received by our sensory memory an passed along for processing and storing.

Short-term (primary) memory is where information is organized and temporarily held for storage in long-term (secondary) memory. While information is received by sensory and temporarily held in short-term memory, true learning occurs when material is stored in long-term (secondary) memory. Rehearsal, memorization, or repeated use of information is necessary for the storage of information in long-term memory. Short-term memory has a limited capacity and may be affected by declines in reaction time speed, while long-term memory is unlimited in its capacity.

Learning, therefore, takes place when information is received (sensory memory), encoded (short-term memory), and stored (long-term memory). Research on recognition and recall (or memory utilization) does not support aging-related declines in the capacity of capacity of these aspects of memory. Older adults, however, may be less efficient in accessing long-term memory and in retrieving information that was stored long ago (Carroll & Linton, 2007; Hooyman & Kiyak, 2008).

Learning and memory in older persons can be maintained or even enhanced through providing stimulating activities and environmental supports. Cognitive performance in memory and learning can be as good as when the person was younger with more time given for task performance; large lettering; adequate lighting; relevant tasks to do; visual, auditory, and gestural cues; nonthreatening environments; and greater opportunity for repetition. Most of the current research evidence supports small aging-related declines, if any,

in intelligence, learning, and memory. By maintaining mentally active lifestyles, most older people can enjoy good mental functioning throughout their later years (Carroll & Linton, 2007; Hooyman & Kiyak, 2008).

Lifestyle and Aging

In spite of gradual and eventual declines in the body's physiological systems with age, the rate of decline can be slowed in many areas of functioning based on lifestyle. Regular exercise, a good diet, and the absence of hazardous health habits (e.g., cigarette smoking) can modify aging-related changes in physical and mental functioning. Older adults who are active, often have quicker reaction time and movement speed compared with sedentary adults. It is widely accepted that lifestyle influences health and functional status in older people. More importantly, however, motivating older adults to engage in healthy lifestyles is an ongoing challenge for many caregivers and family members, at least in the United States (Ferrini & Ferrini, 2008; Hooyman & Kiyak, 2008; Touhy, 2008).

Lifestyle factors (e.g., exercise, eating, and other health habits) have a significant impact not only on the rate of aging decline but also on the quality and longevity of life (Touhy, 2008). A longer expected life has not necessarily meant longer healthy life for many older persons. It is important to differentiate between human life span, life expectancy, and a healthy life in old age.

Life expectancy is the projected number of years that an individual is expected to live beyond a specified time based on environmental conditions and the genetic heritage of the individual. Individuals will have different life expectancies at different points throughout their lives depending upon conditions within that time period and also, the functional status of other members of their families at the same age. Disease, sanitation, health service availability and quality, familial genetic dispositions, and other factors combine to influence the statistically projected life expectancy (Ferrini & Ferrini, 2008).

Life span, on the other hand, is a fixed maximum age for the human species. The maximum life span for the human species is generally thought to be about 120 years (Moody, 2006). That is to say that a very few members of the species will survive past this age if no disease, genetic disposition, or environmental conditions were to affect the life of the individual.

Life expectancy dramatically improved throughout the 20th century and the number of people who survived to 100 years of age also experienced substantial growth. In spite of increased life expectancy in the population, many older people in their 70s, 80s, and 90s experienced aging-related declines that imposed serious impairment to independent functioning and health. Advances in medicine, sanitation, nutrition, and other facets of lifestyle have significantly affected life expectancy, but life span has not been altered as of yet. Certain lifestyle factors and behaviors are especially important in slowing aging-related declines as well as improving the quality of life and independent functioning of older adults. The accumulated effects of the physiological aging process coupled with sedentary living, poor diet, and lifelong participation in hazardous health habits have resulted in a significant portion of the older adult population experiencing impairment, disablement, infirmity, morbidity, and early mortality. Three major areas of lifestyle that are primary targets of health promotion and prevention in older adults are diet, exercise, and the reduction of engagement in health risk behaviors such as smoking and excessive drug/alcohol use (U.S. Department of Health and Human Services, 2000). Healthy People 2010 goals address the following leading indicators via the public health system in the United States: physical activity, overweight/obesity, use of tobacco, substance abuse, responsible sexual behavior, mental health, injury and violence, environmental quality, immunization, and access to healthcare. Improvements in these leading indicator are expected to impact quality of life and the functional independence of older adults. Health and wellness are at the heart of high quality lifestyles for older adults (Touhy, 2008).

Far too many adults in the U.S. are overweight. Obesity is a national concern and specific health threat to older adults. Diet and proper nutrition are current targets of the Public Health Service's national health promotion and disease prevention plan (Public Health Service, 2000; Touhy, 2008). The reduction of body weight and sodium intake are instrumental in controlling the risk of disease, as well as promoting independent functioning in late life. Obesity increases the risk for "hypertension, heart stress, adult-onset diabetes, increase serum fats, respiratory difficulties, and pain from over-stressed joints" (Brookbank, 1990, p. 187). The control of fat, sugar, and overall caloric intake also are dietary concerns of older adults. Diets not exceeding 1800 kcal for women and 2400 kcal for men are recommended for older adults.

A second major lifestyle concern of older adults is the lack of regular physical activity. A significant amount of research supports the impact that exercise has on health, rate of functional declines, and life qual-

ity in general for older adults (Arking, 1991; Brookbank, 1990). For example, regular physical activity promotes the following benefits: (a) increased blood volume; (b) decreased blood pressure; (c) increased maximal stroke volume and cardiac output; (d) improved respiration during exercise; (e) increased bone, ligament, and tendon strength; and (f) increased musculature. Unfortunately, a very low percentage (10%) of the adult population exercises at the minimal amount (e.g., 20 minutes on 3 or more days per week) needed to promote health, improve overall functioning, and slow the rate of aging decline. The problem of inactivity or a sedentary lifestyle is much higher among elderly persons. It is generally observed that more physically active older people are healthier than sedentary persons.

Hazardous health habits are a national concern, as well as problems of older adults. The long-term negative consequences of cigarette smoking and tobacco chewing are widely known. Nicotine is an alkaloid substance that causes heart rate to significantly increase (tachycardia) and vascular contractions that may result in elevated blood pressure (Brookbank, 1990). Tobacco tars are known to cause cancer of the mouth and lungs. Finally, cigarette smoke causes damage to lung function and the uptake of oxygen into the bloodstream. While recent national efforts aimed at reducing cigarette smoking in the U.S. population probably have decreased the overall numbers of smokers, tobacco use continues to present a significant health threat among older adults.

Alcohol abuse (i.e., the consumption of alcohol in harmful amounts) is problematic in the older adult segment of the population much the same as it is in the rest of the population. Barnes (1982) reported that 14% of the males and 7% of the females over age 60 are classifiable as heavy drinkers. It has been estimated that between 2% and 10% of older adults have alcohol problems so severe as to be identified as alcoholics (Brookbank, 1990). In addition to these percentages, periodic overconsumption is not uncommon among older adults. The long-range effects of alcoholic consumption are greater for older adults than they are for younger people due to changes in metabolic and liver function with age. The accumulated effects of alcoholism on cognitive function include losses in visual-spatial ability, sensory-motor functioning, and verbal ability. The aging process has a profound effect on the older person's ability to regain cognitive function that was damaged from alcoholism (Brookbank, 1990).

It is clear from the research that lifestyle factors have a great influence on how individuals are affected by the aging process. The increased risk for health problems and functional declines to the severity that the individual experiences impairment is a direct outcome of lifestyle habits such as poor diet, over consumption of alcohol, cigarette smoking, and lack of regular exercise. On the other hand, a slowing in aging-related decrements in some areas of functioning and an overall increased quality of life, as well as perceived well-being are often experienced by older individuals who engage in positive lifestyles. While it is true and inevitable that all humans age and eventually die, much can be gained by cultivating a health promoting lifestyle.

Summary

It is important to know about the human aging process, for personal as well as professional reasons. Negative myths and stereotypes abound in reference to growing older and being an older adult. By studying *aging*, we can learn more about how aging will affect our own lives, as well as how to provide appropriate activities and programs to older persons whom we serve.

The aging process follows certain patterns of change but is highly influenced by individual genetic makeup, as well as personal lifestyle habits. While many of the body's systems will decline in efficiency, memory and learning abilities hold up quite well through later life. As life expectancy continues to improve for each new birth cohort, the manner in which the society promotes healthy lifestyles will have a great impact on the quality of health and well-being of tomorrow's elderly. In this chapter, we connect the process of aging with the habits of lifestyle in order to help the reader appreciate the role of activities in the overall quality of life of older adults.

Comprehension Questions

The reader can check for comprehension of the material presented in this chapter by answering the following questions:

1. Discuss the difference between gerontology and geriatrics.

2. Describe six patterns that characterize the aging process.

3. Compare and contrast programmed or genetic theories of aging with stochastic theories of aging.

4. Select three physical systems of the human body and briefly describe the aging-related changes that occur in each system.

5. Describe how aging affects intelligence, learning, and memory.

6. Discuss the influence that lifestyle has on the aging process and quality of life for older persons.

References

Arking, R. (1991). *Biology of aging: Observations and principles*. Englewood Cliffs, NJ: Prentice Hall.

Barnes, G. M. (1982). Patterns of alcohol use and abuse among older persons in a household population. In W. G. Wood & M. F. Elias (Eds.), *Alcoholism and aging*. Boca Raton, FL: CRC Press.

Brookbank, J. W. (1990). *The biology of aging*. New York, NY: Harper & Row.

Butler, R. N. (2008). *The longevity revolution: The benefits and challenges of living a long life*. New York, NY: PublicAffairs, Perseus Books Group.

Carroll, D. W. & Linton, A. D. (2007). Chapter 20. Age-related psychological changes. In A. D. Linton & H. W. Lach (Eds.), *Matteson & McConnell's Gerontological Nursing: Concepts and Practices* (3rd ed.). St. Louis, MO: Elsevier/Saunders.

Cattell, R. B. (1963). Theory for fluid and crystallized intelligence: A critical experiment. *Journal of Educational Psychology, 54*, 1–22.

Ferrini, A. F. & Ferrini, R. L. (2008). *Health in the later years*. (4th ed.). Boston, MA: McGraw Hill.

Finch, C. E. (1990). *Longevity, senescence and the genome*. Chicago, IL: University of Chicago Press.

Finch, C. E. & Ruvkun, G. (2001). The genetics of aging. *Annual Review: Genomics and Human Genetics, 2*, 435–462.

Gafni, A. (2001). Protein structure and turnover. In E. J. Masaro & S. N. Austad (Eds.), *Handbook of the biology of aging* (5th ed.). San Diego, CA: Academic Press.

Hooyman, N. R. & Kiyak, H. A. (2008). *Social gerontology: A multidisciplinary perspective* (6th ed.). Boston, MA: Allyn and Bacon.

Horn, J. L. (1988). Cognitive diversity: A framework for learning. In P. L. Ackerman, R. J. Sternberg, & R. Glazer (Eds.), *Learning and individual differences*. New York, NY: W. H. Freeman.

Horn, J. L. (1972). State, trait and change dimensions of intelligence. *British Journal of Educational Psychology, 42*, 159–185.

Horn, J. L. & Cattell, R. B. (1966). Refinement and test of the fluid and crystallized intelligence. *Journal of Educational Psychology, 57,* 253–279.

House-Fancher, M. A. & Lynch, R. J. (2007). Chapter 12. Cardiovascular system. In A. D. Linton & H. W. Lach (Eds.), *Matteson & McConnell's Gerontological Nursing: Concepts and Practices* (3rd ed.). St. Louis, MO: Elsevier/Saunders.

Jett, K. (2008). Chapter 4. Physiological changes with aging. In P. Ebersole, P. Hess, T. A. Touhy, K. Jett & A. S. Luggen (Eds.), *Toward health aging: Human needs & nursing response.* St. Louis, MO: Elsevier/Mosby.

Lach, H. W. (2007). Chapter 6. Gerontology: The study of aging. In A. D. Linton & H. W. Lach (Eds.), *Matteson & McConnell's Gerontological Nursing: Concepts and Practices* (3rd ed.). St. Louis, MO: Elsevier/Saunders.

Linton, A. D. (2007a). Chapter 19. Age-related changes in the special senses. In A. D. Linton & H. W. Lach (Eds.), *Matteson & McConnell's Gerontological Nursing: Concepts and Practices* (3rd ed.). St. Louis, MO: Elsevier/Saunders.

Linton, A. D. (2007b). Chapter 10. Integument system. In A. D. Linton & H. W. Lach (Eds.), *Matteson & McConnell's Gerontological Nursing: Concepts and Practices* (3rd ed.). St. Louis, MO: Elsevier/Saunders.

Linton, A. D. (2007c). Chapter 11. Musculoskeletal system. In A. D. Linton & H. W. Lach (Eds.), *Matteson & McConnell's Gerontological Nursing: Concepts and Practices* (3rd ed.). St. Louis, MO: Elsevier/Saunders.

Linton, A. D. (2007d). Chapter 15. Gastrointestinal system. In A. D. Linton & H. W. Lach (Eds.), *Matteson & McConnell's Gerontological Nursing: Concepts and Practices* (3rd ed.). St. Louis, MO: Elsevier/Saunders.

Linton, A. D., Hooter, L. J. & Elmers, C. R. (2007). Chapter 17 Endocrine system. In A. D. Linton & H. W. Lach (Eds.), *Matteson & McConnell's Gerontological Nursing: Concepts and Practices* (3rd ed.). St. Louis, MO: Elsevier/Saunders.

Millsap, P. (2007). Chapter 14. Neurological system. In A. D. Linton & H. W. Lach (Eds.), *Matteson & McConnell's Gerontological Nursing: Concepts and Practices* (3rd ed.). St. Louis, MO: Elsevier/Saunders.

Moody, H. R. (2006). *Aging: Concepts and controversies.* Thousand Oaks, CA: Pine Forge Press.

Schneider, E. L. (1992). Biological theories of aging. *Generations—Journal of the American Society on Aging, 16*(4), 7–14.

Shock, N. W., Greulich, R. C., Andres, R., Arenberg, D., Costa, P. T., Lakatta, E. G. & Tobin, J. D. (1984). *Normal human aging: The Baltimore longitudinal study of aging.* Washington, DC: U.S. Government Printing Office, NIH Publication No. 84-2450.

Touhy, T. (2008). Chapter 3. Health and wellness. In P. Ebersole, P. Hess, T. A. Touhy, K. Jett & A. S. Luggen (Eds.), *Toward health aging: Human needs & nursing response.* St. Louis, MO: Elsevier/Mosby.

U.S. Department of Health and Human Services. (2000). *Healthy people 2010: Understanding and improving health* (2nd ed.). Washington, DC: U.S. Government Printing Office, Stock Number 017-001-00-550-9.

• CHAPTER 4 •

Social and Psychological Aspects of Aging

Learning Objectives

Describe and compare the various social theories of aging.

1. Discuss stage theories of adult personality.

2. Describe more recent social gerontology theoretical views of aging.

3. Discuss the impact of marriage in later life.

4. Describe the nature of intergenerational relationships and social networks in later life.

5. Explain the impact of widowhood and divorce in later life.

6. Explain the importance of friendship in later life.

7. Explain the impact of retirement on older adult social and psychological adjustment.

Key Terms

- Activity Theory
- Age Stratification Theory
- Aging Well
- Apportioned Grandparent
- Caregiving
- Cohort Effects
- Continuity Theory
- Deep Friendship
- Disengagement Theory
- Ego Integrity
- Empty Nest Syndrome
- Erikson's Psychosocial Model
- Ethnocentric
- Exchange Theory
- Identity Style
- Individualized Grandparent
- Interest Related Friendship
- Jung's Psychoanalytic Perspective
- Modernization Theory
- Remote Grandparent
- Selective Optimization with Compensation
- Social Breakdown
- Socioemotional Selectivity Theory
- Stage Theories of Personality
- Subculture Theory
- Successful Aging
- Symbolic Grandparent
- Symbolic Interactionism

Introduction

The period of older adulthood is a time of many social and psychological changes. Changing roles within the family and work status may challenge the everyday social and psychological well-being of the older adult. Social gerontology is a blending of both social and psychological theories to explain individual aging from a social psychological perspective (Baltes & Carstensen, 1999). Consequently, social gerontology theories have evolved out of two disciplinary traditions: sociology and psychology. Thus, there is a significant range of theories and models to explain how individuals adapt to changes in social roles as well as to the psychological challenges associated with the older adult life stages. A major theme of social gerontology theories is how older adults adapt to the challenges of late life and how mental well-being is maintained. This chapter traces early social gerontology theory through to more contemporary views. The focus is on common psychosocial aspects of the aging process including adult development, mental/emotional well-being and adjustment, common changes in social roles in older adulthood, and the importance of social networks and relationships.

Social Gerontology Theories

One purpose of social gerontology theories is to describe what successful aging means in American society. Before reviewing these theories, it is useful to anchor your thinking in two new and important concepts in the field of social gerontology. These concepts are *successful aging* and *aging well*. Considerable work has been completed in recent years to develop these concepts (Baltes & Baltes, 1990; Johnson, 1995; Rowe & Kahn, 1997). Kahn (2002) noted that the intent behind successful aging is not a matter of the absence of age-related decrements but rather "successful aging means just what it says—aging well" (p. 725). The intention behind both concepts—successful aging and aging well—is to view the aging process not from the disease, decrement, and decline perspectives but rather from the view of adaptation in older adulthood as the key to maintaining a happy, healthy, and satisfying life. Successful aging (Baltes & Baltes, 1990; Rowe & Kahn, 1997, 1998) and selective optimization with compensation (which is discussed later in the chapter) provide the basic conceptual roots for *aging well* (Hawkins, 2003). One of the criticisms of the concept of successful aging is that its opposite presents a very negative view of aging—that is, unsuccessful aging. It

is important to note, however, that both concepts are attempts to present more a positive view of aging.

In general, *aging well* evolves from exercising the choices that create a healthy, successful, and productive life (Krain, 1995). The interaction between the aging process and health is a dynamic process involving the individual in his or her environment, including the historical, social, and cultural contexts. *Aging well* is concerned with the resiliency and adaptability of the aging individual (Johnson, 1995). The individual and the environment are interactive, and the positive behaviors that are associated with *aging well* are a direct result of the adaptation and negotiation that take place within this context.

Most adults want to live long, in good health, and with an overall sense of well-being. *Aging well*, as opposed to a difficult old age, is a construct that is intended to convey positive images and approaches to aging (Johnson, 1995). "As people live longer and fuller lives, negative views of aging and old age are being replaced by appraisals of the aging process and older people that emphasize alternatives and choices" for attaining a good old age (Fontane & Solomon, 1995, p. 118).

With the concepts of *successful aging* and *aging well* in mind, we can now turn our attention to an overview of social gerontology theories. A number of the early theories in social gerontology that were developed ranged from very simplistic to highly complex. The following section briefly highlights some of the major social theories of aging that are commonly discussed in the gerontology literature. As the reader will note, many of them have implications for successful aging or aging well.

Modernization Theory

According to Modernization Theory the status of older people declines as a society increasingly becomes more modern (Hendricks & Leedham, 1991; Moody, 2006). In preindustrial societies, older men owned the land and held the power that accompanied such ownership. As societies industrialized, land became less of a source of power and older men lost their status. According to this theory, the more advanced and technological that society becomes, the status and power of older people decline and further, the need for their wisdom is no longer needed.

Modernization Theory is open to criticism from a number of perspectives. The primary criticism is that it is *ethnocentric*. The power in all preindustrial cultures was and is not based on the ownership of land. Furthermore, lower socioeconomic classes and minority groups who were not or are not allowed to own land are excluded from this model.

Comparison of modern societies to preindustrial societies is difficult due to the great differences that exist between them. In most preindustrial societies, few people lived to an age that is considered old by modern standards. The idea that older people were honored and revered universally in old age is a misconception. Historical evidence indicates older people in many preindustrial societies were victims of harsh treatment (Hendricks & Leedham, 1991).

Modernization Theory becomes even more tenuous in light of increasing longevity of the human species coupled with the notable growth in the number of adults living to older adulthood as well as very old age. By their sheer number, older adults in the 21st century certainly have power and influence in U.S. society.

Disengagement Theory

Disengagement Theory was developed in the early 1960s by researchers working with data from a cross-sectional study of older adults (Cumming & Henry, 1961). The primary tenet of the theory was that old age was a time when both society and the older person engaged in separation from the normal roles of everyday social life, especially in terms of work (Moody, 2006). Disengagement was seen as a natural process for mutual benefit, society would benefit from younger adults entering productive roles and the older individual would be relieved to pursue other forms of activity that would result in higher life satisfaction (Hendricks & Leedham, 1991). Individuals, as they aged, would be released from responsibilities that subsequently would be passed on to younger generations. Personal satisfaction among the older adult population was present when acceptance of withdrawal occurred.

This theory drew immediate criticism from social gerontologists even though many older adults, then and now, exhibit the very behavior described by the theory (Moody, 2006). At the time of the development of this theory, social conditions more closely matched the ideas reflected in the theory. As the 21st century unfolds and the Baby Boomers near their older adult years, disengagement is far from the expected behavior for adults entering this life stage. Nevertheless, efforts to disprove the theory led to research that was critical in the development of other social theories of aging. Additional research was unable to duplicate the original findings and eventually, the authors modified their stance. Today, disengagement theory is rarely referred to as a viable theory.

Activity Theory

Activity Theory is a widely accepted theory of aging that is particularly significant for activity specialists. The popularity of the theory may be due partially to the manner in which it intuitively seems rational (Hooyman & Kiyak, 2008). Activity Theory is based on the premise that high levels of activity are associated with perceptions of high life satisfaction in old age (Havighurst & Albrecht, 1953; Moody, 2006).

Although there has been empirical support for Activity Theory, it has been criticized as being too simplistic to fully explain successful aging and life satisfaction in old age. One limitation is that personal differences in activity level across the life span are not taken into account (Hooyman & Kiyak, 2008). For example, an individual who lived a sedentary lifestyle in middle age may be satisfied with that lifestyle in old age. Additional research has indicated that activity which is personally meaningful does correlate with life satisfaction, while highly structured activity does not (Hendricks & Leedham, 1991; Hooyman & Kiyak; Moody, 2006). Research findings support the impact of social involvement, continued physically active lifestyles, and engagement in productive roles do contribute to positive life satisfaction and mental well-being; however, it is the meaning of these activities to the individual that matters, not mere engagement in them. In other words, it is satisfaction with activity that is associated with well-being, not how much one engages in the activity. It is how one looks at things rather than just the behavior by itself that matters. Another criticism of Activity Theory is how well it explains successful aging or aging well for the very old, especially when activity level naturally lessens (Moody, 2006).

Continuity Theory

Continuity Theory suggests that personality remains stable over the life span (Hooyman & Kiyak, 2008). Relationships and orientations present in mid-life are continued into old age and it is this continuity of habits and activities that contributes to positive aging (Hendricks & Leedham, 1991; Moody, 2006). The older adult will develop new roles to replace lost ones. Based on individual personality characteristics, the older adult develops his or her own expectations for successful aging.

Continuity Theory addresses some of the shortcomings of Activity Theory. Recent empirical evidence does indicate that personality remains stable over the life course (Costa & McCrae, 1989). This theory, however, has its own limitations. The continuation of roles in old age may be difficult for people with functional impairments, illness, or disability (Moody, 2006). In such situations, the inability to change patterns of behavior may be detrimental (Hooyman & Kiyak, 2008).

Subculture Theory

The premise of Subculture Theory is that older adults interact primarily with each other and thus, form their own subculture. It is from this subculture that older people develop their social identities (Hooyman & Kiyak, 2008; Rose, 1965). Demographic trends that support Subculture Theory include the voluntary segregation of older people into retirement communities, and the concentration of older people in urban centers due to the flight of younger residents (Hendricks & Leedham, 1991). Older adults certainly constitute a subculture in the political arena. Social Security and Medicare are examples of government programs administered on the basis of age. In recent years, older people have joined forces to increase their political clout with the government as can be seen through highly effective advocacy organizations such as the AARP—American Association of Retired Persons.

Subculture Theory must be criticized for not taking individual differences into account. In fact, the opposite is true (Hendricks & Leedham, 1991). Individuals do not become more alike as they age; they are the most heterogeneous of all the age groups. Socioeconomic and race differences are discounted by Subculture Theory, as well. Further, the theory tends to isolate and separate older adults from the mainstream of society, thus neglecting their intergenerational roles and responsibilities in a more age-inclusive society.

Age Stratification Theory

At the core of Age Stratification Theory is the concept that people are stratified by society into categories based on age (Quadagno & Reid, 1999; Riley, Johnson & Foner, 1972). Roles, responsibilities, and resources are assigned according to these categories. *Cohort effects* make the aging process for each generation somewhat unique. Cohort effects reflect the impact that historical times have upon a specific age group that distinguish that group from people who grew up during another time period. The coming of the Baby Boomers into the older adult age strata punctuates the impact of cohort effects. The Baby Boomers are not likely to be like the previous generations of older adults and they will probably resist being categorized based on age; in fact, the Baby Boomers may openly resist old myths and stereotypes associated with being older.

Age Stratification Theory does address important considerations for gerontological research. Primarily, it provides evidence that cross-sectional research, which compares members of different cohorts, is not sufficient to explain age-related changes in the older adults. Differences between generations may be due to the historical experiences of a cohort, rather than chronological age. Other criticisms of Age Stratification Theory include that it does not sufficiently take into account individual class, race, and gender differences (Hendricks & Leedham, 1991).

Social Breakdown Theory

Social Breakdown Theory refers to the downward spiral that occurs when criticism and negative feedback of older people leads to lowered self-esteem and subsequent decline in performance, which then leads to more criticism. Loss of self-confidence due to social breakdown may cause older people to reach out for assurance, which may be interpreted as another sign of decline (Hendricks & Leedham, 1991). An increasing cycle of dependency results when older adults reach out for social support because of eroded self-sufficiency (Bengtson, Rice & Johnson, 1999). The negative spiral of social breakdown can be interrupted when older adults are provided with opportunities to demonstrate their abilities. Social Breakdown Theory is particularly useful as a model to guide the planning of therapeutic activity interventions with older people.

Exchange Theory

Exchange Theory is based on the premise of reciprocity and balance (Moody, 2006). For example, in exchange for the care given to children by parents, there is the expectation by parents of reciprocal care when in later life they have a need for care. According to Exchange Theory, individuals and groups in society will act to maximize gains and minimize costs. Relationships are maintained only as long as benefits outweigh costs. Because older adults are often erroneously perceived as not being productive, they have a lowered social status. The major problem with Exchange Theory is the basic assumption that the primary motivation for human behavior is personal gain (Hendricks & Leedham, 1991).

Symbolic Interactionist Theory

Symbolic Interactionist Theory views the interaction of the environment, the individual, and situations as key to the aging process, and in particular, the management of identity in old age (Gubrium & Holstein, 1999; Hooyman & Kiyak, 2008). Older people who believe they are capable of dealing with the demands placed on them by the environment are more satisfied than those whose environment is too challenging or not challenging enough. Individual outcomes can be improved by altering the environment to fit the functional abilities of the older person.

Symbolic Interactionist Theory is a particularly salient perspective for understanding how the older person understands his or her capabilities as shaped by how others interact with him or her (Hooyman & Kiyak, 2008). Adapting to the stereotypic expectations and images conveyed to the older person results in a self-ascribed identity to match the message. This theory is particularly useful for service providers who have control over the level of stimulation in the older person's environment. Unfortunately, circumstances do not always allow for environmental modifications. The person-environment fit model will be further addressed in Chapter 10 and is very applicable under this theory.

Selective Optimization with Compensation Model

The metamodel of Selective Optimization with Compensation (SOC) seeks to describe and explain successful adaption of adults to aging (Carstensen & Baltes, 1999; Baltes & Baltes, 1990). Selective Optimization with Compensation involves three distinct processes—selection, optimization, and compensation—that collectively govern behavior and outcomes in response to life changes. Selection of one's goals and activities is undertaken as a mechanism to optimize and compensate in order to enhance or maintain one's chosen goals. The ultimate goal of SOC is a process by which older adults are able to adapt to physical, social, cognitive, and emotional life changes that come with advancing age, thus maintaining a high quality of life as well as a highly satisfying lifestyle. SOC is another useful perspective for the activity professional who seeks to understand the aging process and how to support adaptation throughout the life course. SOC is not considered to be a theory so much as it represents a model for understanding and supporting successful aging and aging well.

Socioemotional Selectivity Theory

Initially formulated by Carstensen (1991), the Socioemotional Selectivity Theory attempts to explain the decrease in social interaction among adults as the move through their old age. The theory postulates that the shrinking of the social network and decreases in social interaction are a consequence of the older adult's management of narrowing resources. In other words, activities and social interactions are carefully selected to maximize meaningful and close emotional relationships, especially as the social network shrinks.

Based on the theory, an essential set of social goals motivate the individual's social contact throughout life, with goals organized by information seeking and emotional regulation (Baltes & Carstensen, 1999). In older adulthood, social networks become smaller and smaller, and thus, the individual chooses to maintain those relationships that provide the deepest emotional and cognitive meaning. The value of this theory is in its focus on social preferences and social behavior in older adulthood. The theory may be very useful to the activity professional in understanding the kinds of activities and the social meaning of these activities to older adults, especially as they reach very old age and their social networks are decreasing significantly.

Theories of Adult Personality

Prior to the 1930s, psychologists tended to believe that the psychological development of humans was completed by about age 30 and that little, if any, change in personality was evident after this time (Costa & McCrae, 1989). In 1933, Carl Jung presented a bold alternative view in his seminal work, *Modern Man in Search of a Soul*. According to Jung, a number of changes in personality occur throughout the life course. The essence of Jung's theory is that the ego moves through different stages beginning with extroversion (or other directedness) in youth moving through middle age toward introversion (or an inner world focus). Jung also described changes in archetypes with age based on the idea that all humans have both feminine and masculine sides. The idea of archetype means that if male, the feminine side emerges in older adulthood and if female, the male qualities emerge. Thus, in older men we see nurturance and in older women, assertiveness. Jung's work on describing different stages of personality development through to the last stage, dealing with one's ultimate death, set the platform for the emergence of a number of theories of adult development and personality. This section will focus on five of the most important theoretical works: Erickson's psychosocial model, Levinson's life structure approach, Gilligan's work on women's development, Neugarten's cluster of personality types, and Costa and McCrae's work on personality change/stability.

Erikson's Psychosocial Model

Stage Theories of Personality define personality development as a step-by-step growth process. According to Stage Theories, people pass through a series of developmental stages throughout the life course. At each step they are required to complete a developmental task. Failure to complete the task will prevent successful passage to the next step. Erik Erikson's (1959) Psychosocial Model is perhaps the most frequently cited Stage Theory of human development throughout the social sciences. According to Erikson's model, the individual moves through eight stages of development in order to attain the final goal of ego identity (Hooyman & Kiyak, 2008). The final four stages in his model are completed in adulthood. Stage five, ego identity vs. role diffusion, begins in adolescence and involves efforts to clearly define one's identity and social roles. Stage six, intimacy vs. isolation, typically begins in the early to middle 20s and continues into the middle 30s. This stage is characterized by the establishment of long-term intimate relationships. Marriage is more common during this stage. Stage seven, generativity vs. stagnation, generally begins in the middle 30s and continues into the early 50s. Generativity may be defined as the need to build something that lasts, or the need to provide for future generations by looking forward to the future. Parenting and grandparenting are excellent examples of generativity. The final stage, ego integrity vs. despair, is completed in late life. During this stage, the older person strives to establish a sense of meaning and purpose in life. A major task in this stage is the resolution of conflicts in earlier stages of life and integration of past experiences into the present. Successful completion of this final stage should result in higher life satisfaction and acceptance of the inevitability of death.

Erikson's theory is widely applied in the study of personality in older adulthood (Hooyman & Kiyak, 2008). The theory fits well with a person-environment fit perspective on psychological well-being in late life. It also acknowledges that personality is not fixed or static; in other words, personality evolves over the life course and into old age.

Levinson's Life Structure Approach

Levinson (1978) also developed a Stage Theory of adult personality. His work was based on the concept of life structure or the basic patterns of an individual's life during a given period and the dynamics of what is going on in the environment at that time. Life structure encompasses three factors: (a) the individual's participation in the sociocultural world through work, family, and other social groups; (b) the extent to which aspects of the self are expressed or inhibited including wishes, conflicts, and anxieties; and (c) the manner in which the individual participates in the external world.

According to Levinson (1978), the following 10 stages characterize life structures in adulthood:

1. Early Adult Transition (17–22 years): this stage is characterized by severing or altering significant relationships of childhood. During this stage, the individual experiments with relationships, careers, and other aspects of adult life.
2. Entering the Adult World (22–28 years): This stage is characterized by making important decisions about occupation, lifestyle, and relationships, which will determine the life course of the individual. Independence is established during this period.
3. Age-Thirty Transition (28–33 years): This stage is characterized by adjustments made by the individual to tentative decisions made during the previous stage. During this stage, family and occupational choices tend to be more established and permanent.
4. Settling Down (33–40 years): Individuals in this stage have made a strong commitment to family, occupation, and a secure future. Career advancement is important during this stage.
5. Mid-Life Transition (40–45 years): This stage is characterized by a change in life orientation. In the past, achievement was the primary life orientation. During this stage, the individual becomes more reflective and he or she evaluates what has been accomplished in life. The individual may modify his/her life path or form a new one.
6. Entering Middle Adulthood (45–50 years): In this stage, the individual makes choices regarding the life structure of middle age. Changes in feelings toward work and family/marriage may occur during this stage. Divorce, illness, and loss of loved ones may be a theme.
7. Age-Fifty Transition (50–55 years): This stage does not significantly differ from the previous one. According to Levinson, all adults must experience some type of a mid-life crisis. This may occur during this stage.
8. Culmination of Middle Adulthood (55–60 years): This stage is characterized by stability and a solidified life structure.
9. Late-Adult Transition (60–65 years): Middle adulthood is terminated during this stage. Adults prepare a life structure for late adulthood. Levinson did not actually interview people of this age, so his ideas regarding this stage are mostly speculative.

10. Late-Adulthood (65+ years): Levinson did not interview people in this stage either. Consequently, his life structure is not well developed or described.

What About Women's Development?

A criticism of Levinson's and Erickson's work is that both theories were based on research conducted with male samples. Although some research has indicated that the lives of women can be imposed into these stages (Harris, Elliott, & Holmes, 1986; Reinke, Holmes, & Harris, 1985), other research has indicated that women's development is different than men's. According to Gilligan (1982), the emphasis Levinson places on achievement is not appropriate for women.

Gilligan (1982) theorized that women's moral development is based on their involvement in relationships, whereas men's moral development revolves around achievement. In other words, women judge the success of their lives by their ability to maintain relationships with those around them. Men, on the other hand, judge their lives in terms of personal achievement.

Gilligan (1982) identified a common characteristic of women as the *ethic of care*. This concept described the tendency of women to put the needs of others before their own and to make sacrifices in order to provide care for others. Findings from research indicate that giving care is a central theme throughout the lives of many women as they often assume primary caregiving responsibilities for children, aging parents, and their spouse or partner. Nevertheless, women differ from men in patterns of health, lifestyle, life expectancy, and many other personal and environmental factors that influence their experience of aging (Hooyman & Kiyak, 2008). These differences have been poorly accounted for in models and theories of adult development.

The Kansas City Studies

The classic Kansas City studies of personality were conducted by well-known gerontologist and psychologist, Bernice Neugarten (Neugarten & Hagestad, 1976). Data for these studies were collected during the 1960s from adults in the Kansas City area. A cross-sectional comparison of 700 adults ranging in age from 40 to 70 years plus a six-year longitudinal study of 300 individuals ranging in age from 50 to 90 were conducted at this time. The results of the Kansas City studies indicated that there were four clusters of personality types that included most of the adults in the studies. These personality types included:

1. People with *integrated* personalities are older adults who have high life satisfaction, high cognitive skills, and have successfully adjusted to aging. People with integrated personalities may have high, moderate, or low levels of participation in activities. What is important is whether or not their level of involvement is voluntary or involuntary.

2. *Armored or Defensive* people have not adjusted to the idea of aging and are actively combating the effects of aging. Some armored or defensive individuals may be struggling to maintain high levels of involvement in past activities. Other people with this personality type may withdraw from relationships in order to isolate themselves from the losses associated with aging. Armored or defensive people have moderate life satisfaction and high cognitive skills.

3. *Passive/Dependent* people have a lower life satisfaction than the previous groups. Individuals in this group rely on others to meet their physical and emotional needs. Passive/ dependent older adults have moderate to low involvement in activities.

4. People with *unintegrated* personalities have considerable physical and cognitive declines. They have low life satisfaction and involvement in activities. In spite of dysfunction, these individuals are able to remain in the community.

One of the important contributions to the development of social gerontology theory that the Kansas City studies made were the links to activity theory and disengagement theory. The researchers who were involved with these studies debated the tenants of these two theories as the basis to explain individual personality and adaptation in old age. These studies, however, did not pay attention to social structure, which resulted in later publications by Neugarten and her colleagues that incorporated the contribution of social structure to individual personality in old age (Marshall, 1999).

Costa and McCrae: Stability or Change?

Early studies of personality indicated some personality changes in later life. These changes included a tendency for adults to disengage and become more self-oriented in later life. Research also indicated that men and women became more alike in later life. Women took on more masculine traits and became more assertive, while men became more nurturing.

Subsequent research indicated that age was only weakly related to personality (Costa & McCrae, 1989). Adults of all ages show considerable variation in personality, and these individual differences tend to remain stable throughout the adult years, even when individuals perceive that change has occurred. Costa and McCrae (1988) suggested that five factors account for self-characterizations given by adults: neuroticism, openness to experience, agreeableness, extroversion, and conscientiousness. Others who have studied the self in old age also suggested that the most salient dimensions of the self are a blend of sociodemographic characteristics, personal attributes, and social roles (Herzog & Markus, 1999).

Leisure and Life Satisfaction

Many of the various social and psychological theories of aging briefly described in the previous sections are based, at least in part, on the relationships among involvement in activities, quality of life, and satisfaction with life in older adulthood. Based on a substantial body of research, life satisfaction has been found to be positively related to leisure activity (Haley et al., 1987; Hawkins, Foose, Binkley, Cheung, Harahousou & Lamura, 2007; Hawkins, Foose & Binkley, 2004; Kelly, Steinkamp, Kelly, 1986; Riddick, 1985). In fact, the positive relationship between activity and life satisfaction serves as the basis for Activity Theory. More recent theory, such as Socioemotional Selectivity Theory, has been the foundation for investigating the meaning of leisure in late life when illness or disease affects life quality and meaning (cf. Myllykangas, 2004).

Some research findings, however, suggest that the relationship between activity and life satisfaction may not be a straightforward as once believed. In a study of 92 retired older adults, Mannell (1993) found that older adults who had a greater investment in their daily activities tended to have higher life satisfaction than did individuals with a lower level of investment. Consequently, older adults who primarily invested their leisure time in watching television or other passive activities experienced pleasure while engaging in the activity; however, over a period of time these activities contributed little to perceived life satisfaction. Other research findings suggest that it is satisfaction with leisure activity rather than just participation in activity that explains higher levels of global life satisfaction (Hawkins et al., 2007; Hawkins, Foose & Binkley, 2004).

These research findings and others are important for activity professionals to understand. Often specialists who work with older adults are resistant to put forth the energy to invest in potentially highly satisfying activities and they just focus on having a busy calendar of offerings rather than finding out what activities mean the most to the older adult. Activity specialists are challenged to provide programs that do more than amuse. They are encouraged to utilize motivational techniques to ensure participation in high investment activities.

Adjusting to Change in Older Adulthood

Later adulthood is a period of life that is often accompanied by many role changes and stressful life events. Retirement, potential loss of health, and the death of one's spouse, friends, and siblings are all common events at this point in life. The ways that older adults adapt to these events varies greatly between individuals. Some older adults may adjust to significant life changes without much stress, while others may need professional support and guidance.

Whitbourne (1987) developed the concept of *identity style* to explain adaptation to aging and related events. According to Whitbourne, older adults generally fall into one of three types of identity style. The first identity style is assimilative. An individual with this style attempts to integrate new experiences into his/her existing identity. This identity style may lead to denial of the aging process. While older adults with this style generally have a perception of good health, they also may project problems to others instead of themselves (Hayslip & Panek, 1993). Adults with an accommodative identity style take the opposite approach. Accommodators change identity to fit the environment. While accommodation is generally more successful, it may be problematic on occasion. For example, loss of some functional abilities in old age may lead the individual to believe that he or she is *falling apart* and thus, accommodation is a daunting challenge.

Whitbourne (1987) suggested the balanced identity style as the most stable. Individuals with this identity style are able to assimilate or accommodate when necessary. They also tend to have a more realistic view of the aging process. As a consequence, they are likely to take preventive steps to combat the effects of aging, but will seek therapeutic services when necessary (Hayslip & Panek, 1993).

More recent work on identity focuses on management of the self (Coleman & Jerrome, 1999; Ruth & Coleman, 1996). Self-esteem, in this view, is the cornerstone of well-being and quality of life in later life.

The resilience of self-esteem involves strategies for self-maintenance, acceptance of difficulties, and avoidance of problems. Three interdependent processes are essential for maintaining the self across the adult years: immunizing processes such as denial, assimilative or compensatory processes, and accommodative or adjustment processes. In older adulthood, there tends to be a shift from assimilative to accommodative processes as a matter of coping. When this shift fails to occur, depression can be a result (Coleman & Jerrome, 1999). Practitioners who work with older adults can employ life review and life story writing as strategies to help preserve a sense of self and a strong identity in late life.

Self-Concept and Self-Esteem in Older Adulthood

The remainder of this chapter will discuss common role changes and adjustments in later life. In order to understand these changes, it is necessary to discuss a bit more about self-concept and self-esteem. Self-concept refers to the individual's self-identity or self-image. Hooyman and Kiyak (2008) describe self-concept as the "cognitive definition of one's identity" (p. 198). Poor self-concept may be a concern for older adults who base feelings about their identity on a role, such as worker or parent, which may be lost in later life.

Self-esteem can be defined as the emotional assessment of self (Hooyman & Kiyak, 2008). Since self-esteem is related to emotions, it is more likely to be affected by changes in social roles than self-concept. In older adulthood, if the changes in social roles involve loss, the loss very well may have a negative impact on self-esteem. The following strategies as suggested by Morgan (1979) may prove to be useful in supporting and/or maintaining self esteem:

1. Older adults need to define self, free of previous roles. It is more beneficial to focus on internal and individual qualities. For example, "I am a caring person" rather than "I am a good nurse."
2. Older adults need to accept the realities of the aging process. An individual is less likely to suffer loss of self-esteem if he or she is aware of what physical and social losses are inevitable, and what losses can be negotiated or accommodated.
3. Older adults need to be able to reevaluate goals throughout the lifecycle. Life circumstances sometimes change unexpectedly and as a consequence, life goals need to be readjusted to reflect the new circumstances thus enabling adjustment.
4. Older adults need to be able to reevaluate their lives objectively in terms of failures and successes. According to Hooyman and Kiyak (2008), an older adult who can do this will be better able to utilize successful past coping responses in current situations.

Social Networks in Older Adulthood

Social support networks in later life are crucial to the maintenance of well-being and a high level of life satisfaction. The social needs of older adults may be met by both family and friends. The following sections discuss common changes in the social networks of older adults.

Marriage

A majority of older adults are or have been married at some point in their lives. Research indicates that marriages generally remain stable (given that they were stable in middle age) into retirement and old age (Vinick & Ekerdt, 1989). The majority of older couples report satisfaction with their marriage. Comparisons of three generations of spouses indicated that older couples report higher levels of life satisfaction than do middle-aged couples, but lower than newlyweds (Gilford & Bengston, 1979; Markides & Hoppe, 1985). It is well-known that the marital or partner relationship plays a highly important role in ongoing social support in late life (Hooyman & Kiyak, 2008).

Although the quality of marriages appears to remain stable in old age, some changes can be expected to occur. A benefit that many older adults report is an increase in opportunities to spend time with children and grandchildren (Hooyman & Kiyak, 2008). In a study of retired veterans and spouses, about one-half of the respondents reported an increase in companionship activities or activities with the company of others in retirement. Generally, women maintained responsibilities for daily household tasks in old age. Men tended to increase participation in home maintenance tasks, often "projects" they had been saving for retirement (Vinick & Ekerdt, 1989). The *empty nest syndrome* is commonly perceived to be a crisis for older adults, especially women. Some research indicates, however, that children not leaving home at the appropriate time may create more stress for both the parent and the child (Hooyman & Kiyak, 2008; Neugarten & Neugarten, 1987).

Some problems can be expected in later life marriages, as in marriages of all ages. Most late life marriages do not produce serious consequences, however. Women who were used to being at home alone have reported feelings of impingement on their time from their husbands (Vinick & Ekerdt, 1989). Conflict also may arise when one partner is still working and the other retires (Siegel, 1990). Working women may feel disturbed if their retired husband does not assume responsibility for more household responsibilities (Vinick & Ekerdt, 1989). The problem that potentially has the greatest negative impact on a marriage usually arises when the illness or disability of one spouse forces the other into assuming primary care responsibilities (Hooyman & Kiyak, 2008; Shamoian & Thurston, 1986; Vinick & Ekerdt, 1989).

Divorce

While divorce was rare among older adults from a historical perspective, an increasing number of older adults are choosing to divorce (Hooyman & Kiyak, 2008). The rates of divorce today are higher among ethnic minority older adults, and the rate has more than doubled since the 1970s among the general population of older adults. Growth in the divorce rate in the Baby Boom generation will continue to change the nature of later life relationships. The number of never divorced individuals, however, declines with each 10 year cohort (Cherlin, 1981; Hooyman & Kiyak, 2008). When older people do make the decision to divorce, the recovery process may be much more difficult than for younger adults (Grambs, 1989; Shamoian & Thurston, 1986). It also is very difficult for older divorcees to find new partners, this is particularly the case among older women.

Widowhood

Widowhood is a situation that the majority of older women will face (Hooyman & Kiyak, 2008). Widows exceed widowers in the United States by a margin to five to one. This trend is largely due to (a) a longer life expectancy among women, (b) the common practice of men marrying younger women, and (c) the decreased incidence of remarriage by widowed women. Regardless of gender, older adults consider the death of a spouse to be the most stressful life event. Porcino (1983) lists the following situations that are most likely to create high levels of stress for older persons:

- when husbands die unexpectedly,
- when the widow/widower was very dependent on the spouse or the spouse was heavily dependent on him or her for social and emotional support,
- when the widow/widower did not have a career,
- when the widow/widower has attempted to be totally independent of relatives and friends or if his/her life has only revolved around the family,
- when teenage children are at home, and
- when the widow/widower's income drops significantly as a result of the death.

The continuation of long-term relationships with other family and friends provides crucial support to widows and widowers (Heinemann, 1983; Hooyman & Kiyak, 2008). Often these relationships are renegotiated and new roles are defined during the bereavement period. In addition to family support, bereavement support groups and programs may be helpful to the grieving spouse. Regardless of type of support, bereaved individuals need permission and encouragement to express their feelings.

Health declines and/or illnesses often occur during the first year of widowhood. The lack of human companionship that results from the death of a spouse contributes to increased vulnerability for physical and emotional illness (Porcino, 1983). Increased rates of chronic illness, mortality, and suicide also are found. A wide range of emotions (e.g., sadness, longing, loneliness, sorrow, guilt, and anger) are commonly expressed during the grieving process (DeSpelder & Strickland, 1992). These emotions may be evident particularly during holidays, anniversaries, birthdays, or other special days in the couple's life.

Intergenerational Relationships

Relationships with Adult Children

In spite of the modern day myths that older adults are forgotten by their busy children, most individuals maintain satisfying relationships with children and other family members. The extended family of the past was, in fact, never the prominent family arrangement. The nuclear family dominated even in early America when grandparents rarely lived to see their grandchildren (Hareven, 1992). As life expectancy has lengthened in recent decades, modern families find themselves providing increased amounts of intergenerational care. It is not uncommon for older adults to move to be closer to their adult children or vice versa. The ethic of care within families remains a strong theme among adult children (Hooyman & Kiyak, 2008).

The relationship between older adults and their adult children is typically interdependent and mutually satisfying. The relationship between parent and adult child is likely to remain stable until the parent experiences significant losses in functional ability. As health status declines, the adult child may have to assume some caregiving responsibilities.

Caregiving can be defined as provision of emotional support and physical services (Allatt, Keil, Bryman & Bytheway, 1987; Hooyman & Kiyak, 2008). Tasks involved in caregiving may range from daily telephone calls to personal assistance with feeding, bathing, and toileting. Oftentimes, the caregiver assumes responsibilities for infrequent or irregular assistance, and moves into a more time-consuming role as the functional status of the older adult continues to decline.

Grandparenting

The grandparenting role is one many that older adults look forward to assuming in old age. In 2000, about 41% of 10-year-old children had all four grandparents still living (Hooyman & Kiyak, 2008). With increasing life expectancy, more older adults can look forward to enjoying the grandparent role. Nearly 80% of grandparents see their grandchild/children during a month and 50% see grandchildren weekly (Hooyman & Kiyak, 2008). Grandparents who do not live close by are likely to maintain close ties with their grandchildren if they have a close relationship with their child (Kornhober & Woodward, 1981). Also, with increasing life expectancy there has been an increase in the number great grandparents.

A strong relationship between grandparent and grandchild can benefit both. Grandparents can offer children unconditional love and prevent them from developing negative stereotypes of older people (Hooyman & Kiyak, 2008; Kornhober & Woodward, 1981). Grandchildren can provide support and reinforce feelings in the grandparents that the family line will be continued (Robertson, 1977).

Variables that influence the style of grandparent include education, lifestyle, marital status, and age. Wood and Robertson (1976) classified grandparents into four groups:

1. *Apportioned Type:* This grandparent views social norms and personal needs as important in achieving satisfaction in the grandparent role.
2. *Symbolic Type:* This grandparent views social norms as important, but has low personal need. The symbolic grandparent finds the status of grandparent to be most rewarding.
3. *Individualized Type:* This grandparent views the personal benefits of being a grandparent as most rewarding and is less concerned with social norms.
4. *Remote Type:* This grandparent does not draw any satisfaction from personal interactions or the social role.

Generally, the relationship between grandparents and grandchildren is warm and indulgent. Most grandparents do not interfere with the parent/child relationship under normal circumstances. A family crisis, such as divorce, often changes this norm. Grandparents with children who are divorcing often provide financial support and also may provide grandchildren with a place to live during or following the divorce.

Friendships

Friendship networks provide an important social support for older adults. Based on Carstenson's (1991) Socioemotional Selectivity Theory, older adults have benefitted from a lifetime of informal networks of friends. When time becomes narrowed due to advancing age, then a narrowing to the closest friendships can be expected. This narrowing should not be interpreted to represent disengagement but rather it represents the selection of those relationships that offer the most emotional intimacy (Hooyman & Kiyak, 2008). Intimacy, a sense of belonging, and interdependency are needs that are related to the satisfaction that friendships can help to foster. Relationships with friends differ from those with family members due to their voluntary nature and emphasis on mutual gain.

Defining friendship is difficult because of its subjective nature. One definition of friendship relates the importance of mutuality (Stevens-Long, 1984). Specifically, friendship involves mutual self-disclosure, mutual commitment, and mutual expectations. Most friendships can be placed into one of two broad categories: interest-related friendships, and deep friendships (Hayslip & Panek, 1993). Interest-related friendships are developed on the basis of common lifestyles and similar interests between two individuals (Bensman & Lilienfield, 1979). Deep friendships are more intimate and focus less on mutual interests. These friendships tend to last throughout life and the individuals involved are less concerned with equity than the long-term commitment to friendship that they share (Roberts & Scott, 1986).

Not surprisingly, older adults living alone have higher levels of contact with peer friends than those who live with a spouse or other family member (Wister, 1990). Healthy, active older adults also have greater levels of contact with friends. Functional impairment can put older people at risk of losing friends when the impairment prevents the individual from fulfilling obligations and meeting the other person's expectations. Friends provide some informal support for older individuals who are disabled; however, support from family members is preferred by most older people (Adams, 1986). Typically, friends provide support when it is convenient or the need for help is unpredictable. Friendships are extremely important for maintaining intimacy and confidences, especially when family members are physically at a distance or do not fill the need for closeness (Hooyman & Kiyak, 2008).

Based on the importance of friendships to overall health, well-being, and satisfaction with life in older adulthood, different strategies to promote person-environment fit are the focus of current interventions in gerontology practice (Hooyman & Kiyak, 2008). In spite of all the research on practical social networking interventions, we still know very little about the effectiveness of professional work in this area (Hooyman & Kiyak, 2008). While specific strategies have been shown to be effective, such as "community watch" programs and religious/faith-based support networks, there is much to be learned about what kind of support services will be appropriate for new cohorts of older adults such as the Baby Boomers. The challenge is and will continue to be how to effectively support friendship networks through more formal social service programs.

Retirement

Retirement is a social institution largely unique to the 20th century but with the expectation that it will continue in the 21st century. Prior to this timeframe, few individuals lived long enough to reach is considered retirement age. In addition to the longevity that is associated with 20th century higher standards of living, industrialization and surplus labor were major factors in the development of widespread retirement (Hooyman & Kiyak, 2008). The passage of Social Security legislation in 1935 insured the right to financial security in old age. Today, the vast majority of adults can look forward to spending several years in retirement but patterns of retirement have distinctly changed over time. With the coming of the Baby Boomers in the older adult population, retirement patterns are expected to continue to change.

Patterns of employment among older adults from 1994 through to 2007 show an increasing percentage of 65 year old women who are working full-time. For example in 1994, 48.4% of 65-year old women worked full-time, which can be compared with 63.7% in 2007. A parallel increase for 65-year-old men is also true, with 62.3 % engaged in full-time work in 1994 com-

pared with 76.1% in 2007 (Rix, 2008). For adults who are 66–69 years as well as 70 and older, there are similar patterns of increase in the percentage of people who are working either full-time or part-time. These figures illustrate changing retirement/employment patterns from the 1990s through to the first decade of the 21st century (cf. Rix for additional information regarding employment patterns among adults age 55 and older). These shifts are expected to continue with far more people who are 65 and older wanting to or needing to stay employed. Older women and older adults from ethnic minorities are more likely to continue to work based on financial need (Hooyman & Kiyak, 2008).

In the early 21st century, it is clear that older adults prefer to feel productive, either need or desire to remain employed at some level of involvement, and are an important factor in the changing economy and labor force (Rix, 2008). This change from the 1900s when retirement was first institutionalized, however, has not eliminated employment bias due to age. While older workers are more reliable, experienced, and committed to their jobs, some employers still hold ageist attitudes toward employing older workers (Hooyman & Kiyak, 2008). One of the most important points about employment and retirement that activity professionals should keep in mind is that older workers want to work and they are good workers. This source of experienced labor is invaluable in the provision of activity programs to older adults who may need or qualify for therapeutic activity services (e.g., occupational therapy, physical therapy, or recreational therapy).

The majority of American workers find the prospect of either full or partial retirement as desirable (Hooyman & Kiyak, 2008). The exception occurs when retirement is not planned or is not voluntary. Factor that affect the retirement decision include the availability of health insurance, adequate income, health status, the nature of the work environment and work stress as one approaches older adulthood, gender/ethnic minority status, and family/gender roles especially when it concerns caregiving for a family member who is impaired or ill (Hooyman & Kiyak, 2008). On another note, it is important to recognize that in current American society, mandatory retirement is illegal and age discrimination has been somewhat reduced based on the federal Age Discrimination in Employment Act (Hooyman & Kiyak, 2008). Negative stereotypes about older workers, however, continue to exist albeit at a more subtle level. Thus, early retirement from one's full-time career employment may still be involuntary and based on age discrimination. Other factors, however, can influence the decision to retire or no longer participate in the workforce; these factors include adequate income, health status, family preference, informal norms of the workplace, and long range plans (Hooyman & Kiyak, 2008).

As the future unfolds, it is important to keep in mind that Baby Boomers are likely to want a change in the type of work, more flexible work hours, and/or time to reinvent themselves through new career opportunities. The idea of second, third, or fourth careers for Boomers in their mid-50s and early 60s is a trend that has yet to unfold. The future of retirement patterns undoubtedly will be different based on the values and desires of new cohorts of adults who enter older adulthood, changing economic factors, and the availability to younger workers, all of which are unknown at this time.

One persistent theme about retirement is the pursuit of life satisfaction. Health and financial resources are two critical factors that influence satisfaction in retirement (Hooyman & Kiyak, 2008). Research findings show that health status is significantly correlated with retirement satisfaction. Other factors that are important include the perception that what the older adult is doing is useful, that the individual experiences a personal sense of control over his or her life, that the decision to retire is a personal decision, that the individual has a strong social network in place, and that the individual's spouse or partner relationship is strong and supportive. Older adults who retire on a voluntary basis tend to regard retirement more favorably than those who are forced to retire. The ability to sustain one's standard of living also is important. Family relationships and friendships that support the individual's decision to retire as well as provide for mutual engagement tend to produce higher retirement satisfaction than those who are involved in relationships that involve primary care responsibilities. Other factors related to retirement satisfaction include work values, job history, and the perception that daily activities are meaningful and have a purpose (Hooyman & Kiyak, 2008).

In the past, retirement was often viewed as a time of declining vigor, social disengagement, and isolation (Neugarten & Neugarten, 1987). In contract, contemporary older adults view retirement as a time of opportunity and continued activity. The emphasis today embraces a *retirement to something* (e.g., involvement in a retirement lifestyle) rather than a *retirement from something* (e.g., the job) (McCluskey, 1989). Overall, changes in the economy coupled with new cohorts of individuals who are reaching older adulthood will change the nature of retirement. Retirement may be reconceptualized as a time of opportunity rather than a transition to the end phases of life. New cohorts of

older adults are expected to be healthier, have more education and resources, and have higher motivation to push back the frontier regarding the older adult life stages, older adult expectations for productivity and creativity, and the opportunities that come with living long and living well.

Summary

Social gerontologists utilize a number of social and psychological theories to explain aging, as well as to describe successful aging and aging well in modern U.S. culture. Although many of the theories have limitations, some are useful in understanding aspects of the aging process, the experience of growing older, and for guiding activity interventions to meet the needs of older adults. Current national statistics on changing patterns among older adults coupled with research findings show that human aging is malleable based on the social institutions and times in which people live. Social gerontologists recognize that the story of human development within the context of increasing life expectancy and changing social conditions is still unfolding. What we know at this point is that (a) personality remains relatively stable throughout life becoming richer and richer as time goes by; (b) social relationships frequently undergo significant changes in later life based on both losses (e.g. the death of one's spouse or partner) as well as gains (e.g., the development of new intergenerational relationships); (c) the potential for caregiving increases with age and affects the social relationships and physical reserves of all who are involved; (d) many of the issues and challenges experienced by older adults are related to gender (women) and ethnicity; and (e) the nature of involvement in productive activities (paid or unpaid) will continue to evolve based on both personal characteristics and social/economic change .

Retirement is an institution was uniquely established in the 20th century but is clearly evolving as the 21st century ushers in new cohorts of older adults as well as significant economic change. Although retirement was previously viewed as a time of disengagement and inactivity, many older adults now, including the Baby Boomers, view retirement as a time of new opportunities that may involve paid work but clearly represent a time for an active lifestyle. As new cohorts of older adults redefine what retirement means, the ultimate goal for all older adults will be a stage in life that brings a sense of well-being and high satisfaction with life, and a time to experience successful aging and aging well.

Comprehension Questions

The reader can check for comprehension of the material presented in this chapter by answering the following questions:

1. Select two social theories of aging and comparatively discuss them in terms of how well they describe successful aging.

2. Describe how adult personality changes over the adult life stages. Include in your discussion how personality remains stable.

3. How does retirement affect older persons?

4. Discuss factors that influence older persons' social networks and why social networks are very important to the elderly.

5. Describe four types of grandparents.

6. What does it mean to retire in the 21st century? What are some of the factors that influence retirement and/or continued employment? How are the Baby Boomers likely to change what retirement means and what the expectation of retirees will be in the future?

References

Adams, R. G. (1986). A look at friendship and aging. *Generations, 10*(4), 40–43.

Allatt, P., Keil, T., Bryman, A. & Bytheway, B. (Eds.). (1987). *Women and the life cycle.* New York, NY: St. Martin's Press.

Baltes, P. B. & Baltes, M. M. (1990). *Successful aging: Perspectives from the behavioral sciences.* New York, NY: Cambridge University Press.

Baltes, M. M. & Carstensen, L. L. (1999). Chapter 12. Social-psychological theories and their applications to aging: From individual to collective. In V. L. Bengtson & K. W. Schaie (Eds.), *Handbook of Theories of Aging* (pp. 209–226). New York, NY: Springer.

Bengtson, V. L., Rice, C. J. & Johnson, M. L. (1999). Chapter 1. Are theories of aging important? Models and explanations in gerontology at the turn of the century. In V. L. Bengtson & K. W. Schaie (Eds.), *Handbook of Theories of Aging* (pp. 3–20). New York, NY: Springer.

Bensman, J. & Lilienfield, R. (1979, October). Friendships and alienation. *Psychology Today, 13*(5), 55–66.

Carstensen, L. L. (1991). Selectivity theory: Social activity in life-span context. *Annual Review of Gerontology and Geriatrics, 11*, 195–217.

Cherlin, A. J. (1981). *Marriage, divorce, remarriage: Changing patterns in the post-war United States.* Cambridge, MA: Harvard University Press.

Cherlin, A. & Furstenberg, F. F. (1986). Grandparents and family crisis. *Generations, 3*, 26–28.

Coleman, P. G. & Jerrome, D. (1999). Chapter 21. Applying theories of aging to gerontological practice through teaching and research. In V. L. Bengtson & K. W. Schaie (Eds.), *Handbook of Theories of Aging* (pp. 344–395). New York, NY: Springer.

Costa, P. T. & McCrae, R. R. (1989). Personality continuity and the changes of adult life. In M. Storandt & G. R. VandenBos (Eds.). *The adult years: Continuity and change* (pp. 41–77). Washington, DC: American Psychological Association.

Costa, P. T. & McCrae, R. R. (1988). Personality in adulthood: A six-year longitundinal study of self-reports and spouse ratings on the NEO Personality Inventory. *Journal of Personality and Social Psychology, 54*, 853–863.

Cumming, E. & Henry, W. E. (1961). *Growing old: The process of disengagement.* New York, NY: Basic Books.

DeSpelder, L. A. & Strickland, A. L. (1992). *The last dance: Encountering death and dying.* Palo Alto, CA: Mayfield.

Erickson, E. H. (1959). Identity and the life cycle. *Psychological Issues, 1.*

Fontane, P. E. & Solomon, J. C. (1996). Editors' introduction—Aging well in contemporary society, part II—Choices and processes. *American Behavioral Scientist, 39*(3), 230.

Gilford, R. & Bengston, V. (1979). Measuring marital satisfaction in three generations: Positive and negative dimensions. *Journal of Marriage and the Family, 41*(22), 387–98.

Gilligan, C. (1982). *In a different voice: Psychological theory and women's development.* Cambridge, MA: Harvard University Press.

Grambs, J. D. (1989). *Women over 40: Visions and realities.* New York, NY: Springer.

Gubrium, J. F. & Holstein, J. A. (1999). Chapter 16. Constructionist perspectives on aging. In V. L. Bengtson & K. W. Schaie (Eds.), *Handbook of Theories of Aging* (pp. 287–305). New York, NY: Springer.

Haley, W. E., Levine, E. G., Brown, S. L. & Bartolucci, A. A. (1987). Stress, appraisal, coping, and social support as predictors of adaptational outcome among dementia caregivers. *Psychology and Aging, 2*(4), 323–330.

Hareven, T. K. (1992). Family and generational relations in the later years: A historical perspective. *Generations, 17*(3), 17–22.

Harris, R. L., Elliott, A. M. & Holmes, D. S. (1986). The timing of psychosocial transitions and changes in women's lives: An examination of women aged 45 to 60. *Journal of Personality and Social Psychology, 51,* 409–416.

Havighurst, R. J. & Albrecht, R. (1953). *Older people.* New York, NY: Longmans, Green.

Hawkins, B. A., Foose, A. K., Binkley, A. L., Cheung, S. Y., Harahousou, V. & Lamura, G. (September 2007). Satisfaction with life in old age: The contribution of leisure in five countries. IFPRA World — *Journal of the International Federation of Parks and Recreation Administration,* pp. 8–9.

Hawkins, B. A., Foose, A. K. & Binkley, A. L. (2004). Contribution of leisure to the life satisfaction of older adults in Australia and the United States. *World Leisure Journal, 46*(2), 4–12.

Hawkins, B. A. (2003). Aging well: Construct genesis and ideology. *Global Aging Initiative Newsletter,* Spring 2003. Bloomington, IN: Indiana University Center on Aging and Aged.

Hayslip, B. H. & Panek, P. E. (1993). *Adult development and aging.* New York, NY: HarperCollins College Publishers.

Heinemann, G. D. (1983). Family involvement and support for widowed persons. In T. H. Brubaker (Ed.), *Family relationships in later life* (pp. 127–148). Beverly Hills, CA: Sage Publications.

Hendricks, J. & Leedham, C.A. (1991). Theories of aging: Implications for human services. In Paul K. H. Kim (Ed.), *Serving the elderly: Skills for practice.* NY: Aldine de Gruyler.

Herzog, A. R. & Markus, H. R. (1999). Chapter 13. The self-concept in life span and aging research. In V. L. Bengtson & K. W. Schaie (Eds.), *Handbook of Theories of Aging* (pp. 227–252). New York, NY: Springer.

Hooyman, N. R. & Kiyak, H. A. (2008). *Social gerontology: A multidisciplinary perspective.* (8th ed.). Boston, MA: Allyn and Bacon.

Johnson, T. F. (1995). Aging well in contemporary society: Introduction. *American Behavioral Scientist, 39*(2), 120–130.

Jung, C. G. (1933). *Modern man in search of a soul.* New York, NY: Harcourt, Brace, & Company.

Kahn, R. L. (2002). On 'successful aging and wellbeing: Self-rated compared with Rowe and Kahn.' *The Geronotologist, 42,* 725–726.

Krain, M. A. (1995). Policy implications for a society aging well: Employment, retirement, education, and leisure policies for the 21st century. *American Behavioral Scientist, 39*(2), 131–151.

Kelly, J. R., Steinkamp, M. W. & Kelly, J. R. (1986). Later life leisure: How they play in Peoria. *The Gerontologist, 26*(5), 531–537.

Kornhober, A. & Woodward, K. L. (1981). *Grandparents/grandchildren: The vital connection.* Garden City, NY: Anchor Press/Doubleday.

Levinson, D. J. (1978). *The season's of a man's life.* New York, NY: Knopf.

Markides, K. & Hoppe, S. (1985, March). Marital satisfaction in three generations of Mexican Americans. *Social Science Quarterly, 66,* 147–154.

Marshall, V. W. (1999). Chapter 24. Analyzing social theories of aging. In V. L. Bengtson & K. W. Schaie (Eds.), *Handbook of Theories of Aging* (pp. 434–455). New York, NY: Springer.

Mannell, R. C. (1993). High-investment activity and life satisfaction among older adults: Committed, serious leisure, and flow activities. In J. R. Kelly (Ed.), *Activity and Aging: Staying Involved.* Newbury Park, CA: Sage Publications.

McCluskey, N. G. (1989). Retirement and the contemporary family. *Journal of Psychotherapy and the Family, 5*(1–2), 211–224.

Moody, H. R. (2006). *Aging – Concepts and controversies* (5th ed.). Thousand Oaks, CA: Pine Forge Press, Sage Publications.

Morgan, J. C. (1979). *Becoming old.* New York, NY: Springer.

Myllykangas, S. A. (2004). AIDS as a Terminal Illness: The Meaning of Leisure for Female Older Adults and Caregivers. Doctoral Dissertation, Indiana University–Bloomington.

Neugarten, B. L. & Hagestad, G. (1976). Age and the life course. In R. H. Binstock & E. Shanas (Eds.), *Handbook of aging and the social sciences* (pp. 35–37). New York, NY: Van Nostrand Reinhold.

Neugarten, B. L. & Neugarten, D. A. (1987, May). The changing meanings of age. *Psychology Today, 21*(5), 29–33.

Porcino, J. (1983). *Growing older getting better: A handbook for women in the second half of life.* Reading, MA: Addison-Wesley Publishing, Co.

Quadagno, J. & Reid, J. (1999). Chapter 19. The political economy perspective of aging. In V. L. Bengtson & K. W. Schaie (Eds.), *Handbook of Theories of Aging* (pp. 344–358). New York, NY: Springer.

Reinke, B. J., Holmes, D. S. & Harris, S. L. (1985). The timing of psychosocial changes in women's lives: The years 25 to 45. *Journal of Personality and Social Psychology, 48,* 1353–1364.

Riddick, C. (1985). Life satisfaction determinants of older males and females. *Leisure Sciences, 1*(1), 47–63.

Riley, M. W., Johnson, M. & Foner, A. (1972). *Aging and society.* New York, NY: Russell Sage Foundation.

Rix, S. E. (2008). Fact sheet: Update on the aged 55+ worker: 2007. Washington, DC: AARP Public Policy Institute, Fact Sheet Number 142.

Roberts, K. A. & Scott, J. P. (1986). Friendships of older men and women: Exchange patterns and satisfaction. *Psychology and Aging, 1,* 103–109.

Robertson, J. F. (1977). Grandmotherhood: A study of role conceptions. *Journal of Marriage and the Family, 39,* 165–174.

Rose, A. M. (1965). A current theoretical issue is social gerontology. In A. M. Rose and W. A. Peterson (Eds.), *Older people and their social worlds.* Philadelphia, PA: F. A. Davis.

Rowe, J. W. & Kahn, R. L. (1997). The Forum—Successful aging. The *Gerontologist, 37,* 433–440.

Rowe, J. W. & Kahn, R. L. (1998). Successful aging. New York, NY: Pantheon Books.

Ruth, J. E. & Coleman, P. G. (1996). Personality and aging: Coping and management of the self in later life. In J. E. Birren & K. W. Shaie (Eds.), *Handbook of the psychology of aging* (4th ed.) (pp. 308–322). San Diego, CA: Academic Press.

Siegel, R. J. (1990). Love and work after 60: An integration of personal and professional growth within a long-term marriage. *Journal of Women and Aging, 2*(2), 69–79.

Shamoian, C. A. & Thurston, F. D. (1986). Marital discord and divorce among the elderly. *Medical Aspects of Human Sexuality, 20*(8), 25–34.

Smyer, M. & Hofland, B. F. (1982). Divorce and family support in later life. *Journal of family issues, 3,* 61–77.

Sommers, T. (1985). Caregiving: A woman's issue. *Generations, 10*(1), 9–13.

Stevens-Long, J. (1984). *Adult life: Developmental processes* (2nd ed). Palo Alto, CA: Mayfield.

U.S. Senate Special Committee on Aging. (1989). *Developments in Aging* (Volume 1). Washington, DC: U.S. Government Printing Office.

Vinick, B. H., & Ekerdt, D. J. (1989). Retirement and the family. *Generations, 13*(2), 53–56.

Whitbourne, S. K. (1987). Personality development in adulthood and old age: Relationships among identity style, health, and well-being. In K. W. Schaie & C. Eisdorfer (Eds.), *Annual review of gerontology and geriatrics* (pp. 189–216). New York, NY: Springer.

Wister, A. (1990). Living arrangements and informal social support among the elderly. *Journal of Housing for the Elderly, 6,* (1–2), 33–43.

Wood, V. & Robertson, J. F. (1976). The significance of grandparenthood. In J. F. Gubrium (Ed.), *Time, roles, and self in old age* (pp. 278–304). New York, NY: Human Sciences Press.

• CHAPTER 5 •

Common Physical Diseases, Illnesses, and Disabilities

Learning Objectives

1. Explain differences between normal aging versus disease processes in older adults.

2. Describe the "health status" of older Americans.

3. Distinguish between acute and chronic health problems.

4. Describe the common chronic physical health problems of older adults.

5. Define the concepts of activities of daily living (ADLs), instrumental activities of daily living (IADLs), and functional independence.

6. Describe the prevalence of functional limitations among older adult populations.

Key Terms

- Accidents
- Health Status
- Activities of Daily Living (ADLs)
- Heart Disease
- Acute Illness
- Impairment
- Arthritis
- Influenza
- Cancer
- Instrumental Activities of
- Cardiovascular Disease
- Daily Living (IADLs)
- Chronic Conditions
- Metabolic Disease
- COPD
- Oral Disease
- Diabetes
- Osteoporosis
- Functional Independence
- Pneumonia
- Thyroid Disease

Introduction

Good health in later life is of great importance to all adults. Declines in bodily functions that are associated with growing older do not necessarily mean that all adults will automatically suffer from illness, impairment, or disability. Health status, good or bad, is highly individual in the older adult population. There is a great deal of variability in how acute and chronic conditions are experienced from one older person to the next. Older adults are the most heterogeneous of all age groups; that is, older adults are highly individualized.

In this chapter, physical health-related conditions are distinguished from the normal aging process. Health status is discussed, especially as it influences functional limitations and independence. Chronic and acute conditions that are common among older adults are overviewed. The chapter concludes with a discussion of functional independence and the management of physical health status in old age.

Health and Normal Aging

In spite of the inevitable declines in physical functioning that are expected with age, poor health is not necessarily a consequence of growing older. Health status is determined, in large measure, by several factors both within the individual as well as the environment in which he or she lives. A lowered resistance and/or genetic predisposition in older persons may increase the risk for disease or illness in later life from environmental carcinogens and infections. Also, losses in other bodily functions (e.g., bone demineralization) may place an older person at greater risk for accidents or injuries from falls. Selected sociodemographic factors (e.g., poverty, education, race, gender) also are related to increased incidence of illness or disease. Stress may influence the older person's ability to fight infections or cope with long-term disease. Health maintenance and promotion, therefore, are important concerns. Older adults are very aware of the consequences of poor health. For example, the loss of financial security, personal autonomy, and social networks in the wake of one or more chronic conditions can be quite overwhelming and threatening to long-term survival. Based on all these factors, health status is a significant concern of the older population.

Traditionally, the health status of the nation has been measured on the basis of key indicators such as life expectancy, mortality rates, morbidity statistics, and the control of infectious disease (Federal Interagency Forum on Aging-Related Statistics, 2008; U.S. Department of Health and Human Services, 2000). This view,

however, leaves certain gaps in our understanding of the health status of older people. The World Health Organization (1947) envisioned health as more than the absence of disease, illness, or disability. According to the WHO, health is the combination and interaction of physical, mental, and social well-being. Good health is a sense of well-being that is experienced when the body, mind, spirit, and social aspects of life are in harmony.

While growing older may increase the risk of experiencing *chronic* (long-term) disease, the majority of older people perceive their health positively and do not feel that their health is limiting their daily activities (Federal Interagency Forum on Aging-Related Statistics, 2008). Older adults who are happier and more satisfied with their lives, also tend to be healthier. The fact that as age increases there is a higher risk for chronic disease, as well as a lower resistance to *acute* (short-term) illnesses, does not mean that growing old guarantees a poorer health status. Most chronic diseases are the product of long-term engagement in hazardous habits and a lower resistance to disease may be combated by maintaining an active and healthy lifestyle.

Chronic Conditions vs. Acute Illness

Chronic conditions are distinguished from *acute illnesses* in several ways. Chronic diseases or conditions are usually the most troubling in old age because they are difficult to diagnose and manage. As adults experience changes associated with normal aging, the ability to distinguish the symptoms associate with chronic disease is often unclear. Aches and pains, fatigue, transient changes in appetite, vision disturbances, occasional feelings of depression or confusion may be experienced as part of growing old and can be associated with a chronic disease as well (Ferrini & Ferrini, 2008; Jett, 2008).

Chronic conditions are ongoing, have progressive deteriorative effects, and usually are irreversible or incurable. Chronic conditions often start much earlier in life (e.g., heart disease) but become manifest in later life when treatment and management is more difficult, or not possible. It is not uncommon for older persons to experience long-term financial, social, and psychological adversity in the presence of a newly diagnosed chronic disease. The leading ten causes of death among adults age 65 and older in rank order are: heart disease, cancers of all types, cerebrovascular diseases (stroke), chronic lower respiratory diseases,

Alzheimer's disease, diabetes mellitus, influenza and pneumonia, diseases of the kidney, accidents, and septicemia or blood poisoning (Heron, Hoyert, Xu, Scott, & Tejada-Vera, 2008). Of these ten causes, nine (excluding Alzheimer's disease) are associated with lifestyle and eight (excluding accidents) could be considered chronic diseases. Older adults represent 40% of all chronic disease cases in the United States even though they only constitute around 13% of the population. Among the older adult population, more than 80% suffer from at least one chronic condition (Ferrini & Ferrini, 2008).

The older the person becomes, the greater the risk of experiencing one or more chronic condition(s). Among all people over age 65, regardless of age, gender, race, or ethnicity, heart disease and cancer are the two leading causes of death, both of which are chronic conditions caused by unhealthy lifestyle behaviors (Federal Interagency Forum on Aging-Related Statistics, 2008). While some individuals and some chronic conditions do not seriously impair daily functioning, other conditions are devastating. The incidence of chronic disease is much higher among older adults than any other age group in the U.S. population.

Acute illnesses, on the other hand, are episodic and short-term in duration. They are caused by viral, bacterial, or fungal infections. These illnesses come on rapidly and are usually curable through medical treatment. The cost of healthcare for acute illnesses is typically much lower than for chronic diseases due to the short-term, curable nature of acute conditions. Older people have about the same risk for infectious or acute illnesses as do younger people. The complications that may result from an acute illness episode, however, can be deadly for the older person whose immune system resistance to secondary infections is lower. The occurrence of pneumonia and influenza is especially high in the older adult population, and these infections combined account for the seventh leading cause of death among persons over age 65.

The presence of one or more chronic conditions increases the risk for secondary, acute infections. Also, poor management of environmental quality (e.g., clean homes, temperature controlled air) may increase the incidence and severity of acute illnesses among older adults. Some viruses and bacteria remain in the body in a latent state only to recur in older adulthood (e.g., herpes zoster or shingles, tuberculosis). The diagnosis of acute illnesses, like that of chronic conditions, is more difficult in older persons. Symptoms (e.g., loss of interest, depression, fatigue, loss of appetite) may be confused with existing chronic conditions, aging-related declines, or medication interactions. Thus, acute illnesses present special challenges in the diagnosis and treatment, as well as management of health status in the older adult population (Satariano, 2006).

In summary, older people experience more chronic and acute illnesses than do younger persons. The risk for multiple chronic and acute conditions increases with age. These conditions may go unrecognized, and thus untreated, due to the extra attention needed to identify symptoms and to render a proper diagnosis in the older adult. Older persons also have increased susceptibility to secondary infections and adverse drug interactions. The psychological impact of chronic and acute health problems often goes unreported and undetected, thus complicating treatment and health management. Finally, the care and management of health in older persons may be challenged by a shrinking social support system (especially among the very old), as well as a healthcare system that discriminates against older people (Satariano, 2006).

Chronic Conditions Common to Older Adults

Heart disease is the leading cause of death among older persons followed by cancer and cerebrovascular diseases (Heron, Hoyert, Xu, Scott & Tejada-Vera, 2008). These three chronic conditions account for more than the majority of all deaths in people over age 65. Cardiovascular disease increases dramatically with age in both men and women. Other common chronic conditions in older adults include arthritis, osteoporosis, chronic obstructive pulmonary diseases (COPD), diabetes, urinary system diseases, and intestinal diseases (Ferrini & Ferrini, 2008).

Cardiovascular Disease

Heart disease accounts for nearly 50% of all deaths among older people. Atherosclerosis, coronary artery disease, high blood pressure (hypertension), congestive heart failure, stroke, and aneurysms are the most common diseases of the cardiovascular system (Ferrini & Ferrini, 2008).

Atherosclerosis is a narrowing of the blood vessels that occurs over time with the deposition of fat on the lining of the vessel wall. This condition begins in childhood and progresses throughout life as a result of a diet that is high in cholesterol or fat saturated foods. Atherosclerosis is different than arteriosclerosis, which is the hardening of the arteries due to a progressive loss in elasticity in the blood vessel with age. Arteriosclerosis is associated with normal aging and atherosclerosis is a disease condition that results primarily from a diet that is high in animal-based fat. Other factors that increase the risk of atherosclerosis are high blood pressure, stress, diabetes mellitus, obesity, sedentary lifestyle, cigarette smoking, and familial predisposition to heart attacks (Ferrini & Ferrini, 2008).

As atherosclerosis progresses, slowly cutting off blood supply due to thickened vessel walls and fatty deposits, the risk of injury to the affected organ increases. Clogged arteries can occur anywhere throughout the body but the most life threatening areas that can be affected are the coronary (heart) arteries, as well as the vessels leading to the brain. The reduced blood flow to the heart results in coronary artery disease (heart disease). If the blood supply is compromised or blocked too long, then the heart muscle is damaged and a heart attack may ensue. Symptoms of a heart attack are pain in the neck, arm, and/or chest; shortness of breath; weakness; dizziness; confusion; and/or numbness. Symptoms may vary across the genders and individuals. Today, however, it is well-understood that men and women experience the symptoms of a heart attack differently.

Atherosclerosis in the legs can cause cramping and pain in the legs. Coldness or numbness also may be experienced. Modifications in diet, increased exercise, and the cessation of other health risk habits have been shown to slow the development of atherosclerosis.

Hypertension, or high blood pressure, also increases the risk for heart disease and stroke. Blood pressure that is higher than 140 hg systolic and 90 hg diastolic represents an increased risk for organ damage and heart attack. Arteriosclerosis, or hardening of the arteries, will normally elevate blood pressure with age but not to the extent necessary to present a risk factor for a heart attack or stroke. A variety of factors are suspected of causing hypertension including age, gender, stress, genetics, race, diet (especially high intake of salt), and obesity (Ferrini & Ferrini, 2008). In most cases of high blood pressure, however, the cause may not be known. Untreated hypertension results in damage to the heart and other organs of the body. Hypertension may be treated with drug therapy, reduced salt intake, exercise, reduced fat intake, the elimination of cigarette smoking, and reduced alcohol consumption.

Congestive heart failure results when the heart muscle can no longer pump adequately to meet the demands of the body. When the heart is unable to pump sufficiently, damage to other organs results as an insufficient blood supply is delivered to them. Symptoms associated with congestive heart failure are shortness of breath and swelling from the accumulation of blood and fluid in the body (edema). Hypertension is the leading cause of congestive heart failure followed by other causes such as heart attacks, diabetes, and diseased heart valves. Congestive heart failure can be managed with medications, rest, and dietary modifications (Ferrini & Ferrini, 2008; Hooyman & Kiyak, 2008).

Atherosclerosis and arteriosclerosis also can affect the blood vessels to the brain, thus increasing the risk for stroke or cerebrovascular injury. Stroke is the disruption of the blood supply to the brain or an area within the brain, which causes brain injury, malfunction, or death of brain cells. Stroke or cerebrovascular disease is the third leading cause of death among persons age 65 years and older. The risk of stroke increases in persons who have heart disease (Ferrini & Ferrini, 2008; Hooyman & Kiyak, 2008).

Strokes can be caused by either a blood clot (cerebral thrombosis) that cuts off or reduces blood to the brain, or when a weak area of a blood vessel in the brain bursts causing a brain hemorrhage. Hemorrhage occurs primarily among persons with high blood pressure. Strokes caused by clots are more common among older adults in general. Strokes are a major cause of disability among older people. Depending on what part of and how much of the brain is damaged, the stroke victim will experience damaged functioning to some area of the body. Either paralysis to one side of the body and/or damage to the speech center are sometimes permanent. Some areas of functioning, however, can be regained through rehabilitation that makes use of unaffected areas of the brain (Ferrini & Ferrini, 2008; Hooyman & Kiyak, 2008).

The warning sign of a pending stroke is called a transient ischemic attack (TIA) or mini-stroke. TIAs are small disruptions that often only last for a short time; that is, a few minutes to a day. The symptoms associated with TIAs include weakness, dizziness or blackout, disturbances in speech, and changes in personality or affect. Strokes are preventable by reducing the risk factors, which are high blood pressure, medical management of diabetes, and drug therapy to thin the blood (Ferrini & Ferrini, 2008).

Cancer

Cancers, or malignant neoplasms, are the second leading cause of death among all people 65 years and older. There are different types of cancers including the most common, which are lung, colon and rectal, stomach, pancreatic, prostate, and breast cancer (Ferrini & Ferrini, 2008; Satariano, 2006). Lung cancer is the leading cancer-related cause of death in older persons followed by colorectal cancer (American Cancer Society, 2007a).

The incidence of lung cancer is much higher in men than in women; however, more women die from lung cancer compared with breast cancer (American Cancer Society, 2007a). The leading cause of lung cancer is cigarette smoking, which is responsible for more than 90% of all lung cancer. Other causes of lung cancer include environmental toxins such as air pollution, and second-hand cigarette smoke. Smokers are more likely to get mouth cancers and if the smoker also consumes alcohol, the risk of developing oral cancer increases (Ferrini & Ferrini, 2008).

Among women, breast cancer is the second leading source of death followed by colon and rectal cancers (American Cancer Society, 2007a). For men, prostate cancer is the second source of death followed by colon and rectal cancer. Among both men and women, lung cancer deaths have decreased since the 1990s. Colon cancer is more common than rectal cancer. If colon cancer is diagnosed when localized, survival rates are higher; however, if it is not identified until after spreading, survival as seriously diminished. The causes of colorectal cancers are: (a) family history of cancer; (b) persistent colon inflammation; (c) polyps in the colon; (d) high fat, low fiber diet; and (e) sedentary lifestyle. The most common symptom associated with colorectal cancer is rectal bleeding, which is easily detected through regular health screening. Most colon cancer is treated with surgery followed by chemotherapy and radiation to help prevent recurrence. The recurrence rate for colorectal cancer is quite high at 50% (Ferrini & Ferrini, 2008).

Among women, breast cancer is the most frequently diagnosed cancer, however, incidence rates have leveled off since 2003 (American Cancer Society, 2007b). While incidence has leveled off, deaths due to breast cancer in women rises with age. Survival for women is clearly better among younger women compared with women who are 85 and older. Approximately 75% of all breast cancer is diagnosed in older women with the causes still not definitely known. Suspected risk factors include higher levels of estrogen, high fat diet, sedentary lifestyle, obesity, inadequate exposure to sunlight that results in an inadequate production of vitamin D, and family history. Early detection through regular screening and early treatment are effective in reducing the morbidity and mortality rates associated with breast cancer (American Cancer Society, 2007b). The appearance of a suspicious lump is the most common symptom of breast cancer. Treatment can range from radiation and lumpectomy to the removal of the breast (mastectomy) or in some cases, a radical mastectomy to remove the breast, lymph nodes, and sur-

rounding tissue. Radical mastectomy is typically only pursued when the cancer has spread beyond the localized lump to the lymph nodes. Treatment success for breast cancer is quite high, especially with early detection through self-examination and mammography. Older women, however, engage in self-examination and routine mammography screening at a significantly lower rate than do younger women. When breast cancer is identified in older women, aggressive treatment is sometimes not pursued with a parallel vigor to that for younger women. Thus, improvement in the rate of self-examination and more aggressive treatment of breast cancer among older women is a needed service area (American Cancer Society, 2007b).

Men experience prostate cancer that places this type of cancer in first place for new cases and second place as the major cause of death from all diseases (American Cancer Society, 2007a). Prostate cancer is a slow growing cancer, which makes it amenable to early detection and treatment. Risk factors for prostate cancer include age, race (more black men experience cancer than white men), and testosterone levels. Detection is through an annual internal examination for nodules on the prostate and/or a specific blood test. Cancer that is just in the prostate can be surgically removed. If the cancer has spread (metastasized), surgical removal of the testes or hormone therapy is used to manage the disease (American Cancer Society, 2007a).

Skin cancer is the last cancer that will be discussed in this chapter. Death from skin cancer is generally not common; however, the risk of skin cancer with age makes it a concern to older adults. There are several types of skin cancer of which only one is deadly—melanoma. The rate of estimated new cases of melanoma is at 4% among both men and women, which is indicative of the rising concern for this type of cancer in the American population (American Cancer Society, 2007a). The primary cause of skin cancer is exposure to excess sunlight and people with a history of sunburns are at greater risk for skin cancer. With ozone depletion coupled with the social value attached to suntanned skin, the rate of skin cancer is increasing in recent years (American Cancer Society, 2007a). Symptoms of skin cancer include abnormal mole-like growths that continue to grow, change in color, and easily bleed with injury. Through early detection, basal cell, squamous, and melanoma cancers are treatable by surgical removal of the cancer cells. If melanoma has spread to other parts of the body, chemotherapy is used to treat the cancer (American Cancer Society, 2007a).

Often the symptoms associated with cancer are not easy to detect in the early stages because they are confused with normal age-related changes. Weakness and fatigue, depression, weight loss, and changes in appetite are some of the some of the symptoms that difficult to judge as either indicators of cancer or as normal changes associated with aging. The warning signals for potential cancer are: (a) changes in bowel or bladder functions, (b) nagging cough or hoarseness, (c) discharge or bleeding, (d) a lump or thickening in the breast or elsewhere on the body, (e) an unhealed sore, (f) difficulty swallowing or intestinal disturbance, and (g) changes in a wart or mole (Ferrini & Ferrini, 2008). Cancers are typically treated using radiation, chemotherapy, and/or surgery. The course of treatment is determined by the overall health status of the individual, the type of cancer, and the growth rate of the cancer. The high incidence of cancer in older adults may be related with the length of time it takes for most cancers to develop and be detected, in addition to immune system declines with age. A poor diet, an unhealthy lifestyle, and environmental carcinogens also have been implicated in the increasing incidence of cancer.

Chronic Obstructive Pulmonary Diseases—COPD

The occurrence of chronic respiratory conditions increases with age primarily due to declines in pulmonary functioning, genetic disposition, and long-term exposure to environmental carcinogens, of which cigarette smoking is the leading cause. Decrements in the immune system also may contribute to increased episodes of acute respiratory infections that eventually lead to chronic obstructive pulmonary disease (COPD). COPD is characterized by seriously damaged lung tissues that result from several conditions including chronic bronchitis, emphysema, fibrosis, and asthma. These conditions develop slowly, are progressive, may result in frequent hospitalization, produce major changes in lifestyle, and often end in death. Chronic bronchitis, the most common COPD, is characterized by the production of abundant sputum and a chronic cough. Breathing becomes more difficult as the condition progresses (Jett, 2008).

Emphysema is the destruction of the lung air sacs, which reduces oxygen intake and the excretion of carbon dioxide. Emphysema is common among long-time smokers and is irreversible. Modifications in lifestyle and pain reducing exercises can be used to manage the effects of this disease (Ferrini & Ferrini, 2008; Jett, 2008).

The treatment of COPD includes respiratory therapy, drug therapy, breathing exercises, environmen-

tal management to reduce exposure to air pollution, and lifestyle modifications (e.g., smoking cessation). As individuals age, the debilitating aspects of COPD sometimes dominate their attention, thus reducing the ability to attend to other activities. It is not uncommon to find a COPD patient totally preoccupied with their disease (Ferrini & Ferrini, 2008; Jett, 2008).

Diabetes Mellitus

Two types of diabetes are distinguished from one another: (a) Type I or juvenile diabetes, which usually is first diagnosed in youth; and (b) Type II or adult-onset diabetes, which generally presents in middle through later adulthood. The prevalence of diabetes, primarily Type II, in older adults is approximately 20% of all people over age 65. This percent increases among African American, Hispanic, and Native American populations (Ferrini & Ferrini, 2008). Two other disorders are also considered under diabetes; they are, impaired fasting glucose and impaired glucose tolerance (Jett, 2008)

Diabetes is caused by the lack of production or utilization of insulin in the metabolism of glucose (sugar) by the body's cells. In older adults, Type II diabetes is characterized by elevated levels of glucose in the blood and urine. Insulin, even if produced, is inadequately used by the body's cells in the metabolism of glucose. The result is an over-releasing of glucose in the blood by the liver, as well as an elevated production of insulin by the pancreas (Ferrini & Ferrini, 2008; Jett, 2008).

Symptoms associated with Type II diabetes are increased appetite, increased urination, weight loss, fatigue and weakness, excessive thirst, and slower healing of wounds. These symptoms may be confused with other aging-related changes in older adults. The detection of diabetes in older persons is often discovered through routine eye examination, medical testing, and hospitalization for other conditions. Predisposing factors that increase the risk for diabetes in old age include obesity and persistent overeating behavior (Ferrini & Ferrini, 2008; Hooyman & Kiyak, 2008).

The treatment of adult-onset diabetes (Type II) includes (a) weight loss through specified diets that are low in sugar and saturated fats while high in complex carbohydrates and fiber; (b) regular exercise; and (c) medications, in some but not all cases. Diabetes can have long-term, deleterious effects on other body systems including eye infections, vision loss, kidney failure and infections, and poor circulation resulting in peripheral nerve damage (Ferrini & Ferrini, 2008; Hooyman & Kiyak, 2008). It is very important that older adults strictly manage their diets and exercise regimens in order to minimize subsequent damage to other organs. Increased risk of cardiovascular and cerebrovascular disease is common among older adults who have Type II diabetes. Once Type II diabetes is diagnosed, medical management of the disease is required in order to prevent additional complications (Ferrini & Ferrini; Hooyman & Kiyak, 2008; Jett, 2008).

Skeletal Conditions

Osteoporosis and arthritis are the most common chronic skeletal conditions affecting older adults. These conditions often result in functional activity limitations among older adults with the number of activity limitations increasing with age. Not all older persons, however, experience functional limitations, but most suffer from the excruciating pain associated with these skeletal disorders. These disorders are progressive, often beginning in middle adulthood. Arthritis is the leading cause of loss in functioning among all age groups in the United States (Ferrini & Ferrini, 2008; Hooyman & Kiyak, 2008; Jett, 2008).

Arthritis

Arthritis is a class of over 100 inflammatory, degenerative conditions of the skeletal system's joints and bones. Osteoarthritis, the most common type of arthritis, is a degenerative joint disease that occurs through a wearing away of the protective cartilage of the joint. Aggravating causes of osteoarthritis include aging-related deterioration of the joint, wear and tear from overuse, injury, genetic disposition, and obesity. Pain, decreases in function (e.g., range of motion), and joint crackling are commonly experienced symptoms of the disease. Treatment for osteoarthritis includes weight loss, low impact exercise (e.g., walking), heat, and pain killers (Ferrini & Ferrini, 2008; Hooyman & Kiyak, 2008).

Rheumatoid arthritis is caused by persistent inflammation of the joint membranes. The small bones of the feet and hands are more commonly affected but other joints can be involved, also. Rheumatoid arthritis is a degenerative, deteriorative disease of the joints. Left untreated, loss in function will eventually be a result of the disease. Rheumatoid arthritis is episodic; that is, it typically begins by middle adulthood and recurs as acute attacks interspersed with inactive periods. Severe symptoms such as fatigue, weight loss, fever, pain, redness, swelling, stiffness, and malaise may be experienced during acute attacks and as the disease progresses (Hooyman & Kiyak, 2008). Treatment involves rest, exercise, painkillers, as well as other anti-inflammatory medications, and corticosteroid. Joint repair through surgery is used to correct severe degeneration and deformity. Medical management and treatment of rheumatoid arthritis can prevent crippling effects of the disease (Ferrini & Ferrini, 2008; Hooyman & Kiyak; Jett, 2008).

Osteoporosis

Osteoporosis is the aging-related loss of bone mass at an accelerated rate which causes serious structural weakness and vulnerability to fractures. As bone mass is lost, the accumulated effects in later life include weak bones, height loss, slumped posture, dowager's hump, and backache (Ferrini & Ferrini, 2008; Hooyman & Kiyak, 2008; Jett, 2008).

Bone density and bone demineralization are conditions associated with normal aging. The building of bone peaks somewhere between age 20 and 35 after which time progressive, gradual declines in bone mass occur under normal aging conditions (Jett, 2008). Osteoporosis is the abnormally accelerated loss in bone density, which is why it is considered a disease condition. Fractures of the hip are the most common and problematic consequence of osteoporotic bones. Among very old adults (over age 80), hip fractures often portend a poor recovery and an increased risk for placement in a long-term care facility and mortality (Ferrini & Ferrini, 2008; Hooyman & Kiyak, 2008).

The risk factors associated with osteoporosis include family history and genetic disposition, estrogen and calcium losses during menopause, sedentary lifestyle, cigarette smoking, excessive alcohol consumption, race (Caucasian), gender (female), and high caffeine consumption (Hooyman & Kiyak, 2008; Jett, 2008). Prevention is the preferred treatment approach and thus, changes in diet and lifestyle should begin long before old age. Increasing dietary intake of calcium, vitamin D, and fluoride are recommended, as is modified weight bearing exercise (e.g., stair climbing, walking). Therapeutic doses of estrogen also are often recommended for women, especially women in menopause.

Genitourinary Conditions

The incidence of genital and urinary problems increase with age. Chronic conditions are a result of gradual deterioration in the excretory system. As kidney function declines, the probability of disease increases. Incomplete emptying of the bladder in women may bring about inflammation or cystitis. Older men frequently experience a gradual enlargement of the prostate. Noncancerous enlargement is called benign prostatic hyperplasia and is caused by changes in testosterone production. This condition is experienced by as many as 70% of men between the ages of 60 and 70, and 90% of men age 90 and older (Ferrini & Ferrini, 2008; Jett, 2008).

The enlargement of the prostate affects urinary functioning because of the anatomical proximity of the prostate to the urethra. Typical symptoms include hesitancy when beginning urination, reduced force, increased frequency of urination, dribbling, and the lack of ability to completely empty the bladder (Ferrini & Ferrini, 2008). Currently, if proper urinary function is disrupted by an enlarged prostate, minor surgery is used to widen the urethra. Treatment approach depends upon whether the enlarged prostate has spread or not. There is moderate controversy regarding surgery to remove the prostate.

Chronic urinary incontinence is a fairly common problem among older persons, which increases in prevalence with age. The rate of incidence varies for noninstitutionalized older persons compared with those people who are in hospitals or nursing homes. It has been estimated that as many as 30 million people suffer urinary incontinence. This disorder is caused by a number of factors including nervous system problems, infection, muscle weakening, and medication interactions (Ferrini & Ferrini, 2008). Medical management of incontinence ranges from drug therapy to special exercises, biofeedback, surgical repair, urination flow devices, and other supportive measures (Jett, 2008).

Four types of incontinence are experienced by older adults. When uncontrolled leakage of urine coincides with sneezing, coughing, laughing, lifting, or exercise it is called stress incontinence. This form of incontinence is a result of muscle weakness around the bladder and urethra. It is common among women and is related to childbirth, surgery, and estrogen deficiency (Ferrini & Ferrini, 2008; Jett, 2008).

Enlargement of the prostate often influences the ability to sense when the bladder is full, thus resulting in overflow incontinence or when a full bladder leaks out a small amount of urine. Urge incontinence, on the other hand, is the inability to hold urine when experiencing the urge to urinate. Urge incontinence is frequently associated with neurological disorders (e.g., stroke, dementia) or infection (Jett, 2008).

The fourth type of incontinence is a result of an unwillingness or inability to urinate normally. It is called functional incontinence and may be cause by any number of reasons including medications, psychiatric disturbances, the presence of other diseases, or impaired mobility (Ferrini & Ferrini, 2008; Hooyman & Kiyak, 2008; Jett, 2008).

Urinary incontinence presents both a chronic health problem, as well as a social problem. The inability to control continence is socially unacceptable in public while also representing a highly personal health behavior. Incontinence is often one of the deciding factors in nursing home placement. For these reasons and others, the management of this disorder is of great interest and importance to older adults, their caregivers, and the healthcare system (Hooyman & Kiyak, 2008).

Other Chronic Conditions

Older adults also can experience a variety of other chronic health conditions including skin irritations, thyroid dysfunction, oral diseases, and intestinal disorders. While these conditions may be less problematic in terms of long-term survival, they are still bothersome and may create additional difficulties when combined with more serious chronic disease (e.g., cancer). It bears repeating that chronic conditions are the result of poor health habits and lifestyle behaviors and *not* a direct consequence of aging. Most chronic conditions can be avoided or prevented by engaging in healthy, active lifestyles.

Skin Conditions

Older adults often suffer from skin disorders primarily due to gradual changes in the integumentary system, long-term exposure to sunlight, the effects of environmental pollutants, and familial history. Psoriasis, or scaly skin, tends to run in families and can be quite bothersome to the older adult (Hooyman & Kiyak, 2008).

Chronic itching, or senile pruritus, is very common among older adults. This disorder can be very distressing if it is severe. It may be caused by any number of factors including underlying disease (e.g., diabetes, cancer); drug reaction; lice, flea, or mite infestation; or stress, tension, and emotional upset (Hooyman & Kiyak, 2008).

In conclusion, older diabetic adults may experience stasis dermatitis on the legs due to diminished circulation. The skin will appear scaly, reddened, shiny, and will have reduced growth of hair. The treatment of most skin conditions primarily consists of controlling the irritation with creams, relieving symptoms by warm water bathing, light therapy, and prescription drugs to avoid additional infection (Hooyman & Kiyak, 2008).

Thyroid Dysfunction

Older adults, particularly women, may experience thyroid dysfunction either as excess of thyroid hormone (hyperthyroid) or as a deficiency (hypothyroid). Hypothyroidism is the more common of the two conditions and can cause death if not treated. Typical symptoms include constipation, weight gain, cold intolerance, depression, psychic disturbances (e.g., hallucinations), slowed mental processes, and the inability to respond to stress. Treatment is by thyroid hormone replacement and is usually effective in reversing the symptoms of this dysfunction (Ferrini & Ferrini, 2008; Jett, 2008).

The less common hyperthyroidism has the opposite symptoms (e.g., irritability, tremors, diarrhea, weight loss, heat sensitivity, sweating, and increased heart rate). Hyperthyroidism is also treatable.

Intestinal Disorders

Intestinal disorders in older persons are primarily caused by poor or unbalanced diet. Diverticulitis, or inflamed intestinal sacs, are the result of inadequate intake of dietary fiber. Symptoms include disrupted bowel function, bleeding, nausea, discomfort in the abdomen, and nausea. Treatments involving dietary changes and antibiotics are effective in alleviating this condition (Hooyman & Kiyak, 2008).

Older adults also frequently complain about constipation. Most constipation is caused by inadequate exercise, stress, other diseases of the gastrointestinal system, poor diet, and overuse of catheters and laxatives. Probably too much attention by older adults is given to the regularity of their bowl movements, which may result in the inappropriate utilization of laxatives. The overuse of laxatives will eventually damage normal functioning of the intestinal tract.

Oral Diseases

Older adults primarily suffer from the loss of teeth, gum disease, and dental caries of the root of the tooth. As preventive dental care improves, the incidence of these problems may decline among older persons (Jett, 2008).

Acute Health Problems of Older Adults

The two leading causes of acute health problems in older persons are influenza/pneumonia and accidents. Influenza and pneumonia are the seventh leading causes of death among older adults while accidents are the ninth leading cause (Heron, Hoyert, Xu, Scott, & Tejada-Vera, 2008). Because these acute conditions result in high medical care expenditures, they are important considerations in understanding the health status of older people (Ferrini & Ferrini, 2008; Satariano, 2006).

Infections

Older adults frequently suffer from infections for a variety of reasons. Normal aging changes in the immune system that result in a lowered resistance to infection coupled with the presence of one or more chronic conditions often will leave the older adult more vulnerable to infections. Other bodily changes in the respiratory system may increase the risk of pneumonia due to a lowered ability to adequately clear the lungs. Two acute infections that pose significant risks for older adults are influenza and pneumonia. Other infections that may be secondary outcomes associated with chronic disease also are threatening to the health and survival of older people. Finally, latent infections (e.g., tuberculosis, herpes zoster or shingles) can suddenly reoccur in late life, producing episodes of acute illness (Ferrini & Ferrini, 2008).

Respiratory infections, particularly the common cold, flu, and pneumonia, are significant acute illnesses that often increase the risk of mortality among older persons. Increased risk is primarily due to lowered resistance, complications, secondary infection, and a lowered ability to clear the lungs and airways of infectious material. The older the person is, the higher the risk of complications and mortality from acute respiratory infections (Ferrini & Ferrini, 2008; Hooyman & Kiyak, 2008; Jett, 2008).

Diagnosis and treatment of respiratory infection can be complicated when in the presence of a chronic condition. Medications taken for chronic conditions may mask the typical symptoms used to diagnose acute infections (e.g., fever, elevated white blood cell count). Other symptoms (e.g., confusion, fatigue, appetite loss) can be misinterpreted as an age-related change rather than associated with an illness.

Because pneumonia and flu are particularly threatening to older adults, immunizations are highly recommended. Pneumonia, on the other hand, is a serious threat to older people, especially those who are inactive and/or institutionalized in hospitals or nursing homes. Treatment of bacterial pneumonia, which generally is the more dominant type in older persons, is with antibiotics. Vaccines have been developed to protect against pneumonia but they are less effective among very old and frail adults (Gable et al., 1990).

Other infections that are troubling for older people include appendicitis that is caused by bacterial infection, infected diverticula in the intestine, diarrhea, urinary tract infections, genital (vaginitis) infections, bedsores or pressure sores (decubitus ulcers), shingles (latent herpes zoster from childhood chicken pox), tuberculosis, SARS, and AIDS. Among older adults,

AIDS is typically contracted from blood transfusion or homosexual intercourse. The identification of AIDS in older people is confounded by normal aging-related changes and the presence of other chronic conditions. Treatment, likewise, is complicated by lowered immune system functioning and other bodily changes associated with growing older (Satariano, 2006).

Accidents and Injury

Accidents are the ninth leading cause of death in older persons. The most common types are falls, pedestrian accidents, and motor vehicle accidents. Other causes of injury include medical complications, fires, choking, drowning, and poisoning. Falls and motor vehicle accidents are the leading type of accidental death among older people (Ferrini & Ferrini, 2008).

Older adults are more susceptible to accidents and experience more severe injury due to several factors. The most common risk factor is functional loss due to normal aging-related declines. Declines in the nervous and sensory systems result in a slower reaction time and to a decreased awareness of a hazardous situation. Among older adults a lowered perception of temperature extremes, pain, vision, and hearing can contribute to an increased risk for accidents.

Changes in the musculoskeletal system may influence motor abilities (e.g., balance, strength, endurance). Poor nutrition, emotional stress, and medication side effects all may produce lowered capabilities and slower reactions to pending hazardous situations. The presence of other chronic or acute illnesses may further impair the individual's functional capabilities, which consequently increases the risk for injury and accidents. For example, impaired cognition due to diseases of the central nervous system may influence memory and judgment.

Environmental design factors can significantly contribute to the rate of injury and accidents in the older adult population. Personal functional capabilities coupled with poor environmental designs that are not age-friendly produce increased risks for accidents in this population age group. Older people are much more vulnerable to extremes in temperature, slick walking surfaces, stairs without handrails, cluttered environments, and traffic lights that change too quickly, just to name some of the aspects of the environment that pose risks to the health of older people.

In the case of accidents in older people, prevention can be very effective in controlling risk and reducing the incidence of death by accident. The placement and kind of furniture, walking surfaces, handrails, room layout, placement of cupboards and shelves, exterior supports and walkways, lighting, and temperature control are all considerations to which professionals should pay close attention. Injury and accidents can be reduced to some degree through environmental design and management, as well as increased awareness by older adults of their own vulnerabilities.

Impact of Chronic and Acute Illness on Functional Independence

The older person's ability to maintain his or her independent functioning is an important indicator of health status, perceived well-being, and overall quality of life. As the incidence of chronic and acute illness increases, the individual will potentially experience limitations in his or her daily activities. Approximately 42% of all people over age 65 in 2005 experienced some limitation in functioning (Federal Interagency Forum on Aging-Related Statistics, 2008). The main cause of activity limitation is impairment due to chronic conditions, illness, and/or injury. Older women experience higher levels of functional impairment compared with men, and there is a greater frequency of limitation in instrumental activities of daily living (IADLs) than activities of daily living (ADLs).

This section explores what functional independence means to older persons and how functional limitations are impacted by health status. In the health professions, health status is thought to be composed to two elements: (a) the presence or absence of disease, and (b) the degree of functional limitation experienced by the individual (Hooyman & Kiyak, 2008). As adults age, functional limitations may also increase, thus impacting how the older adult may perceive his or her overall health status. Among noninstitutionalized adults who are between the ages of 65 and 74 only about 25% report limitations in activities, however, among people who are 85 and older, this rate increases to 60% (National Center for Health Statistics, 2007). The most prevalent conditions that affect activity limitation are arthritis and other musculoskeletal conditions, heart and other circulatory conditions, diabetes, impaired hearing and vision, and senility or dementia. As age increases, the presence of activity limitation increases, as does the need for assistance.

Functional limitations can be described in two broad categories of activities: activities of daily living (ADLs) and instrumental activities of daily living (IADLs). Typical ADLs are eating, bathing, dressing, getting out of bed or chair, going to the bathroom, walking, and other essential tasks associated with basic daily functioning IADLs are activities that are concerned with the more instrumental tasks of everyday life such as, meal preparation, managing one's finances, shopping, using community services, managing one's home, making phone calls (Hooyman & Kiyak, 2008). Activity limitations begin to occur when an older person needs assistance (partial or full) with one or more of these ADLs or IADLs. Help with one activity does not necessarily mean dependence with others. When older adults need help with three or more ADLs, they are considered unable to perform major activities associated with functional independence. In other words, older adults who need assistance with IADLs may still demonstrate functional independence within their residence; however, when impairment affects ADLs to the extent that partial or full assistance with three or more ADLs is needed, the older person may be considered functionally dependent. Among adults age 65 and older who are living in long-term care facilities, 65% have limitations in three or more ADLs compared with 9% of adults age 65 or over who are living in traditional community-based residences (Jett, 2008). Loss of the ability to perform activities of daily living (ADLs) without assistance often portends increasing dependency on formal systems of healthcare either within the home or in facilities where increasing levels of professional care are provided.

Based on 2005 data from the Centers for Disease Control and Prevention, among community living adults age 65 and older, 23.2% report having difficulty with walking (National Center for Health Statistics, Trends in Health and Aging, accessed on July 26, 2008). Among adults age 65 and over who are living in a facility, the estimate of those who have limitation with walking increases to 58.1%. Among community dwelling older adults, 12.2% report having difficulty getting in and out of bed or a chair, 6.4% report difficulty with dressing, 4.7% have difficulty using the toilet, and 2% report difficulty with eating. As would be expected, these figures are higher among older persons living in a facility as follow: getting in/out of bed/chair (59.4%), bathing (87.7%), dressing (73.6%), using the toilet (71.2%), and eating (49.3%).

In regard to instrumental activities or IADLs, more than one fourth (29.6%) of community dwelling adults over age 65 report having difficulty doing heavy housework, 13.1% had difficulty with shopping 10.9% have difficulty with light housework and less than 10% have difficulty with money management, preparation of meals, and using the telephone. Again, the percentages dramatically increase among adults over 65 who are living in a facility as follows: difficulty with shop-

ping, 82.7%; managing money, 82.7%; and using the telephone, 61.5%. Older adults living in facilities generally do not do housework or prepared meals (National Center for Health Statistics, Trends in Health and Aging, accessed on July 27, 2008). In 2006, 5.9% of adults aged 65–74 reported needing help with routine needs and this figure dramatically increases to 34.6% for adults age 85 and older.

While functional impairment does not necessarily mean a loss of overall quality of life, the interactive effects of functional losses coupled with the presence of chronic and acute illness does place stress on the older person's lifestyle. Good health in older adulthood means more than the absence of disease. Health status, particularly if it is good, impacts functional independence and ultimately increases the quality of life in older adulthood. Assisting older adults in managing, maintaining, and promoting their health will help them to lead active and functionally independent lifestyles into and throughout old age.

Summary

This chapter presented the differences between normal aging-related change, and the illnesses and diseases common among older people. An overview of common chronic and acute conditions that are experienced by older persons helps to clarify this difference. In its broadest sense, health status represents both the presence/absences of illness/disease as well as the degree to functional limitations that the older person experiences. It is clear that health status and healthy lifestyle habits influence quality of life for older adults. Readers who would like to know more about common illnesses and diseases among older adults are encouraged to consult the references that accompany this chapter.

Comprehension Questions

The reader can check for comprehension of the material presented in this chapter by answering the following questions.

1. Define health status.

2. Discuss three factors that influence the health status of older persons.

3. Describe the difference between acute illness and chronic disease.

4. Describe three chronic conditions that are common among older persons.

5. Describe the top three leading forms of cancer that cause death in men and in women.

6. Describe the most common skeletal condition of older women and how they influence everyday functional independence.

7. Why is incontinence a problem among older persons?

8. What is COPD and what treatment approaches can be used with COPD?

9. Describe the two leading acute illnesses common among older persons.

10. Discuss how the ability to perform ADLs and IADLs, or loss thereof, affects the functional independence and life quality of older persons.

References

American Cancer Society. (2007a). Cancer facts and figures 2007. American Cancer Society, 1599 Clifton Road, N.E., Atlanta, GA 30329-4251.

American Cancer Society. (2007b). Breast cancer facts & figures 2007–2008. American Cancer Society, 1599 Clifton Road, N.E., Atlanta, GA 30329-4251.

Gable, C. B., Holzer, S. S., Engelhart, L., Friedman, R. B., Smeltz, F., Schroeder, D. & Baum, K. (1990). Pneumococcal vaccine: Efficacy and associated cost savings. *Journal of the American Medical Association, 264,* 2910-2915.

Federal Interagency Forum on Aging-Related Statistics. (2008, March). *Older Americans 2008: Key Indicators of Well-Being.* Federal Interagency Forum on Aging-Related Statistics. Washington, DC: U.S. Government Printing Office.

Ferrini, A. F., & Ferrini, R. L. (2008). *Health in the later years.* (4th ed.). Boston, MA: McGraw Hill.

Heron, M. P., Hoyert, D. L., Xu, J., Scott, C. & Tejada-Vera, B. (2008, June). Deaths: Preliminary data for 2006. *National Vital Statistics Reports, 56*(16). Hyattsville, MD: National Center for Health Statistics.

Hooyman, N. R. & Kiyak, H. A. (2008). *Social gerontology: A multidisciplinary perspective* (8th ed.). Boston, MA: Allyn and Bacon.

Jett, K. (2008). Chapter 10. Chronic disease in late life. In P. Ebersole, P. Hess, T. A. Touhy, K. Jett & A. S. Luggen (Eds.), *Toward health aging: Human needs & nursing response.* St. Louis, MO: Elsevier/Mosby.

National Center for Health Statistics. (2007). Health, United States, 2007, with Chartbook on trends in the health of Americans. Washington, DC: U.S. Government Printing Office, Library of Congress Catalog Number 76-641496.

National Center for Health Statistics. *Trends in health and aging.* [Data source: Activities of Daily Living by Sex, Race, and Age, Selected Years. LSOA, LSOA II (LSOAADLS)] Retrieved July 26, 2008, from http://www.cdc.gov/nchs/agingact.htm.

National Center for Health Statistics. *Trends in health and aging.* [Data source: Difficulty Performing Instrumental Activities of Daily Living, by Age, Residence, Sex, Race and Ethnicity: Medicare Beneficiaries from the Medicare Current Beneficiary Survey, 1992–2005. (MAIADL05)] Retrieved July 27, 2008, from http://www.cdc.gov/nchs/agingact. htm.

National Center for Health Statistics. Trends in health and aging. [Data source: Needing Help with Routine Needs by Age, Sex, and Race/Ethnicity: United States, 1997–2006. NHIS (NHII06a)] Retrieved July 27, 2008, from http://www.cdc.gov/nchs/agingact.htm

Satariano, W. A. (2006) Epidemiology of aging – An ecological approach. Sudbury, MA: Jones and Bartlett Publishers.

U.S. Department of Health and Human Services. (2000). Healthy people 2010: Understanding and improving health (2nd ed.). Washington, DC: U.S. Government Printing Office, Stock Number 017-001-00-550-9.

World Health Organization. (1947). Constitution of the World Health Organization. Chronicle of the World Health Organization, 29–43.

• CHAPTER 6 •
Psychological Illnesses and Psychiatric Disorders

Learning Objectives

1. Identify conditions and diseases that cause cognitive impairment in older persons.

2. Describe the types, origins, causes, and symptoms of organic cognitive disorders in the older adult population.

3. Describe the types, origins, causes, and symptoms of functional mental disorders in the older adult population.

Key Terms

- Alcoholism
- Group Therapy
- Alzheimer's Disease
- Hallucinations
- Anosognosia
- Iatrogenic Disorders
- Antidepressant Drugs
- Multi-Infarct Dementia
- Anxiety Disorders
- Organic Cognitive Disorders
- Bereavement
- Paraphrenia
- Bipolar Disorders
- Paranoia
- Counseling
- Perseveration
- Delirium
- Polypharmacy
- Delusions
- Pseudodementia
- Dementia
- Psychosis
- Depression
- Psychotherapy
- Drug Abuse
- Schizophrenia
- Electroconvulsive Therapy
- Sundowning
- Excess Disability
- Tardive Dyskinesia
- Family Therapy
- Wandering
- Functional Mental Disorders
- Cognitive Impairment
- Frontal Lobe Dementia
- Vascular Dementia

Introduction

Psychological and psychiatric disorders/diseases of the older adults are often neglected or thought to be of little importance and consequently, they may receive minimal attention. Depression and organic brain syndrome are the most common disorders exhibited by older adults. While anxiety and depression are the most common mental health problems of older adults, organic brain syndrome is the most feared and the least understood mental disorder (Carroll & Linton, 2007; Edinberg, 1985; Jenike, 1989).

Diseases that cause cognitive impairment in older adults are overviewed in this chapter. Organic cognitive disorders are discussed with an emphasis on dementia and its various types including Alzheimer's disease, multi-infarct dementia, Pick's disease, and other dementia-related syndromes. An introduction to the factors that characterize delirium and other reversible causes of mental impairment is included.

Functional mental disorders of depression, anxiety, psychotic illness, alcoholism, and drug abuse are also discussed in the chapter. It is difficult to determine whether the symptoms of cognitive impairment and organic mental syndromes accurately depict true disorders of aging, reactions to stressful life events and circumstances, or the overt expression of enduring disorders.

Diseases that Cause Cognitive Impairment

The term *cognitive impairment* is used to characterize a range of disorders in cognitive function (Touhy, 2008a). Cognitive impairment includes disturbances in emotions, mental function (e.g., intelligence, problem solving, judgment, learning), orientation, concentration, attention, and memory. Cognitive impairment is often characterized by dementia, delirium, and depression because these are the most common symptoms associated with mental diseases in older adults. It is important to recognize that disorders in cognitive functioning are differentiated from normal changes in mental function due to aging.

Diseases and disorders of older adults that cause cognitive impairment may be divided into two general categories: organic and functional. Organic mental syndrome is not a diagnosis; instead, it refers to psychological and behavioral symptoms such as loss of orientation to person, place, and time without reference to a specific cause for the symptoms. *Organic cognitive disorder* is the designation for a particular variety of organic mental syndromes for which the cause has

been identified. The most well-known organic mental disorders are delirium and dementia, especially dementia of the Alzheimer's type (Carroll & Linton, 2007; Edinberg, 1985; Jenike, 1989; Touhy, 2008a).

Organic brain syndromes are recognized by various symptoms including: (a) changes in judgment (decision making, evaluation, and comprehension); and (b) changes in affect (flat affect or excessive display of emotions such as looking frightened or agitated). Other symptoms common to organic brain syndromes are memory impairment; loss of cognitive skills (e.g., mathematical or learning abilities); and loss of orientation to time (day, date, month, year), place (current location), and person (identity of self and others) (Touhy, 2008a).

Multiple psychological and social factors are involved in both organic mental disorders and impaired cognitive functioning. It has been estimated that 15 to 25% of people over the age of 65 suffer from mental illness; however, true prevalence figures are compromised by the underutilization of services and the underreporting of symptoms (Carroll & Linton, 2007; Hooyman & Kiyak, 2008). For example, it has been estimated that less than 25% of older persons in need of services ever actually obtain treatment (Hooyman & Kiyak, 2008). Depression and anxiety are considered the most prevalent mental disorders among older adults; however, many other conditions such as alcoholism, drug abuse, and schizophrenia also are common. Additionally, psychiatric symptoms often occur in older persons suffering from Alzheimer's disease and other chronic medical conditions (Butler, Lewis & Sunderland, 1991).

Organic Cognitive Disorders

Approximately 25% of older adults suffer from serious diseases of the brain at some point in their lives (Jenike, 1989; Katzman, 1985). Primary *organic cognitive disorders* are termed dementias. *Dementia* is widely used in reference to many cognitive disorders of older adults. There are more than 70 known causes of dementia of which Alzheimer's disease is the most common (Touhy, 2008a). Dementia is defined as a loss of intellectual abilities to the degree that it interferes with social or occupational functioning; memory impairment; and at least one of the following: impairment in abstract thinking, judgment, higher cortical function, or personality change (American Psychiatric Association, 2000).

The onset and course of dementia is insidious, slow, and often undetected until progression of losses become obvious (Touhy, 2008a). Most dementias are considered to be irreversible. Dementias that are irreversible and progressive are known as primary dementias and are caused by pathological conditions. Primary dementias include Alzheimer's disease, vascular disorders, Pick's disease, Creutzfeldt-Jacob's disease, and human immunodeficiency virus (HIV) (Hooyman & Kiyak, 2008; Touhy, 2008a). Secondary dementias are those that may be reversible to an extent depending upon the cause and the course of treatment (Butler et al., 1991). Other conditions can cause secondary dementia including alcoholism, drugs and medication interactions, nutritional deficiencies, thyroid dysfunction, and depression.

Dementia is characterized by a complex set of symptoms that may be caused by a variety of disorders and dementia is more accurately described as a syndrome rather than a diagnosis (Katzman, 1985; Touhy, 2008a). The vast majority of dementias are caused by specific brain diseases, lack of adequate blood supply to the brain, or a combination of the two. A careful medical evaluation is required in order to exclude other causes which may be reversible (Butler et al., 1991; Edinberg, 1985; Touhy, 2008a).

Common symptoms that are associated with dementia are summarized in Figure 6.1. *Perseveration*, the tendency to emit the same verbal or motor response continually and *anosognosia*, "the apparent unawareness of or failure to recognize one's own functional defect" (Butler et al., 1991, p. 159) also are associated with dementia. Jenike (1989) reported, however, that many patients with progressive dementia are clearly aware of their impairments.

Alzheimer's Disease

The most prevalent dementia is *Alzheimer's disease*, which accounts for 50% to 60% of all dementia (Touhy, 2008a). This disease may be referred to as primary degenerative dementia, primary degenerative dementia of the Alzheimer's type, Alzheimer's disease (AD), and senile dementia. It is the most common form of dementia in the United States. Alzheimer's disease has been diagnosed in more than 5 million Americans over the age of 65 (Touhy, 2008a). The likelihood of developing dementia of the Alzheimer's type increases dramatically with age (Blazer, 1990; Jenike, 1989) and it occurs more frequently in women than in men, apparently due to their longer life expectancy (Ferrini & Ferrini, 2008). AD is also more prevalent in Blacks and Hispanics, as well in persons with lower educational attainment (Ferrini & Ferrini; Touhy, 2008a).

Although a specific cause for Alzheimer's disease has not been found, several types of brain abnormali-

ties that are related to Alzheimer's disease have been discovered. Low levels of acetylcholine, which appear to be related to loss of memory functions, have been found in older persons with dementia. Senile plaques, which exist in small amounts in all older adults' brains, correlate positively with loss of orientation (Edinberg, 1985). Neurofibrillary tangles in the brain may be related to problems in protein metabolism. They also represent degeneration, interfere with nerve transmission, and lead to the death of brain cells (Butler et al., 1991; Edinberg, 1985; Touhy, 2008a).

Alzheimer's disease is a devastating, progressive brain disease (Touhy, 2008a). The predominance of behavioral symptoms in Alzheimer's disease distinguishes it from many other brain disorders (Cohen, 1989; Touhy, 2008a). Memory loss is progressive and severe, and marked by few complaints or concerns about the loss. Memory loss for recent events is greater than for events from the distant past. Impairment in intelligence and cognition are common with difficulties in abstract thinking, simple calculations, understanding directions and questions (perceptual problems), and communication. With AD, attention as well as orientation to time, place, and person become impaired (Blazer, 1990; Edinberg, 1985; Touhy, 2008a). Difficulties in judgment include the inability to plan or make decisions. Judgmental problems may be increased by a lack of interest in the activities of living. Lapses in self-care often become evident and can present management problems (Edinberg, 1985; Touhy, 2008a).

Wandering is a demanding problem of persons with Alzheimer's disease. Those who do wander are potentially at risk for harm. There are many possible causes for wandering including physical discomfort, disorientation, restlessness, and agitation. Wandering in some individuals becomes greater at night (Leng, 1990).

Early in the disease, moderate to severe depression is a common symptom (Touhy, 2008a). As the disease progresses, victims can become agitated, restless, and uncooperative. Suspiciousness, paranoia, delusions, and hallucinations may occur and are often accompanied by angry outbursts and verbal abuse. Incontinence, speech difficulties, disturbed sleep patterns, and eating problems also can emerge in the final stages of the disease.

Clinical diagnosis of Alzheimer's disease has improved markedly and currently approaches 90% accuracy (Touhy, 2008a). If the patient's dementia has had a deceptive onset, a generally progressive and deteriorating course, and the patient meets the other criteria for dementia, a clinical diagnosis of Alzheimer's disease may be made. All other specific causes of dementia must be excluded by history, physical examination, and laboratory tests. The importance of evaluating demented patients in order to document the course of illness should be emphasized, thereby further increasing the accuracy of diagnosis in patients suspected of having the disease. The onset of Alzheimer's disease is between ages 40 and 90, most often after the age of 65, and the diagnosis of probable Alzheimer's disease is supported by a family history of similar disorders (Jenike, 1989). With more recent drug therapy using cholinesterase inhibitors, treatment in the way of enhanced function and the slowed progression of decline has offered hope to sufferers and their caregivers (Touhy, 2008a).

Multi-Infarct Dementia or Vascular Dementia

The second most common form of dementia is *multi-infarct dementia* or *vascular dementia*. In this disorder, the dementia results as a consequence of multiple

Area of Loss	Symptoms	Onset
Cognition	• Loss of memory • Disorientation—confusion concerning time, place, people, eventually forgetting own name • Poor judgment • Decreased abilities in calculation • Impairment in abstract thinking • Anosognosia	• Early onset; gradual and progressive decline • Onset in middle stages • Onset in later stages
Affect	• Excessive, inappropriate or lack of emotional response	• Onset in later stages
Behavior	• Irritability • Withdrawal • Agitation • Apathy • Occasional violence	• Onset at any stage • Onset in middle stages • Onset in later stages
Psychological	• Depression • Denial • Anxiety • Paranoid • Hallucinations • Delusions • Personality change	• Onset at any stage • Onset in later stages
Language	• Speech disorders, including perseveration	• Onset at any stage; progressive decline
Physical	• Visual impairments • Impaired motor function, including perseveration • Incontinence • Sleep disorders • Weight loss • Sexual disorders • Seizures	• Early onset • Onset in later stages

Note: Developed from information contained in Butler, Lewis & Sunderland, 1991; McKhann, Drachman & Folstein, 1984; and Reisberg, Ferris, DeLeon & Crook, 1982.

Figure 6.1 Symptoms Associated with Dementia

small strokes throughout the brain (Touhy, 2008a). Although the symptoms are similar to those described for Alzheimer's disease, the course of multi-infarct dementia is not gradual. It occurs rather unevenly and the deficits tend to be differentiated (e.g., agitation and depression can be severe, but memory loss may only be minimal) (Blazer, 1990). Multi-infarct dementia is a chronic disorder and can occur simultaneously with Alzheimer's disease in the same patient. Onset is generally between the ages of 50 and 70 and is usually associated with hypertension (Butler et al., 1991).

Infarcts occur randomly in multi-infarct dementia, therefore, the course of illness is difficult to predict and symptoms vary greatly between patients (Stuart-Hamilton, 1991). Many multi-infarct patients die but those who survive may experience a remission of symptoms with varying amounts of intellectual impair-ment (Butler et al., 1991; Touhy, 2008a). Figure 6.2 summarizes the differences between depression, Alzheimer's disease, and multi-infarct dementia.

Pick's Disease or Frontal Lobe Dementia

Pick's disease or *frontal lobe dementia* is clinically very similar to Alzheimer's disease and differentiation may be impossible until autopsy. The age of onset is usually between 40 and 60 years. Behavioral symptoms can include a lack of initiative, early language dysfunction, social misconduct, early personality change, and variable memory impairment (Butler et al., 1991; Jenike, 1989; Touhy, 2008a).

The cause of Pick's disease is unknown, but genetic factors appear to be relevant. The prognosis is always fatal with survival ranging from 2 to 15 years. The course of illness is steadily progressive and the

	Depression	Alzheimer's Disease	Multi-Infarct Dementia
Onset	Relatively rapid changes in mood and behavior	Deceptive; poorly defined	Abrupt; step-wise
Mood and Behavior	Stable, depressed, or agitated	Unstable and/or depressed	Variable with periods of recovery
Mental Competence	Unaffected except for attention, concentration, and interests	Increasingly defective	Defective with recovery; step-wise losses
Complaints	Memory; concentration; self-image; overly concerned with symptoms; loss of interest	Others' complaints about him or her; denial of symptoms	Memory and behavioral losses appropriate to area of infarct
Somatic Symptoms	Anxiety, sleep, eating, fatigue	Sleep disorders, anxiety	Anxiety, neurological disorders
Prognosis	Generally self-limited; 20–30% of cases are chronic	Chronic and progressive	Progressive unless treatable
Past History	Episodes of depression	None specifically related	Hypertension
Brain Scan	Normal	Generalized atrophy	Localized evidence of stroke
EEG	Normal	Generalized slowing	Localized abnormalities

Note: Developed from information contained in Belsky, 1990; Jenike, 1989; and Zung, 1980.

Figure 6.2 Comparative Differences between Depression, Alzheimer's Disease, and Multi-Infarct Dementia

treatment of symptoms is all that can presently be done (Butler et al., 1991). Pick's disease patients are often more difficult to manage than patients with Alzheimer's disease. Nursing home placement is often indicated at earlier stages of the illness (Butler et al., 1991; Jenike, 1989).

Other Dementia-Related Syndromes

Parkinson's, Creutzfeldt-Jacob, and Huntington's disease are often accompanied by dementia. In Parkinson's disease, the clinical symptoms may include forgetfulness, slowing of thought processes, altered personality, and other impaired intellectual functioning. The characteristic features are involuntary movement, rigidity of muscles, slowness of movement, and tremor (Butler et al., 1991; Jenike, 1989; Leng, 1990; Touhy, 2008a). The overt motor functioning of Parkinson's patients can differentiate them from those suffering from the other dementias (Butler et al., 1991; Leng, 1990). Patients with Parkinson's disease receive drug therapy, however, accurate diagnosis and treatment are essential (Butler et al., 1991; Jenike, 1989).

Creutzfeldt-Jacob disease is a rare form of dementia and is known as transmissible spongiform encephalopathy (e.g., mad cow disease, Touhy, 2008a). The disease is transmitted from individuals who are infected and symptoms occur around age 60. The mortality rate is high at about 90% within one year. Memory failure, behavior changes, motor difficulties, and disturbances in vision are all common (Touhy, 2008a).

Huntington's disease is hereditary and usually begins in middle age. The early symptoms of the illness are involuntary movements (Leng, 1990; Stuart-Hamilton, 1991). Subsequently, Huntington's disease patients develop symptoms of dementia. Huntington's disease is progressive and life expectancy is usually about 15 years. It is also characterized by cognitive impairments such as loss of memory, and decreased skills in organizing and sequencing (Butler et al., 1991; Stuart-Hamilton, 1991).

There is no cure for Huntington's disease and treatment is disease-specific. Treatment is directed at controlling and reducing the symptoms and preventing complications. A variety of medications help to control movement problems and emotions including antipsychotics, antidepressants, and tranquilizers. These drugs, however, can produce fatigue, restlessness, and hyperexcitability. Lower dose regimens, therefore, are preferred by healthcare practitioners.

Prolonged use of alcohol also may cause dementia (Touhy, 2008a). Alcohol abuse and drug misuse are common problems among older adults. In order to make the diagnosis of dementia associated with alcoholism, all other causes of dementia should be excluded and three weeks must have elapsed since the prolonged heavy ingestion of alcohol (Jenike, 1989).

Delirium

Delirium is an organic psychiatric syndrome characterized by acute onset and impairment in cognition, perception, and behavior (Beresin, 1988). Delirium also is termed transient cognitive disorder (McPherson, 1991) and acute confusional state, which refers to confusion with a relatively sudden onset that is potentially of limited duration (Leng, 1990; Stuart-Hamilton, 1991). Delirium is often caused by the effects of drugs on brain function, the result of surgery where general anesthesia was used, or as a complication of illness (Touhy, 2008a). From 14% to 80% of all older adults will be affected with delirium.

Delirium is characterized by acute and sudden episodes of confusion, fluctuating levels of awareness, and impairment in attention (Touhy, 2008a). Hallucinations and delusions may be present (Hooyman & Kiyak, 2008). A predominant feature of delirium is disturbance in the sleep-wake cycle and impairments are usually most severe at night. The term *sundowning* is used to describe the agitated and confused behaviors that often occur in the evening and night. Disorganized thinking also is indicated by rambling, irrelevant, or incoherent speech (Blazer, 1990; Butler et al., 1991; Jenike, 1989; Touhy, 2008a). There are many possible causes of delirium. Overmedication, medication interactions, and improper use of medication by older clients are among the most common sources of delirium in older adults (Touhy, 2008a).

Delirium is a critical symptom in older adults. As many as 15% to 40% of delirious patients will progress to stupor, coma, and death (Butler et al., 1991; Liston, 1982). Delirium is frequently undiagnosed; however, when diagnosed and treated early, delirium is often completely reversible (McCartney & Palmateer, 1985).

Treatment of delirium must include attending to any organic or disease-related factors (Jenike, 1989). The immediate environment of the delirious patient is extremely important. The environment must be consistent, familiar, and simplified in order to moderate sensory input, personal contact, activities, and physical aspects of the environment. Supportive reassurances may be provided to diminish anxiety, provide comfort, and promote an affirmation of reality (Butler et al., 1991; Jenike, 1989).

Reversible Causes of Mental Impairment

Dementia that is associated with depression in older adults is perhaps the most important of all the reversible dementias. Antidepressant medications are available for this condition, yet a large percentage of depressed patients are consistently misdiagnosed as suffering from dementia (Butler et al., 1991; Touhy, 2008b). Complaints of poor memory may accompany depression and disappear when the depression is treated (Jenike, 1989).

The term *pseudodementia* is often used to describe reversible depression-related cognitive disorders (Jenike, 1989). A lack of progressive symptoms is a typical characteristic of pseudodementia. Patients who are pseudodemented are usually oriented to time and place, whereas demented patients are not. Pseudodemented patients often perform better in the afternoon than in the morning. Also, patients who are pseudodemented are usually aware of their poor performance; however, true dementia victims may not be reconciled with their deficiencies. The intellectual performance of pseudodemented patients often improves as the depression is treated (Jenike, 1986; Kermis, 1986; Sahakian, 1991; Stuart-Hamilton, 1991).

Cognitive impairment in depression is distinct from that of the dementias. More than 50% of depressed older adults subsequently develop true dementia (Reding et al., 1986; Sahakian, 1991; Stuart-Hamilton, 1991). The impact of depression compounded with dementia increases cognitive impairment to a degree greater than either disorder alone—a state referred to as *excess disability*. When excess disability is treated, an increase in overall functional capacity of patients with dementia may occur. Only with the passage of time does the patient regress and display further deterioration (Cohen, 1988).

Other reversible causes of mental impairment can include cardiopulmonary and cardiovascular disease, malnutrition and anemia, infection, head trauma, alcoholism, diabetes, dehydration, emphysema, brain tumors, liver failure, thyroid disorders, cancer, vitamin deficiencies, environmental changes, exhaustion, and grief reactions or bereavement (Ferrini & Ferrini, 2008; Hooyman & Kiyak, 2008; Touhy, 2008a). With the increasing use of drug treatments in the medical and psychiatric management of older adults, drug reactions also are a significant cause of reversible mental disorders.

Due to multiple chronic conditions, more than 85% of older adults are prescribed a variety of different drugs, which can lead to *polypharmacy* (Gulick & Jett, 2008). Polypharmacy is the concurrent use of two or more medications, particularly in excessive doses or inappropriate combinations. It is because of polypharmacy that *iatrogenic disorders* among older adults are common. Iatrogenic disorders are those pathological brain conditions that result unexpectedly from medications, diagnostic procedures, or therapies and not from any physical dysfunction. There is no substitute for careful monitoring of the individual patient (Butler et al., 1991; Gulick & Jett, 2008; Harper, 1991).

Functional Mental Disorders

Functional mental disorders are those in which behavioral problems or distresses are not due to physical disease processes (Edinberg, 1985). Mental health conditions in older adults are fairly common. Anxiety in older adults is estimated to be 10% to 15% and minor depressive symptoms to occur in 8% to 20% of people over age 65 (Carroll & Linton, 2007; Hooyman & Kiyak, 2008; Touhy, 2008b). Less than 1% of older adults experience major depression. Minor and major depressive symptoms are higher among older women and the rates increase with age. The majority of older adults with mental disorders reside in the community. In nursing homes, however, it is estimated that 20% to 30% of older residents suffer from some depression. Since older persons often do not seek treatment for mental health disorders, it is difficult to estimate the true extent of the problem (Hooyman & Kiyak, 2008; Touhy, 2008b).

Depression

Depression is a very common functional mental disorder and it is important to distinguish between major and minor depression. *Depression* is likely to be misdiagnosed and poorly treated in older persons partially due to the influence of different beliefs and values of different cultural groups (Touhy, 2008b). Depression has such broad effects and has a range of biopsychosocial causes. Depression is viewed as a function of genetic and biological factors, environmental stresses, and habitual ways of thinking and acting. For many older adults, these factors interact in a complex manner that causes or maintains depression (Hinrichsen, 1990). There is considerable evidence regarding a hereditary contribution to depression, however, research has suggested that genetic causation of depressive disorders in late life is weaker than at other stages of the lifecycle (Hopkinson, 1964; Mendlewicz, 1976; Touhy, 2008b). The desire to restore functioning in spite of the inevitable losses in late life is a major developmental task of aging individuals, but older adults also must recognize and accept their declines (Cath, 1965).

Depression impacts and interacts with many physical and psychological functions (Touhy, 2008b). The physical functions of energy, appetite, digestion, sleep, and metabolism are suppressed. Cognitive functions of memory, reasoning, concentration, and problem solving are affected. Disturbances of mood, lack of interest, helplessness, anger, and lowered frustration tolerance are displayed in depressed elderly individuals. Decreased functioning also is exhibited in a lack of meaning in life, pessimism, and hopelessness. Depressed patients generally complain of insomnia and loss of interest in activities such as one's job, hobbies, social situations, and sex. Feelings of guilt, lack of energy, the inability to concentrate, confused thinking, and suicidal thoughts also may be present. In order to be diagnosed, a major depressive episode must last for at least a two-week period and represent a change from previous functioning (Jenike, 1989; Touhy, 2008b).

Other risk factors for developing depression in the older person include the presence of chronic illness, bereavement, caregiver burden, medication interactions, living alone, widowhood, and dealing with accumulating losses (Touhy, 2008b). Family history, gender, and socioeconomic status can increase the risk of developing depression in late life. Previous episodes of depression earlier in life can increase the risk for depression in late life.

Older adulthood often is accompanied by change. The relative stability of middle age may lead to transitions in late life that may or may not have been expected. Late life stresses often involve loss such as of one's partner, friends, money, and health. Older persons have had many years to develop attachments, and they also are the most likely to suffer from loss of people and things to which they have become attached. Despite losses during late life, the majority of older people maintain good emotional health. For some older persons, however, the stresses of late life increase their risk for depression (Hooyman & Kiyak, 2008; Touhy, 2008b).

In older age groups, the depressed patient may not admit to the symptoms of depression, but anxiety, physical symptoms, chronic pain, loss of concentration, memory problems, and pseudodementia are frequent. One of the most common situations that contribute to depressive symptoms is *bereavement*, a universal human experience and the normal response to the loss of a loved one, a job, economic security, or one's home (Blazer, 1990; Jenike, 1989; Touhy, 2008b).

Any medical condition associated with bodily systems and metabolic disturbances can have an impact on the mental functioning of older adults. The most common are fever, dehydration, and electrolyte disturbances. Cancer, heart failure, strokes, and Alzheimer's disease often are associated with depression. Drugs and medication also may cause depressive symptoms in a great many cases (Gulick & Jett, 2008). There is no substitute for systematic monitoring of the older individual using repeated measures of cognitive performance to identify toxic drug effects (Gulick & Jett; Morrison & Katz, 1990).

The clinical treatment and management of older persons suffering from depression includes *antidepressant drugs*, *electroconvulsive therapy*, *counseling*, and *family therapy* (Gulick & Jett, 2008; Touhy, 2008b). Considerable evidence indicates that antidepressant medication is more effective when used in combination with some type of counseling (Goff & Jenike, 1986), however, electroconvulsive therapy may be the only choice of treatment in the older adult depressed patient whose illness is accompanied by self-destructive behavior such as suicide attempts or refusal to eat (Jenike, 1989; Weiner, 1982).

Often older persons do not tolerate antidepressants well (Gulick & Jett, 2008). Heart problems are the most serious side effect. Dryness of the mouth, constipation, blurring of vision, and confusion are the most frequent and disturbing side effects. There is a potential for addiction and overdose with several of the antidepressant drugs (Gulick & Jett, 2008).

Electroconvulsive therapy is a treatment option for depressed older adults. It involves causing a series of seizures in patients with severe depression. The seizure itself, rather than the electrical stimulation, is the therapeutic agent. Electroconvulsive therapy is more effective and faster-acting than drugs in the treatment of depression, and is both safe and effective for the treatment of affective illness in older adults (Hooyman & Kiyak, 2008).

Individual *psychotherapy* and *counseling* are the basis of psychological intervention (Touhy, 2008b). The themes in psychotherapy with older persons are generally different than those of younger persons. Older persons frequently deal with cumulative losses, preparation for life's end, maintenance of personal independence, physical health concerns, family relations, and the preservation of self-worth and self-esteem. A final consideration for the treatment of depressive symptoms in older adults must be their consequences for independent functioning. Without intervention, those persons who are depressed will stay depressed, and everyday functioning and adaptation will be limited (Murrell & Meeks, 1991).

Counseling differs from psychotherapy in that it is less focused on maladjusted behavior. Counseling is concerned with providing information, advice, resources, and referrals to "normal individuals" in order to attain concrete goals. Examples of issues that may be addressed in counseling situations include stress management, relaxation techniques, leisure involvements, and communication skills (Kemp, 1986).

Group therapy approaches to psychological problems are beneficial for several reasons. They are economical and present opportunities for socialization and learning from peers. They are more multidisciplinary, often including physical exercise, psychotherapy, education, and recreation (Kemp, 1986).

The family plays a large role in the well-being of older disabled persons and cannot be excluded from treatment. Treatment of the whole family is both an effective and efficient form of therapy (Kemp, 1986; Touhy, 2008b). The goal of family intervention is to improve the functioning of the family system. The focus of *family therapy* is on the physical functioning and relationships of the older person, as well as the person's support systems (Edinberg, 1985).

Suicide

The seriousness of depression in older adults is demonstrated by an increase in and success of suicidal attempts in this age group (Hooyman & Kiyak, 2008). One estimate proposes that up to 25% of all suicides in the United States are completed by people age 65 and older. Depression is related in two-thirds of the suicides committed by older persons (Gurland & Cross, 1983). Older adults comprise the age group that is most at risk for suicide, and the highest rates of suicide are among males age 85 and older, especially Black men in this age group (Hooyman & Kiyak, 2008). Older suicidal patients tend not to contact crisis intervention workers, but they may contact physicians or other health service providers. More than 70% of older adults who commit suicide visit a physician prior to completing the act but their disturbances were either undetected or overlooked (Hooyman & Kiyak, 2008).

Many older adults provide clues to their impending suicidal behavior. Clues to suicide may be classified as verbal, behavioral, situational, or syndromatic. Verbal clues may be direct or indirect. An example of a direct verbal clue would be "I am going to kill myself." Direct suicidal threats always should be taken seriously. Indirect verbal clues are more subtle than direct suicidal threats, but they also should be taken seriously. Indirect verbal clues include statements such as "I'm tired of life" and "my family would be better

off without me." Some verbal clues require interpretation to detect the self-destructive intent such as "You shouldn't be having to take care of me any longer" (Osgood, 1985).

Behavioral clues also may be either direct or indirect. The most direct behavioral clue is the suicide attempt. Most older adults who attempt suicide kill themselves within one to two years after an attempt. Indirect behavioral clues include putting personal and business affairs in order, giving away money and/or possessions, changes in behavior, general confusion, and loss of judgment or memory (Osgood, 1991).

Syndromatic clues consist of the psychological syndromes that often are associated with suicide. Depression, when accompanied by anxiety, appears to be the most important clue to suicide in older persons. Stress, agitation, guilt, isolation, and dependency are other important syndromatic clues (Hooyman & Kiyak, 2008; Osgood, 1985; Osgood, Brant, & Lipman, 1989).

Accurate assessment in the aged is crucial to suicide prevention. The key factors in recognizing suicidal older adults may be discovered by using the *ASK* approach (Pavkov, 1982):

- Attention to expressed suicidal interests,
- Symptomatic variations, and
- Keen observation of attitudinal and/or activity change.

In the final analysis, older people in the United States may kill themselves because old age has nothing worthwhile to offer them. When old age is viewed as a valued status by society, then the number of suicides by older adults may be significantly reduced.

Anxiety

Anxiety disorders are among the most common problems experienced throughout the life cycle and may include panic disorders, phobias, post-traumatic stress disorders, physical disorders accompanied by anxiety, and generalized anxiety disorders (Carroll & Linton, 2007). Anxiety is a state of inner distress composed of dread, fear, or anticipation of imagined harm that is accompanied by various symptoms including shortness of breath, dry mouth, dizziness, increased heart rate, trembling, sweating, and/or chills. In order to diagnose an anxiety disorder, four or more attacks must have taken place within a four week period or at least a month of persistent fear of having another attack must have occurred. Also, organic factors cannot be established as the cause of the disturbances (Jenike, 1989; Shamoian, 1991).

Among older persons, phobias, generalized anxiety, late life onset of obsessive-compulsive disorder (OCD), and posttraumatic stress disorder (PTSD) are common (Carroll & Linton, 2007). Phobias are the most prevalent among these disorders. About 3% to 12% of older persons have unfounded fears about situations or things. Generalized anxiety disorder, the second most frequent disorder, affects about 0.7% to 7.1% of older adults (Carroll & Linton, 2007). Prevalence rates for late life OCD are around 1.5% and while PTSD can occur at any time in life, it is common among older veterans. PTSD can also manifest in older people who are not adjusting well to aging, especially to losses associated with death of loved ones, relocation, financial stability, and isolation (Carroll & Linton, 2007).

The presence of anxiety symptoms alone often does not cause patients to seek help. Even patients with severe anxiety symptoms wait, on the average, a period of 12 years before seeking treatment for the symptoms. Another difficulty that older patients with anxiety disorders may experience is physical complaints and these may hide the underlying anxiety disorder (Jenike, 1989).

Unrealistic or excessive worry about problems is a distinguishing characteristic of anxiety disorders (Carroll & Linton, 2007). Anxiety symptoms often are a component of many emotional problems that afflict older adults. Anxiety can arise in older persons who reflect upon their lives and their positions in society. Older adults may become aware of a sense of "nothingness" or insignificance in life. This type of anxiety can accompany and exaggerate anxiety from other sources.

Anxiety disorders may be treated with medications; however, manipulation of environmental factors or discussion of the patient's problems is considered when an older person suffers from anxiety (Carroll & Linton, 2007). Many older patients respond favorably to counseling techniques.

Coping with stress can provide a means for developing practical knowledge, wisdom, and positive self-esteem (Touhy, 2008b). Stress management techniques such as meditation, relaxation, and exercise or physical activity often prove useful in the treatment of elderly anxiety disorders. Coping skills may be indicated, such as effective communication, assertiveness, and positive thinking. Social support provides a sense of competence to anxious and stressed elderly individuals (Touhy, 2008b).

Psychosis

Psychosis involves major distortions in reality and is used to describe many general behaviors. Among these behaviors are *hallucinations*, which are psychotic symptoms involving sensory perceptions of sights and sounds that are not actually present. Auditory hallucinations are particularly common in older adults due to decreased hearing capacities. *Delusions* and *paranoia* also may be present in psychosis. Delusions are false personal beliefs that are firmly upheld despite external reality. Paranoid thoughts involve suspiciousness or the sense of being treated unfairly. The instances of paranoia increase with age. Specific risk factors for paranoia include sensory impairment, brain damage, and social isolation (Butler et al., 1991; Touhy, 2008b).

Schizophrenia

Schizophrenia patients have characteristic disturbances in several of the following areas: content and form of thought, perception, affect, sense of self, behavior, and relationship to the external world. A continuous six-month period of symptoms is required for diagnosis (Jenike, 1989). Onset of schizophrenia most often occurs before age 45, however, late-life schizophrenia does occur (Touhy, 2008b). Older schizophrenics generally display differences in symptoms with their delusions focused on sex and personal possessions (Edinberg, 1985). Schizophrenia with a late life onset is termed *paraphrenia* and affects 1–2% of individuals over the age of 65. Paranoid behaviors are the prominent symptoms of persons experiencing paraphrenia. The behavior of the paraphrenia sufferer becomes increasingly bizarre and self-neglect is a pronounced feature. The condition usually improves in response to drug treatment (Stokes, 1992). The life expectancy of people suffering with schizophrenia is as much as 20% lower than nonsufferers (Touhy, 2008b).

Major tranquilizers are used to control psychotic symptoms in all age groups (Carroll & Linton, 2007; Touhy, 2008b). The most commonly used antipsychotic drugs are Thorazine, Haldol, and Mellarill. The side effects of major tranquilizers are potentially serious. Side effects include visual problems, vulnerability to heat or cold, sensitivity to the sun, weight gain, seizures, drowsiness, confusion, anxiety, agitation, and movement disorders (Edinberg, 1985; Jenike, 1989).

Tardive dyskinesia is a side effect of antipsychotic drugs and involves involuntary movement that may appear after 3–6 months of treatment with antipsychotic drugs. It is characterized by involuntary movements of the tongue, face, trunk, and extremities (American Psychiatric Association, 2000). Tardive dyskinesia has been reported in more than 50% of older adults who are on long-term drug therapy (Kazamatsuri, Chien & Cole, 1972).

The goals of intervention with older schizophrenics are generally adaptive (Touhy, 2008b). Rehabilitation of the patient focuses on behavior and socialization. Exercise and counseling often are employed (Edinberg, 1985; Harper, 1991).

Bipolar Disorders

In *bipolar disorders*, the depressive state cannot be distinguished from other types of depression. Bipolar disorder, often termed manic-depressive illness, is characterized by severe mood swings from depression to elation (Touhy, 2008b). A history of manic episodes in the patient or in his family is central to the diagnosis (Butler, et al., 1991; Jenike, 1989). Lithium carbonate is widely accepted as the treatment for bipolar illness and is indicated for older patients (Cade, 1949; Jenike, 1989; Sheard, 1975; Touhy, 2008b).

Alcoholism and Other Drug Abuse

Alcoholism or *alcohol* dependence, in older adults is often difficult to diagnose and often arises as a coping strategy (Touhy, 2008b). Prevalence estimates suggest that between 2% to 17% of adults age 60 and older suffer from alcohol dependence and alcohol related problems (Ferrini & Ferrini, 2008; Hooyman & Kiyak, 2008). This prevalence may increase with the aging of the Baby Boomers, a group of people who have had higher rates of alcohol consumption compared with previous generations. Alcoholic men outnumber women about 5 to 1. About two-thirds of older alcoholics were alcohol dependent as younger adults. Alcoholism dramatically drops off in the over age 80 population, most likely due to the lack of survival among older adult alcoholics. Older adults who are alcohol dependent tend to avoid contact with agencies or professionals who may notice signs of alcoholism. The signs of alcoholism are similar to those of other physical and emotional problems commonly diagnosed in older adults and the residual effects of alcoholism complicate the diagnosis of other conditions (Touhy, 2008b). The majority of elderly alcoholics abused alcohol as younger adults and can be viewed as having a lifelong problem that has persisted into older adulthood. Some older patients, who are referred to as late-onset alcoholics, did not have problems with alcohol until later maturity. Often, late life alcohol dependence is a consequence of poor coping with stressful life events and changes (Touhy, 2008b).

Current criteria for and indications of alcohol abuse include: physical symptoms such as shaking and black outs, psychological dependence on alcohol, failure to carry out major role obligations, substance related legal problems, health problems, and difficulties with family and friends (see DSM-IV, APA, 2000; Touhy, 2008b). Alcohol generally has a more profound effect on older adults than on younger persons due to age-related physical changes that result in the slower metabolism of alcohol (Edinberg, 1985). Prolonged alcohol abuse also can lead to a progressive dementia similar to Alzheimer's disease (Touhy, 2008b).

Every effort should be made to ensure that older adult alcoholics actually present themselves for treatment (Jenike, 1989). Treatment for alcoholism may include Antabuse, a drug that inhibits alcohol consumption, paired with social support from peers. Acute alcohol withdrawal symptoms can be a serious problem for older adults who do not metabolize the substance as quickly as younger persons. Benzodiazpine is used to help with withdrawal symptoms and tranquilizers help with anxiety (Ferrini & Ferrini, 2008; Touhy, 2008b). Alcoholics Anonymous is a program of self-help support groups that is broadly available at no cost across the country in rural and urban communities. Therapeutic intervention with the family also is essential in order to avoid a return to alcohol abuse.

Although less is known about *drug abuse* in older adults, it appears that for every five alcoholics there is at least one person who also abuses other drugs (Redick, Kramer & Taube, 1973; Reifler, Raskind, & Kethley, 1982; Hooyman & Kiyak, 2008). Sedatives are known to escalate alcohol problems (Touhy, 2008b). Particularly problematic is the use of psychoactive drugs among older women (Touhy, 2008b). Older persons comprise the largest group of drug consumers and this fact may increase the potential for drug misuse and abuse (Harper, 1991). The over age 60 age group have high consumption of over-the-counter medications and prescription drug abuse is common among the aged. Over-the-counter drugs are frequently abused including laxatives, sedatives, pain relievers, and cold medications. The fact that drugs are easily obtained, generally inexpensive, and perceived as completely safe by many older persons promotes frequent abuse (Jenike, 1989).

Additionally, overuse of caffeine with the consumption of coffee, tea, and soft drinks contributes to anxiety, panic disorders, heart irregularities, gastric problems, and osteoporosis in older persons (Heaney, 1981; Kofoed, 1984). While these drinks are legal, it is difficult to measure their effects on the mental health status of older adults.

Prescription drug abuse may be difficult to detect in older adults due to the multiple legitimate reasons that older persons have for taking medications. Some of the warning signs associated with prescription drug abuse in older adults include pain disorders, depression, organic cognitive disorders, poor social functioning, changes in tolerance to drugs, proneness to accidents, and defensiveness (Ferrini & Ferrini, 2008; Hooyman & Kiyak, 2008).

Older persons usually respond quite well to emotional support, encouragement, and improvements in their social systems. Family involvement also enhances treatment outcomes (Finlayson, 1984; Touhy, 2008b). Although substance abuse problems are relatively uncommon in older adults, they can be difficult to treat. Once dependence is recognized, hospitalization will likely be required for management of withdrawal symptoms and observation. Education and correction of associated psychological problems such as anxiety, loneliness, grief, and depression usually will improve the situation.

Summary

This chapter provides a general description of the diseases that are associated with cognitive impairment in older persons. The psychological and psychiatric conditions that affect older persons are often neglected by care providers or underestimated due to low reporting of symptoms by older adults. Depression is perhaps the most common condition and many older persons suffer from minor depression. Organic brain disease is also common among older adults. These conditions may affect memory function, as well as the emotional state of the individual. A broad range of treatments can be employed to help the older person cope with or recover from emotional disturbance or cognitive impairment. Functional mental disorders such as depression, anxiety, and alcoholism are treatable conditions for which the activity specialist may have an important role to play in the treatment process.

In conclusion, it is important to remember that all persons respond on some level to emotional and social support, although they may not respond in the manner that is expected. Formal contact might seem impossible yet presence, touch, favorite music, and quiet affirmation of care and concern all may be received beyond the states of awareness that are normally comprehended or displayed. "The force of love remains eternal, giving of itself in faith and hope with no need of reciprocity" (Karr, 1991, pp. 69–70).

Comprehension Questions

The reader can check for comprehension of the material presented in this chapter by answering the following questions:

1. Describe dementia in older adults, including incidence and common symptoms.

2. What are functional mental disorders?

3. Discuss depression in older persons, including risk factors and treatment approaches.

4. Discuss the impact that alcohol and other health risk behaviors have on the mental health of older persons.

References

American Psychiatric Association. (2000). *Diagnostic and statistical manual of mental disorders* (4th ed.). Washington, DC: The Association.

Belski, J. K. (1990). *The psychology of aging: Theory, research, and interventions* (2nd ed.). Pacific Grove, CA: Brooks/Cole.

Beresin, E. V. (1988). Delirium in the elderly. *Journal of Geriatric Neurology, 1,* 127–143.

Blazer, D. G. (1990). *Emotional problems in later life: Intervention strategies for professional caregivers.* New York, NY: Springer.

Butler, R. N., Lewis, M. I. & Sunderland, T. (1991). *Aging and mental health: Positive psychosocial and biomedical approaches* (4th ed.). NY: Merrill.

Cade, J. F. J. (1949). Lithium salts in the treatment of psychotic excitement. *Medical Journal of Australia, 36,* 349–352.

Carroll, D. W. & Linton, A. D. (2007). Chapter 20. Age-related psychological changes. In A. D. Linton & H. W. Lach (Eds.), *Matteson & McConnell's Gerontological Nursing: Concepts and Practices* (3rd ed.) (pp. 631–684). St. Louis, MO: Elsevier/ Saunders.

Cath, S. H. (1965). Some dynamics of middle and later years: A study in depletion and restitution. In M. A. Berezin & S. H. Cath (Eds.), *Geriatric psychiatry: Grief, loss, and emotional disorders in the aging process* (pp. 21–72). NY: International Universities.

Cohen, G. D. (1988). *The brain in human aging.* New York, NY: Springer.

Cohen, G. D. (1989). The interface of mental and physical health phenomena in later life: New directions in geriatric psychiatry. *Gerontology and Geriatrics Education, 9*(3), 27–38.

Edinberg, M. A. (1985). *Mental health practice with the elderly.* Englewood Cliffs, NJ: Prentice-Hall.

Ferrini, A. F. & Ferrini, R. L. (2008). *Health in the later years.* (4th ed.). Boston, MA: McGraw Hill.

Finlayson, R. E. (1984). Prescription drug abuse in older persons. In R. E. Atkinson (Ed.), *Alcohol and drug abuse in old age* (pp. 61–70). Washington, DC: American Psychiatric Association.

Goff, D. C. & Jenike, M. A. (1986). Treatment-resistant depression in the elderly. *Journal of the American Geriatrics Society, 34*, 63–70.

Gulick, G. G. & Jett, K. (2008). Chapter 12. Geropharmacology. In P. Ebersole, P. Hess, T. A. Touhy, K. Jett & A. S. Luggen (Eds.), *Toward health aging: Human needs & nursing response* (pp. 294–322). St. Louis, MO: Elsevier/Mosby.

Gurland, B. J. & Cross, P. S. (1983). Suicide among the elderly. In M. K. Aronson, R. Bennett, & B. J. Gurland (Eds.), *The acting-out elderly* (pp. 456–465). New York, NY: Haworth Press.

Harper, M. S. (1991). *Management and care of the elderly: Psychosocial perspectives*. Newbury Park, CA: Sage Publications.

Heaney, R. P. (1981). Nutritional factors in post-menopausal osteoporosis. *Roche Seminar on Aging, 5*, 8–12.

Hinrichsen, G. A. (1990). *Mental health problems and older adults*. Santa Barbara, CA: ABC-CLIO.

Hooyman, N. R. & Kiyak, H. A. (2008). *Social gerontology: A multidisciplinary perspective* (6th ed.). Boston, MA: Allyn and Bacon.

Hopkinson, G. (1964). A genetic study of affective illness in patients over 50. *British Journal of Psychiatry, 110*, 244.

Jenike, M. A. (1989). *Geriatric psychiatry and psychopharmacology*. St. Louis, MO: Elsevier/Mosby.

Karr, K. (1991). *Promises to keep: The families' role in nursing home care*. Buffalo, NY: Prometheus.

Katzman, R. (1985). Aging and age-dependent disease: Cognition and dementia. In Institute of Medicine and National Research Council, *Health in an older society* (pp. 129–152). Washington, DC: National Academy.

Katzman, R. (1988). Alzheimer's disease as an age-dependent disorder. *CIBA Foundation Symposium, 134*, 69–85.

Kemp, B. J. (1986). Psychosocial and mental health issues in rehabilitation of older persons. In S. J. Brody & G. E. Ruff (Eds.), *Aging and rehabilitation: Advances in the state of the art* (pp. 122–158). New York, NY: Springer.

Kermis, M. D. (1986). *Mental health in late life: The adaptive process*. Boston, MA: Jones and Bartlett.

Kofoed, L. L. (1984). Abuse and misuse of over-the-counter drugs by the elderly. In R. M. Atkinson (Ed.), *Alcohol and drug abuse in old age* (pp. 49–59). Washington, DC: American Psychiatric Association.

Leng, N. R. C. (1990). *Psychological care in old age*. London: Hemisphere.

Linton, A. D. (2007). Chapter 7. Pharmacological considerations. In A. D. Linton & H. W. Lach (Eds.), *Matteson & McConnell's Gerontological Nursing: Concepts and Practices* (3rd ed.) (pp. 138–168). St. Louis, MO: Elsevier/Saunders.

Liston, E. H. (1982). Delirium in the aged. *Psychiatric Clinics of North America, 5*, 49–66.

McCartney, J. R. & Palmateer, L. M. (1985). Assessment of cognitive deficit in geriatric patients: A study of physician behavior. *Journal of the American Geriatrics Society, 33*(7), 467–471.

McKhann, G. M., Drachman, D. B. & Folstein, M. F. (1984). Clinical diagnosis of Alzheimer's disease. *Neurology, 34*, 939–944.

McPherson, S. (1991). Transient cognitive disorders in the elderly. In M. S. Harper (Ed.), *Management and care of the elderly: Psychosocial perspectives* (pp. 180–188). Newbury Park, CA: Sage Publications.

Mendlewicz, J. (1976). The age factor in depressive illness: Some genetic considerations. *Journal of Gerontology, 32*(3), 300–303.

Morrison, R. L. & Katz, I. R. (1990). Drug-related cognitive impairment: Current progress and recurrent problems. *Annual Review of Gerontology and Geriatrics, 9*, 232–279.

Murrell, S. A. & Meeks, S. (1991). Depressive symptoms in older adults: Predispositions, resources, and life experiences. *Annual Review of Gerontology and Geriatrics, 11*, 261–286.

Osgood, N. J. (1991). *Suicide among the elderly in long-term care facilities*. New York, NY: Greenwood Press.

Osgood, N. J. (1985). *Suicide in the elderly: A practitioners guide to diagnosis and mental health intervention.* Rockville, MD: Aspen Publishers.

Osgood, N. J., Brant, B. A. & Lipman, A. A. (1989). Patterns of suicidal behavior in long-term care facilities: A preliminary report on an ongoing study. *Omega Journal of Death and Dying, 19*(1), 69–78.

Pavkov, J. R. (1982). Suicide in the elderly. *Ohio's Health, 34*, 21–28.

Redick, K. R. W., Kramer, M. & Taube, C. A. (1973). Epidemiology of mental illness and utilization of psychiatric facilities among older persons. In E. W. Busse & E. Pfeiffer (Eds.), *Mental illness in later life* (pp. 199–231). Washington, DC: American Psychiatric Association.

Reding, M. J., Orto, L. A., Winter, S. W., Fortuna, I. M., DiPonte, P. & McDowell, F. H. (1986). Antidepressant therapy after stroke. *Archives of Neurology, 43*, 763–765.

Reifler, B. V., Raskind, M. & Kethley, A. (1982). Psychiatric diagnoses among geriatric patients seen in an outreach program. *Journal of the American Geriatrics Society, 30*, 530–533.

Reisberg, B., Ferris, S. H., DeLeon, M. J. & Crook, T. (1982). The global deterioration scale for assessment of primary degenerative dementia. *American Journal of Psychiatry, 139*(9), 1136–1139.

Sahakian, B. J. (1991). Depressive pseudodementia in the elderly. Special issue: Affective disorders in old age. *International Journal of Geriatric Psychiatry, 6*(6), 453–458.

Shamoian, C. A. (1991). What is anxiety in the elderly? In C. Salzman & B. D. Lebowitz (Eds.), *Anxiety inolder adults: Treatment and research* (pp. 3–15). NY: Springer.

Sheard, M. H. (1975). Lithium in the treatment of aggression. *Journal of Nervous Mental Disorders, 160,* 108–118.

Stokes, G. (1992). *On being old: The psychology of later life*. Washington, DC: Falmer.

Stuart-Hamilton, I. (1991). *The psychology of ageing*. London: Jessica Kingsley.

Touhy, T. A. (2008a). Chapter 23. Cognition and caring for persons with cognitive impairment. In P. Ebersole, P. Hess, T. A. Touhy, K. Jett & A. S. Luggen (Eds.), *Toward health aging: Human needs & nursing response,* (pp. 548–581). St. Louis, MO: Elsevier/Mosby.

Touhy, T. A. (2008b). Chapter 25. Emotional health in late life. In P. Ebersole, P. Hess, T. A. Touhy, K. Jett & A. S. Luggen (Eds.), *Toward health aging: Human needs & nursing response,* (pp. 597–638). St. Louis, MO: Elsevier/Mosby.

Weiner, R. D. (1982). The role of electroconvulsive therapy in the treatment of depression in the elderly. *Journal of the American Geriatrics Society, 30,* 710–712.

Zung, W. W. K. (1980). Affective disorders. In E. Busse & D. Blazer (Eds.), *Handbook of geriatric psychiatry* (p. 357). NY: Van Nostrand Reinhold Co.

UNIT III

Program Planning and Implementation Processes

Activities are used with older adults to enhance health, well-being, and quality of life. Also, therapeutic activities can be used for intervention and rehabilitation purposes when functional impairment and/or disability are present. The process of planning and implementing activity programs involves several considerations. Activity specialists use assessment, activity analysis, environmental design, motivational techniques, and a systematic program planning processes in the provision of high quality activity programs and services to older clients.

Unit III covers information that is central to the development and implementation of high quality activity programs and services for older adults. The unit is organized according to the core elements in the provision of activity programs. Chapter 7 covers assessment, activity analysis, and program planning processes. Chapter 8 details the role and function of assessment. Chapter 9 addresses adaptation, autonomy, and resilience in older adulthood, which collectively constitute personal attributes that the older adult brings to the activity program environment. Chapter 10 completes the unit with information on environmental design for active engagement of the older adult in healthy and active lifestyle. Upon completing the unit, readers should have an understanding of the basic elements of high quality and successful activity programs for older adult clients.

• CHAPTER 7 •

Programming for Therapeutic Outcomes

Learning Objectives

1. Describe how therapeutic activity intervention can be used to meet the physical, social, emotional, and cognitive needs of older adults.

2. Identify the phases of systematic therapeutic activity intervention programming.

3. Distinguish between the use of therapeutic activity to attain promotion, preventive, maintenance, and rehabilitative treatment goals.

4. Discuss individual treatment goals and objectives in therapeutic activity intervention.

5. Identify categories of activities used in therapeutic intervention with older adults.

6. Identify barriers to participation in therapeutic activity intervention programs.

Key Terms

- Activity Analysis
- Planning
- Assessment
- Preventive
- Deconditioning
- Promotion
- Evaluation
- Rehabilitation
- Individual Treatment Plan
- Therapy
- Intervention
- Therapeutic
- Maintenance

Introduction

The purpose, content, process, and outcomes of therapeutic activity intervention with older adults are presented in this chapter. The use of activities to reach therapeutic goals, thus enhancing the well-being and overall quality of life of older adults, is discussed within the context of functional decline. Losses in functioning may be due to the accumulated effects of aging-related changes, the need to preserve remaining abilities, or disablement resulting from disease. The intervention process is outlined including assessment, activity analysis, program planning, implementation, and evaluation. Important principles and sample tools guiding steps in the process are presented. Categories of activities that can be used to reach therapeutic outcomes also are introduced. The chapter concludes with a brief discussion of motivation as a leading barrier to participation in therapeutic activity intervention.

The Purpose of Therapeutic Activity Intervention

As adults age, the accumulated effects of the aging process eventually impress every individual with the importance of maintaining his or her personal health and functional capabilities. Older people want to remain independent in as many areas of functioning as possible, especially as they reach the 80s, 90s, and 100s. Independence also is a salient issue for any aging adult who happens to experience an injury or major disease. A sense of well-being, perceptions of life satisfaction, and quality of life are often affected by how independent and active the older person is able to be a daily basis. The use of activities to promote health, to prevent impairment and dependence, to maintain optimal functional capability, and/or to rehabilitate provide the underlying rationale for therapeutic activity intervention.

The word *therapeutic* distinguishes the use of activities for purposive as opposed to diversionary reasons (Hamill & Oliver, 1980). A therapeutic approach is one that is intended to stimulate a change in behavior and this change will be directed by one or more goals in the different areas of functioning (e.g., physical, emotional, mental, social; Smith & Couch, 1990; Stumbo & Peterson, 2009). The goal might be the *promotion* of optimal health, well-being, and vitality in older adulthood through engagement in a sport skill class, or the goal might be the *prevention* of accelerated declines that result from sedentary living or the presence of chronic disease. Activities that are of interest to the participant also can be used to *rehabili-*

tate when there are functional losses due to injury, disability, disease, or illness. This use is another example of goal-directed intervention that distinguishes therapeutic activity from diversionary activity programs. An illustration of a *rehabilitation* goal might be the use of bibliotherapy to stimulate memory and regain communication skills following a stroke. Therapeutic activity intervention, therefore, is fundamentally concerned with the use of activities for the purposes of inducing, facilitating, and/or maintaining independent functioning in the older adult to the degree that is possible within the individual's immediate environment, capabilities, and circumstances. Behavioral change may be achieved through promotion, prevention, maintenance, and rehabilitation goals, or any combination thereof.

It is not uncommon in the healthcare and human service professions to use the terms *treatment, therapy, intervention,* or *rehabilitation* interchangeably (Stumbo & Peterson, 2009). They all imply a process by which positive change is the intended goal. Stumbo and Peterson described the process as involving "(a) an assessment of need; (b) a statement of the problem; (c) formulation of treatment goal(s); (d) design of a treatment plan; (e) implementation, monitoring, and progress reporting; and (f) designation of criteria for decision making regarding termination, continuation, or change" (p. 41).

Figure 7.1 illustrates the continuum of therapeutic purposes and treatment goals that guide activity intervention. As can be seen in the chart, promotion goals at the right end of the continuum are typical in situations where more independent functioning exists and the older person needs fewer supports. Promotion goal-directed activities are targeted toward fostering and maintaining optimal functioning in the individual. These types of intervention activities may be incorporated into the normal routines of everyday life and are often less clinical in nature.

Prevention and maintenance goal-directed activities are at the mid-range of the continuum. Older adults involved in prevention and maintenance activities understand that the behaviors produced through attaining these goals are essential for managing their risk for further decline and increasing dependency. *Deconditioning* is a leading reason underlying the use of prevention and maintenance activities. Deconditioning is the added and accelerated loss in functioning beyond that which is associated with normal aging-related change. Deconditioning is perpetuated by disuse due to illness or sedentary living (Saltin & Rowell, 1980). Deconditioning is reversible whereas the effects of normal aging-related changes are not (Asmussen,

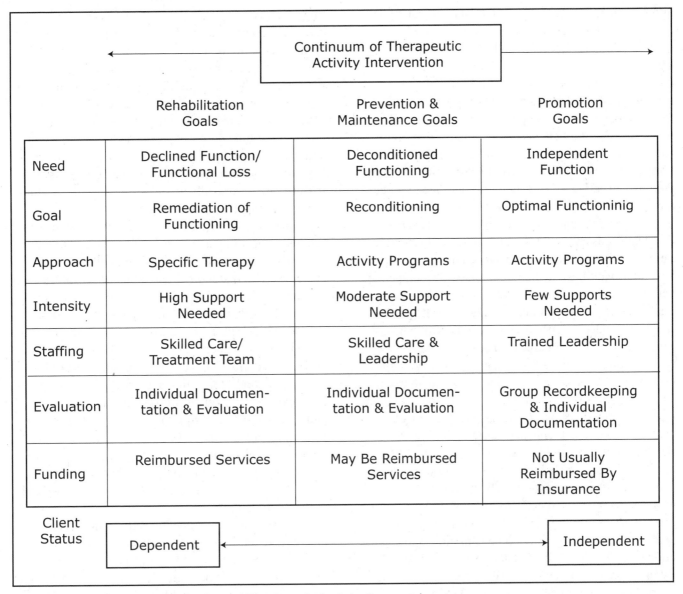

	Rehabilitation Goals	Prevention & Maintenance Goals	Promotion Goals
Continuum of Therapeutic Activity Intervention			
Need	Declined Function/ Functional Loss	Deconditioned Functioning	Independent Function
Goal	Remediation of Functioning	Reconditioning	Optimal Functioninig
Approach	Specific Therapy	Activity Programs	Activity Programs
Intensity	High Support Needed	Moderate Support Needed	Few Supports Needed
Staffing	Skilled Care/ Treatment Team	Skilled Care & Leadership	Trained Leadership
Evaluation	Individual Documen- tation & Evaluation	Individual Documen- tation & Evaluation	Group Recordkeeping & Individual Documentation
Funding	Reimbursed Services	May Be Reimbursed Services	Not Usually Reimbursed By Insurance
Client Status	Dependent ←		→ Independent

Figure 7.1 Continuum of Goal-Directed Therapeutic Activity Intervention

1980). Deconditioning is amenable to therapeutic activity intervention and is most appropriate following extended bed rest due to illness, or in response to the propensity of adults to become increasingly sedentary, both mentally and physically, with age. *Reconditioning*, therefore, is a guiding principle for prevention and maintenance goal-directed activity interventions. Deconditioning can be reversed through the prescriptive use of activities that are low impact, progressive in intensity, regular in frequency, and of an adequate duration to cause change or reconditioning. Physical activities typically characterize reconditioning activity interventions but carry over effects have been demonstrated in other areas of functioning (e.g., increased mental alertness, improved sociability, and greater independence in activities of daily living; Larson & Bruce, 1986; Vallbona & Batzer, 1984).

Rehabilitation goals are directed by significant functional losses that have resulted in impairment or disability to the extent that increased support is needed through individual skilled therapy. Progress is closely monitored and documented from one session to the next. Long-term rehabilitation goals are often broken down into short-term goals that have task-specific components. Maintenance of declined functioning, or the expected continued decline of the individual as in the case of progressive disease, may be inherent in rehabilitation situations. A close communication between therapist, participant (client), and other caregivers (family and/or professionals) is an important part of rehabilitation goal-directed activity intervention.

The intent of Figure 7.1 is to illustrate how activities have therapeutic, goal-directed outcomes ranging from one end of the continuum to the other, depending upon the needs of the individual. Certainly, other goals have been associated with therapeutic activity intervention (Cook & Ball, 2007; Smith & Couch, 1990). They include the use of activities as (a) avocational outlets, (b) to assist in adapting the environment to support greater independence, (c) to support coping through the provision of opportunities for achievement, (d) to promote the use of residual skills, (e) to enhance social skills and personal relationships, and (f) to promote community membership. Direct activity therapy and activity-based support groups are important therapeutic treatment modalities (Cook & Ball, 2007).

While treatment goals are developed based on individual needs and circumstances, ultimately all participants will experience an enhanced quality of life as a result of well-designed and implemented therapeutic activity intervention. The hallmarks of an enhanced quality of life are (a) an improved health status, (b) functional independence or enhanced control when functionally dependent, (c) a sense of well-being, (d) perceptions of life satisfaction, (e) increased self-esteem, and (f) an enhanced personal/social network. These benefits of participation should be apparent and understood by older participants, since the recognition of these benefits will enhance their motivation to participate (McGuire, 1985; Stumbo & Peterson, 2009).

The use of a skilled therapist or activity specialist is essential to effective therapeutic activity intervention. Skilled activity specialists utilize a systematic process of programming that involves assessment, activity analysis, planning, implementation, and evaluation (Stumbo & Peterson, 2009). Therapeutic activity intervention, or goal-directed activity, is distinctly shaped by the functional status and needs of the individual. Declines in physical, social, emotional, and mental functioning are of immediate concern, as are other aspects of the person's life such as financial resources, social networks, and the design of the individual's daily life environment. Explicit in effective therapeutic activity intervention is the activity specialist's understanding of the programming process and the systematic delivery of intervention services.

Systematic Activity Intervention Programming

Why use activities to intervene in the lives of older adults? In the preceding section, the purposes of goal-directed therapeutic activity intervention were discussed. The author of this text has directly observed the effectiveness of recreation activities in meeting therapeutic goals with aging adults in a variety of set-

tings. These settings include adult day care, senior center programs, nursing homes, assisted living facilities, rehabilitation centers, hospitals, and through home delivered care. Explicit in all these settings are the needs of the older adult for support, care, and treatment. Otherwise, the program of activity offerings would serve more diversional purposes and would not be within the purposes associated with therapeutic activity intervention. Diversional activity programs are beyond the scope of this text. The material contained in this book specifically addresses the use of activities to meet therapeutic treatment goals.

Once again, the question arises, "Why use of activities to meet therapeutic goals?" Activities that are normally pursued during leisure time reflect certain characteristics that motivate participation while also producing desired affective and physical states. Activities typically thought of as recreation activities are associated with pleasure, creativity, personal choice, preference, enjoyment, and satisfaction. Recreation activity is central to maintaining an active lifestyle in older adulthood. Recreation activities also foster positive health and perceived well-being, enhance social and personal relationships, and provide opportunities for human growth and development. The use of recreation activities in intervention programming to facilitate behavior change that produces therapeutic goal-directed outcomes is an appropriate and effective tool in the treatment process.

In this context, therapeutic activity intervention is like therapeutic recreation. The central functions of therapeutic recreation are to (a) promote functional independence; and (b) to enable older individuals to attain a higher level of health, well-being, and satisfaction in later life. The use of activities as therapy using a systematic process of program planning parallels the same steps used in the delivery of therapeutic recreation services. In the following sections, a process of systematic program planning and implementation is presented that builds on the programming literature from both therapeutic recreation and gerontology (cf., Austin & Crawford, 2001; Elliott & Sorg-Elliott, 1991; Hamill & Oliver, 1980; Howe-Murphy & Charboneau, 1987; Kraus & Shank, 1992; O'Brien, 1982; Stumbo & Peterson, 2009; Thews, Reaves & Henry, 1993). Five major steps comprise the process: (a) assessment, (b) activity analysis, (c) program planning, (d) program implementation, and (e) documentation and evaluation.

Assessment

Assessment is the first and a critical recurring step in the process of effective therapeutic activity intervention. Assessment is both client focused, as well as concerned with the environments in which the person functions on a daily basis. Assessment follows specific pragmatic techniques and procedures to construct a precise picture of the older person and his or her environment. Assessment of the individual and the environment allows the activity specialist to plan ahead for the best activities, methods for implementing the activities, and procedures for meeting the individual's need for support.

Multidimensional geriatric functional assessment is covered in detail in Chapter 8. This step in the process provides complete documentation about the person's functional status—physically, socially, emotionally, and mentally. A complete assessment also will include information about past activity participation, specific activity preferences and interests, and other pertinent background information (e.g., financial need, social support, insurance). In treatment facilities (e.g., long-term care, nursing homes) where Medicare and Medicaid are used for service reimbursement, the MDS (Minimum Data Set) will form the first standard assessment to be administered. The MDS is a federally mandated process for the assessment of all people living in certified nursing facilities. This tool will be supplemented with other instruments to provide complete client information. Short, easy to complete inventories and scales will be used to collect information about skill strengths and special abilities, functional declines, and problem areas in which the individual may need extra assistance. Comprehensive assessment of the individual also includes a medical history, the evaluation of functional competence in activities of daily living (ADLs) and instrumental activities of daily living (IADLs), a social history, and a mental status examination.

The World Health Organization developed the International Classification of Functioning, Disability, and Health (ICF), which is a standard system for of 1,424 categories that are used to classify components of health (Mayo, Poissant, Ahmed, Finch, Higgins, Salbach, Soicher & Jaglal, 2004). The ICF is useful in determining an individual's capacity for activity participation and his or her actual performance in activities of daily living (e.g., IADLs and ADLs). For example, a person may be able to walk but chooses not to walk because using a wheelchair is easier. The ICF allows for qualifying the degree of severity of impairment and capacity.

The goal of a thorough assessment is to collect and analyze information about the individual that will support the activity specialist in identifying capabilities,

problems, needs, strengths, residual skills, and special abilities. This information is instrumental when selecting, planning, modifying, implementing, and evaluating effective therapeutic activity interventions. The initial assessment begins the programming process but also is an inherent part of ongoing intervention as the reassessment of skills, interests, needs, and strengths is used to evaluate progress and make changes in treatment.

Along with individual client assessment, the activity specialist will assess the physical and social environments in which the client functions on a day-to-day basis. Environmental factors that will potentially influence client functioning will be identified and evaluated in regard to their impact on performance (Ferrini & Ferrini, 2008). Architectural barriers and arrangements will be described and evaluated. For example, are temperature, lighting, walking surfaces, and furniture layout appropriate for the individual's level of functioning, or do any of these environmental factors present potential barriers or hazards? A systematic assessment will consider elements of the exterior and interior of the residential environment. Walkways, handrails, step surfaces, lighting, carpeting and walking surfaces are all evaluated for safety, as well as needed supports. Living areas are reviewed for cluttered furniture and the soundness of any furniture that may be used for additional mobility support. The spatial layout of cabinets and closets, as well as safety features of appliances, and the overall safety of the bathroom should be assessed. In the bedroom, adequate night lighting and a clear pathway to the bathroom should be provided and appropriate for the needs of the individual. In general, the mobility, safety, and comfort of the individual in his or her residence, as well as daily activity environments, are addressed through a detailed assessment and evaluation.

The social attitudes of family members and significant others, caregivers, and other program participants is evaluated to identify potential barriers or problems. The social atmosphere, cultural background (including values, beliefs, and customs), and family functioning (such as family support) are important and will have a direct impact on the individual's needs and potential success in therapeutic activity intervention. The social environment can support or detract from success of the individual and therefore, must be taken into consideration during the assessment phase.

Adaptive devices, environmental redesign or modification, special equipment and materials, and support services each need to be considered as they may be instrumental in the success of activity intervention. As each individual becomes a potential client receiving activity intervention, these aspects of environment are equally important to individual functioning at the assessment phase, as well as in the program planning and implementation phases.

Based upon a thorough individual and environmental assessment, the activity specialist will be able to identify the daily demands placed on the individual's functional competence as well as any limitations imposed by the environment. A goal of this step in the therapeutic activity intervention process is to optimize the fit between the individual, the environment, and the therapeutic activity intervention. If the demands of the environment exceed the individual's needs and capabilities, then negative consequences rather than therapeutic goal attainment may result.

As a result of this initial and important step in the process, the activity specialist is able to identify a list of potential treatment goals and objectives that are appropriate for the individual. Environmental considerations and needs also will be known. The treatment goals may be both long-range and short-range. Global goals may be further subdivided into smaller, more task-specific objectives. Finally, treatment goals may be grouped according to their primary purpose; for example, rehabilitation, prevention, maintenance, and/ or health promotion. The grouping process is useful in distinguishing the level of need for skilled individual therapy from group interventions, which is helpful to the activity specialist in organizing overall service delivery for a number of clients.

Activity Analysis

Activity analysis is the next step in the systematic process of programming for therapeutic activity intervention. Selecting just any activity to use in reaching a treatment goal is not an effective approach to ensuring that the most appropriate activity has been employed. Therefore, activity analysis is a systematic evaluation of activities for appropriateness and utility in attaining individual treatment goals for each client.

Individual activities are identified and analyzed on the basis of psychosocial and physical components, as well as any specific skills that are required to engage in the activity. The activity specialist is concerned with whether or not the activity can be graduated or modified in order to accommodate the client's physical, mental, and emotional capabilities, as well as residual skills. Is the activity amenable to adaptation? Does the activity present increasing complexity so that skill advancement can be fostered? Will the activity be directly applicable in meeting the individual's treatment goals or several treatment goals? Activities that are

analyzed should include those that meet key psychosocial needs such as identity, affiliation, control, autonomy, security, self-esteem, inclusion, and meaningfulness (Zgola, 1987). If these psychosocial needs also are considered, then the personal value of the activities to the individual is more likely to be realized. These are pertinent questions that the activity specialist will ask when analyzing activities to meet treatment goals.

Elliott and Sorg-Elliott (1991) developed a simple, efficient, and effective activity analysis form to assist the activity specialist (see Figure 7.2). This tool can be easily applied when conducting an activity analysis at this step of the systematic program planning process. The analysis process examines the demands of the activity on the participant in the following specific areas: physical, cognitive, and social.

Zgola (1987) suggested that activities be graded according to the degree of environmental demand on the participant. Figure 7.3 presents a grading hierarchy. Each activity should be evaluated regarding task demand ranging from the lowest level of involvement, which is passive attending, to the highest level where active planning and implementation are done by the participant. Grading activities will assist the activity specialist in a number of important ways including: (a) helping to increase motivation for participation, (b) assisting in the tracking of progress in treatment, and (c) enhancing a better client-treatment fit with the selected activities.

Stumbo and Peterson (2004) present nine factors to consider when identifying and analyzing activities for treatment-based application:

1. "Activities must have a direct relationship to the client goal." (p. 220)
2. "Functional intervention activities should focus on the ability of the activity to help the client reach his or her goals, rather than on the activity for activity's sake." (p. 221)
3. "Functional intervention and leisure education activities should have very predominant characteristics that are related to the problem, skill, or knowledge being addressed." (p. 221)
4. "Activity characteristics are important considerations for the successful implementation of a program." (p. 222)
5. "Clients should be able to place an activity in some context in order for them to see it as useful and applicable to their overall rehabilitation or treatment outcomes." (p. 222)
6. "A single activity or session is not likely to produce a desired behavior change." (p. 223)

Activity: _____   Rater: _____

Description: _____

_____

Directions: For each category and item below, evaluate the requirements of participation in the mentioned activity. Use the following scale to mark the appropriate number for each item: 0 = None; 1 = Very Low/Little; 3 = Intermediate/Medium; 5 = Very High/Very Much. For example, if no body movements are needed for the activity, mark the [0] at the "sedentary" end.

Physical Aspects   Comments:

Body Movements:	sedentary [0] [1] [3] [5] bending/stooping	
Arms/Hands—Range of Motion	little [0] [1] [3] [5] full	
Dexterity:	little [0] [1] [3] [5] great	
Lifting:	light [0] [1] [3] [5] heavy	
Legs/Feet—Joint Motion:	none [0] [1] [3] [5] much	
Flexibility:	little [0] [1] [3] [5] much	
Coordination—Body Parts:	none [0] [1] [3] [5] precise	
Hand/Eye:	none [0] [1] [3] [5] precise	
Endurance:	little [0] [1] [3] [5] much	

Cognitive Aspects

Concentration:	none [0] [1] [3] [5] great
Memory Retention:	short-term [0] [1] [3] [5] long-term
Verbalization:	none [0] [1] [3] [5] much
Skill Level:	low [0] [1] [3] [5] high
Sensory Discrimination:	
Sight:	low [0] [1] [3] [5] high
Smell:	low [0] [1] [3] [5] high
Touch:	low [0] [1] [3] [5] high
Hearing:	low [0] [1] [3] [5] high
Taste:	low [0] [1] [3] [5] high

Affective/Social Aspects

Interaction:	low [0] [1] [3] [5] high
Physical Contact:	low [0] [1] [3] [5] high
Competition:	low [0] [1] [3] [5] high
Emotional Response:	low [0] [1] [3] [5] high

Source: Modified from Elliott & Sorg-Elliott, 1991, pp. 14–15.

Figure 7.2 Recreation Activity Analysis

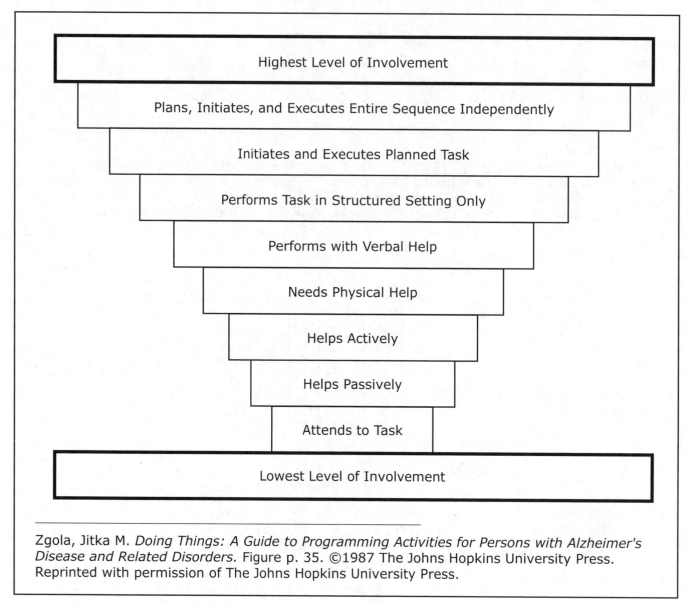

Highest Level of Involvement

Plans, Initiates, and Executes Entire Sequence Independently

Initiates and Executes Planned Task

Performs Task in Structured Setting Only

Performs with Verbal Help

Needs Physical Help

Helps Actively

Helps Passively

Attends to Task

Lowest Level of Involvement

Zgola, Jitka M. *Doing Things: A Guide to Programming Activities for Persons with Alzheimer's Disease and Related Disorders.* Figure p. 35. ©1987 The Johns Hopkins University Press. Reprinted with permission of The Johns Hopkins University Press.

Figure 7.3 Activity Grading Hierarchy

7. "Consider the types of activities in which people will engage when they have choice." (p. 224)
8. "Program to the client's outcomes and priorities." (p. 224)
9. "Client involvement in activities should be enjoyable (or at least not drudgery)." (p. 225)

In the process of identifying and analyzing activities to meet client need-based treatment goals, the activity specialist is on a constant watch for additional activities that can be used in the treatment plan, as well as in the overall activity program for the facility. Elliott and Sorg-Elliott (1991) pointed out that activity analysis is useful to the professional in helping to assure that a well-rounded, client-oriented activity program is developed.

Program Planning

When client and environmental assessment information is complete and combined with the activity analysis data, the activity specialist is prepared to engage in the program planning phase. At this step in the process several tasks are to be accomplished including: (a) goals and objectives will be stated, (b) specific activities will be selected, (c) resources and problems will be identified, (d) alternative plans of action will be outlined, and (e) a clear plan of action will be articulated in writing. It is important that careful consideration be given to each of these aspects of the plan. The focus will be on the individual, the environment, and the overall program. An individual treatment plan, plus an overall activity program, is developed in writing. At this stage, the activity specialist is still engaged in planning what and how therapeutic activity intervention will be provided.

In developing the individual treatment plan, defining specific treatment goals and objectives are matched with selected intervention activities. Treatment objectives will have three parts: (a) the target behavior, (b) the conditions under which the target behavior will be facilitated, and (c) how progress or change will be measured for the target behavior (Zimmerman, 1988). Clear, measurable treatment goals and objectives are placed within a target time frame for accomplishment. Specific and necessary conditions are specified such as the kinds of supports that the client will need in order to attain the target behavior. Outcomes measurement and evaluation constitute the documentation that the behavior has been attained.

Specified treatment goals and objectives with target behaviors form the basis of the written individual treatment plan. For example, a treatment goal for Mrs. A could be to improve her ability to independently transfer from her wheelchair to the toilet by engaging in regular upper body strength training. A target behavior under this goal might be that Mrs. A will perform the "hands to shoulders" exercise independently for a minimum of 10 repetitions on 3 separate occasions per week following a 6-week training program. This target objective could be further graded to a series of smaller, task specific objectives with specified conditions for measuring progress. To illustrate this grading, Mrs. A will perform the "hands to shoulders" exercise at 5 repetitions with 75% assistance for 3 different occasions during the first week of therapeutic intervention. This task specific objective can be graded by changing the assistance over the 6-week program, eventually attaining no assistance. The number of repetitions also can be increased over time. The goal of the treatment program is that Mrs. A will have attained adequate upper body strength to independently transfer from her chair to the toilet after the 6-week intervention.

As can be seen in this brief example, the objectives are measurable and progressively move the client toward attaining the long-range treatment goal. Objectives have clearly specified performance criteria; whereas, goals specify the outcome expected by meeting the treatment objectives (O'Brien, 1982). Specific activities are selected as they match treatment goals and provide the best conditions for meeting individual needs. A processing form for organizing and utilizing the results from the analysis of activities is recommended (see Figure 7.4).

As activities are selected to meet individual treatment goals, the activity specialist considers the resources that are needed and available for delivering the activities. Problems and possible constraints (e.g., inadequate space, money, or staff) will be identified and carefully evaluated for potential impact on the delivery of the program. Often, the activity specialist discovers that problems and constraints are resolvable by considering them at this step in the process and seeking solutions. In the instance where a potential consequence provides a formidable barrier (e.g., legal liability risks) and is not readily resolvable, it may be appropriate to redesign the program to reflect a more feasible plan of activities. This situation also provides the appropriate time to make backup or alternative written plans to safeguard against uncontrolled circumstances (e.g., inclement weather) that will prevent the original plan of activities. Troubleshooting in advance can help to assure implementation of a rewarding and successful therapeutic activity intervention program.

It is important to build consensus and commitment to the treatment plan among all the people who will be involved in safeguarding its success. First and foremost, the client must be consulted and ideally, he or she should approve the individual treatment plan. Other staff and activity leaders also can be involved in this phase. Often, it is also appropriate to involve family members and other caregivers by informing them about the decisions that are made at this point in planning. With a developed and agreed upon plan in place, the activity specialist is ready to move on to the implementation phase.

Program Implementation

When the activity specialist has completed the planning phase with careful consideration given to client needs, therapeutic goals, activity selection, and program design, then it is time to implement the plan. During the implementation phase, the activity specialist engages in the process of (a) staffing, (b) scheduling, (c) supervising or directing the delivery of therapeutic activities, (d) managing the environment where service delivery is occurring, (e) attending to safety and the management of risk, and (f) managing the funding aspects of the program. Each of these tasks is important components of successful program implementation.

Staffing entails selecting, training, and supervising all staff (paid professionals and volunteers) who are in leadership roles, or who provide support services that are needed to safeguard client participation (e.g., aids), or who are associated with program management (e.g., clerical). Staffing is critical to program success. Selecting and hiring staff with the necessary qualifications for the direct delivery of therapeutic activity intervention is a special consideration. Hiring professionals

Activity											
Physical Aspects:											
Bending											
Range of Motion											
Dexterity											
Lifting											
Leg/Feet											
Flexibility											
Coordination of Body Parts											
Hand/Eye Coordination											
Endurance											
Cognitive Aspects:											
Concentration											
Memory Retention											
Verbalization											
Skill Level											
Sight											
Smell											
Touch											
Hearing											
Taste											
Affective/Social Aspects:											
Interaction											
Physical Contact											
Competition											
Emotional Response											

Source: Modified from Elliott & Sorg-Elliott, 1991, p. 16.

Figure 7.4 Therapeutic Intervention Activity Program Analysis

with a degree and/or certification specifically in therapeutic recreation, rehabilitation science, gerontology, or general recreation programming will help to ensure high quality service delivery. There is no substitute for professional leadership; however, many programs also rely on volunteer staff in addition to qualified professionals. Beyond the hiring of qualified staff, such as the Certified Therapeutic Recreation Specialist (CTRS), the development of leadership skills is incorporated into staff training.

The activity staff will benefit from continual training to learn about different disabling conditions and the effects of these conditions on behavior. Technical skills training should be routinely offered. The following topics are examples of technical training skill areas: (a) transferring from bed to wheelchair and chair to toilet, (b) behavior management in dementia treatment, (c) motivation and control, and (d) safety procedures for handling wheelchairs and other assistive devices. Other topics that can be regularly included in staff training are: environmental design and modification, activity intervention techniques, communication skills, and caregiving strategies. Regular staff meetings and educational sessions will help to guarantee a well-trained, smooth working staff. Technical skills plus leadership preparation are critical components of a quality program.

A well-designed program plan is one with structure but not rigidity. Scheduling is an important step in matching the daily life routines of individuals with their treatment plans and management considerations (e.g., staffing). Balancing treatment plans while considering personal daily rhythms, as well as the overall program and facility schedule, can be challenging. A clearly defined schedule with attention given to (a) individual needs; (b) program and group structure; (c) staff and program resources; and (d) overall facility time, space, resources, and operation is the goal of a well-developed and smoothly implemented plan. The ability to be flexible is part of balancing a structured schedule with unexpected circumstances that can frequently arise.

Solid program implementation and management means being attentive to participants, staff, the environment, and the overall atmosphere created with the merging of these elements during activity intervention. The activity specialist is responsible for making sure that the environment is accessible, spacious, stimulating to the senses, safe, and organized for maximum ease of use. Is the activity area arranged to foster socialization, as well as provide a quiet place for privacy or rest? Are participants involved in how the environment is arranged or used? Is there an adequate number of staff immediately available, if needed? The management of participants, staff, environment, and program are all important aspects, as is fiscal management. Maintaining program funds and resources is essential to full program implementation.

Finally, as the program plan moves through full implementation, the activity specialist will attend to the evaluation phase. In reality, evaluation is inherent in all phases of programming, from beginning to end. In addition to ongoing evaluation, at the end of a program or a specific activity intervention, an overall program evaluation is completed as a distinct step in the process of service delivery.

Evaluation

The successful operation of a therapeutic activity intervention program is the ultimate goal of using a systematic programming process. Evaluation provides feedback through documentation, recordkeeping, and decision making that are all necessary to measure success at each phase, as well as at the end of the program. Evaluation is concerned with appropriateness, effectiveness, acceptability, efficiency, adequacy, efficacy, and impact. Did the client receive the benefits expected from the activity intervention? Did staff receive adequate training necessary to the provision of professional care and intervention? Was the environment appropriately designed and managed to support the client's full participation and progress? These and other questions will form the evaluation phase and a feedback loop to assessment, activity analysis, planning, and implementation. This systematic approach to programming is intended to be dynamic and ongoing; therefore, the feedback gained through evaluation is essential in the ongoing programming process.

Evaluation as it relates to assessment and intervention will focus on a careful appraisal of client needs, treatment goals and objectives, progress measurement, and the overall efficacy of the intervention in terms of bringing about targeted behavior changes specified in the individual treatment plan, as well as overall program goals and objectives. In addition to staff progress notes and the documentation of client performance on standard assessment instruments, the activity specialist also will seek interview data from the client. The interview will request feedback on aspects of the program, including the individual's perceptions of social and psychological benefits of participation in therapeutic activities. This careful documentation of client progress and feedback is essential in program evaluation, as well as for service reimbursement purposes. In addition to these sources of information, observational data from activity leaders and volunteers regarding psychosocial benefits of participation also can be utilized in program evaluation. These observations may be found in staff meeting minutes, staff log books, or in anecdotal recollections after the program or activity intervention has ended.

In addition to the essential evaluation of client treatment goals and progress, the activity specialist will want to appraise other aspects of the program including: (a) staff performance, (b) the cost-effectiveness of the program, (c) environmental quality and management, (d) risk management and safety, and (e) scheduling. Staff meeting minutes, administrative records, critical incident documentation, and cost-benefit statistical information serve as evaluation indicators.

Evaluating the quality of the program helps to assure accountability of the activity staff and facility. It is a measurement process that should be guided by stated programmatic goals and objectives beyond those that are client specific. Therefore, it is the responsibility of the activity specialist to state overall programmatic and administrative goals at the beginning of the programming process in order to be certain that adequate and appropriate evaluation data are collected. Salamon (1986) suggested five broad questions to shape and direct evaluation efforts:

1. "What" is to be evaluated? If it is to be staff, program/activities, scheduling, management, or participants, be certain to clearly and operationally define both the long-term goals and specific program objectives.
2. "Who" will be evaluated—staff, program participants, volunteers? Be certain that the role and expectations associated with the "who" are clear and specific.
3. "Where" will the evaluation information or data come from—do they already exist or will they need to be collected; what are the sources—people, documents, records, observations?
4. "When" will the evaluation information be collected—when the program begins, during, or after? Are there multiple times that evaluation should take place?
5. "How" will the evaluation information be analyzed—statistically, qualitatively, or both?

Evaluation in systematic program planning and implementation binds the entire process together. The resulting information is used in a feedback loop that sustains the programming cycle. Figure 7.5 illustrates this systematic process and the dynamic nature of the relationship among all the phases.

Activity Categories and Barriers to Participation

Activities that are being considered for meeting individual and group treatment goals can be organized according to the major areas of functioning (e.g., physical, cognitive, and psychosocial). This organizational scheme can help to give direction to the systematic programming process described in the previous section. Activities within these categories subsequently can be analyzed for their contribution to attaining therapeutic intervention goals and objectives in the activity analysis and planning phases. Based on the outcome of client assessment, activity analysis, and treatment program planning, specific activities will emerge as having the best potential for meeting the intentions of therapeutic intervention.

Three major categories of activities are those that are physical, cognitive, and psychosocial in their general nature. Each of these categories is described in greater detail in Chapters 12, 13, and 14. A chapter on leisure education (Chapter 11) also is included as an integral service function associated with therapeutic activity intervention. The rationale for including leisure education is that activity intervention embraces more than direct skilled intervention using activities. Therapeutic activity intervention can impact the development of awareness, values, attitudes, knowledge, and skills that are fundamental for daily leisure involvement and achieving a high quality of life for all older adults. The systematic process of teaching and facilitating independent decision-making and problem-solving skills associated with the wise use of leisure is central to any activity intervention that is used for attaining prevention and health promotion goals. As clients move along the continuum from rehabilitation to prevention and promotion goals, leisure education will enable their progress and achievement.

Leisure education focuses on the use of task analysis, learning, and motivating behaviors that support an active, healthy lifestyle. Another purpose for providing leisure education, therefore, is to enable older adults to develop and maintain independent, healthy, socially acceptable, and satisfying leisure pursuits after leaving the intervention program.

Activity interventions in the physical, cognitive, and psychosocial areas, along with leisure education, are collectively aimed at promoting optimal functioning, preventing further decline, and rehabilitating functional losses. Physical activities include games, sports, outdoor pursuits, exercise, and fitness-related movement. Cognitive activities are directed toward memory skills and

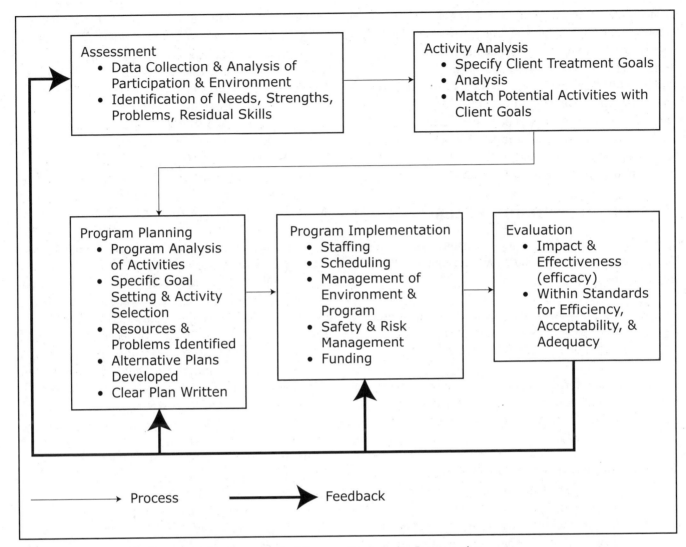

Figure 7.5 Systematic Programming Process for Therapeutic Activity Intervention

learning. They include, for example, games, bibliotherapy, debate groups, reading, and others. Psychosocial activities are those that address adjustment, socialization, social relationships, and community membership. They include such activities as parties, visiting, reminiscence groups, remotivation therapy, relaxation, and others.

One of the most formidable barriers to activity participation among elders is motivation. It is so important that an entire chapter in this book is devoted to motivation and control (Chapter 9). In order to promote the participation of older adults in activity intervention programs, several factors will need to be considered. A leading factor is the individual's personal motivation for behavior change. If the activity program is perceived to be meaningful to the individual, enjoyable, and within the person's capabilities, motivation to participate will be enhanced.

How an activity intervention is structured also is important to participant motivation. The removal of social and physical barriers is crucial. Making the participant feel welcomed and part of the group is the first step. Providing adequate time for the individual to become oriented to the other participants, the place, and the structure of the activity intervention also is instrumental in motivating or demotivating the participant. Sharing and building commitment are necessary for staff to attain motivation with more hesitant participants. Learning when and how to approach, as well as step back, when working with older adults is an important part of the overall therapeutic activity intervention process. Understanding motivation is central to achieving program success; it must not be overlooked in the process of planning and implementing successful therapeutic activity interventions.

Summary

Therapeutic activity intervention is aimed at meeting prevention, health promotion, and rehabilitation goals based upon the client's functional status and the nature of his or her impairment or disability. Activity intervention follows a systematic process that includes assessment, activity analysis, planning, implementation, and evaluation. Activity specialists develop goal-directed interventions using activities from four main categories: physical, cognitive, social, and leisure education. This chapter sets the stage for chapters 8, 9, and 10, which provide greater detail about assessment, motivation and control, and environmental considerations in therapeutic activity intervention.

Comprehension Questions

The reader can check for comprehension of the material presented in this chapter by answering the following questions:

1. Describe how therapeutic activity intervention can be used to meet promotion, prevention, rehabilitation, or maintenance goals.

2. Explain three categories that can be used for grouping therapeutic activities and why these categories are pertinent to the functional status of older adults.

3. Identify barriers to successful activity intervention with older clients.

4. What are the major phases in developing and implementing systematic therapeutic intervention programming?

References

Asmussen, E. (1981). Aging and exercise. In S. M. Horvath & M. K. Yousef (Eds.), Environmental physiology, aging, heat and altitude: Proceedings of Light, Heat, and Altitude Conference (pp. 419–428). NY: Elsevier.

Austin, D. R., & Crawford, M. E. (Eds.). (2001). *Therapeutic recreation—An introduction*. Boston, MA: Allyn and Bacon.

Cook, J. H. & Ball, C. M. (2007). Chapter 24. Therapeutic groups for older adults. In A. D. Linton & H. W. Lach (Eds.), *Matteson & McConnell's Gerontological Nursing: Concepts and Practices* (3rd ed.) (pp. 748–758). St. Louis, MO: Elsevier/Saunders.

Elliott, J. E. & Sorg-Elliott, J. A. (1991). *Recreation programming and activities for older adults*. State College, PA: Venture Publishing, Inc.

Ferrini, A. F. & Ferrini, R. L. (2008). *Health in the later years*. (4th ed.). Boston, MA: McGraw Hill.

Hamill, C. M. & Oliver, R. C. (1980). *Therapeutic activities for the handicapped elderly*. Rockville, MD: Aspen Publishers.

Howe-Murphy, R. & Charboneau, B. G. (1987). *Therapeutic recreation intervention—An ecological perspective*. Englewood Cliffs, NJ: Prentice-Hall.

Kraus, R. & Shank, J. (1992). *Therapeutic recreation service—Principles and practices* (4th ed.). Dubuque, IA: Wm. C. Brown.

Larson, E. B. & Bruce, R. A. (1986). Exercise and aging. *Annals of Internal Medicine, 105,* 783–785.

Mayo, N. E., Poissant, L., Ahmed, S., Finch, L., Higgins, J., Salbach, N. M., Soicher, J. & Jaglal, S. (2004). Incorporating the International Classification of Functioning, Disability, and Health (ICF) into an electronic health record to create indicators of function: Proof of concept using the SF-12. *Journal of the American Medical Informatics Association, 11*(6), 514–522.

McGuire, F. A. (1985). Recreation leader and co-participant preferences of the institutionalized aged. *Therapeutic Recreation Journal, 19*(2), 47–54.

O'Brien, C. L. (1982). *Adult day care—A practical guide*. Belmont, CA: Wadsworth.

Salamon, M. J. (1986). *A basic guide to working with elders*. NY: Springer.

Saltin, B. & Rowell, L. B. (1980). Functional adaptations to physical inactivity and activity. *Federal Proceedings, 39*(5), 1506–1513.

Smith, J. & Couch, R. H. (1990). Adjustment services and aging. *Vocational Evaluation and Work Adjustment Bulletin, 23*(4), 133–138.

Stumbo, N. J. & Peterson, C. A. (2009). *Therapeutic recreation program design: Principles and procedures* (5th ed.). San Francisco, CA: Pearson/Benjamin-Cummings.

Stumbo, N. J. & Peterson, C. A. (2004). *Therapeutic recreation program design: Principles and procedures* (4th ed.). San Francisco, CA: Pearson/Benjamin-Cummings.

Thews, V., Reaves, A. M. & Henry, R. S. (1993). *Now what? A handbook of activities for adult day programs*. Winston-Salem, NC: Bowman Gray School of Medicine, Wake Forest University.

Vallbona, C. & Batzer, S. B. (1984). Physical fitness prospects in the elderly. *Archives of Physical Medicine and Rehabilitation, 65,* 194–200.

Zgola, J. M. (1987). *Doing things—A guide to programming activities for persons with Alzheimer's disease and related disorders*. Baltimore, MD: The Johns Hopkins University Press.

Zimmerman, J. (1988). *Goals and objectives for developing normal movement patterns*. Rockville, MD: Aspen Publishers.

• CHAPTER 8 •

The Role and Function of Assessment

Learning Objectives

1. Understand the purpose and function of multi-dimensional geriatric assessment in the care of older adults.

2. Describe how a functional assessment in conjunction with a medical history can assist in the identification of specific problems that interfere with daily life functioning.

3. Explain how information from a multidimensional assessment may be used for program planning and evaluation purposes.

4. Describe the differences between a functional assessment and a medical assessment.

5. Discuss several assessment instruments that are appropriately used with older adults.

Key Terms

- Active Rehabilitation Programs
- Activities of Daily Living (ADLs)
- Assessment
- Environmental Assessment
- Formal Functional Assessment
- Functional Assessment
- Health/Wellness Status Assessment
- Informal Functional Assessment
- Instrumental Activities of Daily Living (IADLs)
- Leisure Activity Assessment
- Medical Assessment
- Multidisciplinary Assessment
- Multidisciplinary Team
- Observation
- Preventive/Maintenance Programs
- Psychiatric Assessment
- Screening
- Skill Performance
- Social-Role Performance
- Sociocultural/Socioeconomic Assessment

Introduction

The care and daily life functioning of older adults may be enhanced through the knowledgeable use of assessment tools and techniques. This chapter provides the rationale for the ongoing assessment of older individuals. Information about the objectives and functions of the assessment process with older adults also is described.

The chapter outlines the elements of a multidimensional geriatric assessment including the evaluation of medical, psychiatric, sociocultural/socioeconomic, activity, and environmental factors. Functional assessment and its components, such as activities of daily living (ADLs) and instrumental activities of daily living (IADLs), are defined. Information is offered regarding several assessment instruments. The chapter concludes with some general guidelines for the implementation of assessment procedures.

Rationale for Assessment

Aging may be viewed according to two basic principles. First, specific aging-related changes in the physical, psychological, behavioral, and social areas of an individual's life occur at various intervals throughout life. The progression of aging from the physical, psychological, behavioral, and social perspectives, however, is not uniform from one individual to the next. Thus, the second basic principle of aging indicates that there is a significant degree of heterogeneity among older people regarding the rate and progression of aging-related change. As Moody (2006) pointed out that while aging is a universal human experience, the older we become the more dissimilar we are one from another. We each enter older adulthood with our own life histories, lifelong experiences and lifestyle(s), and genetic heritage. Heterogeneity is greatest in older adulthood compared with any younger time period of development. Thus, any assessment of health and functional status must consider each individual on the basis of his or her individuality.

Assessment of individual health and functional status is the centerpiece of care and intervention service delivery (Lach & Smith, 2007a). The importance of functional assessment emerged from the combined efforts of the U.S. Commission on Chronic Illness and the WHO (World Health Organization) to develop a foundation for measurement (Lach & Smith, 2007a). The assessment of an older adult requires gathering information from several sources on a variety of characteristics and focusing upon the individual's circum-stances. A comprehensive assessment will take into consideration the interrelationship between changes in functional status and the impact of these changes upon the daily and basic living skills of the older individual. The results of a functional assessment will be instrumental in the design and delivery of individually appropriate services that are intended to improve care.

It is well-accepted in the health services sector that functional status is positively correlated with a sense of well-being and that it is also a useful predictor of health service consumption (Lach & Smith, 2007a). Assessment information is useful in decreasing the inappropriate use of healthcare services, preventing the waste of resources, and contributing to a reduction in the diagnosis of disability when early declines are detected and treated. Proper assessment will lead to improved diagnosis, more appropriate placement of persons within the healthcare system, less dependency on skilled nursing facilities, improved functional status, and more appropriate use of medications and other medical supports (Koff, 1988).

An interdisciplinary team of professionals who assess older adults typically include allied health professionals (e.g., activity therapists), social workers, and healthcare providers such as geriatricians (medical doctors who specialize in caring for older adults), nurses, and therapists or specialists of various types (Lach & Smith, 2007a). Ongoing or periodic functional assessment can help to ensure continuity of care and the prevention of further or accelerated decline.

Assessment Defined

Assessment represents a systematic approach to identifying and describing the individual older adult's changes in functional status (Lach & Smith, 2007a). Assessment is a complex process that involves gathering information across a range of areas including the biopsychosocial domains. Assessment is a method of viewing the problems of an older adult, placing the concerns and issues with the context of the older person's life circumstances, identifying specific problems, and determining what can be done to alleviate or eliminate these problems (Lach & Smith, 2007a; Butler, Lewis & Sunderland, 1991). Competent care of older persons requires a broad and comprehensive outlook because often they are vulnerable to disability from a variety of perspectives such as chronic diseases or other socioeconomic conditions (Gallo, Fulmer, Paveza & Reichel, 2000).

A careful assessment will accomplish several objectives and functions:

- Documentation of an individual's situation, circumstances, and problems;
- Determination of conditions that need additional care, services, or support;
- Documentation of minor changes in functioning over time;
- Provision of accurate diagnosis of problems;
- Provision of a process for monitoring progress;
- Assistance in the prediction of outcomes or decisions; and
- Obtaining critical information in an efficient and comprehensive manner.

Many problems experienced by older adults are hidden; that is, they are problems that are not frequently mentioned because of embarrassment, negativity, shame, modesty, or ignorance. Professionals who assess older adults should possess sufficient knowledge of and experience with the common health problems of older adults (e.g., arthritis, high blood pressure, diabetes, heart disease, health risk behavior). A sound understanding of the normal changes with age is also a prerequisite skill for the practitioner who conducts functional assessments. They must not only be good listeners, but they also must ask the right questions in order for the assessment to achieve its fullest potential in the identification and clarification of problems (Gallo et al., 2000; Ham, 1989; Lach & Smith, 2007a). Lach and Smith (2007a) offer the following key points in the assessment of older adults:

1. Identify personal biases/stereotypes about older adults so they can be avoided.
2. Be aware of age-related changes in each body system.
3. Distinguish between normal and pathological changes.
4. Know the atypical presentations of illness.
5. Allow time for trust to develop and gather assessment information.
6. Make accommodations for any impairments to promote comfort.
7. Screen for conditions common in the older adult population.
8. Be alert to signs and symptoms of elder abuse and neglect.
9. Always consider medications and their effects as a cause/contributor to a problem.
10. Use collateral sources to validate the patient's report. (p. 30)

A thorough and appropriate assessment constitutes the basis for any rational, systematic, and effective treatment program for an older adult. For the majority of frail or ill older persons, a comprehensive assessment should initially be undertaken and repeated at periodic intervals. According to Kemp and Mitchell (1992), geriatric assessment is pursued for one or more of the following reasons:

- To establish a diagnosis;
- To determine the personal, social, and environmental dynamics that maintain, control, and influence behavior;
- To establish baseline measures and information from which to assess the effects of treatment or natural changes in the client's status; and
- To assess the ability to care for oneself and to function in various environments.

Assessment is a tool for encouraging the maintenance of good health and well-being. Assessment information can aid in the identification of resources within the individual, the family, and the environment that can contribute to the overall quality of life of the older adult. Frail older persons are highly vulnerable to adverse changes in their environments; therefore, the available resources of family, home, social network, formal care system, and access to transportation are important components of both individual assessment and care plans (Koff, 1988).

Multidimensional Assessment

Assessment is at the heart of geriatric practice and activity specialists utilize the information from a *multidimensional assessment* to assist in the development of appropriate activity interventions. Assessment of the problems and needs of the older adult may be directly translated into an appropriate plan for therapeutic activity intervention and additional care giving needs. Because of the complex and individual nature of many older adults' problems, comprehensive evaluation can be a time-consuming and costly process. Multidimensional assessment broadens the traditional medical approach to include the assessment of mental status and affect, functional status, social situations, economic circumstances, values assessment, and preventive strategies (Jett, 2008; Lach & Smith, 2007b; Gallo et al., 2000; Kane, Kane & Rubenstein, 1989).

The use and coordination of the *multidisciplinary team* may allow for minimal redundancy in the assessments that are conducted. The value of assessment exists in its consequent actions and strategies that make the process more efficient (Kane, Kane &

Rubenstein, 1989). Geriatric assessment usually involves professionals working together, a distinct set of criteria for evaluating older adults, and three levels of intensity for the assessment—brief, intermediate, or comprehensive—based upon individual needs (Butler et al., 1991). Frail older persons usually will require many different professionals and services if optimal functioning and independence are to be achieved. It is appropriate, therefore, to make the comprehensive assessment of the older adult a collaborative, information-sharing experience. The use of a multidisciplinary approach can assist in the creative deployment of existing health services and the active development of additional services in areas where they are lacking (Ham, 1989).

The principles that are applied in rehabilitation of the aging client depend upon the nature of the intervention to be performed. The information derived from the multidisciplinary assessment is instrumental in decisions concerning appropriate intervention approaches. *Active rehabilitation* programs involve the performance of skilled therapy. *Preventive/maintenance* programs utilize interventions that are integrated into the everyday life of the older adult. Multidimensional geriatric assessment can assist in guiding and selecting active rehabilitation interventions, as well as in monitoring medical and preventive/maintenance interventions (Jett, 2008; Lach & Smith, 2007b; Robinson, 1989).

Multidimensional geriatric assessment may be accomplished through the use of broadly designed scales such as the Older Americans Resources and Services Functional Assessment Questionnaire (OARS; Fillenbaum, 1988; Lach & Smith, 2007b). The OARS was designed to assess the overall functional status and service use of older adults. Because older adults tend to experience chronic impairments, concern must focus less upon cure and more on the maintenance of personal welfare and independence (Fillenbaum). The OARS was developed to have relevance for a diverse group of practitioners and service providers; therefore, it may serve multiple purposes including program evaluation, needs assessment, and resource allocation decision-making (Kemp & Mitchell, 1992).

Another broad-based tool, the Comprehensive Assessment and Referral Evaluation (CARE) was developed to provide extensive, reliable, multidimensional information on older people in urban communities (Gurland et al., 1977). The assessment of psychiatric, medical, nutritional, economic, and social problems are accomplished using this scale. Shorter versions of the scale also are available (Gurland & Wilder, 1984).

Screening and Observation

A distinction should be made between screening and assessment. *Screening* is a preliminary assessment based upon quick and often observational measures. Screening is used to identify people who need a more thorough assessment. *Formal assessment* is a longer process conducted with the identified "at risk" client. Formal assessment is used in the diagnosis and treatment process to identify the full range of health problems and functional abilities/deficits, as well as to monitor progress during treatment (Kane & Kane, 1981; Lach & Smith, 2007b).

Several factors should be considered when selecting a screening tool (Lach & Smith, 2007b). The purpose, ease of administration and scoring, clinical relevance, testing environment and equipment needs, and the training require to administer the instrument are important considerations. In addition, any tool that is used should be appropriate as indicated by published evidence of validity and reliability for use with older adults. Depending upon the situation, the instrument should be sensitive enough to produce specific and useful information.

The basis of assessment of human behavior is *observation* and evaluation. Although a care provider may feel that he/she knows a person well, systematic and formal observations are necessary to confirm the actual functional and health status of the individual. Another important reason for observation is to assess a person's ability to engage in activities that may be used in the treatment/intervention process (Jett, 2008; Lach & Smith, 2007b).

General Guidelines for Assessment

The practitioner who conducts a geriatric assessment needs to establish rapport and a trusting relationship with the client. Older people may feel uncomfortable or anxious during assessment sessions, which can lead to poor or decreased performance. Establishment of rapport and explanation of the purposes of testing to the older client have added meaning for accurate assessment (Lach & Smith, 2007b).

Another consideration is keeping the assessment sessions as short as possible, especially for ill or heavily-medicated clients. The phrasing of questions can be critically important. Discrepancies also may arise between different informants. Tests should not be used by themselves to make decisions about the care and living arrangements of older persons. Rather, they should be considered as a part of the assessment process (Jett, 2008; Kane, Ouslander & Abrass, 1989; Lach & Smith, 2007b).

Elements of Basic Geriatric Assessment

Typically, a basic assessment will include: (a) general personal information, (b) physical health/medical assessment, (c) mental status/psychiatric assessment, (d) sociocultural/ socioeconomic assessment, (e) activity assessment (f) evaluation of living environment and resources, and (g) functional assessment (Lach & Smith, 2007b). A completed assessment provides baseline information and measurement of the individual's present status, as well as a standard against which to evaluate future changes. Many older adults, particularly frail persons, will need various services for the remainder of their lives and therefore, the collection of assessment information provides useful information in the current and future implementation of treatment interventions. An incomplete or haphazard approach to assessment is neither time-saving nor considered appropriate care (Butler et al., 1991).

Medical Assessment

A physical health/medical evaluation of the older individual focuses particular attention upon present illness and chronic conditions, as well as past medical problems (Jett, 2008; Lach & Smith, 2007b; Stoukides, Holzer, Ritzau & Burbank, 2006). Medical assessments involve the examination and evaluation of all body systems including: (a) vital signs; (b) analysis of the skin, head, mouth and teeth, eyes, ears, nose, and throat; (c) inspection of the neck; (d) testing of the heart, lungs, and musculoskeletal system; (e) exploration of the abdominal area, breasts, gastrointestinal system, and genitourinary tract; and (f) neurologic assessment. Laboratory analysis will include information about hematologic values, renal function, thyroid capacity, and glucose intolerance (Gallo et al., 2000; Jett, 2008). *Medical assessment* should be comprehensive, multiphasic, and repeated on a regular basis. It is usually completed by a physician or a nurse. It should be emphasized that Medicare programs do not cover routine checkups, which makes it extremely difficult for older persons to take advantage of early detection and prevention through regular physical examinations (Butler et al., 1991; Jett, 2008).

Psychiatric Assessment

In the *psychiatric assessment*, the health professional must be aware of the possible presence of reversible delirium, functional disorders, and reactions to stress (e.g., situational depression) (Jett, 2008; Lach & Smith, 2007b). Much of what is viewed as "old age" may have a psychiatric component that deserves proper diagnosis and treatment. Both adaptive and maladaptive characteristics accompany adults into old age. Only through careful evaluation of the client's life history can a differentiation be distinguished between those qualities possessed by the individual throughout life and those that first occurred in old age due to personality reorganization (Butler et al., 1991). When judging the adaptation of older persons, it should be remembered that older individuals commonly deal with more stresses than any other age group. Maintenance of the status quo may be all that is possible, and pride in present accomplishments is both significant and appropriate.

The psychiatric assessment often is termed a mental status examination (Lach & Smith, 2007b). A traditional mental status assessment encompasses an evaluation of behaviors and mental capability over a range of intellectual functions. Assessment may include: (a) level of consciousness; (b) attention; (c) language and communication skills; (d) short-term and long-term memory; (e) interpretation of proverbs; (f) perception of similarities and differences; (g) calculations; (h) writing ability; and (i) the capacity for construction. Well-established mental status assessment instruments that can be utilized with older persons are the Short Portable Mental Status Questionnaire (Pfeiffer, 1975), the Folstein Mini-Mental State Examination (Folstein, Folstein, & McHugh, 1975), and the Kokmen Short Test of Mental Status (Kokmen, Naessens, & Offord, 1987). The Geriatric Depression Scale (Yesavage & Brink, 1983) and the Beck Depression Inventory (Beck & Beck, 1972) also are appropriate in psychiatric assessment.

Psychiatrists are not the only persons who are qualified to complete psychiatric evaluations. In community mental health centers, psychiatric hospitals, and other environments serving older persons, a team of professionals from many disciplines may conduct a joint mental status evaluation. Also, paraprofessionals with appropriate training often can assess the psychiatric condition of older persons (Butler et al., 1991).

Sociocultural/Socioeconomic Assessment

A sociocultural/socioeconomic assessment includes information concerning family structure, housing, work or retirement, friendship patterns, economic circumstances, social roles, activities, and interests (Lach & Smith, 2007b). An evaluation of the family is crucial because the onset and maintenance of disorders often can be identified from the family context. It is inappropriate to routinely judge all older persons as helpless or fragile. Many older individuals still retain substantial influence over family and friends (Butler et al., 1991).

It is important to assess the support system of the older adult. The informal social network, the formal support system, and semiformal supports are considered elements of the older person's total support system. These categories are reciprocal in nature. The informal support system includes family and friends. Formal supports are comprised of Medicare, Medicaid, Public Health Department, Area Agencies on Aging, and other social welfare agencies. Semiformal supports refer to neighborhood organizations such as churches and senior citizen centers.

An adequate evaluation of social support will also determine the older person's healthcare coverage and economic circumstances (Jett, 2008; Lach & Smith, 2007b). It is usually necessary to appraise the individual's ability to pay for treatment. Personal financial responsibility, however, is generally not very useful because of the escalating costs in healthcare, the denial of adequate income programs, and the availability of job opportunities for older persons (Butler et al., 1991).

Sociocultural and socioeconomic assessment generally is completed by a social worker or other members of the social services staff; however, therapeutic activity specialists also can be involved in this type of assessment because of its relevance for activity programming. The Family or Friends APGAR (Adaptation, Partnership, Growth, Affection, and Resolve) (Smilkstein, Ashworth, & Montano, 1982) and the Social Resources component of the OARS assessment (Duke University Center for the Study of Aging and Human Development, 1988) are useful instruments for conducting the socio-cultural assessment of older adults. Additionally, the OARS can be used to estimate the economic resources of older adults.

Activity Assessment

Activity assessment may be separated into two distinct components — an general appraisal of health/wellness status and assessment of leisure-time use skills. Both of these evaluations may be completed by the activity specialist or in conjunction with other members of an interdisciplinary team (Hawkins, 1988).

The purpose of the *health/wellness status assessment* is to identify strengths and weaknesses of the older adult in order to optimally enhance the leisure or recreation needs of the individual. The basic components of a comprehensive health and wellness assessment include: (a) general health status evaluation, completed by or with the guidance of a physician; (b) physical fitness appraisal; (c) nutritional analysis, which is usually accomplished by a dietician; and (d) stress or emotional adjustment appraisal (O'Donnell & Ainsworth, 1984).

The assessment of physical fitness typically involves: (a) an exercise history, (b) body composition,

(c) flexibility, (d) muscle strength and endurance, (e) balance and equilibrium, (f) cardiopulmonary capacity, and (g) contraindications for exercise. A qualified activity specialist (e.g., Certified Therapeutic Recreation Specialist) and an exercise physiologist generally can conduct an assessment of the physical fitness of older adults (Touhy, 2008). Examples of physical fitness assessment instruments may be found in Dishman (2008), Ford (1985), and Katch and McArdle (1983).

A stress or emotional adjustment appraisal is generally useful in activity programming with older persons. This assessment includes documentation of the events that have produced stress in the individual's life and how he or she reacts to anxiety-producing circumstances. By developing an understanding of the older person's responses to stress and situations that elicit stress reactions, a more effective management of behaviors and social milieus can be facilitated. In addition, activities often are the logical intervention when stressful situations occur (Hawkins, 1988, 1997).

Leisure activity assessment is essential in the development of an appropriate therapeutic activity program for older persons. Leisure activity assessment involves gathering a variety of information (Hawkins, Ardovino, Rogers, Foose & Ohlsen, 2002). The activity specialist, as well as other interdisciplinary team members, will solicit information concerning the older person's repertoire of activities, interests, preferences, desires, and specific skills that support independent functioning (Hawkins et al., 2002). These data can be accumulated by using qualitative methods and/or standardized instruments such as the Linear Model for Individual Treatment in Recreation (Compton & Price, 1975), the Recreation Therapy Assessment (Cousins & Brown, 1979), and the Leisure Assessment Inventory (Hawkins et al., 2002). Leisure activity assessment clearly provides a picture of the individual's leisure activity participation patterns, their independent leisure decision making, barriers to activity involvement, and some assessment of the overall satisfaction that leisure provides in the person's daily life.

Environmental Assessment

Environmental assessment is closely related to sociocultural/socioeconomic assessment. Typically, the social worker or activity specialist will initiate an evaluation of the older person's community resources. Available community services are appraised in order to improve the appropriate utilization of community-based services and professionals (e.g., visiting nurses, occupational therapists, and senior service volunteers) in the ongoing care and evaluation of older clients

(Butler et al., 1991). The identification of supports that are needed in order to maintain community involvement may become the deciding factor between enabling the older person to remain at home or be placed in an institutional setting such as an assisted-living facility or nursing home.

An important goal in the care and treatment of older persons is the restoration and/or maintenance of an optimal level of independent functioning in the most personally desired environmental setting. Because chronic functional impairment becomes more prevalent in old age, personal independence becomes a primary concern to the older client. Due to the substantial burden of functional impairment in older persons, reliable objective assessment of the role of environmental support and design in relationship to functional loss is critical for the delivery of preventive, maintenance, and rehabilitative services to older adults (Lach & Smith, 2007b; Jett, 2008).

Functional Assessment

An assessment of functional competence or independence is an important part of any diagnostic process (Lach & Smith 2007a, 2007b). It is relevant to assess functional status because a physical health/medical diagnosis alone will not predict all the final outcomes from professional interventions or the ability to live independently. The capacity of the individual to function independently or with assistance in the home is poorly described or predicted by medical condition alone. It is not enough to diagnose medical problems and treat them in isolation from the other aspects of the individual's life (e.g., family members, social constraints). When medical illness is determined, it affects the older person's total life including their functional capacity, thus underscoring the dynamic relationship between functional competence and health status (Gallo et al., 2000).

The functional assessment informs all members of the care team (including aides and activity specialists) as to the older person's performance and need for support. Allied health professionals who conduct a functional assessment will provide (a) detail of the individual's overall functional status, (b) define all factors interfering with or modifying normal function, (c) identify all correctable factors in order to optimize functioning, (d) judge appropriateness of current and future environments, (e) objectively chart mental status, (f) evaluate rehabilitation potential, (g) define existing support services, (h) evaluate overall prognosis, and (i) construct a plan for the future (Gallo et al., 2000).

Functional assessment is both formal and informal in nature (Robinson, 1989). *Formal functional assess-*ment is useful in determining health status, compensation for health insurance benefits, level and amount of social services required, and the most beneficial type of living arrangements or environments for the individual. Furthermore, the planning of treatment interventions and the prediction of treatment outcomes are enhanced through accurate formal functional assessment (Jett, 2008; Lach & Smith, 2007b).

Informal functional assessment involves the collection and integration of functional data that complement traditional formal assessment procedures. The older adult and his/her support persons are asked questions in a simple, open-ended manner. The questions address survival skills, the support system, the barriers to optimal functioning, stress-related problems, and other issues of concern (Robinson, 1989).

The functional assessment is targeted at measuring and quantifying human behavior in regard to the performance of survival skills in day-to-day living. It focuses upon what clients can do and what they desire to do. It also provides data upon which to base and evaluate therapeutic activity intervention recommendations to older clients and their families (Mezey, Rauckhorst & Stokes, 1993). Routine functional assessment of persons over 65 years of age can be incorporated into the annual physical examination. Functional assessment also is indicated when the individual's status suddenly changes, as well as at regular intervals for *at risk populations* such as individuals with Parkinson's disease, frequent falls, or severe arthritis (Mezey et al., 1993).

Functional assessment usually includes areas that are known as *activities of daily living* (ADLs) and *instrumental activities of daily living* (IADLs) (Gallo et al, 2000; Lach & Smith, 2007b). Assessment includes skill performance and social-role performance. ADLs are generally divided into seven tasks: eating, dressing, grooming, toileting, bathing, transferring, and mobility. These seven abilities constitute the skills of self-maintenance or basic self-care activities, and are recognized as including the basic independence-promoting activities that are progressively lost in the declining older person. Other basic areas of activities of daily living or ADLs may include communication, continence, vision, and use of the upper extremities. The functional abilities necessary for basic ADL performance include endurance, strength, range of motion or flexibility, and coordination.

Instrumental activities of daily living (IADLs) are the more complex activities that are necessary to lead an independent life (Gallo et al., 2000; Lach & Smith, 2007b). IADLs refer to the skills and behaviors that are needed to survive in the community. IADLs include the following: money management, household chores, use of transportation to access the community, shopping, taking care of one's health, communicating with others, and safety preparedness.

Social-role performance is another component of functional competence and ability. This area consists of role performance as a member of society, as well as interpersonal functioning. Factors related to social-role performance include the following: job performance, friendships, intimacy, parenthood/grandparenthood, recreation, assisting others, and self-maintenance. These abilities also include the skills of self-preservation (Kemp & Mitchell, 1992). *Skill performance* is another area included under functional status and located between IADLs and social-role performance in terms of complexity and the level of skills. These skills involve intellectual, motor, and personality traits.

The use of instruments to assess the functional status of older persons may not be commonly employed by physicians but is highly relevant to activity specialists. Functional assessment is critical because the ability of older individuals to remain independent may depend upon their competence to perform essential activities of daily living. There are many geriatric functional assessment instruments available for use in this area (Gallo et al., 2000; Lach & Smith, 2007b). The Katz Index (Katz et al., 1963) is one of the most well-known and widely-used of the ADL instruments. It is so popular that it has been used as a guide for the development of other ADL scales. The Barthel Index and Barthel Self-Care Ratings also are widely known and often used scales with demonstrated reliability and validity (Mahoney & Barthel, 1965).

The Performance Test of Activities of Daily Living (Kuriansky & Gurland, 1976) is a structured performance test of ADLs based upon actual observation of the individual's performance. Observation of the person's performance and reaction to various tasks provides information regarding mental status and its effect upon ADL activity. The Physical Self-Maintenance Scale and Instrumental Activities of Daily Living Scale measure ADLs and IADLs among community and hospitalized older adults (Lawton & Brody, 1969).

The Blessed-Roth Dementia Rating Scale (Blessed, Tomlinson, & Roth, 1968) and the Direct Assessment of Functional Status Scale (Lowenstein et al., 1989) were designed to measure the ADL and IADL status of clients with cognitive impairments such as Alzheimer's disease and other forms of dementia. These scales rely on information from a caregiver, relative, or other persons who are in close contact with the older individual.

Information from these scales is best interpreted when used in conjunction with other measures of cognitive status (Jett, 2008; Lach & Smith, 2007b).

Summary

Multidimensional assessment of older adults is a challenging but essential aspect of the care and treatment process. Professionals who assess the physical, mental, social, activity, economic, and environmental conditions that impact the well-being of older persons can become more effective and knowledgeable through the utilization of standard evaluation techniques (Gallo et al., 2000; Jett, 2008; Lach & Smith, 2007a, 2007b; Stoukides et al., 2006). Assessment is a valuable tool for the preservation of health status, well-being, and quality of life of older persons. Assessment is useful in the identification of individual, family, and environmental resources that are instrumental in the care and treatment process. It can assist in understanding the value and significance of the environment for the maintenance of well-being and provide goals for improvement. Assessment also may define a plan for realistic expectations of family members' participation in the care of their older relatives.

Comprehension Questions

The reader can check for comprehension of the material presented in this chapter by answering the following questions:

1. Discuss why a multidisciplinary geriatric assessment is desirable when planning the care and treatment of older persons.

2. What are the components of a functional assessment? Name an assessment tool that can be used in each assessment area.

3. What is the difference between a functional assessment and medical evaluation?

4. Describe the assessment information that activity specialists will utilize in planning a therapeutic activity intervention with an older client.

References

Beck, A. T. & Beck, R. W. (1972). Screening depressed patients in family practice: A rapid technique. *Postgraduate Medicine, 52,* 81–85.

Blessed, G., Tomlinson, B. & Roth, M. (1968). Association between quantitative measures of dementia and of senile change in the cerebral grey matter of elderly subjects. *British Journal of Psychiatry, 114*, 797–811.

Butler, R. N., Lewis, M. I. & Sunderland, T. (1991). *Aging and mental health: Positive psychosocial and biomedical approaches* (4th ed.). New York, NY: MacMillan.

Clark, G. S. (1984). Functional assessment in the elderly. In T. F. Williams (Ed.), *Rehabilitation in the aging* (pp. 111–124). New York, NY: Raven Press.

Compton, D. & Price, D. (1975). Individualizing your treatment program: A case study using LMIT. *Therapeutic Recreation Journal, 9,* 127.

Cousins, B. & Brown, E. (1979). *Recreation therapy assessment.* Jacksonville, FL: Amelia Island ICF/MR.

Dishman, R. K. (2006). Chapter 16. Measurement of physical activity. In L. W. Poon, W. Chodzko-Zajko, & P. D. Tomporowski (Eds.), *Active living, cognitive functioning, and aging* (pp. 91–111). Champaign, IL: Human Kinetics.

Duke University Center for the Study of Aging and Human Development. (1978). *Older Americans Resources and Services (OARS) methodology: Multidimensional functional assessment questionnaire* (2nd ed.). Durham, NC: Author.

Fillenbaum, G. G. (1988). *Multidimensional functional assessment of older adults: The Duke Older Americans Resources and Services procedures.* Hillsdale, NJ: Erlbaum.

Folstein, M. F., Folstein, F. E. & McHugh, P. R. (1975). Mini-mental state: A practical method for grading the cognitive state of patients for the clinician. *Journal of Psychiatry Research, 12,* 189–198.

Ford, R. (1985). *Health assessment handbook.* Springhouse, PA: Springhouse.

Gallo, J. J., Fulmer, T., Paveza, G. J. & Reichel, W. (2000). *Handbook of geriatric assessment* (3rd ed.). Gaithersburg, MD: Aspen Publishers.

Gurland, B., Kuriansky, J., Sharpe, L., Simon, R., Stiller, P. & Birkett, P. (1977). The comprehensive assessment and referral evaluation (CARE): Rationale, development, and reliability. *International Journal of Aging and Human Development, 8,* 9–42.

Gurland, B. J. & Wilder, D. E. (1984). The CARE interview revisited: Development of an efficient, systematic, clinical assessment. *Journal of Gerontology, 39,* 129–137.

Ham, R. J. (1989). Functional assessment of the elderly patient. In W. Reichel (Ed.), *Clinical aspects of aging* (3rd ed.) (pp. 26–49). Baltimore, MD: Williams & Wilkins.

Hawkins, B. A. (1988). Leisure and recreational programming. In M. P. Janicki, M. W. Krauss & M. M. Seltzer (Eds.), *Community residences for persons with developmental disabilities* (pp. 217–227). Baltimore, MD: Paul H. Brookes.

Hawkins, B. A. (1997). Chapter 2. Health, fitness, and quality of life for older adults with developmental disabilities (pp. 29–35). In T. Tedrick (Ed.), *Older adults with developmental disabilities and leisure: Issues, policy and practice— Activities, Adaptation and Aging.* NY: Haworth Press.

Hawkins, B. A., Ardovino, P., Rogers, N. B., Foose, A. & Ohlsen, N. (2002). *Leisure Assessment Inventory.* Ravensdale, WA: Idyll Arbor.

Jett, K. (2008). Chapter 6. Health assessment in gerontological nursing. In Ebersole, P., Hess, P., Touhy, T. A., Jett, K. & Luggen, A. S. (Eds.), *Toward health aging—Human needs & nursing response* (7th ed.) (pp. 104–119). St. Louis, MO: Elsevier/Mosby.

Kane, R. A. & Kane, R. L. (1981). *Assessing the elderly: A practical guide to measurement.* Lexington, MA: D. C. Heath and Company.

Kane, R. A., Kane, R. L. & Rubenstein, L. Z. (1989). Comprehensive assessment of the elderly patient. In M. D. Petersen & D. L. Wilhite (Eds.), *Health care of the elderly.* Beverly Hills, CA: Sage Publications.

Kane, R. L., Ouslander, J. G. & Abrass, I. B. (1989). *Essentials of clinical geriatrics* (2nd ed.). New York, NY: McGraw-Hill.

Katch, F. I. & McArdle, W. D. (1983). *Nutrition, weight control, and exercise.* Philadelphia, PA: Lea & Febiger.

Katz, S., Ford, A., Maskowitz, R., Jackson, B. & Jaffe, M. (1963). Studies of illness in the aged. The Index of ADL: A standardized measure of biological and psychosocial function. *Journal of the American Medical Association, 185,* 914–919.

Kemp, B. J. & Mitchell, J. M. (1992). Functional assessment in geriatric mental health. In J. E. Birren, R. B. Sloane, G. D. Cohen, N. R. Hooyman, B. D. Lebowitz, M. Wykle & D. E. Deutchman (Eds.), *Handbook of mental health and aging* (2nd ed.) (pp. 671–697). San Diego, CA: Harcourt, Brace, Jovanovich.

Koff, T. H. (1988). *New approaches to health care for an aging population.* San Francisco, CA: Jossey-Bass.

Kokmen, E., Naessens, J. M. & Offord, K. P. (1987). A short test of mental status: Description and preliminary results. *Mayo Clinic Proceedings, 62,* 281–288.

Kuriansky, J. & Gurland, B. (1976). Performance test of activities of daily living. *International Journal of Aging and Human Development, 7,* 343–352.

Lach, H. W. & Smith, C. M. (2007a). Chapter 2. Assessment: Focus and Function. In A. D. Linton & H. W. Lach (Eds.), *Matteson & McConnell's Gerontological Nursing: Concepts and Practices* (3rd ed.) (pp. 25–51). St. Louis, MO: Elsevier/Saunders.

Lach, H. W. & Smith, C. M. (2007b). Chapter 3. Tools for Screening and Assessment. In A. D. Linton & H. W. Lach (Eds.), *Matteson & McConnell's Gerontological Nursing: Concepts and Practices* (3rd ed.) (pp. 52–81). St. Louis, MO: Elsevier/Saunders.

Lawton, P. & Brody, E. (1969). Assessment of older people: Self-maintaining and instrumental activities of daily living. *Gerontologist, 9,* 179–186.

Lowenstein, D., Amigo, E., Duara, R., Guterman, A., Hurwitz, D., Berkowitz, N., Wilke, F., Weinberg, G., Black, B., Gittleman, B. & Eisdorfer, C. (1989). A new scale for the assessment of functional status in Alzheimer's disease and related disorders. *Journal of Gerontology, 44*(4), 114–121.

Mahoney, F. & Barthel, D. (1965). Functional evaluation: The Barthel index. *Maryland State Medical Journal, 14,* 61–65.

Mezey, M. D., Rauckhorst, L. H. & Stokes, S. A. (1993). *Health assessment of the older individual* (2nd ed.). New York, NY: Springer.

Moody, H. R. (2006). *Aging – Concepts and controversies* (5th ed.). Thousand Oaks, CA: Pine Forge Press.

O'Donnell, M. P. & Ainsworth, T. H. (1984). *Health promotion in the workplace*. New York, NY: John Wiley & Sons.

Pfeiffer, E. (1975). A short portable mental status questionnaire for the assessment of organic brain deficit in elderly patients. *Journal of the American Geriatrics Society, 23,* 433–441.

Rzetelny, H. & Mellor, J. (1981). *Support groups for caregivers of the aged*. NY: Community Service Society.

Robinson, K. M. (1989). Module 2.B: Rehabilitation services. In B.A. Hawkins, S. J. Eklund & R. Gaetani (Eds.), *Aging and developmental disabilities: A training inservice package* (pp. 1–44). Bloomington, IN: Indiana University.

Smilkstein, G., Ashworth, C. & Montano, D. (1982). Validity and reliability of the family APGAR as a test of family function. *Journal of Family Practice, 15,* 303–311.

Stoukides, J., Holzer, C., Ritzau, J. & Burbank, P. (2006). Chapter 2. Health care strategies for frail older adults. In P. Burbank (Ed.), *Vulnerable older adults—Health care needs and interventions* (pp. 25–54). New York, NY: Springer.

Touhy, T. A. (2008). Chapter 3. Health and wellness. In P. Ebersole, P. Hess, T. A. Touhy, K. Jett & A. S. Luggen (Eds.), *Toward health aging: Human needs & nursing response* (pp. 43–64). St. Louis, MO: Elsevier/Mosby.

Yesavage, J. A. & Brink, T. L. (1983). Development and validation of a geriatric depression screening scale: A preliminary report. *Journal of Psychiatry Research, 17,* 37–49.

• CHAPTER 9 •

Adaptation, Autonomy, and Resilience in Older Adulthood

Learning Objectives

1. Understand the importance of autonomy, motivation, and control for older adults in treatment settings.

2. Differentiate between independence, interdependence, and autonomy.

3. Describe the concepts of *motivation* and *control* as they apply to older adults.

4. Discuss resilience and problems associated with a lack of motivation and control.

5. Explain techniques to improve motivation among older persons.

6. Identify common behavior management techniques.

Key Terms

- Amotivation
- Antecedents of Behavior
- Autonomy
- Blocks to Communication
- Compliance
- Consequences of Behavior
- Control
- Direct Versus Designated Autonomy
- Disruptive Behavior
- The Elderly Mystique
- Environment
- Extrinsic Motivation
- Independence
- Intrinsic Motivation
- Interdependence
- Nonverbal Techniques
- Objective Autonomy
- Physical Restraint
- Privacy
- Rapport
- Resilience
- Self-Determination
- Subjective Autonomy
- Wandering Behavior

Introduction

Perceptions of autonomy and control can positively influence the physical and psychological well-being of older adults. Uncontrollable situations may have detrimental effects on thinking and behavior. This chapter discusses the importance of resilience and adaptation as influenced by autonomy, motivation, and personal control in older adults. Issues related with independence and interdependence also are reviewed.

This chapter describes various motivational techniques to use with older clients such as improvement of rapport, application of nonverbal cues, and behavior modification strategies through environmental management, relaxation, and communication. Problems associated with the infringement of individual rights are explored by examining aspects of disability programs. The chapter concludes with the suggestion that complex matters of autonomy should be resolved jointly by older adults and their caregivers.

Importance of Autonomy, Motivation, and Control for Older Adults

Older individuals who reside in restrictive settings (e.g., assisted-living facilities, nursing homes) are often alienated, less satisfied, and highly dependent upon other persons. *Resilience, autonomy,* and *control* are central concerns in any environment that provides intensive care and support to the older client. Resilience is related to the processes by which the older adult copes and adapts to changes and stressors in later life (Touhy, 2008). Resilience manifests as a set of beliefs, values, behaviors, and physiology that helps the person adapt to or cope with challenging situations. Some people do better than others; some older adults are more resilient than others. Resilient individuals have a more positive outlook that helps them to maintain their sense of control over things through demonstrating greater adaptability. Resilience and a general hardiness help older adults continue to participate in decisions that affect their lives, thus buffering losses in independence. In highly resilient people, there is a sense of interdependence in stressful and challenging situations. Total independence is less relevant when resolving difficulties and making important decisions. It is interdependence that maintains an active and mutual engagement of the client with caregivers in decision making.

Opportunities for clients to make choices and control events that influence outcomes should be promoted (Langer & Rodin, 1976). A belief in one's control over an undesirable event can reduce aversion to that situation. Perceptions of control also may have positive effects upon psychological functioning, performance, and physical well-being (Touhy, 2008). At the same time, uncontrollable situations can have detrimental effects upon thoughts and behaviors and create severe stress and anxiety (Geer, Davison, & Gatchel, 1970).

Perceptions of control are expected to change with age and more resilient people do better in situations where control must be shared (e.g., assisted-living or nursing facilities). The loss of valued social roles, the normal biological changes associated with aging, and the occurrence of major life events such as retirement, bereavement, or moving into congregate care may challenge one's sense of control. For many older persons, these events can alter their explanations and interpretations of less significant occurrences, which further may erode feelings of competency, autonomy, and self-worth (Rodin & Langer, 1980). For older residents in restricted environments, choices about clothing, diet, and other aspects of daily living have the potential to enhance perceptions of control and mastery over the environment (Touhy, 2008).

Privacy is another aspect of environmental control that is related to autonomy, interdependence/independence, and self-concept. When personal space is unavailable, many individuals withdraw from social interaction. Privacy can be enhanced through the use of physical room dividers, a decrease in noise levels, the closing of room doors, rearrangement of furniture, and the provision of private areas or rooms where confidential conversations may occur (Moos, 1976).

Motivation, like resilience, is comprised of those sources that energize behavior in general and in particular situations. Motivation helps to maintain a person's goal-directed behavior, as well as contributes to the continuity and persistence of certain behaviors (Touhy, 2008). Motivation refers to a prompt for action or a desire that makes an action pleasant or necessary. In psychology, motivation is viewed in terms of a physiological or psychological need or drive that stimulates behaviors in an attempt to reduce the drive or need. Older adults will be more highly motivated when they perceive that caregivers respect their autonomy and competence to make decisions for themselves (Deci & Ryan, 2000a, 2000b). Motivation and resilience are considered to be important factors in individual behavior with the implication that if motivation and resilience are improved, then performance might also improve (Carroll & Gray, 1981).

Independence, Interdependence, and Autonomy

The issue of *independence* can be viewed in terms of the right to flourish. The right to flourish implies that there are many routes to independence that may exist, even in what may seem like inconsequential areas of choice (Cohen, 1992). The independent living movement views services for older persons as either enhancing or limiting independence. Services can be controlled and directed by consumers or by agencies. Consumer-directed services accept risk-taking and uncertainty, and are directed at a level of involvement that gives meaning to life. The independence strived for by the independent living movement means more than mere survival with the limited goal of preventing institutionalization (Berkowitz, 1987).

Throughout the years, however, a greater recognition of the importance of *interdependence* has reshaped how older consumers and professionals work cooperatively for the greatest good of the client. Interdependence is the recognition that no one is alone in this world and to attain optimal outcomes, older clients and their caregivers work together toward goals that in the best interest of the older adult.

Among older adults who have disabilities, most will spend a significant amount of time free of disability in later life. It is not until very advanced age (80s, 90s, 100s) that many adults must learn to cope with the disabling effects of arthritis, osteoporosis, cardiovascular disease, blindness, diabetes, and other ailments. *The elderly mystique* as described by Rosenfelt (1965) is the common myth that disability in old age indicates inevitable decline, demise, and a significant end to skill and mastery. According to this myth, older adults who become disabled are no longer able to travel, to eat the foods that they prefer, to engage in physically demanding activities, to maintain schedules, or to exercise authority. *The elderly mystique* is one that many disabled older adults have come to accept as the essence of aging (Cohen, 1992), which is unfortunate because it does not help older individuals to adapt and remain resilient.

The belief that others must control the intellectual tasks of the older adult regarding autonomous decision making is unfounded. This belief suggests that older persons consider themselves to be less competent than many persons and more dependent upon particular individuals to complete various cognitive tasks. Even if the older adult is not influenced by theses negative stereotypes about aging, the older individual may believe that adaptation requires relinquishing primary control

in favor of assuming control through secondary sources (Rothbaum, Weisz, & Snyder, 1982; Schulz, 1987). The process of self-fulfilling prophesy renders many older adults as expressing a learned helplessness when it comes to making important decisions in their lives (Touhy, 2008). Replacing these negative, inappropriate stereotypes with more positive approaches that utilize interdependent decision-making strategies will be more effective for the activity professional in terms of motivating older clients to engage in activities.

All too frequently, policymakers, program planners, and practitioners consciously and unconsciously support and encourage the elderly mystique. Programs for the older adults often utilize and promote activities based upon a model of incompetence (Minkler, 1990). Because interdependence cannot be easily measured, it is often considered to be without meaning. Healthcare, rehabilitation, and social service program providers must explore the similarities and differences between and among younger and older persons with regard to their attitudes toward rehabilitation, decision-making, interdependence, control, activities, and role expectations (Cohen, 1992).

Autonomy refers to self-rule or self-determination and includes the attributes of liberty, independence, interdependence, and freedom of choice (Lucke, 2007). Autonomy means that the older adult "will be respected as decision makers about their own care" (Lucke, p. 203). The feeling of autonomy is similar to a sense of control; that is, feeling in control rather than believing that one is controlled by others. Autonomy includes both an objective and a subjective component. The objective aspect refers to the enhancement of self-determination through the removal of apparent barriers, while the subjective portion includes the more personal experience of self-determination—the feeling of control over one's life (Tobin, 1991).

Objective autonomy is most often the focus in the care of older adults. The presence of barriers such as the choice of clothing, bed times, and the types of food should be minimized. Autonomy also must be expanded to incorporate a personal sense of autonomy within each individual. The enhancement of *subjective autonomy* is more difficult to achieve than merely removing objective barriers. An increased subjective sense of personal autonomy for the older adults often may involve active fostering of interdependent relationships with other individuals (Tobin, 1991).

The justification for autonomy of older adults is based in law (Lucke, 2007). All persons should receive due process and equal protection even though they may be older and/or chronically impaired. A second justification for older adult autonomy is intrinsic to medical ethics, which require health professionals to utilize their knowledge and skill to find the greater balance of good over harm in treatment and care. This responsibility may lead to paternalistic behaviors that impose on the autonomy of older individuals. A third justification is concerned with how to modify policies and practices when a cure is not possible or probable. In the situation where a cure is unattainable, the relationship of the client with physicians and other healthcare professionals is clearly different. The client often exhibits a greater degree of awareness about their adaptation to the disease or disability than do "expert" health professionals. The challenge then is to modify professional judgments to include greater sensitivity to the potential adverse consequences of treatment, policies, and practices (Tobin, 1991).

Care providers have certain responsibilities when protecting the autonomy of older clients.

> These include (1) recognizing and acknowledging the validity of the values and beliefs of the older person, especially when the clinician differs with those values and beliefs; (2) assisting the older person to identify relevant values and beliefs; (3) assisting the older person to express a value-based preference; and (4) refraining from interfering with the implementation of that preference by the older person, or assisting with its implementation as necessary, given the limitations on the older person's ability. (Lucke, 2007, p. 203)

It remains unclear, however, why there is a tendency to turn every decision in the lives of older persons into a healthcare decision. Older nursing home residents generally desire more control over many areas of their lives; however, many older persons state that they currently possess little control (Kane, Caplan, Freeman, Aroskar, & Urv-Wong, 1990). A solid commitment to the value of human life, even when the life may no longer be that of a human person as personhood is normally understood, provides insurance against discrimination, repression, and death at the hands of others.

Autonomy should be promoted because it advances individual welfare and generally, most individuals know how to further their own interests better than anyone else (Lucke, 2007). Some older adults have varying capacity to make decisions and these persons must be encouraged to make decisions by providing assistance and support, even in difficult or nearly impossible situations. Far too little attention is given to understanding older persons as they really are and

assisting them in being themselves; an omission that occurs even when there are the best of intentions.

Direct versus designated autonomy means making decisions and/or acting on one's own or granting the authority to others to decide or to act. It is often necessary to combine both with explicit, mutually-accepted responsibilities. The inability of many mentally-impaired older adults to make rational decisions must be considered. Even when the older adult demonstrates choices that may appear unreasonable, best practices requires that caregivers and professions show respect. In many instances, there is no simple answer regarding professionally responsible behavior (Lucke, 2007). Just because autonomy is promoted does not ensure that client satisfaction is guaranteed. Certainly, no one person receives everything that he or she desires. Autonomous individuals do require the ability to exercise at least some small amount of choice and control.

Autonomy is not merely an end state. It also comprises the use of particular skills, abilities, desires, and preferences that are the products of past efforts and interactions (Lucke, 2007). One's abilities and capacities are subject to interpretation by others in a complex and dynamic manner. Autonomy means to freedom to experience the world within the framework of personal habit, choice, necessity, insight, and validation. Autonomy exists and is best understood on an individual basis with no preset standards or criteria. It is spontaneous within events and environments in which caregivers are responsive to being a part of a true community (Agich, 1993).

Motivation

Motivation refers to the desire to initiate, direct, and sustain behavior. *Intrinsic motivation* refers to behaviors that are engaged in for their own sake—for the pleasure and satisfaction that is gained. *Extrinsic Motivation* refers to behaviors that are performed in order to acquire or to avoid some consequence and they are not performed merely for the experience of engaging in them (Deci & Ryan, 1985, 2000a, 2000b).

In addition to intrinsic and extrinsic motivation, *amotivation* also can be considered. *Amotivated* behavior is neither intrinsically nor extrinsically motivated. *Amotivated behavior* is behavior in which the individual perceives a lack of dependence or interconnection between their behavior and the outcome(s). For example, a nursing home resident may state that she really does not know why she plays cards—that playing cards does not accomplish anything for her. There are no intrinsic or extrinsic rewards, and participation in the activity will decline and eventually cease. Learned helplessness can be a consequence of amotivation. Amotivated behavior is the least self-determined. There is no sense of purpose, no expectation of reward, nor the chance to change the progression of events (Deci & Ryan, 1985, 2000a, 2000b).

Motivation is central in the care of older persons in congregate care environments. It represents a quality and an attitude of mind that provides a sense of direction and purpose, a desire and willingness to participate. Chronically ill older adults often do not possess the necessary resources or skills to remain active and involved in everyday life. These clients generally want to remain independent, and maintain both physical and mental activity (Hunt, 1988). Motivation, or the lack of it, possibly is the most frequently used explanation for success and failure in rehabilitation settings and clinical practice (Kemp, 1986).

There are several theories of motivation. Humanistic theory is useful and relevant for explaining mature adult behavior. A hierarchy of needs is associated with humanistic theory, including physical concerns, safety, belonging, love, esteem, self-actualization, desire for knowledge and learning, and aesthetic or beauty interests. Humanistic needs are motivating, and older adults with impairment or degeneration may feel threatened at any or all levels of need (Dreher, 1987).

In motivating older adults, caregivers should consider the circumstances that encourage or support behavior, as well as the conditions that discourage or prevent behavior. Motivation is most desirable when (a) the person knows what he or she wants and expects that it can be obtained, (b) the associated rewards are meaningful and timely, and (c) the consequences of the behavior are not negative or substantial. To improve motivation, strategies are undertaken that will maximize the chances of the individual receiving what he or she wants, promoting his or her belief and expectation that what is wanted can be obtained, rewarding progress toward that goal, and minimizing any undue costs of the behavior (Kemp, 1986).

Age-related differences in motivational level may affect the rehabilitation of older persons. Older adults require more and different reinforcements than do younger individuals. Rehabilitation activities are usually harder for older adults. It is generally less useful to promise benefits that are far in the future because the emergence of disability can indicate the approach of life's end (Riley & Foner, 1968). Older individuals respond best to concrete goals that affect the functions of daily living. A concern for safety and security are more significant than are career, future achievement, financial compensation, and materialism (Neugarten, 1968).

Self-determination is a necessary condition for the enhancement of motivation. Self-determination allows the individual to attempt new activities, to explore unfamiliar territories or arrangements, and to experience satisfaction from the exploration (Deci, 1980).

Older adults need to be supported in their attempts to engage in enjoyable and challenging activities of their own choosing. Participation in self-selected activities can enhance motivation and are more often related with positive consequences. A focus upon the nature of encouragement for participation in the activities of daily living should be a consideration. If older adults feel compelled by others to engage in particular activities, intrinsic or self-determined extrinsic motivation toward certain activities may be reduced (Vallerand & O'Connor, 1989). Many older adults have decreased expectations concerning their abilities and potentials. Without a positive belief in oneself, behavior can be undecided and easily suppressed.

Control

The fear of **loss of control** over one's environment is a common concern among older adults. *Loss of control* is frequently associated with a loss in independence (Feingold & Werby, 1990). A person's beliefs concerning *loss of control* may be the result of an inability to engage in and to complete various tasks of everyday life. The idea of control over the environment is a powerful force that also serves as a motivator. Yet, caregivers generally do not trust the decision-making capabilities of the older client (Chowdhary, 1990). It has been demonstrated that restricted opportunities for control will limit the positive effects of interventions that are designed to increase the competence of older clients (Timko & Moos, 1989).

Behavior that increases control in a manner that is mutually beneficial to both the client and the staff has been shown to result in positive outcomes. Nursing home staff members, however, often reinforce dependent rather than independent behavior. Personal choice increases perceived control and, as a consequence, motivation and performance are enhanced. Attempts to encourage self-determination will consider the amount of control desired by the individual because there is much diversity in preferences for control among older adults. Too much choice or control can sometimes be as overwhelming and detrimental as too little (Rodin, 1987).

Individuals who have experienced more negative life events and those who are more functionally impaired often display a greater decline in perceived control (Arling, Harkins & Capitman, 1986). A significant number of the oldest residents who are in congregate care are more likely to have the desired amount of control when compared to younger nursing home residents who are the least satisfied with the amount of control afforded them. Residents of nursing homes and other facilities who have high degrees of desired control also are generally in poorer health with decreased functional abilities (Mullins, 1985).

Lack of control has been associated with poor mental and physical health outcomes. Control is likely to be an issue in old age because of the accumulated losses related with the aging process. It has been confirmed that control directly affects health status by altering an individual's physiological processes (Rodin, 1986). Reliance upon one's own efforts or skills to attain goals can facilitate the development of efficient coping strategies to deal more successfully with the many problems identified with old age. Aging may simply become another obstacle for which effective coping strategies are determined and then utilized (Die, Seelbach, & Sherman, 1987). Enhancement of the older adult's perceptions of control can include (a) the promotion of choice and the elimination of learned helplessness stereotypes, (b) encouragement of positive accomplishments and a sense of responsibility, (c) provision of success experiences and modification of unrealistic goals, and (d) the utilization of communication skills that reinforce control (Teitelman & Priddy, 1988).

Physical Restraint

In any discussion of control the issue of *physical restraint* must be addressed. It has been confirmed that restrained older adults are likely to be ill, frail, and at risk of death during hospitalization or institutionalization (Strumpf & Evans, 1988). The reasons offered for restraint of the older client include prevention of falls, impaired mental status, and facilitation of treatment. In contrast, clients rarely cite the need for restraints, even to prevent falls or for other safety reasons. A strong emotional response to the application of restraint may be explained by the fact that so few older persons perceive the need for restraints (Strumpf & Evans, 1988).

Responses to the experience of restraint vary in intensity and reflect feelings of denial, discomfort, anger, and resistance. Yet, many staff members often are unable to propose alternatives to physical restraint. Older adults can provide several practical suggestions. When restraints are used, they must be considered as a special treatment requiring further assessment, intensive monitoring, and consultation with healthcare team members. Alternative interventions should be attempted. The possible elimination of restraining devices ex-

cept under the most extreme, short-term circumstances is recommended (Strumpf & Evans, 1988).

Motivational Techniques

The extent to which the older adult participates in the decisions about activities, the nature of participation in activities, and the progression of the activities will, in part, determine the level of success with motivation and adaptation. Older adults become discouraged and less satisfied with their lives if they perceive themselves as lacking control. Older persons may then perform less well and experience low motivation for participation. Lower participation increases the risk for illness and injury. Activity professionals who work with older adults should carefully consider all the factors that influence motivation. Providing opportunities for autonomy and choice are instrumental for increasing motivation (Vallerand & O'Connor, 1989).

Activity leaders maximize a sense of control and autonomy by offering activities in which choice is promoted. Through experiencing personal control over decision making and participation, older clients will overcome a fear of failure and learn to more realistically assess the demands of their environments.

The development of trust is essential to a group leader's success in the encouragement of participation. As much time as is necessary should be spent in the establishment of *rapport*. An especially useful motivational technique is the provision of snacks. Refreshments can be utilized as a means to secure additional interest and to provide a period of relaxation during activities that require a high degree of mental, emotional, or physical involvement (Salamon, 1986).

Motivation may be based upon giving participants recognition. The participation of a visitor in an activity also can be a powerful motivator. The importance of motivation must not be minimized. Imagination and creativity are required for thoughtful programming that attracts the greatest number of participants (Salamon, 1986).

Older individuals who have received control-enhancing interventions (e.g., stress-management, relaxation, instruction in self-responsibility, physical fitness, nutritional awareness, and spirituality) have experienced significant improvements in their levels of perceived control and well-being (Slivinske & Fitch, 1987). The practitioner's challenge is to accurately assess the older individual's need for therapy, leisure education, or voluntary recreation participation and then to provide relevant activities that have the potential for autonomy and perceived control within the activity. Respect for individual human rights and dignity should be the standard in all activity programs (Luttrell & Fisher, 1997). Individual differences must be considered with an emphasis upon previous lifestyles, leisure interests, former roles, individual personality, and personal values when programming relevant activity interventions.

Older clients who are frail or infirm should not be overstimulated. Impaired or disabled older persons tend to perform less well when arousal is too great. When the arousal states caused by anxiety and stress are reduced, the performance of older individuals tends to improve. Meaningful material will more often be remembered and the material is also more motivating if it is relevant. Unique experiences may be remembered well; however, individuals can more clearly remember if they realize that the information to be recalled has some priority or personal meaning (Carroll & Gray, 1981).

Motivation for involvement is influenced by several factors including a desire for change. Hamill and Oliver (1980) noted other relevant aspects of motivation to be the desire to please others, the need for approval, associations between past experiences and the present, social rewards gained from sharing, a sense of creativity, curiosity, achievement and recognition, and the need to improve competence.

Older participants will be more highly motivated when they are related to as adults. "They deserve respect and will respond to it" (Hamill & Oliver, 1980, p. 30). Activities should be offered that are based upon goals determined by and shared with participants. The recognition of any degree of progress can be rewarding. Ongoing staff-participant interaction must occur in order to ensure that needs and goals are met.

Although nonverbal techniques may be as effective as verbal motivational techniques, *nonverbal techniques* often are neglected. By providing a shoulder touch or a gentle hand squeeze or a hug, the individual will feel reinforced. Smiles and laughter are also effective motivational cues. Sincerity is essential when utilizing verbal and nonverbal techniques. It is important to remember that older adults of different cultural, racial, and ethnic backgrounds may respond differently to the various nonverbal techniques (Leitner & Leitner, 1985).

The specific benefits of an activity and how those benefits relate to the particular needs of an individual should be emphasized. Personal invitations and the provision of leadership roles for clients can be an effective motivational strategy. Another practical technique concerns the use of peer influence as a motivator of participation. Further, the enhancement of self-image is important in motivating client involvement and

also is a significant outcome of participation in activities (Leitner & Leitner, 1985).

An important motivational tool is to encourage participation in a broad range of challenging activities that are within the individual's capabilities. The older client's capacity for self-direction will remain underutilized as long as the idea of providing more and more staff-directed activities is maintained. Value must be assigned to a person's own accomplishments, nevertheless encouragement and recognition are always necessary.

Behavioral Techniques and Strategies

The appropriate assessment of behavior problems in older persons may lead to treatment planning that utilizes reinforcement, the shaping of desired behaviors, and the learning of new skills. *Antecedents of behavior* require evaluation before behavioral interventions can be applied. Antecedents are the events and circumstances that immediately precede the problem behavior. Antecedents can be related to location; that is, when the behavior occurs at a certain place. Some antecedents are cognitive; that is, when they reflect certain thought patterns or feelings within the client. Additional antecedents are social, for example other persons can trigger problem behavior. Any or all antecedents can be related to the maintenance of problem behavior (Edinberg, 1985).

The *consequences of behavior* also must be determined. It is critical to examine the positive rewards that result from client behavior and to alter the outcomes until the problem behavior is discontinued (Edinberg, 1985). Positive reinforcement is necessary for every client. Older adults who are apparently unmotivated to attend activities may become involved by holding smaller activity groups in the clients' rooms. There is a tendency for older individuals to avoid association with clients who function at lower levels than themselves. It is apparently too great a reminder of the declines associated with individual's aging and the additional care that is required (Elliott & Sorg-Elliott, 1991).

The terms *motivation* and *compliance* are often confused. Compliance refers to obedience or submission to the desires of another person. Motivation refers to self-directed behavior. Persons who appear to be unmotivated often are described as passive, indecisive, and easily frustrated. When an older adult does not perform or respond in the way that someone else believes is appropriate or when others cannot understand or control the behavior, the individual often is labeled as unmotivated (Kemp, 1986). In fact, nothing could be further from the truth. These apparently *unmotivated* persons must work hard at attaining their goals, even though they may be entirely different from the goals that staff members have established for them.

Relaxation

Relaxation is a technique that can be utilized in corrective, adaptive, enrichment, and preventive interventions (Touhy, 2008). It is focused upon the moderation of internal feeling states such as anxiety and anger. Relaxation may be viewed as a natural way of being, a stage of self-awareness, or simply the absence of excessive anxiety.

Relaxation has been utilized as a treatment intervention with a wide range of older persons (Touhy, 2008). With certain adaptations, relaxation techniques can be used with persons of limited cognitive abilities and those who function independently. With impaired older individuals, the instructions must be clear and simple while not requiring significant memory for detail. The strengths of relaxation are its flexibility and proven effectiveness in combination with other forms of treatment. Relaxation techniques also may be practiced on the client's own time and in their own environments as reinforcement of previously learned skills.

Environmental Management with the Confused or Disruptive Client

The physical *environment* should be organized so that impaired individuals have access to relevant information without having to ask others in the environment. A variety of aids such as names on doors, calendars, clocks, and posted activity schedules are helpful. It also is useful to maintain a consistent daily routine. Major daily events (e.g., group meetings and activities, meals, and everyday living functions) should occur at the same time each day. A *reality board* can serve as a valuable aid. These boards commonly provide information regarding time, place, date, weather conditions, and perhaps the next meal. To be most effective, reality boards should be positioned at eye level (including wheelchair users) and in a conspicuous location. Boards are frequently referred to during daily reality orientation to reinforce their use (Edinberg, 1985).

The provision of an environment in which achievement is possible can be important when working with older adults who have disabilities. Clients who are confused often display frustration or restlessness, and appear worried again and again over the same problem. Refocusing their efforts and attention should provide troubled clients with something else to

think about and a sense of purpose. The challenge for staff members is to assign a task before the older client reaches a state of agitation. This idea is not practical with all confused clients; however, it has proven useful with many impaired individuals. The most appropriate tasks are those that are familiar or comfortable, and the client must feel that the task is helpful. Some examples of successful repetitive tasks are dusting, polishing shoes or silverware, sorting silverware, cleaning tables, folding laundry or towels, and rolling yarn into balls (Elliott & Sorg-Elliott, 1991).

Disruptive behavior, such as angry outbursts or throwing things, should be deterred by assisting the agitated individual to express emotion in a more socially acceptable manner. After a direct response to the distressed behavior, quiet and nonthreatening activities may be attempted such as listening to music or eating a snack. Other activities that might be appropriate for some disturbed individuals include carpentry, creating with clay, or physical exercise (Hamill & Oliver, 1980).

Many confused older adults remain ambulatory and are at risk for *wandering behavior*. In the past, the solution to wandering has been the use of physical restraints. However, the use of restrains almost always results in the deterioration of the individual to the point of little or no responsiveness.

Following their request, older clients may be permitted short walks on the facility grounds or within the facility when accompanied by a staff member. When older clients realize that a walk can be taken at most any time, wandering may decrease. Activity staff and nursing personnel join efforts in the provision of a walking program. Many patients regress because they are forced to refrain from an activity that apparently provides enjoyment (Elliott & Sorg-Elliott, 1991).

Communication

Staff attention also should focus upon the skills necessary for the exchange of information with older clients. *Blocks to communication* may include the following partial list:

- Ordering, directing, commanding;
- Warning, reprimanding, threatening;
- Inciting, preaching, moralizing;
- Providing solutions;
- Lecturing or arguing;
- Judging, criticizing, blaming, ridiculing; and
- Interpreting, analyzing, diagnosing, and probing.

Active listening attends to the feelings of others and to one's own feelings or reactions. Active listening is useful when communicating with all adults. The genuineness of the staff member's communication is critical to the success of this approach. A great number of problems encountered by older clients will require more direct intervention. However, due to a lack of meaningful roles and relationships, active listening and genuine communication can provide much needed emotional support to older individuals (Edinberg, 1985).

Summary

Although many older adults maintain their autonomy and independence, they do so in a society that cares little for their dilemma or for their quality of life, or for human nurturance. Independence has often been emphasized in legal terms, yet physicians, social workers, therapists, other healthcare personnel, and adult children continue to assume that dependence is the norm. Issues related to independence, interdependence, control, and autonomy should not be considered as conflicts, but as complex circumstances that older adults, caregivers, and most healthcare providers can resolve together. It is imperative that public policy be influenced in a manner that is consistent with an individual's right to pursue his or her full potential, regardless of age.

The importance of autonomy, motivation, and control for older persons is considered in this chapter. Independence and interdependence were recognized as existing in many areas of choice. The existence of *the elderly mystique* is the belief that disability in old age indicates an unavoidable decline in functioning. The elderly mystique is acknowledged as frequently being supported by policymakers, program planners, and practitioners, especially in congregate care settings.

Motivational techniques are reviewed, such as the development of rapport and the implementation of nonverbal approaches. Behavioral techniques and strategies including relaxation, environmental management, and effective communication also are described. In conclusion, the autonomy of older adults is determined to be contingent upon the interdependence between older adults and their caregivers working together to maximize the potentials of all involved.

Comprehension Questions

The reader can check for comprehension of the material presented in this chapter by answering the following questions:

1. Distinguish among autonomy, independence, and interdependence.

2. Discuss adaptation and resilience in older adults.

3. Why is motivation important when working with older clients?

4. Discuss techniques that can be used to enhance motivation and a sense of control in older persons.

5. Why are some older people not motivated?

6. What is meant by *amotivation*?

References

Agich, G. J. (1993). *Autonomy and long-term care.* New York, NY: Oxford University Press.

Arling, G., Harkins, E. B. & Capitman, J. A. (1986). Institutionalization and personal control: A panel study of impaired older people. *Research on Aging, 8*(1), 38–56.

Berkowitz, E. D. (1987). *Disabled policy: America's programs for the handicapped.* Cambridge, England: Cambridge University Press.

Carroll, K. & Gray, K. (1981). Memory development: An approach to the mentally impaired elderly in the long-term care setting. *International Journal of Aging and Human Development, 13*, 15–35.

Chowdhary, U. (1990). Notion of control and self-esteem of institutionalized older men. *Perceptual and Motor Skills, 70*(3), 731–738.

Cohen, E. S. (1992). What is independence? *Generations: The Journal of the Western Gerontological Society, 16*(1), 49–52.

Deci, E. L. (1980). *The psychology of self-determination.* Lexington, MA: D. C. Heath and Company.

Deci, E. L. & Ryan, R. M. (1985). *Intrinsic motivation and self-determination in human behavior.* New York, NY: Plenum.

Deci, E. L. & Ryan, R. M. (2000a). The "what" and "why" of goal pursuits: Human needs and the self-determination of behavior. *Psychological Inquiry, 11*, 227–268.

Die, A. H., Seelbach, W. C. & Sherman, G. D. (1987). Achievement, motivation, achieving styles, and morale in the elderly. *Psychology and Aging, 2*, 407–408.

Dreher, B. B. (1987). *Communication skills for working with elders.* New York, NY: Springer.

Edinberg, M. A. (1985). *Mental health practice with the elderly.* Englewood Cliffs, NJ: Prentice Hall.

Elliott, J. E. & Sorg-Elliott, J. A. (1991). *Recreation programming and activities for older adults*. State College, PA: Venture Publishing, Inc.

Feingold, E. & Werby, E. (1990). Supporting the independence of elderly residents through control over their environment. *Journal of Housing for the Elderly, 6*(1, 2), 25-32.

Geer, J. H., Davison, G. C. & Gatchel, R. I. (1970). Reduction of stress in humans through nonveridical perceived control of aversive stimulation. *Journal of Personality and Social Psychology, 16*, 731–738.

Hamill, C. M. & Oliver, R. C. (1980). *Therapeutic activities for the handicapped elderly*. Rockville, MD: Aspen Publishers.

Hunt, L. (1988). Continuity of care maximizes autonomy of the elderly. *The American Journal of Occupational Therapy, 42*(6), 391–393.

Kane, R. A., Caplan, A. L., Freeman, I. C., Aroskar, M. A. & Urv-Wong, E. K. (1990). Avenues to appropriate autonomy: What next? In R. A. Kane & A. L. Caplan (Eds.), *Everyday ethics: Resolving dilemmas in nursing home life* (pp. 306–317). New York, NY: Springer.

Kemp, B. (1986). Psychosocial and mental health issues in rehabilitation of older persons. In S. J. Brody & G. E. Ruff (Eds.), *Aging and rehabilitation: Advances in the state of the art* (pp. 122–158). New York, NY: Springer.

Langer, E. J. & Rodin, J. (1976). The effects of choice and enhanced personal responsibility for the aged: A field experiment in an institutional setting. *Journal of Personality and Social Psychology, 34*, 191–198.

Leitner, M. J. & Leitner, S. F. (1985). *Leisure in later life: A sourcebook for the provision of recreational services for elders*. New York, NY: Haworth Press.

Lucke, K. T. (2007). Chapter 9. Ethical considerations. In A. D. Linton & H. W. Lach (Eds.), *Matteson & McConnell's Gerontological Nursing: Concepts and Practices* (3rd ed.) (pp. 198–221). St. Louis, MO: Elsevier/Saunders.

Luttrell, S. & Fisher, F. (1997). Chapter 2. Ethical aspects of quality care. In P. P. Mayer, E. J. Dickinson & M. Sandler (Eds.), *Quality care for elderly people* (pp. 17–35). New York, NY: Chapman & Hall Medical.

Minkler, M. (1990). Aging and disability: Behind and beyond the stereotypes. *Journal of Aging Studies, 4*(3), 245–260.

Moos, R. H. (1976). *The human context: Environmental determinants of behavior*. NY: John Wiley & Sons.

Mullins, L. C. (1985). An examination of the locus of desired control among young-old and old-old nursing home patients. *Sociological Spectrum, 5*, 107–117.

Neugarten, B. L. (1968). Perspectives of the aging process. *Psychiatric Research Reports, 23*, 42–48.

Riley, M. W. & Foner, A. (1968). *Aging and society*. New York, NY: Russell Sage Foundation.

Robinson, L., Boyko, E., Lane, J., Cooper, D. & Jahnigen, D. (1987). Binding the elderly: A prospective study of the use of mechanical restraints in an acute care hospital. *Journal of the American Geriatrics Society, 35*, 290–296.

Rodin, J. (1986). Health, control, and aging. In M. M. Baltes & P. B. Baltes (Eds.), *The psychology of control and aging* (pp. 139–165). Hillsdale, NJ: Lawrence Erlbaum Associates.

Rodin, J. (1987). Personal control through the life course. In R. P. Abeles (Ed.), *Life-span perspectives and social psychology* (pp. 103–119). Hillsdale, NJ: Lawrence Erlbaum Associates.

Rodin, J., & Langer, E. J. (1980). Aging labels: The decline of control and the fall of self-esteem. *Journal of Social Issues, 36*, 12–29.

Rosenfelt, R. (1965). The elderly mystique. *Journal of Social Issues, 21*, 37–43.

Rothbaum, F., Weisz, J. R. & Snyder, S. S. (1982). Changing the world and changing the self: A two-process model of perceived control. *Journal of Personality and Social Psychology, 42*, 5–37.

Ryan, R. M. & Deci, E. L. (2000b). Self-determination theory and the facilitation of intrinsic motivation, social development, and well-being. *American Psychologist, 55*, 68–78.

Salamon, M. J. (1986). *A basic guide to working with elders*. New York, NY: Springer.

Schulz, R. (1987). Successful aging: Balancing primary and secondary control. *Adult Development and Aging News, 13*, 2–4.

Slivinske, L. R. & Fitch, V. L. (1987). The effect of control-enhancing interventions on the well-being of elderly individuals living in retirement communities. *The Gerontologist, 27*(2), 176–180.

Strumpf, N. E. & Evans, L. K. (1988). Physical restraint of the hospitalized elderly: Perceptions of patients and nurses. *Nursing Research, 37*(3), 132–137.

Teitelman, J. L. & Priddy, J. M. (1988). From psychological theory to practice: Improving frail elders' quality of life through control-enhancing interventions. *The Journal of Applied Gerontology, 7*(3), 298–315.

Timko, C. & Moos, R. H. (1989). Choice, control, and adaptation among elderly residents of sheltered care settings. *Journal of Applied Social Psychology, 19*(8), 636–655.

Tobin, S. S. (1991). *Personhood in advanced old age: Implications for practice*. New York, NY: Springer.

Touhy, T. A. (2008). Chapter 24. Stress, Crisis, and Health in Aging. In P. Ebersole, P. Hess, T. A. Touhy, K. Jett & A. S. Luggen (Eds.), *Toward healthy aging: Human needs & nursing response* (pp. 582–596). St. Louis, MO: Elsevier/Mosby.

Vallerand, R. J. & O'Connor, B. P. (1989). Motivation in the elderly: A theoretical framework and some promising findings. *Canadian Psychology, 30*(3), 538–550.

• CHAPTER 10 •

Environmental Design for Active Engagement

Learning Objectives

1. Describe Lawton's ecological model of aging.

2. Describe Kahana's congruence model.

3. Explain the importance of home in later life.

4. Discuss problems related to relocation.

5. Discuss how age-related physical changes impact the need for environmental modifications.

6. Describe environmental barriers to active living.

7. Identify four environmental domains and describe how each can be assessed for promoting active engagement by older adults.

8. Discuss how the environment can be modified to facilitate active living among aging adults.

Key Terms

- Active Living
- Age-Friendly Environmental Design
- Aging in Place
- Barriers to Active Engagement
- Environmental Domains
- Environmental Press
- Individual Competence
- Person-Environment Fit
- Prosthetic Approach
- Smart Growth
- Therapeutic Approach

Introduction

Aging, like all other human experience, does not occur in a vacuum. The effect of environment on the aging adult can be profound. A well-designed, age accommodating environment can promote active engagement in activities by older adults. Conversely, a barrier-laden environment can deter and demotivate older adults from involvement. This chapter introduces the reader to environmental considerations in planning therapeutic activities with aging adults. The first part of this chapter provides an overview of conceptual approaches to understanding the impact of the environment on the aging experience. The remainder of the chapter is devoted to discussion of practical environmental considerations for activity planners and leaders.

Conceptual Approaches to Understanding Aging and the Environment

Lawton's Model

An ecological model of aging as developed by Lawton (1982) proposes that behavior is a product of individual competence in interaction with the environmental press (or demands) of the situation. Individual competence refers to the theoretical upper limit of a person's ability to function. Environmental press refers to the demands placed on the individual by the environment—social, physical, or psychological. A high environmental press for one person could be low for another, largely due to the individual capacity of each person to negotiate and function within the environment. When individual competence does not meet environmental demand, maladaptive behavior may occur.

According to Lawton (1982), there are five components of individual competence. The first is physical health status that reflects the absence of disease or impairment. Individual sensory and perceptual capacities compose the second category. Common functional losses in this area include diminished hearing and vision. The third area of competence is motor skills. Older adults with arthritis, kyphosis (osteoporotic curvature of the spine), Parkinson's disease, and other diseases that affect mobility will typically show decline in this area. Cognitive capacity, the fourth competence area, refers to intelligence, learning, and memory (Hooyman & Kiyak, 2008). Depression and irreversible, as well as reversible, dementia are com-

mon disease-related causes of cognitive decline in aging adults. The final area of competence indicated by Lawton is ego strength. This concept refers to the ability of the individual to accept the realities of aging. While ego strength is certainly the most challenging to assess, all the components of competence are quite difficult to assess separate from environmental factors.

Maladaptive behavior due to a lack of congruence between environmental press and personal competence can be modified through reducing environmental stress and thus, enhancing personal competence. Environmental stress may be changed with or without the participation of the older person. Often, a social worker, family member, or care provider can take steps to modify the environment. Activity specialists also may use techniques to adjust the environment to provide greater congruence between individual competence and environmental press. For example, the activity specialist can disguise exits that confused clients should not use in an activity room (Zgola, 1987). Another method of reducing environmental press involves active efforts by the individual to produce change in his or her own level of competence.

Older individuals can assume a passive or active role in raising their level of competence. Many types of rehabilitation and treatment programs do not require participants to initiate any action. Lawton (1982) described active programs as those that elevate competence such as self therapy or growth experiences. Physical therapy programs where participants follow the instructions of a therapist tend to be more passive programs. More active programs that elevate competence include elements of self-discovery and growth. Activity specialists can initiate programs to elevate personal competence. For example, an older adult with signs of cognitive decline may benefit from participation in a guided autobiography program (Birren & Deutchman, 1991). Even though the group leader is providing the writing themes, it is the participant who must explore and express his or her own thoughts and feelings.

Regardless of the approach, the goal of an environmental modification is to create a situation in which the environmental demand is slightly above the older person's accustomed performance level, thereby providing challenge but not high stress or anxiety (Lawton & Nahemov, 1973). One of the most useful aspects of the environmental press model is that it can be applied to almost any intervention situation. Only older adults with the most profound disabilities do not respond to the environment in a way that is readily discernible. Lawton (1982) outlined the benefits of improving the participant's ability to respond to the environment. These include: (a) the utilization of unrecognized potential, (b) an increase in self-esteem as a result of being successful in handling an increase in press, and (c) the affirmation of self by being able to demonstrate control over the nature and intensity of environmental press. Benefits such as these are often central goals in activity programs and this model is helpful in understanding the role of environment in producing positive behavioral gains for aging adults who are engaged in therapeutic activities.

Person-environment fit is applicable to the person's ability to live independently (Schaie & Willis, 1999). Two levels must be considered. At the most basic level is the person's competence to perform basic activities of living such as bathing, dressing, feeding, etc. If the person has challenges in these areas, environmental supports and resources will need to be increased. These supports and resources can include modified physical design as well as in home assistance services. Higher order needs are those that involve socialization and affiliation, privacy and independence. These needs are directly related to perceived well-being and a sense of connectedness with others in the social world.

Kahana's Congruence Model

Kahana's (1982) congruence model is another useful approach for understanding the behavior of aging adults in the context of the environment. Under Kahana's model, it is proposed that it is more likely that older individuals will be situated in environments that match or are consistent with their needs. When a situation arises in which environmental press and personal needs are not in congruence, the individual will typically modify environmental demand or leave the environment. For example, if an older adult signs up to take an exercise class at the local YMCA that it is not adequately challenging, he or she will modify the environmental press by attending a more difficult class or leave in order to pursue other options elsewhere. Problems arise when individuals do not display the power or the ability to modify or leave environments under these circumstances (e.g., assisted living facilities, rehabilitation centers, or nursing home placements). In these situations, stress and discomfort may follow.

Many older adults with disabilities, especially those who are residing in institutional settings, have little opportunity to modify or change their environments. In fact, institutional control has been found to play a significant role in explaining low morale in long-term care facilities (Kahana, 1982). Consequently, activities

designed to improve person-environment fit in long-term care facilities should enhance individual feelings of control, thus facilitating greater congruence. Two types of interventions are included in Kahana's model. The first is the prosthetic approach. This approach assumes that the disability cannot be modified and environmental supports are needed. The therapeutic approach, on the other hand, seeks to create change in the individual's ability to negotiate the environment.

The lack of control over who has access to residents constitutes an important aspect of the environment in most long-term care facilities (Hooyman & Kiyak, 2008). It is difficult to retain a sense of autonomy when one has no control over when one will be bathed, fed, or allowed to engage in activities. Privacy also is needed in order to retain self-identity and engage in self-reflection.

Activity specialists should be aware of and respect older adults' need for privacy. Even though the activity professional may think that participation in social activities is in the best interest of the older adult, the individual's right to spend time alone and not participate must be respected.

Willcocks, Peace, and Kellaher (1987) studied the lives of residents in a variety of long-term care facilities. The results of the study demonstrated that a lack of privacy was an important concern. Older adults expect to exercise control in their homes and not have outsiders violate this autonomy by assuming control. The ability of older adults to maintain control was found to be an important source of personal power.

Hooyman and Kiyak (2008) discussed the special case of person-environment congruence caused by relocation. Moving from one environment to another requires some adjustment for people of all ages. Typically, a successful adjustment is achieved within a relatively brief period of time. For older adults with multiple or severe disabilities, this may not be the case. New floor plans and features in the environment may be a source of great stress for the disoriented or otherwise impaired individual. The need to adjust to the rules and regulations associated with institutional living coupled with a reluctance to move into an institution may compound the stress for the older adult. Simple floor plans, easy to follow signs, adequate lighting, and enhanced accessibility can contribute to successful environmental adaptation. The elimination of extraneous stimuli (excessive noise, bright colors, furniture) also is an important consideration for older adults who are impaired (Zgola, 1987).

Active Aging and Age Friendly Environmental Design

Active aging is accepted world-wide as the "process of optimizing opportunities for health, participation, and security in order to enhance quality of life as people age" (World Health Organization, 2002, p. 12). Active aging is a concept that has wide application for both individuals and population groups. The primary focus of active aging is to improve quality of life for all older adults, even those who are frail or disabled (Hooyman & Kiyak, 2008). The emphasis is on maintaining active lifestyles through choice and autonomy, and through the provision of environmental modifications and design that promote continued participation.

According to the WHO (2002), there are six broad categories of determinants of active aging:

- Social determinants—adequate social support resources and networks, protection from violence and abuse, access to education
- Physical environment—such as accessible and affordable transportation, barrier free community design, safe homes and community buildings, safe water, etc.
- Personal determinants—such as genetic factors and psychological factors
- Health and social services—such as access to disease prevention, curative, and health promotion services
- Behavioral determinants—such as reducing health risk behaviors (e.g., smoking, alcohol and drug abuse), engagement in regular physical activity, oral health, healthy eating, etc.
- Economic determinants—income security, formal social insurance programs (e.g., food stamps, Medicare/Medicaid), access to work, etc.

Implicit in this model for active aging is the need for *livable communities* that promote and sustain active lifestyles for all older adults.

Livable communities are those that contain environmental design features that support older adults to access and use culturally appropriate services, to have safe neighborhoods, to live in appropriately designed homes, and to maintain active lifestyles using community resources and organizations (Silverstein, Johns, & Griffin, 2008). At present, there is no single definition for *livable community* and interpretations tend to be according to the mission of the organization or group that is applying the term (Oberlink, 2008). Some organizations are concerned with the natural and built environment, thus the focus upon the capacity of the community to meet the needs of older adults in terms of housing, transportation, and other services. In a key report from the AARP, six key components provide a useful framework for promoting livable communities:

- transportation and mobility,
- land use,
- housing,
- cooperation and communication,
- understanding community and planning, and
- leadership. (Oberlink, 2008)

Livable community design promotes the development of age friendly environments that can support active aging. Guiding principles for age friendly environments include:

- removing barriers to participation,
- accommodating age-related changes and needs,
- acknowledging and responding to racial and ethnic diversity, and
- promoting active engagement to foster positive health outcomes.

One way to conceptualize the environment is to divide it into four domains: built, program, cultural, and living (Hawkins, Voreis, Hill, Myllykangas, & Spangler, 2007). Based on features associated with these four domains, local community facilities can be evaluated in terms how well they promote active engagement by older adults. Figure 10.1 outlines the basic areas within each domain that can be developed or modified in order to remove common barriers that may deter older adults from participating in community programs and facilities.

The International Council on Active Aging is an organization that is committed to promoting change that supports active living for all citizens. This organization distributes information on programs and services that are successfully achieving active living in barrier free environments. The organization publishes information on preferred vendors, a guide to developing or remodeling centers to be age-friendly, and the *Journal on Active Aging*, which contains state of the art articles on the latest research, policy, successful programs, and industry leaders. Of particular usefulness to the activity specialist is the ICAA *Age-Friendly Facility Checklist* (see ICAA web site for access to publication). This checklist is a short and easy to administer tool that activity specialists and caregivers can utilize when determining the appropriateness of a facility for the older adult consumer.

Built Domain Features
- Land Use Patterns (Streets, Parking Lots, Sidewalks, Paths, Transportation)
- Fixed Elements (Building Structure, Architectural Elements)
- Semi-Fixed Elements (Furniture, Fixtures, Equipment, Arrangement)

Program Domain Features (37 Items)
- Programming (Organized, Supervised, Instructional)
- Staff (Experience, Qualifications, Practices, Development, Training)
- Marketing
- Maintenance

Cultural Domain Features (16 Items)
- Rental Space (Weddings, Birthday Parties, Celebrations, Conferences, Markets)
- Entertainment (Plays, Musical Events, Movies, Dances, Exhibits)
- Sporting Events (Basketball Games, Swimming Matches, Tournaments)
- Food Service and Concessions
- Cultural Items (Flags, Plaques, Awards)
- Works of Art (Paintings, Sculptures, Stained Glass, Wall Murals)
- Items for Sale

Living Domain Features (20 Items)
- Community Partnerships (Health Screening, Shared Resources)
- Participant Autonomy (Volunteers, Unstructured Activities, Self-Monitoring)
- Free Services (No Cost Activities and Use, Scholarships)
- Nature/Life Elements (Plants, Scenic Views, Animals)
- Atmosphere Elements (Noise, Odors, Natural Light, Ambiance)

Figure 10.1 Age-Friendly Environmental Domains

Preference for Home in Later Life

The majority of older adults prefer to *age in place* or remain in their homes for as long as possible, if not for the remainder of their lives. Sixsmith and Sixsmith (1991) indicated that older adults with disabilities prefer to remain in their homes even when negotiating aspects of that environment becomes difficult. In fact, older adults with disabilities view the home as a haven of rest, not a place that "traps" them. Older adults also may find that they can "conceal" their declining abilities better in the home compared with other environments such as institutional care (Willcocks, Peace & Kellaher, 1987). Sixsmith and Sixsmith also found that the home is the best place for preserving independence. Furthermore, as maintaining independence becomes more significant, so does the importance of the home.

Aging in place is the universal desire and preference to stay in one's home throughout the remainder of one's life (Hooyman & Kiyak, 2008). According to research, 90% older adults prefer to *age in place*, even when there are declines in competence and more assistance is needed. Home is typically thought to be the place where the environment is familiar and friends, family, and neighbors can be relied upon to provide assistance when it is needed. Older adults equate *aging in place* with their ability to maintain the greatest control over their lives and environment.

Environmental modifications may be needed in order to support remaining in one's home (Hooyman & Kiyak, 2008). With the availability of new technologies and environmental modifications based upon *universal design* principles, increasing numbers of older adults are able to maintain their homes as an appropriate and nonthreatening environment. Universal design maximizes autonomy while enhancing dignity, both of which are very important aspects of *aging in place*. Homes that are modified using universal design have the goals of preserving independence within an environment that is the most preferred by adults, their home.

Some of the typical modifications in the home are bathrooms with showers that are modified for rolling in and out, hands-free sensors on water faucets, floors covered with nonskid surface materials and low-pile carpets, unified lighting throughout the home, and the installation of elevators when needed (Hooyman & Kiyak, 2008). Handrails and lever handles for doors and faucets are also common as well as ramps in place of stairs/steps. Technological supports include remote controls for windows, thermostats, and window coverings, and sensors to detect falls or other changes in movement patterns that may indicate that the older person is having trouble. Kitchen redesign to promote safety and accessibility are also common environmental modifications.

The home provides a source of personal power beyond that which is promoted through physical independence. While remaining in the home, the individual is able to control what events and activities happen, as well as who enters (Hooyman & Kiyak, 2008; Willcocks, Peace, & Kellaher, 1987). Outsiders are not expected to make major decisions that control the individual's future. Some of the services that may be needed in order to remain in one's home include home care and home improvement services, home-delivered meals, and home health care (Hooyman & Kiyak, 2008).

The home often provides an important link to the past for older adults (Hooyman & Kiyak, 2008; Rubinstein & Parmelee, 1992). Pictures of loved ones, valued possessions accumulated throughout life, and symbols of the individual's family and cultural heritage contained in the home. All of these home environment attributes contribute to the older adult's sense of identity. In one study by Sixsmith and Sixsmith (1991), older adults expressed a strong association between home and the past. This association was so strong for some persons that they felt the "presence" of the deceased partner in the house.

Impact of Relocation

In spite of the fact that the majority of older adults wish to remain in their homes indefinitely or *age in place,* many eventually may need to relocate to a new residence. In many cases, the new place of residence will be a facility that will provide some level of care on a long term basis, probably for the remainder of the individual's life. Relocation, especially if it is not desired or is done at a moment of crisis, can be very stressful. Consequently, service providers including activity specialists must be prepared to assist the older adult in making a positive adjustment to the new residence.

Any new residential environment that involves long-term care that is provided by paid care providers is not viewed as desirable by our society. It also creates discontinuity in person-environment-fit for the older person during the adjustment period to the new surroundings (Hooyman & Kiyak, 2008). Attempts by staff to create a warm and welcoming atmosphere may go unnoticed by new residents of the facility due to their perception that they were pushed out of their own homes into the facility—by necessity and usually, not by choice (Rubinstein & Parmelee, 1992). Negative feelings toward relocation to residential facility also may be created by the perception that this type of living arrangement may represent disengagement from the mainstream of society.

The control and power older adults have in their own homes typically does not exist in long-term care facilities (Hooyman & Kiyak, 2008; Rubinstein & Parmelee, 1992). While the home serves as a link to the older adults' personal and cultural past, residential care environments are "collectively defined spaces" that are not personally meaningful, even when personal items are incorporated into the new living space. Willcocks, Peace, and Kellaher (1987) found the following factors to be important in the social environment: *choice/freedom, privacy, involvement,* and *engagement/stimulation.* Each of these factors need to be considered when facilitating the relocation of an older person to a long-term care facility.

The *choice/freedom factor* refers to the extent that older adults have freedom to make choices about their lifestyle. Within a nursing home setting, there may be very little opportunity for decision making. Scheduling and staffing restrictions may prohibit residents from making even the most routine decisions including when to get up and go to bed, when and what to eat, when to get dressed, and who can enter their personal living space.

Privacy refers both to personal privacy and to interactions with others. Sharing a room with another resident coupled with the need for personal care assistance make it difficult to retain privacy in nursing homes. The public nature of long-term care facilities also makes it difficult to maintain private relationships. For example, a married resident may have great difficulty in finding times for intimacy with his or her nonresident spouse.

Involvement refers to the extent that the resident is participating in the operation of the nursing home. Long-term care facilities tend to have strict rules and policies that must be followed for legal, ethical, and financial reasons. This type of structure allows little opportunity for resident participation in decision making. In some cases, residents may not even understand the rationale behind facility rules and policies.

Engagement/stimulation refers to the degree to which staff members encourage resident autonomy and independence. Taking the time to encourage residents to make decisions may not be a priority in a facility that has a small number of workers who are providing care to a large number of residents. It may be much easier for a staff member to make decisions for a resident than to explain options in order to support resident initiated decision making. Unfortunately, this type of an arrangement can lead to *learned helplessness,* which is clearly not in the best interest of older adults.

Environmental Design and Modifications Associated with Specific Age Changes

Many older adults experience physical changes that directly impact their ability to successfully negotiate their environments. Earlier in this chapter, the importance of person-environmental fit was discussed. A great part of this book is devoted to teaching people strategies for implementing therapeutic interventions with older adults. The remainder of this chapter will focus on a prosthetic approach and suggestions for environmental modifications to enhance person-environment fit within activity programs.

Mobility Changes

Arthritis, osteoporosis, Parkinson's disease, and other disease limit the mobility of many older adults, thus placing them at risk for falling. A well-designed facility for older adults reflects the prevention of accidents and provides for the ease of movement for its participants. Surfaces in such facilities should be level and have a nonslip surface. If the facility has stairs, they should be uniform in size and a handrail must be provided. All program areas should be accessible to individuals who use wheelchairs, canes, or walkers.

Facilities that provide services for older adults, unless affiliated with a church or private club, must be designed in compliance with the Americans with Disabilities Act. If a facility is in compliance, then participants with disabilities will have full access to the facility and its programs. To obtain more information about the Americans with Disabilities Act, readers are encouraged to contact the U.S. Department of Justice, Civil Rights Division, Coordination and Review Section, P.O. Box 66118, Washington, D.C., 20035-6118.

Visual Changes

Changes in vision are a normative aging experience. The decreased ability of older adults to adapt to changes in light is a crucial factor for facility planners and activity programmers to understand. Cataracts, while not a normative part of aging, are prevalent among the older adult population so that they also should be of concern when designing program environments. It is necessary to carefully evaluate and design activity environments to match the visual support needs of all older adults in mind in order to ensure participant safety and comfort. According to Fogg and Fulton (1994), visual clarity considerations in environmental design include: (a) evenness of light; (b) legibility of graphic information; and (c) understandability of design.

Evenness of light can be achieved by providing several indirect sources of light that utilize a higher watt level than normal. It is also important to design the entrances and exits from facilities so that the slower light-to-dark adaptation of older adults is accommodated. For example, on a bright, sunny day it would not be appropriate to have older adults come from the outdoors into a dimly lit entrance of a building. It would be more helpful to have the entrance slightly less bright than the outside, the hall slightly less bright than the entrance, and the program area at the desired level of illumination.

Signs and other types of graphic information are important orientation tools in any facility or program environment. The most effective signs have large letters and use simple terminology. High contrast colors should be used for signs and printed materials; activity staff should be especially careful to avoid using blues and violets together. Signs need to be located so that both adults who walk and those who use wheelchairs can read them. Finally, the use of nonglare glass is highly recommended.

There are several steps that can be taken to enhance the understandability of a facility. Extra orientation aids can be useful. Many facilities use color code doors and walls to assist with orientation to location and layout. In this type of a plan, color lines on a wall lead from a central area, such as a front desk, to different parts of the facility such as the cafeteria or activity room. Color coding also can be used to mark changes in elevation on the walking surfaces.

Hearing Changes

Loss of hearing is another physical change that is normative for the older population. In crowded areas it is often difficult for older adults with hearing loss to distinguish between different frequencies of sound. In some cases, background noise is not distinguishable from the immediate conversation. In such a situation, effective participation in a program may be quite difficult. Activity specialists can help to minimize the impact of hearing loss in a number of ways. It is important that background noise be reduced during programs that involve conversation. Following are some recommendations:

1. Program areas should be located in spaces where participants will not be distracted by noise from another source such as a busy street or a main reception area for the building.
2. Sound proof rooms are costly but are useful for offices, conference rooms, or other rooms in facilities that older adults frequently use.
3. Carpeted floors and textured wall coverings absorb sound better than do other surfaces and consequently, these building materials can be used to reduce background noise.

Environmental Considerations for Persons with Alzheimer's Disease

The design of program spaces is of particular concern to agencies and activity specialists who serve older adults with Alzheimer's disease. Throughout this chapter, the need to provide choice to older adults has been emphasized; however, for persons with Alzheimer's disease or other types of dementia, free choice is usually not appropriate (Bell, Green, Fisher & Baum, 2005). Consequently, in recent years, nursing homes, assisted-living facilities, and adult day programs have developed specialized Alzheimer programs, areas, or units that are designed with the specific needs of older adults with dementia in mind.

Traditionally, the erratic or wandering behavior of many adults with Alzheimer's disease has been treated with chemical or physical restraints (Bell et al., 2005). In more recent years, however, federal policies have discouraged the use of restraints and increased research of behavior management techniques. The result has been the development of less restrictive environments for this special client group. Programmatic changes have focused on adjusting environments to behavior, rather than attempting to alter the person's behavior to fit the environment. In many cases, the results have been substantial and reflect a positive move forward in the care of persons with Alzheimer's disease.

Older adults with Alzheimer's disease are less likely to be confused or disoriented in environments that are free of ambiguities (Zgola, 1987). Environments that are not overly stimulating and that are consistent tend to promote lower levels of disruptive behavior. The following are several suggestions from Zgola from her guidebook on adult day programs for persons with dementia:

1. Floors and walls should be distinct from each other and steps should be clearly marked. Persons with diminished perceptual capabilities may have difficulty judging distances if the floors, walls, and furniture all meld together. The use of contrasting colors can help clients to negotiate their surroundings.
2. Floors should be free of markings such as lines or figures that could be perceived as obstacles. Changes in the texture of the floor also may be perceived as obstacles. For example, a person with the disease may not want to enter a room with a tile floor, walk on a brick sidewalk, or cross over the metal threshold of a door.
3. When an effective arrangement of the facility has been found, it should be kept permanent. Also, it is important to dedicate certain spaces for certain activities. Consistency is important if the client is to feel comfortable in his or her surroundings.
4. The ambiance of the facility should be neutral and subdued. Many bright colors or graphic designs on the wall can be over stimulating and cause agitation.
5. Background noise should be minimized. Techniques for reducing background noise as discussed in another section of this chapter can be used.
6. Washrooms should be marked clearly. Signs that use stick figures or alternative terms for men and women may confuse clients and thus, should be avoided.
7. Large open spaces may be intimidating to persons with dementia. For example, a client may not be willing to cross to the other side of a large activity room. Groups of tables or chairs arranged in small sitting areas within a larger room can help with this problem.
8. Wandering is a behavior that is exhibited by many people who have Alzheimer's disease. This behavior can be especially problematic for staff charged with ensuring client safety, as it is not uncommon for individuals to try and walk out of their programs. As a result,

many Alzheimer's units in nursing homes are locked. If it is not possible or preferred to lock the facility, some other options are available. Providing a space within the facility for clients to wander is one option. Long hallways or fenced outdoor areas also may be suitable options. Staff may find it helpful to simply take a client on a walk outside if he or she seems agitated or upset. Disguising exits from the facility also has been found to be useful. Doors can be covered with fabric or paper, or painted to match the wall. One monitored exit should be left apparent.

Working with Alzheimer's Patients in the Home

Most families prefer to keep their older relatives with Alzheimer's disease at home as long as possible. This can be a trying task for any family. Fortunately, there is support available from local chapters of the Alzheimer's Association. Family members may also find the book, *The 36 Hour Day* (Mace & Rakens, 1991), helpful. Mace and Rabins offer several suggestions for modifying homes to accommodate persons with Alzheimer's disease. The following are helpful suggestions for therapists and activity specialists who are serving this client group:

1. Power tools, knives, small appliances, car keys, medicines, and household chemicals should be locked in a cabinet.
2. The water heater should be turned down so no one can get scalded. Exposed water pipes should be covered.
3. Security locks should be installed on balcony windows and doors.
4. Radiators and furnaces should be blocked.
5. Poisonous houseplants should not be used in any type of program. Pins and buttons should be kept out of reach to prevent choking. Some people with Alzheimer's disease may also try to eat chipped paint.
6. A switch should be installed on the back of the stove to prevent it from being turned on or the knobs should be taken off of it.
7. Gates should be installed at the top of stairs.
8. Patio doors should be marked and storm doors should have grills.
9. Automatic windows on the car may be dangerous. It is also important that the driver of a vehicle be able to control the locks. Some patients may try to get out of a moving car.
10. Smoking can be very dangerous for the patient with Alzheimer's disease. It is possible that the cigarettes can be taken away from the person without incident. If not, smoking should only be allowed under supervision.
11. "Burglar alarms" or gadgets that monitor sound may help the caregiver monitor behavior at night.

It is important to remember that each individual with Alzheimer's disease will respond differently. Some individuals may need a very simple, structured environment, while others are able to function relatively well in an environment with minimum modifications. If aspects of the current environment do not create a safety hazard or serve as a source of distress, modifications are not necessary.

Summary

This chapter stresses the impact of environment on the functional competence of older adults. Two models are commonly used to explain and understand the dynamic relationship between environmental demand and personal performance—Lawton's *Environmental Press Model* and Kahana's *Congruence Model*. These models can be used to guide the design and implementation of activity interventions and program environments for the optimal performance of older adult clients. Other considerations include promoting active living through the development of livable communities and age-friendly environments. The chapter also covered special considerations for adults with cognitive declines (e.g., Alzheimer's disease). Specific pragmatic environmental modifications include lighting, noise, physical layout, and behavioral supports.

Comprehension Questions

The reader can check for comprehension of the material presented in this chapter by answering the following questions:

1. Compare and contrast Lawton's Environmental Press Model with Kahana's Congruence Model regarding the impact that environment has on the older person's behavior and competence in daily activities.

2. Discuss why home is important to older persons and how a residential relocation influences personal competence.

3. Discuss the concepts of aging in place, active living, livable communities, and age-friendly environmental design.

4. How can activity specialists modify the environment to accommodate changes in vision, hearing, and mobility in older adults?

5. Describe the special environmental support needs of persons who have Alzheimer's disease.

References

Bell, P. A., Green, T. C., Fisher, J. D. & Baum, A. (2005). *Environmental psychology* (5th ed.). Fort Worth, TX: Harcourt College Publishers.

Birren, J. E. & Deutchman, D. E. (1991). *Guiding autobiography groups for older adults*. Baltimore, MD: The Johns Hopkins University Press.

Fogg, G. E. & Fulton, R. F. (1994). *Leisure site guidelines for people over 55*. Arlington, VA: National Recreation and Park Association.

Hawkins, B. A., Voreis, J., Hill, J., Myllykangas, S. & Spangler, K. (March 2007). CEPAE – A tool for change. *Parks and Recreation*, 71–76.

Hooyman, N. R. & Kiyak, H. A. (2008). *Social gerontology: A multidisciplinary perspective* (8th ed.). Boston, MA: Allyn and Bacon.

Kahana, E. (1982). A congruence model of person-environment interaction. In M. P. Lawton, P. G., Windley & T. O. Byerts (Eds.), *Aging and the environment* (97–121). New York, NY: Springer.

Kahana, E., Felton, B. & Fairchild, T. (1976). Community services and facilities planning. In M. P. Lawton, R. J. Newcomer, & T. O. Byerts (Eds.), *Community planning for an aging society: Designing services and facilities* (227–239). Stroudsburg, PA: Dowden, Hutchinson, & Ross.

Lawton, M. P. (1982). Competence, environmental press, and the adaptation of older people. In M.P. Lawton, P. G. Windley, & T. O. Byerts (Ed.). *Aging the environment* (33–59). New York, NY: Springer.

Lawton, M. P. & Nahemov, L. (1973). Ecology and the aging process. In C. Eisdorfer & M. P. Lawton (Eds.), *The psychology of adult development and aging* (619–674). Washington, DC: APA.

Mace, N. L. & Rabins, P. V. (1991). *The 36 hour day* (Rev. ed.). Baltimore, MD: The Johns Hopkins University Press.

Oberlink, M. R. (2008). *Opportunities for Creating Livable Communities*. Washington, DC: Public Policy Institute, AARP.

Rubinstein, R. L. & Parmelee, P. A. (1992). Attachment to place and the representation of the life course by the elderly. *Human Behavior and Environmental Advances in Theory Research, 12,* 139–163.

Schaie, W. K. & Willis, S. L. (1999). Chapter 10. Theories of everyday competence and aging. In V. L. Bengtson & K. W. Schaie (Eds.), *Handbook of Theories of Aging* (174–195). New York, NY: Springer.

Silverstein, N. M., Johns, E. & Griffin, J. A. (2008). Students explore livable communities. *Gerontology & Geriatrics Education, 29*(1), 19–37.

Sixsmith, A. J. & Sixsmith, J. A. (1991). Transitions in home experience in later life. *The Journal of Architectural and Planning Research, 8*(3), 181–191.

Willocks, D., Peace, S. & Kellaher, L. (1987). *Private lives in public places*. NY: Tavistock Publications.

World Health Organization. (2002). *Active ageing – A policy framework*. Geneva, Switzerland: Noncommunicable Diseases and Mental Health Chapter, Noncommunicable Disease Prevention and Health Promotion Department, Ageing and Life Course.

Zgola, J. M. (1987). *Doing things*. Baltimore, MD: The Johns Hopkins University Press.

UNIT IV

Categories of Activities for Older Adults

Activities that are used with older persons can be grouped under four broad categories. The following activity areas are covered in Unit IV: leisure education, physical activity and health promotion, mental health activities, and psychosocial activities. Most activity programs that address the needs, interests, and concerns of older adults will fall into one or more of these broad categories.

Each chapter in this unit is organized to address the basic goals and purposes of activity programs within a particular area of functioning; that is, physical, cognitive, and psychosocial. In the case of leisure education, the usefulness of this process is important in meeting the activity needs, knowledge, and skills of older adults in maintaining an active and healthy lifestyle. Common activity approaches are described, a sample program is presented, and additional resources are provided to the reader for use in program development. This unit directly addresses the application of knowledge about human aging within best practices that use activities as the modality for meeting health, well-being, intervention, and rehabilitation purposes.

• CHAPTER 11 •
Leisure Education

Learning Objectives

1. Become familiar with leisure education and describe its applicability in meeting the activity needs of older adults.

2. Describe the purposes and goals of leisure education.

3. Define the content that forms the basis of leisure education and the processes that are used for delivering leisure education to older adults.

4. Describe sample lessons that are used in leisure education.

5. Identify resources that are useful in developing a leisure education intervention program for older adults.

Key Terms

• Active Living/Lifestyle
• Education
• Leisure
• Leisure Education
• Recreation

Introduction

Educating adults for leisure-centered living, or the wise use of leisure time, is an appropriate concern of professionals who are providing activity programs for older adults in a variety of service settings. As life expectancy and years of healthy life continue to improve, the need for leisure education also will increase. Adults who reach later maturity will have increased opportunities to continue lifelong leisure pursuits, to explore new activities, and to experience a rebalancing of time use as the available hours for leisure potentially expand.

The life changes associated with older adulthood can be both instrumental (i.e., retirement) or sudden (e.g., loss of one's partner or spouse) (Kelly, 1994). Both instrumental and sudden life changes bring on new challenges, one of which is the common experience of increase "free" time or leisure time. The meaningful and constructive use of leisure to enhance one's quality of life and improve one's overall health is a desired outcome associated with successful aging and aging well. The high quality use of leisure time is also an explicit goal of leisure education.

The meaning of leisure and the purpose of leisure education in the lives of older adults are explored in this chapter. The scope of content covered in educating for leisure-centered living is discussed including the processes that are used to structure and deliver leisure education programs. A sample leisure education program with suggested activities clustered under five primary content areas is included. The chapter concludes with reference and resource information for use in developing leisure education programs for older adults.

Educating for Leisure-Centered Living

Brightbill and Mobley (1977) observed that leisure may well be:

> "that part of life that comes nearest to allowing us to be free in a regimented and conforming world, which enables us to pursue self-expression, intellectual, physical, and spiritual development, and beauty in their endless forms." (p. 7)

These words express some of the hopes and desires that many older adults feel as retirement approaches. Rarely, however, does the transition from work to retirement happen so smoothly that the "perfect life" is realized.

For many older Americans, there is little preparation for the ideal use of free time when it becomes abundant. The expansion in "free" hours may be especially challenging when life has been filled with work, family responsibilities, and a general sense of the need to be occupied doing something that will benefit others or produce material possessions. Learning to appreciate leisure is a vital first step in preparing for an increase in the number of hours that are available for leisure.

Real leisure is not enforced free time; rather, it is the opportunity to freely choose from a wide variety of experiences that promote self-expression and the pursuit of self-development—intellectually, physically, socially, and spiritually (Brightbill & Mobley, 1977). Over the years, scholars who philosophize about and study leisure have identified key characteristics of leisure to be time, activity, and a state of mind. Embraced by the wide array of definitions of leisure are the ideals of (a) personal freedom to choose what to do, (b) freedom to carry it out, and (c) freedom from obligatory responsibilities (i.e., work, family, school, self-care). Freedom is what makes leisure distinct from work and the other routine obligations of everyday life. Based upon these ideals, participation in leisure is expected to produce feelings of personal satisfaction, pleasure, happiness/joy, fulfillment, creativity, and self-actualization. Perceived freedom, activities that are motivating in and of themselves (i.e., not associated with external rewards such as financial gain), and affective states that embody personal satisfaction, pleasure, and self-actualization are the central ingredients of wholesome leisure (Kelly, 1990; Murphy, 1975; Neulinger, 1974).

If leisure is self-directed activity that produces a state of mind that is personally satisfying, then why the need for leisure education? Most adults anticipate that they will be able to retire from lifelong occupations at some point in their older adulthood; however, when and how retirement happens is somewhat governed by current economic trends and cohort differences that are emerging with the aging of the Baby Boomers. Traditionally, older adults expected that their grown children would be living on their own; however, current circumstances in the United States may see some changes in household living arrangements. It is still expected, however, that older adulthood may be the time and opportunity to embrace a different lifestyle than was experienced during the younger and middle adult life stages. This lifestyle change opportunity is one that embraces expanded free time for engaging in leisure. As shown throughout this text, older adulthood also may present many challenges. These challenges may be associated with physical declines due to disease, illness, impairment, or just growing older. Additionally, older persons may confront changes in their social networks due to the death of their spouse, other family members, and friends. Often, retirement from lifelong work may be seen as a loss by some older persons due to a central belief system that places high value on one's occupational status. A sense of identity for many adults is closely woven into work roles and family responsibilities throughout the younger and middle adult years. Adaptation in older adulthood may be a significant challenge for many people. The process of adjusting to these changes can be greatly assisted by well-designed and implemented leisure education programs.

Leisure education is intended to assist older adults in making a positive transition to retirement and older adulthood. The process and content of leisure education focuses on developing knowledge, attitudes, and beliefs about the value of leisure in enhancing the quality of life in older adulthood. Leisure education involves a systematic program of learning about (a) what leisure is and the instrumental role that it can play in older adulthood; (b) the benefits of leisure in human growth and well-being, especially during the older adult years; (c) the availability of leisure resources and opportunities in one's community including how to access and use them; and (d) how to overcome barriers to developing a fulfilling leisure lifestyle in later life. In this context, leisure education is a program that develops the knowledge and skills necessary to make a smooth and effective transition to the older adult life stages. Leisure education is learning across the lifespan into older adulthood about how to shape an active, healthy, positive lifestyle, especially when increased leisure time is available.

Definitions that have been used to describe leisure education stress the following key ideas:

- enhancing one's quality of life through wholesome use of free time;
- developing knowledge, attitudes, beliefs, and skills that promote constructive use of leisure;
- learning to use leisure to promote self-development and self-actualization;
- learning to accept, appreciate, and enjoy leisure, as well as achieve a sense of personal freedom to pursue leisure;
- recognizing personal needs and abilities that can be satisfied through leisure;
- establishing personal leisure goals and repertoire; and
- empowering the individual to develop his/her own leisure lifestyle.

(Bender, Brannan & Verhoven, 1984; Mundy, 1998; Stumbo, 2002)

Leisure education, therefore, is a process through which activity specialists assist older adults to discover the benefits of leisure and to develop the necessary skills for pursuing an appropriate leisure lifestyle during the older adult life stages. In the next section, the basic content and processes of leisure education are described. The section is then followed by a sample leisure education program with suggested activities and selected resources.

Leisure Education Content and Process

Successful leisure education programs are developed through a careful consideration of both program content and the processes used to deliver the content (Dattilo, 1999; Howe-Murphy & Charoneau, 1987; Mundy, 1998; Stumbo, 2002). Typically, the content of a leisure education program will be developed in the following areas: (a) leisure appreciation, (b) self-awareness and leisure, (c) self-determination and leisure choices, (d) knowledge of leisure opportunities and resources, and (e) decision-making and activity skills (Dattilo, 1999; Mundy, 1998). The leisure education process moves participants through each of these five areas in order to attain the goal of an independent, active, and satisfying leisure lifestyle. The exploration of self-awareness through leisure in later life begins the process of preparing for retirement. Learning about one's preferences, interests, and specific needs enables the individual to seek leisure experiences that are personally relevant and rewarding.

In order for leisure to provide opportunities for self-development, an understanding of the concept of leisure and related concepts (i.e., recreation, play, entertainment, and adult learning) is essential. Placing the individual's understanding of leisure into the context of changing circumstances in older adulthood is part of enhancing leisure awareness. Cultivating an appreciation of leisure, coupled with promoting a sense of freedom and control over one's actions and environment, form the essential building blocks for self-determination in later life with regard to leisure. A guided process for learning to take control over one's destiny, especially when the context of everyday life may be changing dramatically (e.g., as with retirement), is an essential step in the leisure education process. Recognizing that a range of leisure choices exist and that one has personal preferences is the beginning of the process. These learning objectives constitute the first steps in the process of educating for leisure-centered living.

Knowledge of the resources that are available to fulfill one's leisure needs is necessary in order to act on stated activity preferences. Typical settings and resources that were associated with work schedules and work companions may fade in prominence upon retirement. New connections need to be built in order to prevent social isolation or the development of a sedentary lifestyle. The changing social context of the older adult who is retiring or who is entering very late life may necessitate learning about new outlets in the community that are available for maintaining an active leisure lifestyle. Leisure education programs provide the opportunity to learn about the resources and social opportunities that may not have been previously known to the older adult. Knowledge of leisure opportunities, facilities, resources, and programs that are available to older adults can support a smooth and successful transition to retirement, as well as sustaining a leisure lifestyle when reaching very old age. Awareness of resources and social networks also is important to older adults who are making a transition from a healthcare facility back to community-based living.

In addition to knowing about leisure resources, it is important to know about social support networks and services. Leisure education programs can serve a critical function by assisting older adults in learning about individuals, groups, organizations, and social services that are available to them for meeting social interaction needs. Preventing social isolation or, conversely, promoting a feeling of being connected with a social support network, can be an important component of a well-designed leisure education program. Learning about social resources is necessary part of most leisure education programs for older adults.

The last area of content that leisure education programs typically embrace is learning leisure decision-making and activity skills. Decision-making skills are often directly taught when leisure education is being provided to individuals who have impaired cognitive abilities. In this situation, the individual is coached to recognize (a) what resources are needed in order to act on leisure interests, (b) the consequences associated with making one leisure choice over another, and (c) how to proceed once a leisure activity is selected. The teaching of leisure decision-making skills is a very important aspect of leisure education programs that are being delivered in rehabilitation, assisted-living, and long-term care settings.

The learning of new leisure activity skills is the component of leisure education through which participants make personal activity choices. The selection of new activities may require learning how to do the activity. The skill development phase often can be one of the most exciting and rewarding parts in the program for participants who are building new lifestyles or reconstructing their previous leisure lifestyles following an illness or major life change. The discovery and learning of new activities with which to satisfy personal interests can be a capstone experience in life. Further, the development of new skills can be highly motivating and can reinforce the value of the program to participants.

The success of leisure education programming depends upon age-appropriate and need-based content, as well as on effective processes for delivering the content. A general programming process that encompasses the following steps is recommended: (a) delineate the overall purpose of the program, (b) specify the program goals and objectives, (c) identify specific content with implementation procedures and performance measures, and (d) document individual progress and evaluate program outcomes. For each content area of leisure education, specific goals with learning objectives are developed. Appropriate activities are identified to match the learning objectives. The leisure education activities can be adapted from existing materials or developed for the specific group being served. The activities are matched with performance measures that help the program leader to recognize and document when participants have mastered the specific leisure education content and have thus attained the learning objectives. Finally, the program leader is responsible for structuring activities in a manner that is appealing and socially valued by older adults.

Planning the processes for delivering the leisure education content is important to the overall success of the program. Adult learners appreciate learning experiences that utilize life experiences and personal abilities. Incorporating participants into the planning process is an effective strategy for motivating and sustaining participant investment in the program. In situations where leisure education is part of an overall treatment plan (e.g., in assisted-living or nursing facilities and at adult day care), it is incumbent upon the activity specialist to develop and lead a stimulating program format. As with all programming, documenting individual progress and evaluating the outcomes of the leisure education program are essential steps. Documentation and evaluation will enable the program leader to identify successful components of the program, as well as areas that need to be modified or changed.

In summary, the process of planning and delivering an effective leisure education program for older individuals involves (a) identifying educational goals and objectives in the target content areas and based upon individual needs, (b) planning and implementing age and ability appropriate learning experiences, and (c) evaluating learning outcomes. The next section presents a brief example of a leisure education program that focuses on preretirement preparation. The program embraces five leisure education content areas: (a) leisure appreciation, (b) self-awareness and leisure, (c) self-determination and leisure choices, (d) knowledge of leisure opportunities and resources, and (e) decision-making and activity skills.

Preretirement Education for Leisure-Centered Living: A Sample Program

The following brief program example illustrates the use of leisure education to help older persons to prepare for the major life change of retirement. The goals, objectives, and suggested activities have been adapted from general literature on leisure education and the author's practical experience with older adults (Bender, Brannan, & Verhoven, 1984; Dattilo, 1999; Mundy, 1998; Joswiak, 1989). Suggested activities are provided under the following five leisure education content areas: (a) awareness of self and leisure, (b) leisure appreciation, (c) self-determination and leisure choices, (d) knowledge of leisure opportunities and resources, and (e) decision-making and activity skills. In each area, information is provided according to (a) target goal, (b) enabling objectives for attaining the goal, (c) activity format (content and process suggestions), and (d) ideas for implementation and resource materials.

Leisure education programs are typically organized to contain several activities for each content area. Activities may be developed to reflect incremental steps toward attaining an overall goal for each content area. Activity leaders will develop more detailed program plans than what is provided here including: specific information regarding activity format, activity implementation plans, materials list, evaluation methods and procedures, and follow-up activities for participants and/or staff. This chapter outlines the basic content of a program organized by purpose, target goals, enabling objectives, activity suggestions, and implementation ideas.

Program Purpose:

The purpose of this leisure education program is assist adults who are preparing for a near future retirement in the following key ways:

1. To facilitate an understanding of the role of leisure in meeting personal interests and needs in retirement.
2. To explore the possible impact that a change in job/work status may have on personal lifestyle.
3. To investigate ways in which leisure can be instrumental in promoting self-development and adaptation in retirement.
4. To explore potential new leisure interests and activities in the community.

CONTENT AREA I— LEISURE APPRECIATION

Target Goal:

Participants will be able to describe a personal definition of leisure within the context of personal life course and life circumstances.

Enabling Objectives:

- To distinguish leisure from associated concepts (e.g., play, recreation, relaxation, sports, entertainment, cultural events and activities).
- To compare personal definitions of leisure with definitions held by significant others and from literature.
- To understand the role of leisure across the lifespan, from birth to death.
- To identify personal peak leisure experiences and explain why they were peak experiences.

Activity Suggestion: *Autobiographical Sketch of Leisure in My Life*

This activity is completed over several sessions spanning 3–6 meetings of 1–2 hours each in duration. The completed autobiographical sketch includes information about the participant's major work/job experiences, personal relationships and responsibilities, and leisure activities across the life course. Through the process of developing the autobiographical sketch, the participant explores and constructs his or her own definitions for several key concepts including work, family, personal responsibilities, and leisure. He or she discovers how personal life has unfolded and places these perspectives within a developing appreciation of the value of leisure, especially in older adulthood. Each session begins with a focus topic that is introduced by the group leader and is processed through group discussion. The topical discussion is followed by a period of personal reflection and writing time.

Participants may wish to continue the reflection and writing process between sessions and should be encouraged to do so.

Focus topics can be arranged according to major periods of life starting with childhood and may include memories pertaining to work roles, relationships, and favorite leisure activities. Another strategy is to utilize people, places, and events as the focal points for the day. The leader will select the focus topic for each session. The leader will organize topics so that the completed project will result in meeting the enabling objectives specified above.

Implementation and Materials Suggestions:

This activity is recommended for groups that are 4–8 participants in size. A series of 3–6 incremental sessions are needed to complete the activity with ample time for discussion during each session. The activity leader may use guest speakers, slides or video materials, magazines or family photo albums, or genealogical records to assist in focusing the participants on the topics discussed and documented each week.

Participants will need a journal, loose paper for jotting notes, and pens/pencils at each session. Each person should be encouraged to write in his or her autobiographical journal between sessions, as well as take time to review what has already been written. Birren and Deutchmann's, *Guiding Autobiography Groups for Older Adults—Exploring the Fabric of Life* (1991) may be helpful to the leader in terms of assisting participants with writing personal biographies.

Suggested Session Sequence:

Session 1: At the first session following a preliminary meeting that outlines the objectives of the activity and may also include the sharing of a previously completed autobiography, participants will focus on reconstructing their personal leisure activity patterns from a lifespan perspective. Participants will be requested to bring photos, memorabilia, diaries, memories, and any other personal artifacts that can be used to help them reconstruct their major leisure activity patterns across the life course. The leader may wish to use his or her own leisure history, or a sample visual timeline that highlights the major life stages with typical leisure activities, as an example of leisure across the life course.

In this session, the group leader will start the session by drawing a lifecycle line and segmenting it into the following major life stages: birth through to preteen years (i.e., ages 1–10), preteen and teenage years (ages 10–18), college and young adult years (ages 18–25),

early adulthood (ages 25–40), middle adulthood (ages 40–55), the transition years (ages 55–65), later maturity (ages 65 and older). Group discussion will facilitate recollection of the major lifestyle patterns associated with each broad life stage. The second half of the session will be spent in preparing notes and recollections from the brainstorming/recollection discussion period.

The group leader will determine whether participants are able to prepare their written journals for this session during the time between the first and second sessions. In the instance where participants do not wish to work on writing between sessions, the second session should be reserved for the completion of the personal leisure history.

Session 2: For the second session, the leader will invite an expert in the area of recreation and leisure service delivery to come to the group to talk about what leisure means from different perspectives; that is, historically, in contemporary society, and from a developmental/lifespan perspective. The speaker should be requested to cover primary conceptualizations of leisure as they are presented in the literature and relate to different stages across the lifespan. Part of the session should be reserved for discussion of common meanings, allowing for individual questions, summarizing prevalent conceptualizations of leisure, recognizing the benefits of leisure in older adulthood, and encouraging participants to share personal definitions and reflections.

The second half of the session is used for participants to write notes, reflections, and insights into their journals. Participants' journals, when completed, will be used in the development of each individual's autobiographical sketch.

It is the responsibility of the leader to determine whether or not an additional session is needed to complete the writing portion related to the content presented in the second session. It is recommended that participants be encouraged to continue their writing on topics that are presented during sessions one and two so that they can focus their attention on presenting new topics for discussion during future sessions.

Session 3: In this session participants will explore memories of their *peak leisure experiences* from a lifespan perspective. The leader facilitates the session by beginning with a group exploration of the concept—*peak leisure experience*. Each participant will be requested to recall a leisure experience that was the best they had ever experienced. Participants will proceed to define what makes a peak experience. The group leader may use word association techniques to assist the group in developing the definition. For example, the leader may ask participants to use adjectives to describe their peak experiences. By listing the adjectives on a flip chart or blackboard, the leader can then ask participants to group the adjectives into categories and follow this categorization process with identification of the key components of a peak experience. By using this process the group will be facilitated to develop a more wholistic definition of peak leisure experience.

Next participants will list their own personal peak experiences across the life course. For each experience, each participant will identify the reasons why each experience was a peak experience for him or herself. Using a grid composed of each experience listed down the left hand side of the page and followed by several columns labeled *why, what, where, with whom,* and *how.* Each participant will process each experience in regard to identifying the reasons under each column that may have contributed to the high quality of the experience.

Following this evaluation process each participant will be asked to share a peak experience, as well as provide the reasons they listed for why, what, where, with whom, and how it came to be that this experience was perceived as a peak experience. The leader will record notes from group discussion on a blackboard, flip chart, or computer that is connected to an overhead projector. This process will guide participants in discovering what makes selected leisure activities a peak experience.

Following the group discussion, each participant will recollect those experiences across his or her life that were peak experiences. Each participant will modify or develop brief explanations/descriptions of these experiences. Finally, each will prepare journal notes regarding what kind of activities have constituted peak experiences at a personal level. An effective close to this activity is to have participants identify activities that they will want to pursue in the near future in search of the peak experience.

Session 4: Putting it all together. Based on the notes and passages prepared in the previous three or more sessions, this session will be used to prepare a draft version of a autobiographical sketch entitled: *My leisure life.* Participants will be encouraged to use self-directed timeframes and focal points for their autobiographical essays. The role of the group leader is to encourage individual expression and choice of content. The entire session will be spent composing the autobiographical sketch. At the end of the session, participants will be asked if they wish to share or do anything more with their autobiographies. In some instances, participants may wish to put all the autobiographies

together in an anthology; in other instances, the final results are private and should remain as a personal product from participation in this group exploration activity.

CONTENT AREA II—
LEISURE AND SELF-AWARENESS

Target Goal:

The participant will explore the meaning of work and leisure to one's self.

Enabling Objectives:

- To identify any and all personal needs that are fulfilled through work and leisure.
- To classify daily activities into self-defined categories.
- To identify values and benefits received from leisure experiences.
- To compare leisure benefits with those received from work-related activity and personal responsibilities.
- To recognize barriers to leisure involvement and to identify resources necessary to negotiate barriers.

Activity Suggestion: *Leisure and Work Values Debate*

This activity will consist of only one session of about 1–2 hours in duration. The session is structured in order to facilitate discussion and debate of the values, benefits, and constraints associated with work and leisure activities. In the first half of the session, participants engage in small group discussion followed by a debate in the second half. The session uses values-clarification as a process for attitude change and development. The activity is one example of exercises that can be used to assist participants in exploring personal values, attitudes, and beliefs regarding the roles of work, leisure, and personal responsibilities in life.

Implementation and Materials Suggestions:

This session is structured into two distinct components, the preparatory discussion segment followed by the debate. The leader requests that participants form into roundtable discussion groups of 3–4 members in size. Each roundtable is given a flip chart for recording the group's ideas and discussion.

Each roundtable discussion group is instructed to develop a grid on their flip chart. Across the top are three columns labeled *work activities, leisure activities,* and *personal responsibility activities*. Down the left side of the page are listed *values, benefits*, and *barriers*. Each group is then instructed to go around the table with each participant naming an activity that they do and classifying it as work, leisure, or personal responsibility. Then the participant, along with other group members, identifies the values associated with the activity, the benefits gained from engaging in the named activity, and identification of any barriers that constrain participation in the activity (Figure 11.1). This process is continued for 30–45 minutes of discussion so that each roundtable group has several activities under each category that they have discussed in terms of values, benefits, and barriers to participation. The leader should monitor discussion. If groups are having difficulty getting started, then the leader can offer an example from his or her own life experiences. If the groups are deep in discussion when 45 minutes have passed, then the leader should let them continue a little longer so that participants don't feel cut off before getting enough information down on the flip chart.

In preparation for the debate segment of the session, each roundtable is given a set of value statements. If there are two roundtable discussion groups, then they both receive the same set. If there are four or more groups, then the statements are subdivided with different sets being distributed to paired roundtables. In the case of an odd number of discussion groups, one group should divide itself up with members evenly distributing themselves among the other groups.

Roundtable discussion groups will work in pairs to debate value statements according to whether they

	Work Activities	Leisure Activities	Personal Responsibility Activities
Example Activity	Mowing the lawn Delivering meals to home bound	Golfing with friends Listening to the radio	Exercising Preparing meals for self and spouse
Personal Values Associated with the Activity	Helping others makes me feel good, useful Contributing to the quality of life in my community by being a productive member	Maintaining my social network Providing for the aesthetic qualities of my life	Maintaining my health Improving my personal appearance Keeping the social part of eating meals in my daily life
Benefits from Doing the Activity	Maintaining my home in good condition	Good health, good friends, good times, pleasure Continuing my learning of music types	Lower healthcare costs Higher functional status and lower risk for impairment or disability in late life
Barriers that Constrain Personal Participation in this Activity	Sometimes I am too tired to feel motivated for these activities Transportation	Money Available friends	Too tired Living alone No motivation Poor lifelong habits

Figure 11.1 Example of Round-Table Discussion Grid

were randomly assigned by the leader as either assuming the pro or con position for each statement. Participants should be given around 10 minutes to discuss among themselves each value statement in preparation for stating a convincing position for or against the statement. Participants should be encouraged to use the previously discussed values, benefits, and constraints associated with their own activity involvements to help them in structuring their debate.

The following statements are examples of values that can be used in the debate (the leader may wish to develop her or his own statements based on knowledge of the participants or other issues that have surfaced during previous sessions in the leisure education program):

- Idle hands are the devil's workshop.
- All work and no play makes Jack a dull boy (or Jill a dull girl).
- Winning at all costs is the only thing that counts in a game.
- Anything worth doing is worth doing well.
- Work first, play later.
- Play is children's work.
- Families that play together, stay together.

At the end of this session, participants should have experienced a growing awareness of the importance and benefits of leisure to themselves, as well as to other participants in the leisure education program. Through the discussion and debate, some participants may recognize that they have well entrenched attitudes and biases against leisure and for work. If the leader discovers this situation, additional activities may be developed to enhance positive attitudes and values toward leisure.

CONTENT AREA III— SELF-DETERMINATION AND LEISURE CHOICES

Target Goal:

The participant will be enabled to pursue his or her personal interests and preferences through leisure.

Enabling Objectives:

- To understand that pursuing one's interests and preferences through making independent choices in leisure is vital to developing an active and healthy lifestyle.
- To recognize one's personal decision-making style and how it affects personal leisure.
- To identify one's personal leisure preferences, interests, and barriers to participation in leisure.

Activity Suggestion: *Time Diary and Lifestyle Analysis*

This activity will cover 2–3 sessions of 1–2 hours duration each. The activity is intended to move participants through the process of keeping a time diary of their major life activities and conducting an analysis of their lifestyle for the purpose of planning change or maintaining continuity in life activity throughout older adulthood. The time diary and analysis take about 2–3 weeks to complete due to the need for (a) preliminary instructions, (b) a time frame in which to conduct the diary recording process, and (c) debriefing sessions for analysis and the planning to make change if needed. The time diary process and analysis include maintaining a record of activities plus analysis of activity patterns in regard to major categories and personal needs.

Implementation and Materials Suggestions:

Each participant will need a 10–14 day, time incremented diary that is organized into hourly periods. Preliminary instructions are to log in the major activities by time blocks and to complete the diary at the end of each day before retiring to bed. For each activity logged, the participant also will need to record major attributes associated with the activity (Figure 11.2). The key attributes will be determined during the first session as a group activity.

Session 1. During the initial session, the leader will introduce participants to the activity. The leader will explain the purpose and process for developing the 10–14 day diary of daily activities.

The leader will work with participants to decide what criteria will be used to code and record the key characteristics for each activity. For example, each activity can be rated on the following attributes:

- I do this activity because I *want to* (WT) or because I *have to* (HT).
- I do this activity *with others* (WO) or *alone* (A).
- This activity is *physically active* (PA) or *sedentary* (S).
- This activity is done at *home* (H) or in the *community* (C).
- I would classify this activity as **primarily** *recreation* (R), *leisure* (L), *work* (W), *education* (E), *personal maintenance* (PM), *family responsibility* (FR), or *civic involvement* (CI).
- If I had the choice, I *would do* this activity (Y) or I *would not do* this activity (N).

Day #1 Time:	Activity	WT/ HT	WO/ A	PA/ S	R/L/W/ E/PM/CI	H/ C
7:00 a.m.	Exercise	HT	WO	PA	PM	C
8:00	Breakfast	WT	WO	S	PM	H
9:00	Read Paper	WT	A	S	L	H
10:00	Grocery Shop	HT	A	PA	FR	C
11:00	Grocery Shop	HT	A	PA	FR	C
Noon	Snack lunch	HT	A	S	PM	H
1:00 p.m.	Senior Center: Cards	WT	WO	S	R	C
2:00	Senior Center: Cards	WT	WO	S	R	C
3:00	Senior Center: Cards	WT	WO	S	R	C
4:00	Television and nap	WT	A	S	R	H
5:00	Prep Dinner	HT	A	PA	FR	H
6:00	Dinner and News	HT	WO	S	FR	H
7:00	Television	WT	WO	S	R	H
8:00	Television	WT	WO	S	R	H
9:00	Television	WT	WO	S	R	H
10:00	Television	WT	WO	S	R	H
11:00	Bed	WT	WO	S	PM	H
Midnight	Bed	WT	WO	S	PM	H
1:00 a.m. to 6:00 a.m.	Bed	WT	WO	S	PM	H

KEY

WT=want to   HT=have to   WO=with others   A=alone
PA=physical activity S=sedentary   R=recreation   L=leisure
W=work   E=education   FR=family responsibility   PM=personal maintenance
CI=civic involvement H=home   C=community

Figure 11.3 Sample Page from a Time Diary

While the leader should have a set of characteristics in mind that can be used to analyze major activities and life patterns, the group should be encouraged to develop and agree upon the set that will be used for this activity.

Session 2. The second session is intended to follow-up after a 10–14 day cycle of maintaining the activity diary. Participants will bring their diaries to the session for review, discussion, and self-evaluation.

Each participant will review his or her diary entries using the agreed upon criteria. Every day should be summarized according to how much of the day is spent in each of the following main categories: (a) leisure/recreation, (b) work and other forms of obligatory activity, and (c) self-development/self-care such as education or personal maintenance. Furthermore, each category of activity can be evaluated regarding how much of the time was spent with others or alone, was leisure sedentary or active, etc. It is anticipated that by engaging in this process participants will identify at least one or more areas in which they might like to make some changes. Participants should be encouraged to discuss how satisfied they are with the way they are spending their daily lives.

At the close of the second session, participants will determine what criteria they will continue to use in evaluating daily activities, as well as what areas they might like to experiment with making changes. Based on the results of this evaluation process, an additional session is scheduled to follow-up on another 10–14 days of diary keeping during which participants will have decided to consciously change the configuration of daily activities in order to improve their overall lifestyle.

Session 3 (optional). The third session is optional and the intent is to follow-up on the additional days of diary keeping wherein participants consciously tried to alter the balance in daily activity choices and are now reflecting on the outcome of this activity. The same evaluation process can be used as was outlined in the second session. The objective at the end of this session and this overall activity is to continue to empower participants to make a conscious choice for rebalancing their daily life to fully embrace an active and healthy leisure lifestyle.

The ultimate outcome of this activity is to assist participants in clarifying the roles of work, leisure, and personal responsibilities in everyday life by examining the balance among these activity types in their present lives. A follow-up activity to this one is to plan the ideal daily diary for the future retirement years.

CONTENT AREA IV— LEISURE OPPORTUNITIES AND RESOURCES

Target Goal:

The participant will have the necessary knowledge about the full range of leisure opportunities that are available in his or her home and community in order to pursue an active, healthy leisure lifestyle.

Enabling Objectives:

- To identify varied forms of leisure opportunities that are available at home and in the community.
- To identify factors that influence participation in the leisure services and opportunities that are available in one's personal life and community.
- To distinguish among factors that can and cannot be changed, as well as to identify strategies for overcoming barriers to participation.

Activity Suggestion: *Leisure Resource Catalog for Older Adults*

This activity is intended to assist participants in identifying local resources and generating a reference file for their future use. The activity will encompass 3–6 sessions depending upon the size of the community and the detail that participants seek in their final product. Participants will work in teams, as well as on an individual basis, to gather information, evaluate their findings, and compile the results in a usable format.

Implementation and Materials Suggestions:

The final product, *Leisure Resource Catalog for Older Adults*, will take 3–6 sessions to complete with each session encompassing 1–2 hours of meeting time. The leader will need to provide participants with local publications from a variety of sources including the local visitors and convention office, the city and county parks and recreation departments, the local Area Agency on Aging as well as the State Unit on Aging, private and quasi-public organizations that provide leisure opportunities (e.g., YMCA, clubs, special interest groups), newspaper and other printed media, etc. The group will need to determine the final format and content for the *Leisure Resource Catalog* and if they want to also create a digital version that could be put on a CD/DVD or posted to a website. Additional resources or contacts that are needed by the group as they complete the activity will need to be coordinated by the program leader. Finally, the program leader should have a plan for duplication and distribution to the program participants of the final product, including cost estimates and potential underwriters.

Session 1. The first session will introduce the project, outline possible content and format approaches for the final product, determine the scope and depth of detail that will be included in the catalog, and generate a project completion timeline. The participants will be guided through a group discussion that determines each of these aspects of the project. For example, it could be decided that only local leisure resources will be included in the catalog rather than including state or regional level resources. Participants may decide to organize resources by categories; i.e., programs, services, facilities, and other leisure resources. For all resources included in the catalog, the following kinds of information could be collected: cost, design features, leadership, hours of operation, transportation availability, equipment needed or provided, special clothing, special skills, availability and design of restrooms, food services, membership requirements, barriers to participation by seniors, contact information including phone number(s), and potential interest to older adults. Participants will be make all decisions about what will be included and will be encouraged to work in pairs, if possible.

Sessions 2–5. The first organizational session will be followed by several working sessions where participants will meet to share and review findings, make changes or adjustments to their project plan, amend decisions regarding content and format, and keep a working compilation of their project. The program leader is to serve as a consultant and facilitator of the group's work. Each of these sessions should be planned for 1–2 hours in duration. The leader should make sure that the group has ample material and resources to complete their work including flip chart, paper and writing tools, computer access with printer and devices for saving back-up copy, etc.

Session 6. The last session will review and evaluate the product in its final draft form. The group will work with the program leader to make plans for the final production, duplication, and dissemination of the *Leisure Resource Catalog for Older Adults* to members of the program as well as other potential constituents in the community, such as adults who may be newcomers to the community or who live in housing for older adults (e.g., retirement communities). The leader also should plan an evaluation step to determine if participation in this activity helped to expand the par-

ticipants' knowledge about leisure resources that are available in their community.

CONTENT AREA V—
DECISION-MAKING AND ACTIVITY SKILLS

Target Goal:

The participant will create an ideal leisure lifestyle plan for attaining self-fulfillment, health, and active living in retirement.

Enabling Objectives:

- To reevaluate one's personal leisure lifestyle and identify areas for modification or development.
- To identify new leisure activity interests.
- To select and practice the use of at least one new leisure activity.

Activity Suggestion: *(1) Planning My Preferred Leisure Lifestyle* and *(2) Planning and Implementing a Culminating Leisure Event*

This content area is the highest level in the process of education for leisure-centered living. It is designed to bring together all the newly acquired knowledge, values, skills, and attitudes to support the development of a healthy, active leisure lifestyle; especially a lifestyle that will support a high quality of life during the retirement years. Two suggested activities are provided under this content area: (a) planning a preferred leisure lifestyle, and (b) planning and implementing a culminating leisure event for the leisure education program.

The first suggested activity in this area involves making a plan for a personal leisure-based lifestyle. This activity entails four steps: (a) identifying 1–4 goals for your personal leisure lifestyle including the reasons for the goals; (b) identifying 1–4 activities for attaining each goal, as well as listing the expected benefits for each activity; (c) evaluating the identified activities in terms of time, money, skills, equipment, companionship, transportation, and availability; and (d) making a commitment to pursuing at least 3 of the identified activities including a target date for participation. This activity is facilitated by the program leader in a single 1–2 hour session.

The second suggested activity can be used as a means for ending the leisure education program. Participants can share personal leisure goals and activities from the individual leisure plan that each has developed. The group leader can facilitate a brainstorming discussion regarding an activity that the group could do together which would meet at least one goal from each member's personal plan. The outcome from this process would be a culminating leisure event planned and implemented by the group as the finale for the leisure education program. The number of sessions that it would take to complete this second activity will depend upon the group's decision making and commitment to change at this point in the program. It is hoped that independent leisure skills are well in place at this point so that the group's next steps are easily identified and completed under the group's initiative. The program leader should only function as a facilitator and helper at this point in the process.

If, for some reason, the group is unable to arrive at a decision regarding a culminating event, the leader may want to suggest a social gathering in order to bring closure to the program. At this point, the leader can ask for volunteers to help in planning and implementing the social gathering.

Implementation and Materials Suggestions:

The first suggested activity, *Planning My Preferred Leisure Lifestyle*, will involve group process skills on the part of the program leader. The leader will organize the session to guide participants through a process of writing their plans. Participants will need paper, writing implements, and a comfortable place to sit and write. The leader will need at least one of the following: a flip chart, blackboard, or overhead projector to use in guiding each step in the process. The session will last from 1–2 hours with adequate time for discussion and debriefing at the end of the session.

Four steps as follow will be led by the program facilitator. Each participant will first identify 1–4 goals for their preferred leisure lifestyle, including the reasons for the goals. These will be listed on four separate sheets of paper at the top. Next, each participant will identify 1–4 activities that he or she would be interested in pursuing for attaining each goal, listing these activities down the left hand side of the page. Four activities should be listed under each goal along with the expected benefits from each activity, summarized next to each activity in the middle of the page. On the far right hand side of the page corresponding to each activity, the participant will evaluate each activity in terms of the resources that are needed to pursue the activity (Figure 11.3). The needed resource factors can include time, money, skills, equipment, companionship, transportation, money, and availability. Finally, on a fifth sheet of paper, each participant will select

three activities from all those considered and listed; the three selected should be activities that the participant is willing to make a commitment to pursue. For each of these activities, the participant will state a target date for participation and any other details that they need to address in order to ensure that participation takes place.

After completing the above process, the program leader provides a forum for participants to voluntarily share their final plan as written on the fifth piece of paper. Participants should be encouraged to provide positive and constructive feedback to each other, including suggestions for additional activities or ideas on how to negotiate constraints. At the end of this activity, the leader can determine if the group is positioned to consider a planning and implementing a capstone event to close the program. Based on group dynamics, individual and group progress throughout the program, and the demonstration of positive attitudes toward leisure along with strong independent leisure skills, the leader may pose to the group the idea for a closing event of their choosing.

Summary

The sample program for pre-retirement leisure education outlined in this chapter is intended only as an illustration of the content and processes of leisure education with older adults. Any leisure education program that is planned and implemented for a target audience or purpose (e.g., retirement preparation, rehabilitation, etc.) will need to be developed in far greater detail than is provided here. It is highly recommended that the reader consult one or more of the references or resources provided with this chapter to assist in planning and implementing specific leisure education programs.

Using educational tools and strategies to develop the knowledge, values, attitudes, and skills necessary for a healthy, active leisure-centered living is one approach for meeting the needs of older adults as they move through later life events and stages. Leisure education is appropriate for the full range of older adult concerns; that is, from the development of healthy and active lifestyles to rehabilitation following a major health event to adapting one's lifestyle when moving into an assisted-living facility or nursing home. By using the educational process, the activity specialist works in collaboration with the older adult to cultivate independence and control over personal lifestyle. In this regard, leisure education is a highly desired approach with older persons who cherish their autonomy and self-direction.

Potential Goals:
1. Improve overall health status—mentally, physically, and socially.
2. Expand social and friendship network, improve social well-being.
3. Increase number of pleasure-based recreation activities that are outside my home.
4. Exercise my mind through enrolling in an adult learning class.

Selected Goal:
Improve overall health status—mentally, physically, and socially.

Potential Activities:
Swim aerobics, bicycling, yoga, healthy cooking class.

Goal Planner:

Activity	Benefits	Needed Resources
Swim Aerobics	Socialization, improved flexibility, improved muscle strength, better circulation throughout body	Community program availability and access, transportation, money for fees and special equipment, time
Bicycling	Spend time outside, enjoy nature and feel mentally "clear," increase cardiovascular fitness, find a bicycling companion to develop new friendship	Equipment, locate potential biker friends, time, energy, personal motivation
Yoga	Find inner peace, body and mind integration, discover control	Videotape on yoga, motivation, energy
Healthy Cooking Class	Improve meal planning and preparation, learn new alternatives for improving overall diet, socialization, better physical health	Locate available program in community or on television, plan time, transfer program activities to everyday cooking via personal motivation

Figure 11.3 Sample Plan for Future Leisure Lifestyle

Resources for Developing Leisure Education Programs

The following leisure education curriculum materials may be useful in developing a leisure education program for older adults.

1. *Leisure Education Program Planning: A Systematic Approach (3rd ed.)* by John Dattilo, 2008, Venture Publishing, State College, PA. Dattilo provides the most comprehensive and available textbook on leisure education. The author gives a thorough review of related conceptual literature, as well as providing complete guidelines for developing leisure education programs. This text is a must for the activity specialist who intends to develop leisure education programs at senior centers, day activity programs, or skilled nursing facilities.

2. *The Wake Leisure Education Program: An Integral Part of Special Education* by Charles C. Bullock, Leandra A. Bedini, & Linda B. Driscoll, 1991, Center for Recreation and Disability Studies, University of North Carolina—Chapel Hill. This curriculum was initially designed for use in public schools in conjunction

with special education curricula for school children with disabilities. It is useful in planning leisure education programs for older adults in two ways: (a) it is an excellent model from which to build an age-appropriate leisure education program for older adults; and (b) it focuses on the concepts of *transition or adaptation,* which are important aspects of late life development. Leisure education can be instrumental in helping older adults more positively adapt to critical late life transitions (e.g., from work to retirement, from high level health to impairment), and in coping with changes in social networks due to death of family members and friends.

3. The text by Jean Mundy, *Leisure Education—Theory and Practice,* 1998, Sagamore Publishing, Champaign, IL, is an essential resource for professionals who desire to build their expertise in the area of leisure education. Mundy provides an important review of the historical roots of leisure education and outlines a model for implementation that can be adapted for participants of all ages.

4. *Leisure Education: Program Materials for Persons with Developmental Disabilities* by Kenneth F. Joswiak, 1989, Venture Publishing, State College, PA, thoroughly explains the design and implementation of leisure education for people with mental impairment. The concepts and lesson plans in this text can be easily adapted to a wider audience than that of people with mental retardation. The book is very complete and is a valuable resource for any activity professional who may be serving older clients who have cognitive impairments.

Additional useful resources are listed in the References and Resources section at the end of this chapter.

Comprehension Questions

The reader can check for comprehension of the material presented in this chapter by answering the following questions:

1. Identify the overall purpose of leisure education programs for older adults.

2. Describe the content and processes of leisure education.

3. Explain why leisure education is relevant and important for older adults.

4. Describe the goals of leisure education for older adults.

5. Why is the development of a healthy, active leisure lifestyle important for older adults?

6. Briefly describe one content area with sample activities for a leisure education program that prepares older adults for retirement.

References and Resources

Backman, S. J. & Mannell, R. C. (1986). Removing attitudinal barriers to leisure behavior and satisfaction: A field experiment among the institutionalized elderly. *Therapeutic Recreation Journal, 20*(3), 46–53.

Bedini, L. A. (1990). The status of leisure education: Implications for instruction and practice. *Therapeutic Recreation Journal, 24*(1), 40–49.

Bender, M., Brannan, S. A. & Verhoven, P. J. (1984). *Leisure education for the handicapped: Curriculum goals, activities, and resources.* San Diego, CA: College-Hill Press.

Birren, J. E. & Deutchmann, D. E. (1991). *Guiding autobiography groups for older adults—Exploring the fabric of life.* Baltimore, MD: The Johns Hopkins University Press.

Boyd, R. (1990). Participation in day programs and leisure activities by elderly persons with mental retardation: A necessary component of normalization. *Research into Action, 7,* 12–21.

Brightbill, C. K. & Mobley, T. A. (1977). *Educating for leisure-centered living* (2nd ed.). New York, NY: John Wiley & Sons.

Bullock, C. C., Bedini, L. A. & Driscoll, L. B. (1991). *The Wake leisure education program: An integral part of special education.* Chapel Hill, NC: University of North Carolina - Chapel Hill, Center for Recreation and Disability Studies.

Dattilo, J. (1999) *Leisure education program planning: A systematic approach* (2nd ed.). State College, PA: Venture Publishing, Inc.

Elliott, J. E. & Sorg-Elliott, J. A. (1991). *Recreation programming and activities for older adults.* State College, PA: Venture Publishing, Inc.

Gushiken, T. T., Treftz, J. L., Porter, G. H. & Snowberg, R. L. (1986). The development of a leisure education for cardiac patients. *Journal of Expanding Horizons in Therapeutic Recreation, 1,* 67–72.

Herrera, P. M. (1983). *Innovative programming for the aging & aged mentally retarded/developmentally disabled adult.* Akron, OH: Exploration Series Press.

Joswiak, K. (1989). *Leisure education: Program materials for persons with developmental disabilities.* State College, PA: Venture Publishing, Inc.

Keller, M. J., McCombs, J., Piligrim, V. V. & Booth, S. A. (1987). *Helping older adults develop active leisure lifestyles.* Atlanta, GA: Georgia Department of Human Resources.

Kelly, J. R. (1990). *Leisure* (2nd ed.). Englewood Cliffs, NJ: Prentice Hall.

Kimeldorf, M. (1989). *Pathways to leisure: A workbook for finding leisure opportunities.* Bloomington, IL: Meridian Education Corporation.

Mundy, J. (1998). *Leisure education: Theory and practice.* Champaign, IL: Sagamore Publishing.

Murphy, J. F. (1975). *Recreation and leisure service: A humanistic perspective.* Dubuque, IA: W. C. Brown.

Neulinger, J. (1974). *The psychology of leisure: Research approaches to the study of leisure.* Springfield, IL: Charles C. Thomas.

Overs, R. P., Taylor, S. & Adkins, C. (1974). Avocational counseling for the elderly. *Journal of Physical Education and Recreation, 48*(4), 44–45.

Powers, P. (1991). *The activity gourmet.* State College, PA: Venture Publishing, Inc.

Stumbo, N. J. (2002*). Leisure education I: A manual of activities and resources* (2nd ed.). State College, PA: Venture Publishing, Inc.

Stumbo, N. J. & Peterson, C. A. (2009). *Therapeutic recreation program design: principles and procedures* (5th ed.). San Francisco, CA: Pearson/Benjamin-Cummings.

Thews, V., Reaves, A. M. & Henry, R. S. (1993). *Now what? A handbook of activities for adult day programs.* Winston-Salem, NC: Bowman Gray School of Medicine, Wake Forest University.

Wuerch, B. B. & Voeltz, L. M. (1982). *Longitudinal leisure skills for severely handicapped learners. The Ho'onanea curriculum component.* Baltimore, MD: Paul H. Brookes Publishing Company.

Suggested Reading

- *Advanced Concepts for Geriatric Nursing Assistants,* by Carolyn A. McDonald (Venture Publishing, Inc.). This book is designed to allow CNAs to understand the importance of their role in geriatric healthcare, and provide CNAs with a theoretical base so they can provide licensed nurses with improved information about the people for whom they provide care.

- *Assessment: The Cornerstone of Activity Programs,* by Ruth Perschbacher (Venture Publishing, Inc.). While assessment is sometimes viewed as merely paperwork in residential settings for the elderly, Perschbacher shows both why and how assessment can serve to make activity therapy a way of reengaging residents' interest in life by helping them realize dreams and aspirations. A must read for all those involved in recreation and other activity therapy with the elderly.

- *Beyond Baskets and Beads: Activities for Older Adults With Functional Impairments,* by Mary Hart, Karen Primm, and Kathy Cranisky (Venture Publishing, Inc.). According to the authors, *Beyond Baskets and Beads* was born out of love. This book contains all the things the authors wish someone had told them when they started developing activities for older adults with functional impairments.

- *Beyond Bingo: Innovative Programs for the New Senior,* by Sal Arrigo, Jr., Ann Lewis, and Hank Mattimore (Venture Publishing, Inc.). Written by award-winning recreation professionals with many years of experience with seniors, this book is valuable to those working with senior citizen programs in a variety of settings. A must read for those who work in recreation settings with older adults.

- *Beyond Bingo 2: More Innovative Programs for the New Senior,* by Sal Arrigo, Jr. (Venture Publishing, Inc.). This book will provide the reader with many helpful hints and program ideas for senior centers, nursing homes, assisted-living and retirement communities.

• CHAPTER 12 •
Physical Activity and Health Promotion

Learning Objectives

1. Describe recent advancements in the knowledge and understanding of physical activity and quality of life for older adults.

2. Identify the types of activities that are used in physical activity intervention and health promotion with older adults.

3. Compare and contrast the biomedical model of aging with a health and wellness model.

4. Discuss the following components of an exercise program: strength training, aerobic training, and flexibility training.

5. Explain the benefits of an exercise program.

6. Discuss concerns and considerations for implementing a fitness program.

Key Terms

- Active Living
- Aerobic Activity
- Biomedical Model of Aging
- Fitness
- Flexibility
- Health Promotion
- Health Risk Behavior
- Maximal Oxygen Consumption
- Metabolism
- Muscular Endurance
- Physical Activity
- Quality of Life
- Range of Motion
- Strength
- Stress Test
- Weight Bearing
- Wellness

Introduction

Historically, aging has been viewed from a biomedical model. According to Estes and Binney (1989), there are two closely related aspects of this model: "(1) the social construction of aging as a medical problem and (2) the praxis (or practice) of aging as a medical problem" (p. 587). In the 20th century, the dominance of this model led to the belief that disease management was the natural approach to solving the health problems of older adults (Estes & Binney). From the perspective of a biomedical model of aging, the decline in physical performance is expected to be a normative experience in later life; however, more recently another view has surfaced. Based on an growing foundation of scientific evidence, today it is widely accepted that engaging in regular physical activity can and will produce considerable health benefits (Chodzko-Zajko, 2006). In spite of the fact that almost every system of the body deteriorates when it is inactive (Ferrini & Ferrini, 2008), engagement regular physical activity can and will produce different outcomes if such behavior can be motivated in older adults. The facts are, however, that the majority of older adults do not exercise on a regular basis, which is a national health concern (see National Blueprint: Increasing Physical Activity among Adults 50 and Older, The Robert Wood Johnson Foundation, available at http://www.rwjf.org/pr/product.jsp?id=15729).

Critics of the biomedical model have argued that it has created a mentality that supports the extension of life at all costs and does not consider quality of life (Estes & Binney, 1989). Some gerontologists have advocated a shift from the biomedical model of aging, which emphasizes treatment of disease, to a health and wellness model, which requires older adults to take responsibility for their own health (Hooyman & Kiyak, 2008). According to Hooyman and Kiyak, the goal of health promotion is to reduce the incidence of disabling chronic diseases and thereby enhance the functional independence and overall quality of life for older adults. Health promotion does not only focus on the absence of disease, it also embraces active lifestyles as a central to well-being and quality of life. The focus of this chapter is the exploration of current issues and trends in health promotion among older adults. National trends encompasses efforts to create community change/development, programs, and services that promote physical activity and active lifestyles among older persons.

An important part of any health promotion and wellness model is regular physical activity. Unfortunately, the number of older adults who participate in regular physi-cal activity is exceptionally low (Dishman, 2006). Recent statistics show that only about one-fourth of adults between age 65 and 74 engage in regular leisure-time physical activity and this figure goes down to 19.5% for people ages 75 to 84 and even lower to 9.6% among people age 85 and older (Federal Interagency Forum on Aging-Related Statistics, 2008). Physical fitness is clearly an important factor in the quality of life and wellness of many older adults. It is widely recognized that fitness is linked to the ability to live independently, to maintain one's home, engage in leisure activities, and withstand illness and injury (Ferrini & Ferrini, 2008). The benefits of regular physical activity are well established including improved cardiovascular function, better musculoskeletal strength and stability, stronger immune system function, lower body fat and better glucose regulation, improved sleep, lower stress and anxiety, higher life satisfaction, and enhanced mood states, just to name a few (Chodzko-Zajko, 2006). Other research has shown that participation in physical activity is linked with improved measures of mental health; for example, Mactavish and Searle (1992) found that a five-week, self-selected physical activity program had a positive impact on perceived competence, locus of control, and self-esteem in a group of older adults with mental retardation.

An important national health goal for older adults involves increasing physically active lifestyles in order to improve health status. Also important is the reduction of health risk behaviors such as smoking and alcohol/drug abuse, as well as reducing the incidence of obesity. Health is also improved through adequate sleep and proper nutrition (Hooyman & Kiyak, 2008). Keller (1994) recommended the following additional factors as part of a comprehensive approach to health and wellness: stress management, safety, and regular engagement in leisure activities.

Developing a Health Promotion Program

The challenge of facilitating health, wellness, and a high quality of life for older adults is an ongoing concern for activity specialists and other recreation professionals. While the scientific evidence supporting the benefits of regular physical activity is compelling, it continues to be difficult to motivate older adults to engage in physically active lifestyles (Chodzko-Zajko, 2006). Presently, many older adults are at risk for experiencing significant functional declines over time because they are not involved in regular physical activity either through fitness programs or active leisure activity. There are a number of factors that contribute to this situation including:

- the lack of basic physical fitness, poor quality lifestyles, and insidious participation in high risk health behaviors;
- increasing levels of individual and societal stress;
- lack of recognition, preparation, and education for high quality use of leisure time;
- low or no affiliation with others or in community life;
- lack of age-appropriate, high quality social structures, environments, and supports in the work place including job requirements and job expectations;
- inadequate quality, age-appropriateness, and safety in personal communities and residences;
- lack of access to or availability of age-appropriate health-related services; and
- the persistence of detrimental sociocultural norms and values such as pervasive ageism in the media, community, and even within the family. (Hawkins, 1988)

Comprehensive health promotion and wellness programs are designed with all of these factors in mind. According to Butler (1986), age-appropriate health promotion and wellness programs should encourage three types of fitness: personal, social, and physical. The minimum components of a health promotion and wellness program that meet these needs are nutrition, stress management, recreation/leisure activity, and physical activity/exercise. Behavior change is a central part of any health promotion program and health promotion would be incomplete without some discussion of preventive strategies as well as risk reduction. These components are briefly described in the following sections.

Nutrition

There are a number of reasons why older adults are often at risk for problems related to nutrition and health. Several factors are known to contribute to malnutrition including social isolation, problems with dentures or missing teeth, loss of sense of smell or taste, the inability to chew or swallow, and inadequate intake of calories and protein (Ferrini & Ferrini, 2008). It has been estimated that between 10–25% of older Americans are malnourished. While malnutrition is a common problem among older adults, obesity is now recognized to be of national epidemic proportions (Federal Interagency Forum on Aging-Related Statistics, 2008; Ferrini &

Ferrini, 2008). Obesity is determined by a body mass index of 30 or greater, and further, an adult is overweight if his or her body mass index is between 25 and 29. The adverse effects of being either overweight or obese are well-known and these effects create additional health risk among adults as they grow older. As reported by Federal Interagency Forum on Aging-Related Statistics (2008), in 2005–2006 among non-institutionalized adults, 37% of women and 24% of men age 65–74 were obese; among adults age 75 and older, 24% of women and 13% of men were obese. Obesity is considered to be a major cause of disease and mortality due to heart disease, cancer, asthma and other respiratory disease, arthritis, and Type 2 diabetes. Inadequate nutrition can also be related to diminished cognitive function, lack of motivation, fatigue, and depression (Luggen, Bernstein & Touhy, 2008).

A comprehensive discussion of the nutrition requirements for older adults is beyond the scope of this chapter; however, there are some general guidelines that can be followed. The following recommendations for older adults are offered:

- Consume a wide variety of foods, especially more fruits and vegetables than refined carbohydrates and saturated fats.
- Increase consumption of unprocessed foods containing complex carbohydrates (starch and fiber), such as whole grains and legumes.
- Restrict intake of sugar.
- Drink lots of water and nutritional fluids.
- Drink milk (up to 3 cups per day) or consume yogurt, cheese, or equivalent dairy products to ensure adequate calcium
- Be attentive to a balanced diet and any possible insufficiencies that may indicate supplementation. (Ferrini & Ferrini, 2008; Hooyman & Kiyak, 2008; Luggen, Bernstein & Touhy, 2008)

A number of federal, state, and local programs have been designed to meet the nutritional needs of the older population. The Older Americans Act allocates federal funds to each state to provide congregate and home delivered meal programs. Often senior centers operated by parks and recreation departments are utilized as congregate meal sites. The federal government also finances the Food Stamp Program, which is utilized by approximately 2 million lower income older adults (Hooyman & Kiyak, 2008). Even with these federal food programs, many older adults remain malnourished and unable to obtain adequate food to maintain good nutrition.

Activity specialists can impact nutrition in a variety of ways. Nutrition education, cooking classes, and other programs can be offered at senior centers, as part of nursing home activity programs, in adult day care centers, and as part of rehabilitation activity services. Fitness programs also offer an excellent opportunity to educate about nutrition and health. Each class can be followed by a brief discussion or lecture on active lifestyles and the role of proper nutrition in health maintenance. Serving healthy food at programs and facilities is another important step in the process of achieving a positive health status and a sense of well-being in older adults.

Stress Management

A number of life changes in older adulthood can contribute to increased stress including death of a spouse/ partner, friends, or siblings; relocation to a new residence; changes in functional status; onset of an illness or chronic disease; and retirement (Hooyman & Kiyak, 2008). Any event, by itself or in combination with others, places a demand on the older adult to cope with new life demands. Individual personality characteristics coupled with potentially other stressors in the environment can threaten the older person's ability to adapt. Collectively, life change stressors can undermine health and well-being. It's important to distinguish between internally and externally stress producing events. Examples of internal changes that produce stress are (a) disturbances in sleep patterns (i.e., long periods of restlessness without adequate deep sleep cycles), (b) changes in eating habits (i.e., over-eating unfamiliar foods when visiting others or forgetting to eat out of loneliness or lack of motivation to cook), and (c) the impact of a chronic condition that is undermining self-care (e.g., arthritis or diabetes) (Ferrini & Ferrini, 2008). External stressors include stopping a lifelong career, beginning a new job, loosing a significant other, or the necessity of changing one's residence. When life events (such as retirement) happen as expected, or on time, the older person can do much to prepare for the change and the stress that may come with it. When life event changes come too soon or unexpectedly, the stress level can be heightened. Any stress, whether it be expected or unexpected, will result in physiological and psychological responses that can threaten health and well-being (Touhy, 2008a). Regulating stress can contribute to overall health status, as well as the prevention of specific health problems including hypertension and sleep disturbances (Hooyman & Kiyak, 2008).

A number of interventions can be used to manage stress including a variety of types of physical exercise and relaxation techniques. For example, meditation as a form relaxation can help older persons cope with stress (Touhy, 2008a). There are many forms of meditation that can be effectively used. While in a meditative state the individual seeks to find a psychological state that is calming and often may be experience as a form of spirituality (Hooyman & Kiyak, 2008). Biofeedback and autogenic training (self-regulation) are additional techniques that can be used for managing stress (Touhy, 2008a). Yoga and other forms of physical movement (e.g., Tai Chi) have been shown to produce relaxation and stress reduction. Beyond relaxation techniques, arranging one's environment to reduce stress and encouraging the older person to express self-goals and needs are part of an overall approach to stress management.

Leisure and recreation activity

Regular engagement in leisure time activity is an integral component of successful aging. Participation in recreational activities on a regular basis is necessary for a healthy lifestyle. Leisure and recreation activities provide opportunities for older adults to meet a variety of needs, including (a) strengthening self-concept and self-esteem, (b) providing for spiritual satisfaction, (c) promoting a sense belonging, (d) supporting companionship and socialization, (e) improving mental stimulation, (f) supporting a feeling of social usefulness, (g) promoting the occupation of time, and (h) gaining recognition from others in the community (Kaplan, 1960). Music, dance, creative writing, art, and active physical leisure pursuits (e.g., biking, hiking, etc.) all are known to promote a sense of well-being and self-actualization (Touhy, 2008b). Health promotion programs will reflect a more comprehensive approach if they also include recreational activity and leisure education as important components.

Physical activity

Healthy aging is a national concern and priority and increased physical activity has been noted in the nation's Healthy People 2010 plan as a pathway to healthy aging (Touhy, 2008a). As outlined in Healthy People 2010 (U.S. Department of Health and Human Services, 2000), the leading indicators of improved health among older adults are (a) increased physical activity, (b) the reduction of obesity and being overweight, (c) smoking reduction and cessation, (d) reduced substance abuse, (e) improved mental health, (f) the prevention of injury and violence, (g) improved environmental quality, (h) increased immunization, (i) responsible sexual behavior, and (j) access to healthcare. While healthy aging is a wholistic concept that collectively embraces physical health, mental health, and social health, collectively (Rowe & Kahn, 1997; Touhy, 2008a), there is compelling evidence suggesting that physically active lifestyles as having benefits in all these areas (Chodzko-Zajko, 2006). Unfortunately, many older adults believe that they are too old for exercise or to participate in a fitness program. The evidence informs us that the opposite is true. When a fitness or exercise program is customized to the needs and capabilities of the individual, health benefits are clearly possible and probable. Beyond fitness and exercise programs, older adults can and will benefit from engaging in physical leisure activities. Walking is widely recognized as producing a broad range of benefits. There is little excuse for older adults to be sedentary, thus threatening their chances for healthy aging.

Four types of exercises are recommended for improving the health of older adults: endurance exercises, strength training, balance exercises, and flexibility exercises (Touhy, 2008a). Each of these is discussed in the section on developing an exercise program. It is also possible to achieve benefits in all four of these areas by regularly engaging in leisure activities that involve them such as gardening, swimming, walking, hiking, skiing, tennis, bowling, and many others. Comprehensive health promotion programs will seek to offer a broad range of physical activities that promote fitness and healthy aging.

Health risk reduction and prevention strategies

Health risk reduction and preventive health services are as important in health promotion programs as are nutrition, leisure/recreation activity, stress management, and physical activity. Key health risk reduction targets include smoking cessation, weight management, and alcohol/drug abuse intervention. The effects of each of these health risk targets on improved health and well-being are well-documented in the research literature (Ferrini & Ferrini, 2008; Hooyman & Kiyak, 2008; Touhy, 2008a). Health promotion programs that include efforts to help older people reduce their risks for chronic disease and disability due to smoking, obesity, and substance abuse are needed. Change in these high health risk behaviors can be accomplished through support services and behavior change initiatives.

Health prevention services also include (a) influenza vaccination, (b) vaccination to prevent pneumonia, (c) immunizations (e.g., tetanus, hepatitis B), and (d) preventive screening tests (e.g., diabetes, high blood pressure, elevated cholesterol, vision, hearing, cancers, osteoporosis, etc.) (Ferrini & Ferrini, 2008; Hooyman &

Kiyak, 2008; Touhy, 2008a). The importance of health prevention efforts cannot be understated in terms of the role they play in achieving health and wellness outcomes for the older population.

Behavior change

Few health promotion strategies, services, and programs will be successful without the older person's motivation to change his or her behavior. It is well-recognized, however, that behavior change can be challenging with older adults because their patterns of behavior are often long-standing and well-entrenched (Ferrini & Ferrini, 2008). Ferrini and Ferrini outline ten ingredients that are instrumental to achieving behavior change (adapted from Westberg & Jason, 1996).

1. The first step is acknowledgement. In the absence of the older individual's acknowledgement that there is a need to change a behavior that is undermining or detrimental to achieving a positive health status and sense of well-being, there is little reason to continue to urge his or her involvement in health promotion programs.
2. Following acknowledgement is cultivating the belief that one has much to gain by engaging in health promotion activities, initiatives, programs, or services.
3. Older people, as is true of people of all ages, need to feel that they have self-worth and can be effective in changing; therefore, self-worth and self-efficacy are important.
4. Older adults, like younger adults, also need to feel a sense of ownership over their planned behavior change.
5. Doable plans and realistic goals are a fifth ingredient that is essential for sustained behavior change.
6. Success breeds success, especially when it is rewarded by positive reinforcement. Finding out the kinds of rewards that are motivating to individuals is another important ingredient in a successful health behavior change program.
7. Most of us do not live in isolation; therefore, enlisting the involvement and support of others will further enhance the older person's ability to make and sustain a behavior change. Friends, family members, and peer mentors all are useful strategies for building the social support needed for behavior change.
8. Without ongoing progress monitoring and evaluation, long-term behavior change may fail.

9. Follow-up goes hand-in-hand with progress monitoring and periodic evaluation. Even when goals are met, reverting back to old behavior patterns is always a liability.

10. Finally, patience and practice are watchwords for ensuring that any ongoing health behavior change "sticks." Older adults are constantly challenged by changing life events that may threaten their health behaviors. Practice and patience are integral in times of backsliding as well as in times of achievement, albeit small steps toward behavior change.

Five common steps in behavior change are relevant to health prevention and health promotion behaviors: precontemplation, contemplation, preparation, action, and maintenance (Ferrini & Ferrini, 2008; Touhy, 2008a). Activity specialists can be instrumental in assisting older adults through these steps as they seek to reduce or cease health risk behaviors and develop health promotion lifestyle patterns.

Developing an Exercise Program

An exercise program that is designed to promote healthy aging will include a variety of types of exercise that target different aspects of physical functioning. Exercise may be aerobic or anaerobic. Aerobic exercises elevate the heart rate for a sustained period of time to improve cardiovascular endurance. Anaerobic exercises are designed to increase muscle strength and flexibility. A combination of both types is recommended. The remainder of this section will describe the primary training targets for any exercise program that is intended to improve endurance, balancing, strength, and flexibility.

Strength Training

Strength training programs should be designed to increase muscular endurance and strength (Ferrini & Ferrini, 2008). Muscular endurance refers to the ability of a muscle to sustain work over a period of time. Strength is the ability of an individual to apply force by muscle contraction. Increased muscle strength can improve older adults' speed of walking and enhance their ability to climb stairs, rise from a chair, get in and out of a bathtub or bed, and perform other important daily activities (Ferrini & Ferrini).

Among people age 65 and older the leading cause of injury-related deaths is falls (CDCP and The Merck Foundation, 2007). Often, early admission to a nursing home is the result of a fall. Loss of independence and the onset of disability are also common outcomes from falls. There is also considerable financial burden as a consequence of a fall-related injury. Strength training to improve balance is one of many factors that can help to prevent falls by older adults. Vision problems and medications also are contributing risk factors for falls along with unsafe environmental hazards. For many older adults falls can be devastating with significant social, psychological, and physical consequences. Older adults with chronic illnesses or disabilities that affect balance can benefit greatly from strength training. Strengthened muscles and ligaments help the older adult to maintain balance (Chodzko-Zajko, 2004). A general exercise and fitness program for older adults can use walking, flexibility, and strength exercises to improve posture, stability, and balance (Chodzko-Zajko, 2004). Finally, strength training helps reduce muscle tremor, which is particularly a problem for individuals with Parkinson's disease and other neuromuscular diseases.

Weight bearing exercise is crucial for women with or at risk for osteoporosis. Exercises such as walking, aerobic dancing, or weightlifting can increase bone mineral content and bone strength, and reduce the incidence of broken bones (Ferrini & Ferrini, 2008). Special attention should be given to exercises that prevent bone mass loss in the hips, spine, and wrists, since these are the bones most likely to fracture. In addition to reducing risk of injury, weight bearing exercise helps facilitate healing if orthopedic injury occurs (Hooke, 1992).

Aerobic Activity

Any exercise or activity that elevates the heart rate over a sustained period of time is considered aerobic. Common aerobic exercises include walking, swimming, jogging, bicycling, and aerobic dance. Aerobic exercise strengthens the heart muscle and increases pumping efficiency. Consequently, the individual who exercises regularly can perform activities with less strain. "The goal of aerobic is to fortify the body against stress" (Touhy, 2008a). The heart and circulatory system, vital lung capacity, metabolism, blood sugar levels and cholesterol levels, immune system, affect, sleep, and mental functioning all can benefit from a sustained program of aerobic fitness activities. Overall, older people who engage in a regular program of aerobic exercise seem to be healthier and happier, and even may appear to look younger than those who do not.

Maximal oxygen consumption, or uptake, refers to the amount of oxygen taken in and distributed to working muscles during exercise at maximum rate (Ferrini

& Ferrini, 2008). As people age, their vital lung capacity and maximal oxygen uptake generally decrease (Jett, 2008). Adults who have led sedentary lives may experience a 50% decrease by age 60, which leads to decreased function of the lungs and heart (Jett). Older adults who engage in regular vigorous aerobic activity, however, may maintain relatively high maximal oxygen uptake levels.

Aerobic exercise reduces the risk of heart disease in a number of ways. A regular aerobic program will result in a lowered level of LDL (bad) cholesterol and an increase in HDL (good) cholesterol. These changes in cholesterol levels may lower the risk of heart disease. The progression of atheroscerosis also may be slowed with regular exercise by a change in the proportion of blood lipids (Ferrini & Ferrini, 2008; Jett, 2008; Touhy, 2008a).

Basal metabolism, or the minimum amount of energy needed to maintain the body while at rest, declines over the life course (Jett, 2008). As a result, people should decrease caloric intake or maintain or increase levels of physical activity to prevent weight gain. In addition to improving cardiovascular function, aerobic exercise causes a temporary increase in metabolism (the rate at which the body burns calories) that persists for a few hours after exercise.

Persons who maintained a sedentary lifestyle for most of their lives should start an aerobic exercise program with a schedule of 20 minutes of aerobic exercise 3 times a week and progress to 30 to 50 minutes 3–4 times a week. Some older adults who walk to the store or do light housework on a regular basis may mistakenly believe that they are engaging in sufficient exercise. For any activity to be effective, it must elevate the heart rate for a sustained period of time and be repeated on a regular basis (Ferrini & Ferrini, 2008; Touhy, 2008a).

A treadmill stress test or some other method of assessing baseline fitness should be conducted before the older adult begins a fitness program. This assessment makes it possible for an individualized exercise program to be prescribed, which will provide for maximum results. In addition to a stress test before initiating an exercise program, participants should be taught to monitor their own heart rate so they can report any irregularities to their instructor (Penner, 1989). A common method of monitoring whether or not you are exercising at the appropriate level is the talk test. If you cannot carry on a conversation without becoming breathless, you are working too hard (Cheney, Diehm, & Seeley, 1992).

Flexibility

Flexibility refers to the ability to move joints through the entire range of motion (Ferrini & Ferrini, 2008; Touhy, 2008a). When full range of motion cannot be achieved, it may be difficult to accomplish normal tasks such as reaching, grasping, pinching, stooping, and walking. Adults typically loose muscle elasticity and experience thickening of tissue around the joints as they age (Jett, 2008). Exercise can counteract this deterioration by stretching the muscles to prevent them from becoming short and tight. Regular flexibility training also may help retard the development of arthritis.

Starting an Exercise Program

It is important to recognize that there are some risks associated with exercise programs that involve aging and aged adults. Muscle soreness, shin splints, tension strains, stress fractures, bone bruises, joint pain, and low back pain are not uncommon. Many injuries can be avoided by designing programs that minimize the risk of falls and teach participants the appropriate posture to use while exercising. Older adults with certain health conditions might not be good candidates for engaging in vigorous aerobic activities, and all older adults are wise to check with their primary physicians regarding any concerns or precautions. Conditions that are of concern include angina, irregular heartbeat, congestive heart failure, severe hypertension, anemia, and obesity (Ferrini & Ferrini, 2008). In some cases, patients with these conditions may participate in an exercise program, but only under strict medical supervision.

An exercise program should be initiated only after a medical assessment has been completed (Chodzko-Zajko, 2004; Ferrini & Ferrini, 2008). The medical assessment should include a treadmill or similar test to determine the older adult's baseline for a physical fitness program (Hooyman & Kiyak, 2008). The American College of Sports Medicine promotes the use of exercise tolerance testing (ETT) to help determine target heart rate and metabolic equivalents for the individual (Luggen & Touhy, 2008). An exercise prescription should be developed by the older client and a trained professional following a thorough assessment. The exercise program should be prescribed according to the individual's abilities and also should consider individual motivation and potential barriers. Common barriers to engaging in physical activity programs by older adults fall under the following categories:

1. Individual or psychological constraints such as feeling too tired or concerns about being too tired, not feeling confident, perceptions of a lack of fitness needed to engage, and fears about getting hurt.
2. Barriers associated with facilities and services such as lack of or poor quality of facilities, program times and schedules, lack of time to access facilities and programs, and other limitations associated with facilities/services.
3. Issues associated with finances and accessibility such as lack of transportation, inability to afford the facility or service fees, and the time it takes to get to the facility or programs.
4. Lack of partners to do activities with, for example no spouse or partner, friends don't like physical activity/exercise programs, and friends don't have time to participate. (Alexandris, Barkoukis, Tsorbatzoudis & Grouious, 2003)

Exercise programs are likely to vary from person to person in terms of type, intensity, duration, frequency, and progression of exercise (Luggen & Touhy, 2008). Sustained involvement in an exercise or fitness program is enhanced through the following characteristics:

- The program involves group participation in an environment of social pleasure.
- Typically, low to moderate intensity exercise, and a regular frequency of engagement with modest duration works best for most older persons.
- Use of recreation activity and games enhances pleasure and promotes variety.
- Setting personal goals enhances commitment and motivation.
- Evaluation of personal improvement as well as perceptions of the programming is important.
- Involving family and friends provides reinforcement.
- Use of environmental enhancements (music, ambience, etc.) provides motivation and pleasure.
- Use of positive feedback by program leaders at each and every session is important.
- Having positive role models and skilled leaders who are enthusiastic will promote commitment and motivation by older adult participants. (Luggen & Touhy, 2008; Orsega-Smith, Payne & Godbey, 2003)

The program should be monitored by the client and professional on a regular basis. If improvement is not evident after a few months, the rigor of the program may need to be increased.

Individual preferences will vary regarding what time of day is best to engage in an exercise program. Popular times are early morning and later afternoon before dinner. The preferences of participants can be used as the primary determinant of when to hold the program. It is important to remember, however, that many older adults may experience stiffness in the morning and might prefer to wait until at least a half hour after they get up to exercise in order to avoid injury (Cheney, Diehm & Seeley, 1992). Programs should not be held until two hours after eating because digestion makes heavy demands on the circulatory system (Cheney, Diehm & Seeley, 1992). Other considerations regarding the time of day to hold the program include facility availability, weather, transportation, and program schedules. Exercise programs should not be conducted in extremely hot or humid weather. If you live in a warm climate, try to secure an air-conditioned facility in which to conduct the program.

Exercise programs should always have a defined emergency plan that is familiar to all staff and participants. The leader of any exercise program should maintain current cardiopulmonary resuscitation (CPR) certification (Beal & Berryman-Miller, 1988; Penner, 1989).

A Sample Program

The following program demonstrates the types of activities that can be used in a physical fitness program. The program is appropriate for a nursing home, assisted living facility, adult day care, retirement community, senior center, or fitness center. Adaptations can be made to each recommended activity in order to accommodate a variety of skill levels and motivational factors of individual participants.

Program Purpose:

The purpose of this program is to provide older adults with an opportunity to participate in physical activity that is designed to facilitate high level health and wellness through the improvement of the physical, mental, social, and spiritual self. The program is based on the following principles:

1. Older adults have the ability to assume responsibility for their quality of life through health and wellness programs that promote physical activity and fitness.
2. The utilization of a variety of local agencies with expertise in recreation, nutrition, exercise, and stress management will contribute to the success of a holistic health and wellness program.

3. Older adults prefer to be involved in the planning, implementation, and evaluation of activities and programs, policies, and procedures that are designed to meet their health and wellness needs.

ACTIVITY AREA I—
AEROBIC ACTIVITIES

Target Goal:

Participants will be able to walk or engage in aerobic activity continuously for a minimum of 20 minutes 3 times a week, or the length and frequency specified in their individual treatment plans.

Enabling Objectives:

*   To plan and implement a varied program of physical activities that target aerobic exercise.
*   To determine a baseline level of aerobic fitness for each participant through a treadmill or other exercise tolerance test.
*   To develop an individual health and wellness plan for each participant based on their fitness assessment.
*   To train staff in facilitating and/or leading a variety of aerobic exercise programs.
*   To identify and modify a variety of aerobic physical activity programs appropriate for a diverse older population.
*   To regularly monitor changes in level of aerobic fitness of program participants.

Activity Suggestions:

An ideal aerobic exercise program is one that is flexible enough to accommodate participants with a wide range of fitness levels, functional abilities, and motivational levels. Also of consideration are individual barriers that impede involvement in regular physical activity such as transportation, personal fears of injury, lack of friends, economic concerns, program/facility hours, and other environmental accessibility considerations. Older adults are least likely to have a history of regular participation in regular physical activity and/or exercise programs compared with people of other ages and therefore, they may feel uncertain about their ability to be successful in an exercise/physical activity/fitness program. Consequently, programs should be designed to let the participants feel an immediate sense of ownership and accomplishment. It is also important to start participants at a level where they will feel challenged, but not discouraged.

Walking is an excellent activity choice for many older adults. Strain on joints is minimal in walking since it is low impact. Swimming is another activity that is good for people with injured joints or people who are obese. Caution is recommended, however, for older adults with osteoporosis who need to engage in weight bearing activity. In addition to the physical benefits of walking or swimming, there is the opportunity for socialization. Beginning exercisers are more likely to continue participation if someone participates with them.

An effective strategy for promoting exercise is to organize a walking program that involves staff, clients, friends, and volunteers at the facility. A "Walk Around the Country" program has been suggested by Elliott and Sorg-Elliott (1991). In this program, staff, and residents work together to build up mileage that is needed to walk across the country to major national attractions. Participants select places of interest and map a route prior to starting the program. Once a route has been established, a chart which indicates progress is located in a prominent area of the facility. Any mileage accumulated while walking, running, or biking for exercise by staff or participants is recorded on the chart. When the "travelers" reach the first "destination" a theme party including slides/videos of the destination, local cuisine, and decorations can be held for all participants. This destination event provides a goal for the exercise participants, as well as an opportunity for staff and participants to socialize.

Dance is another type of aerobic exercise program that provides participants with multiple benefits. According to McAdam (1988), dance produces the following benefits: the opportunity to artistically express thoughts, socialization, the opportunity to be creative, and the physical benefits of an aerobic exercise program.

The ideal dance class lasts for 50 minutes to an hour (McAdam, 1988). This timeframe includes: 10–15 minutes of warm-up, 10–30 minutes of aerobics, 5 minutes of cool down, and 10–30 minutes of strength and flexibility training. The purpose of the warm-up period is to gradually elevate the heart level to the desired training level. Walking in time to music or learning new dance steps for the aerobic training are good warm-up activities. The aerobic period consists of rhythmic steps that allow people to keep the heart rate at a target training level. The steps should be simple, of moderate tempo, and have long repetitive phrases. In addition, dances are choreographed in a sequence that minimizes stress to any one joint, avoid hops and jumps, and provides a low-impact option that does not require elevation for people with painful joints. A simple walk with large arm movements is recommended for the cool-down period. The cool-down period helps keeps blood from pooling. Some type of cool-down activity is essential and highly recommended. Suggestions for the strength training and flexibility periods are discussed later in this chapter.

Implementation and Materials Suggestions:

Good form and posture are essential for participants in order to avoid injuries. The proper form for walking involves a heel-to-toe movement. The weight of the body should be transferred smoothly from one foot to the other, with one foot always on the ground. The heels should be centered with the foot pointing slightly out. The body should be kept erect by leaning slightly from the ankles. Arms should be loose at the sides and moving in opposition to the legs (Hooke, 1992).

Dance participants should hold their shoulders slightly back and down. The pelvis should be tilted in and the abdominal muscles held in to prevent back injury. Knees should be soft or slightly bent throughout the routine to avoid hyperextension. Elevation of feet off the floor should be minimized. High impact moves, which are popular in many aerobic dance routines, can cause excessive stress to the joint and result in injury (Beal & Berryman-Miller, 1988).

Little equipment is needed for most aerobic exercise programs. Participants in the walking program should have comfortable and appropriate footwear that provides ample support. If participants will be walking outside, they should dress in layers that can be easily removed if needed. The dance program requires music, mats for stretching (if participants will be on the floor), straight chairs without arms for participants who exercise from a sitting position, and a microphone for the instructor, if needed. Optional equipment includes balls, hoops, and ribbons/scarves that can be incorporated into the dance sequence. Dance program participants should wear comfortable and appropriate footwear that provide ample support and comfortable clothes that do not restrict movement. Some participants may feel self-conscious about their bodies and prefer to wear baggy clothes to the program. The primary problem with this attire is that it prevents the instructor from monitoring posture and form during the program, which could lead to potential injury.

Due to the possibility of impact injuries, the preferred location of aerobic programs is a space that does not have a concrete floor. If a concrete floor is unavoidable, then only low impact activities should be utilized and proper shoes must be worn. The space should have good lighting, proper ventilation, an open space large enough to allow the participants to move

freely, the availability of water, and places for sitting for rest. Indoor walking programs require a circular route that is level and contains benches/seats for resting. If an outdoor walking space is available, it should be secured by a fence to prevent confused clients from wandering away from the path. Again, shaded places to sit and rest, and the availability of water for hydration are essential. Utilization of a variety of plantings along the walkway will add interest to the area.

ACTIVITY AREA II— STRENGTH TRAINING

Target Goal:

Participants will be able to complete 20 repetitions of strength exercises specified in their individual health and wellness plans.

Enabling Objectives:

- To plan and implement a varied program of strength training physical activities.
- To determine target muscle groups for each individual based on the assessment of muscular strength and endurance.
- To train staff in facilitating and/or leading a variety of strength training activity programs.
- To identify and modify a variety of strength training activities that are appropriate for a diverse older population, including older adults who use wheelchairs and those who must remain in bed due to a disabling or medical condition.
- To regularly monitor changes in strength level of program participants.

Activity Suggestions:

Strength training programs consist of resistive exercises. Participants may participate in isotonic exercise in which resistance is provided by a weight or isometric exercise in which resistance is created by contracting a muscle group statically (Lasko & Knopf, 1988). The advantage of isometric exercise is that it does not require equipment or space to perform. It is, however, generally not as effective as isotonic exercise so the transfer to functional activities may not be as great. Strength training has been shown to be effective of older and very old adults, especially in improving mobility, the ability to perform activities of daily living, and overall independence. A major barrier to engaging in strength training programs by older adults is that the lifting of weights or use of resistance training equipment is not very appealing.

Greninger and Kinney (1988) recommend the three Is for localized strength training:

- Identify the muscle or muscle groups you wish to exercise.
- Isolate the muscle group by placing the body in the appropriate position. This step is key to preventing injuries and gaining maximum benefits.
- Intensify the muscle group by using weight or resistance to gravity.

In addition, localized strength exercises should only involve one joint at a time. All strength exercises should be done slowly and movements should be made through the full range of motion.

Another approach to strength training is to identify and select physical activities that promote increasing strength through a program of active involvement in them. For example, swimming is an activity that improves muscle strength, endurance, and circulation (Luggen & Touhy, 2008). To date, however, the main approach to strength training is through specific exercises (such as lifting weights) that are incorporated into an exercise training protocol for older adults (see ASCM, 1995).

Implementation and Materials Suggestions:

It is recommended that one set (8–12 repetitions) of 8–10 resistance exercises be completed by healthy older adults at least 2 days a week (American College of Sports Medicine, 1990; 1995). Localized exercises may be performed standing, sitting, or lying down. According to Hooke (1992), the following posture tips should be followed to reduce the risk of injury and decrease muscle fatigue:

- Standing position—The body should be erect and relaxed with the head held over the spine. The shoulders should be down, level, and back and the chest should be lifted. The abdominal muscles should be drawn in and the pelvis tucked forward. Knees should not be locked or hyper-extended and feet should be shoulder width apart, with body weight slightly forward of the ankles.
- Sitting position in a chair—The body should be erect and relaxed with a 90 degree angle at the hips. The hips should be tilted forward to prevent back injury. The head should be held directly over the spine. The shoulders should be held level and back, the abdominal area drawn in, and the thighs supported by the seat of the chair. Feet should be flat on the floor and placed shoulder width apart.
- Sitting position on the floor—The upper body should be erect and relaxed with a 90 degree angle at the hips. Head, shoulder, and abdomen positions should be similar to the chair position. Feet should be slightly apart and knees may be straight or bent.
- Lying on the floor or other flat surface—The knees should be bent with feet shoulder width apart and flat on the floor. A small pillow should be placed under the head to support the head and neck.

A variety of equipment has been developed for strength training programs. Small hand held weights are available in a variety of sizes. Weights of 1, 3, 5, and 10 pounds are sufficient for most programs. Ankle weights also are useful, however, sandbags may be draped over the ankle and used for leg exercises. If cost is a concern to participants, especially those who are exercising at home, program leaders may use soup cans, books, water filled jugs, or other household goods instead of weights. Many programs utilize resistance bands for strength training. These bands are fairly inexpensive and are particularly useful for strengthening the arms and legs.

ACTIVITY AREA III— FLEXIBILITY PROGRAMS

Target Goal:

Participants will be able to move targeted joints through the full range of motion or appropriate level as determined through assessment.

Enabling Objectives:

- To plan and implement a varied program of flexibility exercises or physical activities that promote flexibility.
- To develop an individual plan for each participant based on the results of a fitness assessment.
- To train staff in facilitating and/or leading a flexibility training program.
- To identify and modify a variety of flexibility exercises or physical activities that involve flexibility movements.
- To regularly monitor changes in level of flexibility of program participants.

Activity Suggestions:

A flexibility program is a necessary element of any well-rounded fitness program. Flexibility exercises may be done on their own or in conjunction with aerobic exercise and/or strength training activities. Specific flexibility exercises may be the focus or the use of physical recreation activities that involve flexibility movement patterns.

Stretching to music adds interest to a flexibility program. New age music or sounds of nature are soothing and conducive to the slow movements that are part of a flexibility program. Ribbons or brightly colored scarves may be incorporated into the routine for additional interest.

Yoga, a very popular physical activity and highly recommended, is an ancient form of exercise that encourages physical, mental, and spiritual development (Girdano, Everly & Dusek, 1990; Luggen & Touhy, 2008). Yoga has both physical and mental benefits. It also can be engaged in by all older adults, regardless of physical condition. Hatha yoga is a popular form of yoga in the Western cultures. This type of yoga utilizes positions and exercises to promote harmony between the physical self and the mental self. Although some yoga positions and exercises may be too advanced for older adults, many are easily adapted to individuals who are frail or unsure about flexibility exercises. Local parks and recreation departments or college physical education departments may be able to recommend an instructor for the yoga program. Yoga programs also may include an educational element wherein participants learn about the various levels of yoga and the culture from which it originated.

More recently Tai Chi has become a popular form of exercise that has application in flexibility, strength, mobility, and balance training (Luggen & Touhy, 2008). Other benefits include improved breathing, relaxation, pain management, and sense of well-being. Resources are now available on Tai Chi for older adults (Tai Chi, 2006), and some groups have promoted forms of Tai Chi that are motivating and challenging to older persons (Arthritis Foundation, 2006).

Implementation and Materials Suggestions:

Prior to beginning stretching, participants should take a walk for three to five minutes or engage in some other type of warm-up activity (Hooke, 1992). Following the warm-up, general stretches such as long stretches from the toes to fingertips, side stretches, and relaxing shoulder movements are implemented. Stretches for specific muscles may then be done. All major muscle groups should be stretched individually (Clements, 1994).

A number of safety concerns should be addressed when doing stretching exercises. The body should be positioned within its normal range of motion (Clements, 1994). Smooth, gentle movements or static stretching are recommended for older adults (Hooke, 1992). The participant should move very slowly into the stretch and hold it for a period of 10 to 20 seconds before slowly returning to the starting position. Participants may try to "bounce" while they are stretching in order to reach further but this should be discouraged. It is important to emphasize that everyone has a different level of flexibility, so progress in this area must be measured on an individual level. All participants should understand that stretching exercises should feel good. Participants should feel "pull, but not pain" (Hooke, p. 263).

ACTIVITY AREA IV— STRESS MANAGEMENT

Target Goal:

Participants will develop the skills to incorporate stress management techniques into their lives on a daily basis and as needed.

Enabling Objectives:

- To plan and implement a varied program of stress management activities.
- To determine an individual stress management plan that is appropriate for the needs of each participant.
- To train staff in facilitating and/or leading a variety of stress management programs.
- To identify a number of stress management programs appropriate for a diverse older population.
- To regularly monitor perceived changes in level of stress, as well as the reduction of physical manifestations of stress (e.g., ulcers, high blood pressure).

Activity Suggestions:

An ideal stress management program is one that contains a variety of techniques (Touhy, 2008a). Individual preferences for techniques will vary. It is the task of the instructor or facilitator to introduce these techniques and let the participants decide which are most effective for them. Relaxation, meditation, changing one's environment to promote stress relief, biofeedback, self-regulation, and self-care are all methods that can be used to reduce and manage stress (Touhy, 2008a). Some specific physical activities/exercises include yoga, aerobic activities like walking, and Tai Chi are just a few of the popular approaches to stress management.

Yoga or stretch-relaxation exercises like Tai Chi, help to reduce stress through the reduction of muscle tension. A general lack of physical activity coupled with chronic sitting contribute to shortened muscles, tendons, and ligaments and muscle tension in older persons. Older adults that experience chronic back or neck pain, or headaches may be feeling the effects of a lifetime of sedentary living and/or poor posture. Stretching is a natural reflex after the muscles have been tightened or experienced tension and can be used to prevent tension pain in the body (Girdano, Everly & Dusek, 1990).

Aerobic activity is an excellent stress reducer, such as walking, swimming, hiking, etc. All humans have an innate need to respond to stress with physical activity. During stressful situations, the human body produces adrenal hormones which ready the body to "fight or flight" (Girdano, Everly & Dusek, 1990). In modern times, the "fight or flight" response is typically not an appropriate response to a stressful situation. As a result, the increased hormones are not utilized and can contribute to ulcers, cardiovascular disease, and a number of other physical illnesses. These resulting health conditions can be prevented with the regular exercise that promotes a healthy and appropriate outlet for stress.

There are many other techniques in addition to exercise that can be used to manage stress. Many of the techniques are simple to teach and can be easily incorporated into daily life as needed. The following is a brief description of three techniques that are described in *The Relaxation and Stress Reduction Workbook* (Davis, Eshelman & McKay, 1988):

- Progressive Relaxation—Progressive relaxation is used to identify tension in particular muscle groups. While using this technique, participants focus on specific muscle groups, contract those muscles, visualize the tension in the muscles, and then relax the muscle. This sequence is repeated for the following muscle groups: (a) hands, forearms, and biceps; (b) head, face, throat, and shoulders; (c) chest, stomach, and lower back; and (d) thighs, buttocks, calves, and feet.
- Breathing—Although breathing is an automatic natural action, we do not all breathe correctly. Our breathing may be altered by poor posture,

tight clothing, disease, or stress. Taking the time to learn proper breathing techniques can contribute to overall health status and reduce the effects of stress. It is difficult to remain stressed or anxious when you are taking slow, deep breaths. There are many breathing techniques that can be used for stress management. They all involve good posture, deep full breaths, and appropriate use of the diaphragm.
- Meditation—Meditation involves focusing your attention on one thing at time. The goal is to become so focused on one object so that the participant "lets go" of worries, fears, hate, and other negative emotions. Meditation has long been used by Eastern cultures as a method of strengthening the spirit and the mind. There are three basic types of meditation that can be easily learned. Mantra meditation involves focusing on a word or syllable that you like or find pleasing. Breath counting meditation utilizes counting slow, relaxed, and unforced breaths. Gazing meditation utilizes an object as the center of attention, rather than a word or syllable.

Summary

This chapter outlines the basic elements of physical activity programs that are designed to meet the health promotion and wellness needs of older adults. These activities can be implemented in a variety of settings and can be adapted to a variety of physical health levels. A variety of resources are available to help in the development and implementation of an exercise and wellness program (Figure 12.1). Additional texts are listed in the References and Resources section at the end of the chapter.

Comprehension Questions

The reader can check for comprehension of the material presented in this chapter by answering the following questions:

1. Describe the components of a health and wellness program for older adults.

2. Discuss the three basic components of a fitness program for older adults. Explain why each of these components are necessary?

3. Identify and discuss barriers to participation in physical activity programs by older adults.

Activities, Adaptation & Aging published monthly by Haworth Press Inc., 28 E. 22nd St., New York, NY, 10010. This publication contains valuable articles and other resource materials.

Administration on Aging (n.d.). The fitness challenge...In the later years: An exercise program for older adults. (DHHS Publication No. OHD 75-20802). Washington, DC: U.S. Government Printing Office.

Aerobics and Fitness Foundation, telephone 1-800-233-4886.

American Association of Retired Persons, 1909 K St., N.W., Washington, DC, 20049 (brochures and audiovisual materials available).

American Arthritis Foundation: Aquatic program (website): www.arthritis.org/events/get involved/ProgramsServices/aquaticprogram.asp.

American Arthritis Foundation: Tai Chi from the Arthritis Foundation (website): www.arthritis. org/events/getinvolved/ProgramsServices/taichi.asp.

American College of Sports Medicine. (1991). Guidelines for exercise testing and prescription (4th ed.). Philadelphia, PA: Lea & Febiger.

American Diabetes Association, 505 8th Avenue, New York, NY, 10017.

American Heart Association, National Center, 7320 Greenville Avenue, Dallas, TX, 75231.

Arthritis Foundation, 1314 Spring Street N.W., Atlanta, GA, 30309.

Beal, R. K. & Berryman-Miller, S. (1988). Dance for the older adult. Reston, VA: The American Alliance for Health, Physical Education, Recreation, and Dance.

Clements, C. B. (1994). The Arts/Fitness Quality of Life Program: Creative ideas for working with older adults. Baltimore, MD: Health Professions Press, Inc.

Corbin, D. E., & Metal-Corbin, J. (1990). Reach for it: Handbook of health, exercise and dance for older adults (2nd ed.). Dubuque, IA: Eddie Bowers Publishing Company.

Easy Yoga for Seniors. Videotape by Video Vacation, 306 West Avenue, Lockport, NY, 14094, telephone 1-800-441-3006.

Fitness for the Good Years. Videotape by Parade Video, Newark, NJ.

Greninger, L. O. & Kinney, M. B. (1988). Therapeutic Exercises for Older Adults. Dubuque, IA: Eddie Bowers Publishing Company.

Hooke, A. P. (1992). Active older adults in the YMCA: A resource manual. Champaign, IL: YMCA of the USA.

Lewis, C. B. & Campanelli, L. C. (1990). Health Promotion and Exercise for Older Adults. Rockville, MD: Aspen Publishers.

National Resource Center on Health Promotion and Aging, AARP, 601 E. Street, N.W., Washington, DC, 20049.

Penner, D. (1989). Eldercise: A health and fitness guide for older adults. Reston, VA: American Alliance for Health, Physical Education, Recreation, and Dance.

President's Council on Physical Fitness and Sports, 450 5th Street, N.W., Suite 7103, Washington, D.C., 20001, telephone 1-202-272-3430.

Rejeski, W. J. & Kenney, E. A. (1988). Fitness motivation: Preventing participant dropout. Champaign, IL: Life Enhancement Publications.

Tai Chi for Health Institute. (2006). Tai Chi for seniors (website): www.taichiforseniorsvideo.com/

Figure 12.1 Additional Resources

4. Discuss the benefits of physical activity health status, wellbeing, and quality of life.

5. Discuss considerations for implementing a physical activity/fitness/exercise program for older adults.

References

American Association of Retired Persons. (n.d.). *Pep up your life: A fitness guide for seniors.* [Brochure]. Washington, DC: Author.

American College of Sports Medicine. (1990). The recommended quantity and quality of exercise for developing and maintaining cardiorespiratory and muscular fitness in health older adults. *Medicine and Science in Sports and Exercise, 22*(2), 265–274.

American College of Sports Medicine. (1995). *ACSM's guidelines for exercise testing and prescription* (5th ed.). Philadelphia, PA: Lea & Febiger.

Beal, R. K., & Berryman-Miller, S. (1988). *Dance for the older adult.* Reston, VA: The American Alliance for Health, Physical Education, Recreation, and Dance.

Butler, R. N. (1986). Wellness and health promotion for the elderly: An overview. In K. Dychtwald (Ed.), *Wellness and health promotion for the elderly.* Rockville, MD: Aspen Publishers.

Centers for Disease Control and Prevention and The Merck Company Foundation. (2007). *The state of aging and health in America 2007.* Whitehouse Station, NJ: The Merck Company Foundation.

Cheney, W. J., Diehm. W. J., & Seeley, F. E. (1992). *The second fifty years: A reference manual for senior citizens.* New York, NY: Paragon House.

Chodzko-Zajko, W. (2004). Topic 20. Physical activity and aging: Implications for health and quality of life in older persons. In C. B. Corbin, R. P. Pangrazi, & B. D. Franks (Eds.), *Toward a better understanding of physical fitness and activity–Selected topics, volume two* (191–200). Scottsdale, AZ: Holcomb Hathaway, Publishers.

Chodzko-Zajko, W. (2008). Chapter 1. National blueprint: Increasing physical activity among adults 50 and older: Implications for future physical activity and cognitive functioning research. In L. W. Poon, W. Chodzko-Zajko & P. D. Tomporowski (Eds.), *Active living, cognitive functioning, and aging* (pp. 1–14). Champaign, IL: Human Kinetics.

Davis, M., Eshelman, E. R. & McKay, M. (1988). *The relaxation and stress reduction workbook.* Oakland, CA: New Harbinger Publications, Inc.

Dishman, R. K. (2006). Chapter 16. Measurement of physical activity. In L. W. Poon, W. Chodzko-

Zajko & P. D. Tomporowski (Eds.), *Active living, cognitive functioning, and aging* (91–111). Champaign, IL: Human Kinetics.

Dishman, R. K. (1990). Determinants of physical activity and exercise for persons 65 years of age and older. In W.W. Spirduso and H. M. Eckert (Eds.), *The Academy Papers: Physical activity and aging.* Champaign, IL: Human Kinetics.

Elliott, J. E. & Sorg-Elliott, J. A. (1991). *Recreation programming and activities for older adults.* State College, PA: Venture Publishing, Inc.

Estes, C. L., & Binney, E. A. (1989). The biomedicalization of aging: Dangers and Dilemmas. *The Gerontologist, 29*(5), 587–596.

Federal Interagency Forum on Aging-Related Statistics. (2008, March). *Older Americans 2008: Key Indicators of Well-Being.* Federal Interagency Forum on Aging-Related Statistics. Washington, DC: U.S. Government Printing Office.

Ferrini, A. F. & Ferrini, R. L. (2008). *Health in the later years.* (4th ed.). Boston, MA: McGraw Hill.

Girdano, D. A., Everly, G. S., Jr. & Dusek, D. E. (1990). *Controlling stress and tension: A holistic approach.* Englewood Cliffs, NJ: Prentice Hall.

Greninger, L. O. & Kinney, M. B. (1988). *Therapeutic exercises for older adults.* Dubuque, IA: Eddie Bowers Publishing Co.

Hawkins, B. (1988). *Health promotion and high level wellness in health, physical education, and recreation.* Bloomington, IN: School of Health, Physical Education, and Recreation.

Hawkins, B. A. (1999). Population ageing: Perspectives from the United States. *World Leisure & Recreation Journal, 41*(3), 11–15.

Hawkins, B. A. (2005). Aging well: Toward a way of life for all people. Invited editorial. *CDC Preventing Chronic Disease, Public Health Research, Practice, and Policy.* Online, refereed journal, Centers for Disease Control and Prevention, U.S. Public Health Service.

Hawkins, B. A. (2006). Aging well. In N. J. Salkind (Ed.), *The Encyclopedia of Human Development.* Thousand Oaks, CA: Sage Publications.

Hooke, A. P. (1992). *Active older adults in the YMCA: A resource manual.* Champaign, IL: YMCA of the USA.

Hooyman, N. R. & Kiyak, H. A. (2008). *Social gerontology: A multidisciplinary perspective* (6th ed.). Boston, MA: Allyn and Bacon.

Jett, K. (2008). Chapter 4. Physiological changes with aging. In P. Ebersole, P. Hess, T. A. Touhy, K. Jett & A. S. Luggen (Eds.), *Toward health aging: Human needs & nursing response.* St. Louis, MO: Elsevier/Mosby.

Kaplan, M. (1960). *Leisure in America: A social inquiry*. NY: John Wiley & Sons.

Keller, M. J. (1994). Wellness programs with older adults residing in retirement communities. In M. J. Keller & N. J. Osgood (Eds.). *Dynamic leisure programming with older adults*. Arlington, VA: National Recreation and Park Association.

Konstantinos, A., Barkoukis, V., Tsorbatzoudis, H. & Grouios, G. (2003). A study of perceived constraints on a community-based physical activity program for the elderly in Greece. *Journal of Aging and Physical Activity, 11,* 305–318.

Lasko, P. M. & Knopf, K. G. (1988). *Adapted exercises for the disabled adult: A training manual.* (2nd ed.). Dubuque, IA: Eddie Bowers Publishing Co.

Lewis, C. B., & Campanelli, L. C. (1990). *Health promotion and exercise for older adults.* Rockville, MD: Aspen Publishers.

Luggen, A. S., Bernstein, M. & Touhy, T. A. (2008). Chapter 9. Nutritional needs. In P. Ebersole, P. Hess, T. A. Touhy, K. Jett & A. S. Luggen (Eds.), *Toward health aging: Human needs & nursing response* (pp. 194–221). St. Louis, MO: Elsevier/Mosby.

Luggen, A. S. & Touhy, T. A. (2008). Chapter 7. Managing basic physiological needs. In P. Ebersole, P. Hess, T. A. Touhy, K. Jett & A. S. Luggen (Eds.), *Toward health aging: Human needs & nursing response* (pp. 120–156). St. Louis, MO: Elsevier/Mosby.

Mactavish, J. B. & Searle, M. (1992). Older individuals with mental retardation and the effects of physical activity intervention on selected social psychological variables. *Therapeutic Recreation Journal, 26*(1), 38–42.

McAdam, M. (1988). Dance as a vehicle to fitness for the healthy older adult. In R. K. Beak & S. Berryman-Miller (Eds.), *Dance for the older adults* (16–27). Reston, VA: AAPHERD.

Orsega-Smith, E., Payne, L. L. & Godbey, G. (2003). Physical and psychosocial characteristics of older adults who participate in a community-based exercise program. *Journal of Aging and Physical Activity, 11,* 516–531.

Penner, D. (1989). *Eldercise: A health and fitness guide for older adults.* Reston, VA: American Alliance for Health, Physical Education, Recreation, and Dance.

Rejeski, W. J. & Kenney, E. A. (1988). *Fitness motivation: Preventing participant dropout.* Champaign, IL: Life Enhancement Publications.

Rowe, J. W. & Kahn, R. L. (1997). Successful aging. *The Gerontologist, 37*(4), 433–440.

Tai Chi for Health Institute. (2006). *Tai Chi for seniors.* Retrieved March 20, 2009, from www.taichiforseniorsvideo.com

Touhy, T. A. (2008a). Chapter 3. Health and wellness. In P. Ebersole, P. Hess, T. A. Touhy, K. Jett & A. S. Luggen (Eds.), *Toward health aging: Human needs & nursing response* (43–64). St. Louis, MO: Elsevier/Mosby.

Touhy, T. A. (2008b). Chapter 27. Self-actualization, spirituality, and transcendence. In P. Ebersole, P. Hess, T. A. Touhy, K. Jett & A. S. Luggen (Eds.), *Toward health aging: Human needs & nursing response* (666–696). St. Louis, MO: Elsevier/Mosby.

U.S. Department of Health and Human Services. (2000). *Healthy People 2010* (2nd ed.). Washington, DC: U.S. Government Printing Office.

• CHAPTER 13 •
Mental Health Activity Intervention

Learning Objectives

1. Identify therapeutic activities that may be used to support mental health and well-being in older adults.

2. Describe common treatment modalities that are used with older adults with and without impaired mental functioning.

3. Discuss the following common therapeutic mental health activity approaches: reminiscence and life review, validation therapy, reality orientation, sensory training, spiritual activities, therapeutic humor, remotivation, and resocialization.

4. Describe a sample mental health activity program for older clients.

5. Explain common motivational and leadership techniques that can be used to enhance participation by older adults in therapeutic activities that promote mental health and well-being.

Key Terms

• Life Review

• Sensory Stimulation

• Motivation

• Spirituality

• Reality Orientation

• Therapeutic Humor

• Reminiscence

• Triggers

• Remotivation

• Validation Therapy

• Resocialization

Introduction

Non-hospital based or outreach programs that provide mental health support are limited and often may not meet the broad range of mental health needs prevalent among older adults. Older adults are challenged by issues that affect mental well-being, especially when dealing with losses that are common in late life (e.g., loss of loved ones, loss of independent physical functioning, declining health, or loss of a job or primary source of income). Older adults also tend to receive much less therapy or skilled outpatient care than is recommended for depression, anxiety, alcohol or drug use and abuse problems, and other mental disorders that are prevalent among this segment of the population (Kane & Kane, 1989). Some of the most common mental health concerns among older adults include Alzheimer's disease, depression, inadequate cardiovascular functioning that affects mental function, mood disorders related to medication use, and conditions associated with metabolic functioning (Stoukides, Holzer, Ritzau & Burbank, 2006). Comprehensive geriatric assessments may miss psychiatric diagnoses and similarly, physicians in geriatric practice may only inadvertently recognize issues related with mental health (Waxman, Carner & Berkenstock, 1984).

The situation described above continues to be problematic as we begin the 21st century. It is further exacerbated by the inadequate supply of trained geriatric health practitioners. Consequently, activity specialists who work in nursing homes, senior centers, adult day care centers, in-home care, assisted-living facilities, and rehabilitation facilities may encounter older adults who are in need of activities to help them achieve and maintain a sense of mental well-being, regardless of whether or not there is a formal diagnosis of mental health disease or disorder.

This chapter discusses strategies that are responsive to changes in the mental health and well-being of older adults. Stressful events in older adulthood that are often the impetus for mental health concerns in late life are explained. The chapter presents an overview of various activities that are used in therapeutic programs with older persons. The following activity modalities are described: reality orientation, sensory stimulation, spiritual activities, therapeutic humor, remotivation therapy, and resocialization activities. Common motivational and leadership techniques that enhance participation in activities that strengthen mental well-being are considered. The chapter concludes with a sample intervention program.

Rationale for Mental Health Activity Intervention

Therapeutic activity intervention is similar to generic rehabilitation programming because the goals involve positive behavioral changes in the cognitive, sensorimotor, and affective domains (Stumbo & Peterson, 2009). Specifically, activity programs based upon individual needs can facilitate positive behavioral change. The older adult who is able to adapt to changes may be more likely function as a complete human being through the integration of these changes into all areas of his or her environment (Greenblatt, 1988). This chapter addresses therapeutic activities that target behavioral change which supports positive mental health and well-being.

In Chapter 6 of this text, several psychological illnesses and psychiatric disorders commonly experienced by older persons were presented. Typical disruptions in the functional mental health of older adults include depression, anxiety disorders, psychotic illnesses, alcoholism, and drug abuse/misuse. Organic diseases, on the other hand, encompass dementia-related syndromes including Alzheimer's disease. Whether the older individual suffers from a cognitive disease or temporary decline in mental health due to depression, therapeutic activity intervention will focus on enhancing overall mental health in areas such adjustment, judgment and decision-making, memory (long- and short-term), affect and emotional stability, reasoning, orientation, and self-identity. Because as high as 20% of the older population experiences depression or other form of mental illness, therapeutic mental health activities are recognized as an important aspect of any activity program for older persons (Stoukides et al., 2006).

Meeting Mental Health Needs Through Activity Intervention

Impaired mental health and well-being in older persons may be caused by either organic brain disease (e.g., Alzheimer's disease or multi-infarct dementia) or difficulties in mental functioning as associated with depression, drug misuse/abuse, alcoholism, adjusting to loss, etc. In any case, the older person displays the need for mental health support and therapy. Reminiscence, life review, validation therapy, reality orientation, sensory stimulation, spirituality, therapeutic humor, remotivation, and resocialization are common approaches that are covered in this chapter.

Reminiscence and Life Review

Reminiscence refers to the vocal or silent recall of events in a person's life, either alone or with other persons. The term *life review* is usually applied to a guided process of reviewing, organizing, and evaluating one's life, in general, in order for the individual to consider his/her life as unique. It is focused on integrating events and experiences into themes as a way to bring one's life into full relief so that one can gain fuller understanding, appreciation, and meaning. The themes generated through life review generally reflect the person's own hopes and expectations (Carroll & Linton, 2006; Woods, Portnoy, Head & Jones, 1992).

Reminiscence groups, on the other hand, are generally a less formal psychotherapeutic approach to recollecting life experiences (Carroll & Linton, 2006). These groups are often used to strengthen self-concept during stressful situations and have the benefit of setting the stage for empathetic support from others in the group. Reminiscence can involve certain positive qualities such as fantasy, simplicity, fun, comfort, empathy, affiliation, history, heritage, legacy, and self-preservation. Reminiscence also is intellectual, rational, emotional, therapeutic, and cultural, as well as involves both passive and active components (Ebersole, 1988). Reminiscence is also distinguished from life review in that life review is commonly a task to be completed in the final phase of life. Life review also embraces the positive functions of reminiscence. Both life review and reminiscence are useful in personal adaptation and produce social benefits as well. Life review may be thought of as a form of structured reminiscence (Butler, 1963).

Assisting older persons with life review promotes self-acceptance and strengthens self-concept (Carroll & Linton, 2006). It is not unlikely that the nature of life review will evoke a sense of regret and sadness at the brevity of life; however, most older adults have the capacity to reconcile their lives and to find meaning, especially with the support of others. The success of life review is difficult to determine because much of the process often occurs within an individual and overt indications of change are not always apparent. For the most part, it's best to encourage achievements within the reminiscence session rather than analyze changes and positive results that may occur outside of the group (Butler, 1963; Woods, Portnoy, Head & Jones, 1992).

Ebersole (1988) provided the following considerations when using reminiscence groups as therapeutic activity:

- Smaller groups work best, maximum size to be no more than six people.
- Maintain a regular schedule in terms of time and place.
- Both short-term and long-term reminiscence groups are effective.
- Use objects (food, pictures, memorabilia) to aid recollections and discussion.
- It is helpful to begin and end with exercises that help participants to relax, stimulate their thinking, and get ready to talk.

Reminiscence and life review have not always been recognized as valuable experiences for older persons and staff members. Reminiscence has been viewed by some as a negative attribute of older persons. Dwelling in the past and repeating stories about the old days were seen as indicators of regression. In more recent years, however, the therapeutic power associated with guided reminiscence and life review have been recognized as valuable at any life stage and most particularly, during periods of transition (Carroll & Linton, 2006; Woods, Portnoy, Head & Jones, 1992).

Group reminiscence can be used to meet many levels of human need. As older persons socialize, they express themselves, share, and mutually value each other for their contributions. In group reminiscence, participants can develop the strength and self-esteem required to actualize their potentials (Carroll & Linton, 2006; Ebersole, 1988). In order to accomplish predetermined treatment goals and objectives, it is helpful to begin with each individual and to focus upon abilities rather than impairment or disabilities.

The overall aims of a reminiscence group include: (a) improved affect, (b) strengthened self-concept, (c) increased socialization, and (d) increased opportunity for others to listen to excerpts from the participant's life. Reminiscence stimulates interest, attention, and interaction, and can be enjoyed by all who are involved, including the activity leader. There also is hope that staff members will retain the knowledge learned about residents during reminiscence and utilize this information during other caregiving activities (Carroll & Linton, 2006; Woods, Portnoy, Head & Jones, 1992).

Reminiscence groups provide a supportive setting for the discussion of problems and the expression of feelings. They promote elevation of mood through enjoyable, entertaining activity. Reminiscence also facilitates supplementary description of self to others, offers opportunities for continuity, and contributes to autonomy and perceived control over one's life. The activity specialist can utilize reminiscence sessions for the evaluation of treatment efficacy by monitoring client confusion, depression, social interaction, and self-esteem prior to the intervention, during the activity, and after termination of the group. Older adults who exhibit impaired memory processes and low self-concept often have the ability to discuss events from the past because of the richness of the association with strong affective memories, repetition, and possibly, memory storage in different areas of the brain other than those that have been damaged by dementia or other illnesses (Burnside & Schmidt, 1994; Harrison, 1980; Holland, 1987; Morris & Koppelman, 1986).

In the course of reminiscence, *triggers* or props are employed and they may be specific or implied. *Triggers* are any type of stimuli that prompt recall. Music, photographs, food, poetry, faces, colors, objects, and odors all may act as triggers. These triggers can be utilized intentionally to facilitate or access particular memories, or used spontaneously during ongoing conversation. Random environmental events also can function as triggers and questions alone may be appropriate to inspire and focus recall (Woods, Portnoy, Head & Jones, 1992).

Validation Therapy

Validation therapy was originated by Naomi Feil (2002) as a communication technique to be used with older adults who are experiencing cognitive disorders or dementia. Specific communication strategies were based on reciprocal respect and acknowledgment. In other words, the central focus of validation therapy is that disoriented older people need to be afforded genuine respect for their feelings rather than simply being dismissed as if their feelings were somehow no longer valid. Feil classified people with disorientation or dementia according to four stages: mal orientation, time confusion, repetitive motion, and vegetative state. The basic principles behind validation therapy include treating all people as unique individuals who are valuable regardless of how disoriented they might be. Nonjudgmental acceptance of older adults with dementia is an essential part of building a trusting and respectful relationship so that broader goals associated with balance and resolution may be attained. The processes of validation therapy are not intended to restore damaged brain tissue, but rather as a means for it can assist in the stimulation of dormant yet intact capacities by acknowledging basic human needs. Validation therapy does not judge, analyze, or intend to change the disoriented person. The goals of becoming and remaining oriented are not emphasized. Validation therapy is used to assist the older disoriented individual in attaining his or her own goals. A validation approach promotes the acceptance of the feelings of the older person with dementia.

Validation is a humanistic approach for providing disoriented older persons with the opportunity to resolve their unfinished conflicts through (a) the expression of their feelings, (b) acknowledgement of their lives through reminiscence, and (c) a coming to peace with their losses (Babins, 1988; Feil, 1989). Validation includes reflection of a person's feelings, assistance in the expression of unmet human needs, restoration of well-established social roles, facilitation of perceptions of well-being, and stimulation of interactions with others (Feil, 1989).

Reality Orientation

Reality orientation is a psychological treatment approach for attending to the problems of confused older adults (Ferrini & Ferrini, 2008; Folsom, 1986). The specific procedures for reality orientation are pragmatic, focused upon daily routines and behavior, and utilize principles of reinforcement to assist clients in maintaining a sense of self, time, and place. Reality orientation concentrates upon supporting clients at their highest level of current functioning and actively presenting them with reality though environmental management, teaching/training, and consistent attitudes of family and staff members (Bowlby, 1993; Edinberg, 1985). Continual consistent and repetitive reminders help to keep the older person oriented to the environment. The effectiveness of reality orientation depends upon this repetitiveness by every person who comes into contact with the confused older person, which can become challenging for caregivers and therapists.

Sensory Stimulation

Sensory stimulation is an individual or group activity for cognitively impaired older adults who have difficulty in relating and responding to their environments. Meaningful and familiar smells, movements, sights, sounds, tastes, and tactile sensations from the immediate and larger surroundings are systematically presented in a format that can be understood by the individual. By focusing attention on specific, concrete, sensory cues, individuals can explore and relate "sensory props" to familiar life experiences. From this process, they are enabled to make appropriate responses to the world. Sensory stimulation is designed to compensate for the sensory deprivation that older persons often suffer as a result of dementia. It has been suggested that individuals who have the ability to participate in the social and self-care aspects of their lives function at a higher level, have higher self-esteem, are calmer, and tend to be more alert (Bowlby, 1993).

Spirituality

Spirituality and religious activity may not necessarily be a part of the daily life experiences of all older adults nonetheless they are considered to be instrumental to happiness, health, and morale (Touhy, 2008). For those persons to whom religion has played a continuing and significant role, they may rely heavily upon maintaining their involvement as a major contributor to self-respect and perceived well-being. Religious behavior is reported to be an effective means of coping and is common among older adults regardless of sex, race, socioeconomic status, or place of residence. There is a significant correlation between positive morale and involvement in religious activities (Bowlby, 1993; Touhy, 2008).

As a lifelong means of coping with stress, personal spirituality and religious practices are negatively affected by the progression of dementia. Individuals afflicted by dementia will require additional support and assistance in order to adapt their means of coping through participation in religious activities. Religious activities can be modified to be compatible with the individual's present abilities. Inclusion in religious activities must be based upon enduring experiences and practices (e.g., weekly devotions, celebration of religious holidays and events), and may be supported by the use of a peer companion system. Spiritual and religious activities should continue to be purposeful and adult-oriented. Religious activities represent a unique method of communication that can provide opportunities for reminiscence, as well as offering meaning, even when standard communication has regressed (Bowlby, 1993; Touhy, 2008).

Therapeutic Humor

There is a complex system of mutual functioning between the human psychological and physiological processes. Laughter is an observable reaction to humorous situations in which muscles are stimulated, heart rate is intensified, and respiration is increased, thereby expanding the exchange of oxygen (Fry, 1971). However, the natural healing powers of the body are often ignored. It is important to recognize that positive emotions (e.g., the experience of humorous moments or material) may produce chemical changes in the brain that are effective in the obstruction of pain. Laughter also facilitates the reduction of stress and therefore, the remission of stress-related illnesses and related pain (Adams & Mc-Guire, 1986; Touhy, 2008).

Improvements in quality of life for those elderly persons who view humorous movies, television programs, or live performances are possible and have been documented. Activity interventions that are founded upon the effective use of humor are beneficial in the care and treatment of older persons. The application of *therapeutic humor* activities that promote amusement and laughter are exceedingly valuable, especially in the later stages of life when additional challenges and compromises in health may be present (Adams & McGuire, 1986).

Remotivation and Resocialization

Remotivation activity intervention attempts to make older adults aware of current surroundings while providing opportunities for socialization. It is a useful intervention with older adults who are withdrawn and have some cognitive impairment (Hooyman & Kiyak, 2008). Remotivation activities employ the practice of memory and/or cognitive skills, as well as verbal abilities, through which the participant gains a sense dignity and self-esteem. Remotivation groups consist of structured sessions that are usually held once or twice a week for 12 sessions. Meetings last from 30 minutes to one hour depending upon the attention of the group (Dennis, 1994).

Resocialization activity intervention is a less structured discussion approach used to maintain cognitive functioning, as well as to focus upon relationships and feelings. Resocialization is a method utilized for the readjustment of confused or withdrawn clients (Edinberg, 1985). Resocialization groups provide the older client with opportunities to establish new relationships, as well as to renew long-term friendships (Herrera, 1983). The differences among reality orientation, remotivation, and resocialization are described in Figure 13.1.

Motivational and Leadership Techniques

Motivation can be defined as a process that arouses and instigates behavior, provides purpose and direction, permits behavior to continue, and guides behavior preferences (Wlodkowski, 1978). Some factors that may be effective in motivating desired behaviors include: explanation of benefits; avoidance of pretense; opportunities for competition; and attractive, supportive environments (Teaff, 1985). Other motivating factors include: (a) a comfortable, relaxed, nonthreatening environment; (b) a structure based upon success experiences; (c) the promotion of dignity; (d) the availability of trained, competent leadership; and (e) the

Reality Orientation	Remotivation	Resocialization
Structured	Structured	Unstructured
Refreshments may be served	Refreshments not served	Refreshments served
Reminds of who, where, why, and what	Stimulates desire to function in society	Encourages participation
Group size: 3 to 5	Group size: 5 to 12	Group size: 5 to 17
Meeting one-half hour daily	Meeting one to two times per week for one-half to one hour	Meeting three times per week for one-half to one hour
Planned procedures; reality-centered objects	Preselected and reality-centered objects	No planned topic; group-centered feelings
Periodic reality orientation	Progress ratings	Periodic progress notes
Emphasis on time, place, person	No discussion of religion, politics, or death	Any topic freely discussed
Use of part of the mind still intact	Untouched area of mind	Store of memories and experiences
Greeting, handshake and/or physical contact upon leaving	No physical contact	Greeting, handshake upon leaving
Conducted by trained aides and activity assistants	Conducted by trained psychiatric aides	Conducted by RN/LPN, aides, and program assistants

Note: Adapted from Barnes, Stack & Shore, 1973.

Figure 13.1 Differences between Reality Orientation, Remotivation, and Resocialization

use of persuasive, informative promotion of activities (McGuire, 1987).

A responsibility of the activity specialist is to enhance motivation for participation and this may require considerable leadership creativity. Activities generally are not longer than two hours, with 45 minutes to an hour being most appropriate duration. The length of an activity depends upon its nature, number of rest periods provided, and interest and endurance of the participants. The physical setting where activities are conducted also is an important consideration. It is difficult to conduct discussion groups in a large room where other activities are being accommodated. If a small, quiet room is not available, the manipulation of furniture to provide a secluded corner for discussion may be an acceptable alternative (Salamon, 1986).

If there is only one group leader, it is better to keep group size small—six to eight members. The intensity of a group experience is likely to diminish proportionately as membership increases. It is best not to mix participants who have high levels of cognitive impairment with alert individuals in the same group, which might create additional problems. The group is placed in a circle to maximize vision and hearing. Individual attention is provided at the beginning and end of a group session. Personal names are used often. It is a good idea to keep a small number of simple rules. The purposes and goals of the group are developed in collaboration between the leader and the group members. Touching and closeness are of critical importance. The group leader will share things about herself or himself; group members often will not allow the leader to escape being an active member of the group. Dealing with sad themes is also a part of the group leader's role (Burnside & Schmidt, 1994).

Leadership involves human behavior and social interactions. Because older people are a heterogeneous group, optimizing performance in learning, problem solving, and memory tasks may require special methods during certain activities. In various learning tasks, the activity specialist enhances participation through the use of:

- slow, preferably self-paced, instruction;
- concrete, directly relevant material;
- repeated exposure to the material to be learned;
- a narrow focus to avoid diffusion of interest;
- generalization;
- a structured learning process; and
- multiple opportunities for feedback (Patrick, 1987).

The "here and now" can be effectively used to initiate a group. The use of common topics, such as the weather or the seasons, is acceptable for beginning a group session. Through the use of praise and compliments that are sincere and free-flowing, self-esteem is nurtured. The group leader also must be willing to express his or her own feelings (Burnside & Schmidt, 1994).

Activity programs emphasize the dignity of the individual. Depersonalization occurs when programming details and rules take precedence over the specific needs of the participants. Choice, independence, and control in activity programs is encouraged for all persons who are involved in the program. Those individuals who take part in activity programs prefer to have input into all aspects of the program including activities, leadership, scheduling, and accessible locations. Strong activity programs reflect flexibility in order to address the needs of the participants rather than forcing individuals to meet fixed requirements. Individuals need challenges and excitement in their lives. Stimulation is vitally important for persons who reside in nonstimulating institutions or live fairly passive lives. Activity programs can incorporate stimulation into the daily routines of elders through incorporating variety and progression (McGuire, 1987).

Additional motivational techniques may include (a) praise after successful completion of a task, (b) opportunities for participants to feel useful, (c) the use of frequent reminders, (d) being careful to speak directly to the individual, (e) providing continual reinforcement of reality, and (f) by extending personal invitations. Other areas to consider when attempting to motivate and encourage participation are promoting self-esteem

and status, relating to lifelong interests, overcoming boredom, socializing, building legitimacy and relevancy of the activity tasks, and providing refreshments (Cunninghis, 1989).

A Sample Program (Cognitive Remediation)

The following program is suggested as representative of the types of therapeutic activities—reminiscence and life review, validation therapy, reality orientation, sensory stimulation, spirituality, therapeutic humor, and remotivation and resocialization—that can be used to remediate the cognitive abilities of older adults when impairment is present. The program is adaptable to a variety of surroundings such as public recreation facilities, senior centers, adult day care, assisted living facilities, retirement communities, rehabilitation centers, and nursing homes. The activity specialist will develop additional program components such as facility preparations, equipment and supplies, expenses, staffing, and publicity in order to effectively utilize the proposed framework.

Program Purpose:

The purpose of this program is to provide older adults with an opportunity to experience a diversity of cognitive activities that influence awareness, promote self-esteem, reduce feelings of isolation, encourage interaction with others, reinforce desired behaviors, challenge and stimulate the client, and provide an environment where achievement and recognition are possible. The program is based upon the following principles:

1. Older persons prefer a variety of unique program activities in order to address individual cognitive abilities, interests, and requirements. The following objectives are relevant for enhanced activity involvement:
   (a) to support recognition of surroundings,
   (b) to foster appreciation of self,
   (c) to maintain supportive environments,
   (d) to cultivate and nurture supportive relationships,
   (e) to arouse the senses,
   (f) to provide opportunities for mastery,
   (g) to enhance possibilities for acknowledgment, and
   (h) to inspire pertinent emotion and behavior.

2. The utilization of local community resources, associations, and agencies to assist in meeting

the mental health needs of older adults will contribute to the success of a therapeutic cognitive activity program.

3. Older individuals prefer activities that encourage self-renewal.

4. Older persons prefer to be involved in the planning, implementation, and evaluation of activities and programs, policies, and procedures that are designed to meet their mental health needs.

ACTIVITY AREA I— REMINISCENCE AND LIFE REVIEW

Target Goal:

Reminiscence and life review activities are planned and implemented in order to provide the following benefits to older adult participants:

(a) reduce apathy and confusion,
(b) relieve depression,
(c) increase social interaction,
(d) increase life satisfaction,
(e) improve morale,
(f) enhance self-esteem,
(g) evoke creativity,
(h) increase control over the environment, and
(i) evaluate ego integrity (Burnside & Schmidt, 1994).

Enabling Objectives:

▪ To assess the interests of potential group members and to provide a variety of program formats that correspond to these interests.

▪ To determine resources that are required for successful reminiscence group activities.

▪ To devise an agenda of prospective reminiscence topics or themes, and to gather provoking reinforcements.

▪ To evaluate reminiscence activities and group participants for progress and changes, as needed.

Activity Suggestions: *Memory Stimulation*

A number of topics can be effectively used to stimulate reminiscence and life review in group or individual discussion sessions (Jones, 1992). Suggested topics are organized in Figure 13.2.

In addition to using a topical approach, lead questions also produce quality reminiscence or life review sessions. Haight (1992) recommended the use of the following lead questions:

1. If you could stay the same age all of your life, what age would you choose? Why?

2. What are the best things about the age that you are now?

3. What are the worst things about being the age you are now?

4. What are the most important things to you in your life today?

5. What do you fear will happen to you as you grow older?

6. What do you hope will happen to you as you grow older?

7. Have you enjoyed participating in the review of your life?

With any group process, there are certain procedural steps that will enhance a successful outcome for the participants. Orienting the participants to the environment, each other, and the goals of the group is the first step. As discussion is set up by the suggestion of a topic or a lead question, group leader can facilitate conversation by seeking a response from participants who are known to be more comfortable in group situations. As discussion progresses, the regulation of participation to ensure involvement of all participants will be an important task for the leader. Pointing out important relationships, events, and happenings on an individual basis and linking them across participants helps the group to develop an "identity." Finally, closing the discussion with a summary of the main contributions, as well as issues that may need to be continued for resolution is important to the overall success of reminiscence or life review as a group activity. A positive experience for all participants is enhanced by creating an environment of support and acceptance. Two-way communication, a lack of pressure, room for sharing personal mementos, and affirmation of the importance of each participant are just some of the ways to build a supportive environment for reminiscence or life review activities.

Life review and reminiscence need not only be undertaken as a group activity. Individuals can be encouraged to engage in bibliotherapy as a means for completing a life review. For individuals who are not interested in writing, the audiotaped or videotaped life review can provide both therapeutic benefits and a documented record for other family members (Dreher, 1987).

Implementation and Materials Suggestions:

There are several important factors to consider in selecting the members for reminiscence or life review groups. Potential group members are approached individually

Childhood:
    Games played, hobbies
    Favorite toy
    Favorite food
    Where did you grow up?
    What did you want to be?
    Family stories, traditions
    Celebrations, holidays, movies
    Schooling, clubs
    Religious beliefs and practices

Adolescence:
    Entering high school
    Graduation
    Clubs, activities, music
    Favorite books
    Best friends
    Hobbies
    Part-time jobs
    Clothing, cards, dating
    Radio programs, television programs

Early Adult Years:
    Dating
    First paycheck, salary
    When did you move from your parents' home?
    Entertainment
    Furnishing own home
    Things done alone
    Where did you meet spouse?

Marriage:
    How long did you know spouse before
      marriage?
    Age at marriage
    Wedding—best man, maid of honor
    Planning for marriage
    First home as married couple
    Adjusting to marriage
    Were you surprised to marry person that
      you did?

Childbearing/Family Building:
    How many children?
    Special events in their lives
    Help from spouse in rearing children
    Positive and negative aspects of being a parent
    Child's first words
    Children moving from home

Work and Avocations:
    Clubs and Organizations
    Church
    Politics
    Type of work
    Changes in work

Health:
    Major illnesses
    General health
    Fitness
    Involvement in activities

Memories of People/Pets:
    Parents, brothers, sisters
    Grandparents
    Relatives
    Friends
    Teachers, actors, heroes
    Pets
    Helping mother and father

Memories of Places:
    Holidays, vacations
    Hideaways
    Bedroom, home
    Where have you lived?

Memories of Events:
    Holidays, vacations
    Celebrations

Other Memories:
    Historical events
    How did you view self?
    Being an American

Favorite Things:
    People
    Places
    Events

Seeking Advice:
    Getting along with others
    Marriage, rearing children
    Work, handling finances
    Preparation for retirement

Hardest Times and Things that Might
Have Happened Differently:
    Job loss
    Parents' death
    Children leaving home

Note: Developed from information contained in Jones & Miesen, 1992.

Figure 13.2 Examples of Stimulus Topics for Reminiscence and Life Review

and following an explanation of the purpose of the group, a verbal contract is established. Personal choice and an understanding of the commitment needed for participation in the group significantly add to active involvement in the group process. It also is important to inform each prospective member of the other group membership. It is unrealistic to expect people to gather arbitrarily and share important memories without an orientation to the process and the other members of the group (Ebersole, 1988).

Reminiscence groups meet regularly at the same time and place each week. Group meetings become an anticipated, which adds to the structure of the participants' lives. Occasionally, a group member may be unable to get out of bed or attend the group meeting. Barring restrictive factors, the group can meet at the member's bedside or contact the absent participant. Consideration of the relevance for such an action would include: meaning to other members, adaptability of the group, and the possibility of manipulation (Ebersole, 1988).

The group process includes a beginning, a working phase, and termination. The working phase may present the most difficulty when occasions arise that the reminiscence group leader is facilitating group members with sad subject matter. Termination also can be painful, but if planned early in the group, it can contribute to growth experiences (Ebersole, 1988).

Short-term groups are more effective when there is more structure. For longer term groups, as the group members become more familiar with each other, the group process should flow with a lessening of structured content. In either case, maintaining the flexibility needed to meet the needs of the participants is important. The content areas for reminiscence can be enhanced by the use of music, bright visual aids, and objects or memorabilia that are not fragile or difficult to handle. Various scents and aromas are among the most powerful stimuli for reminiscence (Ebersole, 1988).

Short-term reminiscence groups (10 weeks or less) should be small and focused upon particular group needs. Long-term groups can be conducted indefinitely with periodic reassessment and redefinition of goals. Group members should be actively involved in the process and in the admission of new members once the group is well-established. It also is important to consider all personnel affected by group meetings because they will impact the success or failure of the group. Other staff members can assist by reminding group participants of meeting times, and by helping them to prepare for and attend the meetings on time (Ebersole, 1988).

Reminiscence may be transformed into a social visit or occasion on an individual basis by conducting the session in a resident's room or in other areas in which the resident may feel comfortable such as the lounge, cafeteria, or garden. Occasionally, a family member of the resident can be present in order to provide *triggers* that may elicit a response or to confirm factual details in the life review process (Woods, Portnoy, Head, & Jones, 1992). Community outings also are an important adjunct to reminiscence groups. Attending a nostalgic movie, seeing a band concert in the park, viewing a live fireworks display, or eating at a restaurant with a memorable decor are all catalysts for reminiscence (Ebersole, 1988).

ACTIVITY AREA II— VALIDATION THERAPY

Target Goal:

The use of validation therapy with confused, disoriented, or demented older persons is targeted toward assisting them to be as happy as possible by accepting them as they are, thereby reducing anxiety and frustration. It is anticipated that personal well-being will be promoted through the use of validation therapy (Feil, 1989).

Enabling Objectives:

- To assess the capacities of potential group members and to supply purposeful activities that satisfy the needs of the individual.
- To ascertain the resources essential for successful implementation of various validation activities.
- To plan a feasible program of topics and themes, and to determine positive reinforcements.
- To evaluate validation activities and group members for progress and to make alterations, as needed.

Activity Suggestions: *Unresolved Conflicts*

Issues and themes for discussion usually include death, family relations, loneliness, and disappointments. The selection of a topic is based upon areas of conflict for the individual. Questions, manipulation of an assortment of items, singing, acting out, and role play are methods that can be used by clients to express themselves (Babins, 1988).

Implementation and Materials Suggestions:

Validation therapy can be used in association with other programs without attempting to alter the older person's concept of reality. A group of five or six people can meet in a group to converse about unresolved personal conflicts. The activity specialist facilitates the discussion by posing basic questions such as who, what, where, and when. These questions provide opportunities for individuals to describe relevant events in their lives (Babins, 1988).

Individualized plans will consider the older adult's abilities for attaining desired outcomes. Through the use of tolerance and recognition, activity leaders and other group members will have the ability to validate and affirm the value of each individual. Validation requires that meaningful expressions of the person's inner-self are acknowledged and accommodated (Taft, Delaney, Seman & Stansell, 1993).

ACTIVITY AREA III— REALITY ORIENTATION

Target Goal:

According to Herrera (1983), reality orientation activities can be effectively used to reach several treatment goals:

- To promote the awareness of daily living factors in the immediate environment.
- To develop and/or maintain interactions with surroundings, peers, and caregivers.
- To supply information regarding person, time, place, and things.
- To correct disoriented information.
- To reinforce behaviors that approximate or reflect meaningful interactions with the environment.

Enabling Objectives:

The above treatment goals are attained through the following enabling objectives:

- To assess the needs and abilities of potential group members, and to provide meaningful reality orientation activities that address these needs and capacities.
- To determine the resources necessary for successful implementation of reality orientation activities.
- To devise a probable agenda of topics and themes, and to gather motivating reinforcements.
- To evaluate reality orientation activities and group participants for progress and for changes, as required.

Activity Suggestions: *Reinforcement of Person, Time, and Place*

Basic, current, and personal information are presented and reviewed with group members. The group leader should attempt to improve the ability of members to identify information related to person, time, and place, and to act upon the information in an appropriate manner. The reinforcement of members for correct responses and the repetition of information are aspects of the treatment process. Discussion is centered on a variety of subjects that are related to the interests of the participants such as holidays, weather, and current events (Herrera, 1983; Williams, 1994).

Implementation and Materials Suggestions:

Instructional tools such as large calendars, clocks, telephones, mailboxes, and a reality orientation board are utilized to stimulate the group. Verbal and nonverbal communication is used to emphasize various concepts. Positive reinforcement is employed within a strategy of active or passive friendliness, depending upon the preferences of the client (Herrera, 1983; Williams, 1994).

ACTIVITY AREA IV— SENSORY STIMULATION

Target Goal:

The target goal of activities in this area is to stimulate the individual senses on a regular basis in order to maintain their functional abilities in daily life (Herrera, 1983).

Enabling Objectives:

- To assess the needs and abilities of possible group members, and to provide beneficial sensory stimulation activities that consider these needs and capacities.
- To determine the resources required for effective implementation of sensory stimulation activities.
- To prepare a reasonable schedule of subjects and themes, and to consider potential motivating reinforcements.
- To evaluate sensory stimulation activities and group members for progress and for changes, as needed.

Activity Suggestions: *Touch, Vision, Hearing, Taste, and Smell*

Activities that stimulate the senses can follow any of the following strategies (Elliott & Sorg-Elliott, 1991):

- the participant's skin can be stroked with various textures.
- hand gestures may be used to act out hello, stop, thin, tall, etc.
- the participant can clap hands, reach out, make a fist, laugh, smile, frown, etc.
- a tape recording of people laughing, crying, clapping, etc. may be played in order to determine if the participant can identify the actions.
- different sizes and textures of balls may be passed, squeezed, and kicked.
- the participant can be asked to recognize other persons by name.
- a ball may be bounced and the participant can count the number of times that it is bounced.
- the game "Simon Says" may be utilized to accomplish exercises such as lifting the arms over the head, moving the arms to the side, stepping to the front and stepping to the back, etc.
- a telephone can be used with the participant being encouraged to answer the phone when it rings.
- a variety of short songs can be played on a portable radio/CD player near the participant.

Implementation and Materials Suggestions:

A variety of activities and objects may be used to awaken the senses such as:

(a) flashlights in a darkened room and colorful objects to stimulate vision;
(b) sharp smells contrasted with sweet smelling substances to exercise the sense of smell; and
(c) recordings, musical instruments, and whispering to provide a diversity of sounds that augment hearing.

Candy, pickles, and potato chips can demonstrate differing types of taste. Soft, hard, smooth, rough, hot, and cold objects should offer stimuli for the sense of touch (Herrera, 1983).

ACTIVITY AREA V— SPIRITUALITY

Target Goal:

Spiritual activities are used to provide a means of coping with stress, promote self-esteem, and foster a general sense of well-being (Bowlby, 1993).

Enabling Objectives:

- To assess the needs of individual participants in regard to spiritual needs.
- To provide meaningful religious activities that address these needs.
- To determine the resources and services that are available in the community for meeting the religious needs of the program participants.
- To maintain a reasonable schedule of spiritual activities as motivation and reinforcement of personal religious beliefs for participants of various faiths.
- To evaluate spiritual activities, group members, and spiritual changes, if any, in individual participants.

Activity Suggestions: *Religious Services*

Spiritual activity groups can serve the purposes of worship, education, support, and introspection. Spiritual gatherings may include recurrent worship services, religious discussions, singing of hymns, world religious education sessions, and intergenerational religious projects (Szekais, 1986).

Implementation and Materials Suggestions:

Generally, younger participants are involved in more formal or organized religious activities, and older individuals engage in more private devotional endeavors. The spiritual well-being of older persons is enhanced by the relationship one has with one's God, self, community, and the environment. Engaging in organized religious activities is a means for affirming, nurturing, and celebrating the wholeness of life (Young & Dowling, 1987).

Spiritual groups can be structured to meet the needs individuals at the same level of impairment, or to include individuals of various functional skill levels. Regular worship, as well as the sharing of spiritual beliefs and values through discussion groups, are activities that are responsive to the innermost needs of many elderly persons (Szekais, 1986).

ACTIVITY AREA VI—
THERAPEUTIC HUMOR

Target Goal:

Participants in activities that use therapeutic humor receive many benefits. The goals of therapeutic humor activities are to enhance self-concept, provide a means for coping with stress, and promote positive affect and psychological well-being (Martin, Kuiper, Olinger & Dance, 1993).

Enabling Objectives:

- To assess the interests and abilities of older persons for their involvement in activities and events that involve humor and laughter
- To provide activities that satisfy these interests and abilities.
- To determine the resources necessary for the beneficial implementation of humorous activities.
- To maintain a feasible schedule of humorous and laughter-provoking activities, and to clarify appropriate reinforcements for the perpetuation of humor and laughter.
- To evaluate the use of therapeutic humor with individual group members, and to make changes as needed.

Activity Suggestions: *Evoking Laughter*

Reminiscence activities such as humorous anecdotes, favorite stories, and viewing old television comedy shows (e.g., *I Love Lucy* or *The Honeymooners*) and comedy movies can reaffirm the pleasures of life. Sing-alongs, topical or thematic parties, humorous readings, and the use of exaggeration and absurdity also are effective for evoking laughter and enjoyment (McGuire & Boyd, 1993).

Implementation and Materials Suggestions:

The physical act of laughing; the social act of joke telling; and involvement in movies, other humorous activities, and productions may each result in better physical and emotional health (Touhy, 2008). The ability to see the humor in detrimental situations also is an effective way to alleviate potentially harmful or unhealthy consequences. Humor can be used to transform difficult circumstances into humorous situations. Laughing with others is natural and communicates the themes of community, vitality, and disclosure (McGuire & Boyd, 1993).

ACTIVITY AREA VII—
REMOTIVATION AND RESOCIALIZATION

Target Goal:

Remotivation and resocialization activity programs target several treatment goals for participants (Burnside & Schmidt, 1994; Dennis, 1994). These treatment goals include:

- To establish a climate of acceptance.
- To create a bridge to reality.
- To share and to appreciate the function of the world.
- To maintain an atmosphere of appreciation.
- To improve communication.
- To decrease withdrawal and isolation.
- To care for and enjoy other persons.

Enabling Objectives:

- To assess the interests and abilities of potential group members.
- To provide beneficial remotivation and resocialization activities that address these interests and capabilities.
- To determine the resources necessary for the successful implementation of remotivation and resocialization activities.
- To maintain a reasonable schedule of remotivation and resocialization activities, and to discover acceptable reinforcements.
- To evaluate resocialization and remotivation activities and group members in order to determine progress and to make changes, as needed.

Activity Suggestions: *Discussion Groups and Word Games*

Topics for remotivation groups include: vacations, holidays, hobbies, gardening, sports, pets, art, nature, transportation, weather, and animals (Dennis, 1994). Familiar activities such as spelling bees, Name That Tune, finish the proverb or weather saying, and simple math problems may be utilized in resocialization groups. Other examples of resocialization activities might include: well-known topics and objects, open ended statements, word scrambles, special dinners, and It's on a Penny (Elliott & Sorg-Elliott, 1991).

Implementation and Materials Suggestions:

Each remotivation session is based upon a different topic. The topics that are used will represent the diverse backgrounds, experiences, and interests of elderly group members, and must directly tempt as many senses as possible. Visual aids and appropriate objects can be used to maintain a high level of attention, interest, and response. Visual aids are passed from one person to another in order to encourage communication among group members. The group is structured to focus discussion on the things that constitute the real world of the participants (Dennis, 1994).

Resocialization groups provide elderly participants with frequent exposure to experiences which promote the feeling that life is worth living. Group members focus upon their relationships with each other. The group leader provides a model of behavior with his or her actions during the group, recognition of group members, and nonevaluative conversation. Resocialization activities should establish an atmosphere of acceptance and freedom of expression where group participants may discuss the concerns of daily living and enjoyable experiences that conceivably might be dismissed as insignificant (Herrera, 1983).

Summary

A variety of therapeutic cognitive activities are introduced in this chapter including reminiscence and life review, reality orientation, sensory training, spiritual activities, the application of therapeutic humor, remotivation, and resocialization. The use of these activities is intended to emphasize abilities rather than to focus upon impairment or disability. The human needs of older persons require that activity staff positively and creatively work to meet the mental health concerns of the aging participant. Interventions and methods are designed to nurture the potentials of elderly individuals, as well as to assist in their adjustments and transitions that often accompany the older adult life stages.

Various motivational and leadership skills and techniques are presented at the end of the chapter along with a listing of additional activity resources (see Figure 13.3). The sample program of therapeutic cognitive activities illustrates programming to meet the cognitive and affective needs of older persons. Supportive, caring environments that actualize control, choice, adaptation, and coping skills can effectively influence the well-being of elderly individuals.

Comprehension Questions

The reader can check for comprehension of the material presented in this chapter by answering the following questions:

1. Describe four different activity types that can be used in cognitive intervention with older adults.

2. Outline a sample activity program to use with older adults who have cognitive impairment. Include the target goals, enabling objectives, suggested activities, and implementation plan.

3. Discuss motivational and leadership strategies that can be effectively used with older adults who have cognitive impairment to enhance their participation in therapeutic activity programs.

References

Adams, E. R. & McGuire, F. A. (1986). Is laughter the best medicine? A study of the effects of humor on perceived pain and affect. In P. M. Foster (Ed.), *Therapeutic activities with the impaired elderly* (157–175). New York, NY: Haworth Press.

Babins, L. (1988). Conceptual analysis of validation therapy. *International Journal of Aging and Human Development, 26*(3), 161–168.

Barnes, E., Stack, A. & Shore, H. (1973). Guidelines to treatment modalities and methods for use with the aged. *Gerontologist, 13*(4), 513–527.

Bowlby, C. (1993). *Therapeutic activities with persons disabled by Alzheimer's disease and related disorders.* Gaithersburg, MD: Aspen Publishers.

Burbank, P. M. (Ed.). (2006). *Vulnerable older adults: Health care needs and interventions.* New York, NY: Springer.

Burnside, I. M. & Schmidt, M. G. (1994). *Working with older adults: Group processes and techniques* (3rd ed.). Boston, MA: Jones and Bartlett.

Butler, R. N. (1963). The life review: An interpretation of reminiscence in the aged. *Psychiatry, 26*, 65–76.

Carroll, D. W. & Linton, A. D. (2007). Chapter 20. Age-related psychological changes. In A. D. Linton & H. W. Lach (Eds.), *Matteson & McConnell's Gerontological Nursing: Concepts and Practices* (3rd ed.). St. Louis, MO: Elsevier/Saunders.

Cunninghis, R. N. (1989). The purpose and meaning of activities. In E. S. Deichman & R. Kociecki (Eds.), *Working with the elderly: An introduction* (151–170). Buffalo, NY: Prometheus Books.

Dennis, H. (1994). Remotivation groups. In I. M. Burnside & M. G. Schmidt, *Working with older adults: Group processes and techniques* (3rd ed.) (153–162). Boston, MA: Jones and Bartlett.

Activities, Adaptation, and Aging is a practical journal published quarterly and including articles on activities.
   Address: Haworth Press, 10 Alice Street, Binghamton, NY 13904-1580
   Telephone: 800-429-6784
   Product Details: ISSN: 0192-4788 Electronic—ISSN: 1544-4368 SKU: J016v32

ElderCare Activities Guide (formerly *Activity Director's Guid*e) is a bimonthly magazine that provides useful activities, calendars, therapeutic activities and programs, feature stories, specialized activities for Alzheimer's patients and other disease conditions, professional news, medical news and much more!
   Address: Freiberg Press, Inc., P.O. Box 612, Cedar Falls, IA 50613
   Telephone: 800-354-3371; Fax: 319-553-0644
   Online: http://www.activities4elders.com/E-mail: klynch@cfu.net

The American Association of Retired Persons (AARP) offers resources for reminiscence, intergenerational programs, and other books on various topics, as well as audiovisual materials for loan. American Association of Retired Persons, 1909 K Street, NW, Suite 400, Washington, DC 20036
   Telephone: 202-296-5960

Eldergames Inc. offers a variety of materials for various functional levels such as memory games, trivia questions, and fabric books for stimulation.
   Address: Eldergames, 11820 Parklawn Drive, Suite 200, Rockville, MD 20852
   Telephone: 301-881-8782

Eldergames Project is based on the importance of play for older adults. The project is developing information technology based games with therapeutic value.
   ElderGames Project: Malena Fabregat and Francisco Ibanez
   E-mail: eldergames@aiju.info

National Council on Aging (NCOA) has many resources for purchase including games for older adults, reminiscence books, trivia books, and programming guides.
   Address: NCOA, 1901 L. Street, NW, 4th Floor, Washington, DC 20036
   Telephone: 202-479-1200
   Online: http://www.ncoa.org

Therapeutic Recreation Directory is an online resource that contains links, games, and a directory of contacts. The directory has no affiliations with organizations and is an independent web site.
   Online: http://www.recreationtherapy.com

Figure 13.3 Resources for Cognitive Remediation Programs

Dreher, B. B. (1987). Communication skills for working with elders. *Springer Series on Adulthood and Aging, 17*. New York, NY: Springer.

Ebersole, P. P. (1988). Establishing reminiscing groups. In I. M. Burnside (Ed.), *Working with the elderly: Group processes and techniques* (2nd ed.) (236–254). North Scituate, MA: Duxbury.

Edinberg, M. A. (1985). *Mental health practice with the elderly*. Englewood Cliffs, NJ: Prentice-Hall.

Elliott, J. E. & Sorg-Elliott, J. A. (1991). *Recreation programming and activities for older adults*. State College, PA: Venture Publishing, Inc.

Feil, N. (1989). Validation therapy with late-onset dementia populations. In G. M. M. Jones & B. M. L.

Miesen (Eds.), *Caregiving in dementia: Research and applications* (199–218). NY: Routledge.

Feil, N. (2002). *The validation breakthrough: Simple techniques for communicating with people with Alzheimer's-type dementia* (2nd ed.). Baltimore, MD: Health Professions Press. (revised by V. De Klerk-Rubin)

Ferrini, A. F. & Ferrini, R. L. (2008). *Health in the later years*. (4th ed.). Boston, MA: McGraw Hill.

Folsom, G. S. (1986). "Worth repeating" reality orientation: Full circle. In P. M. Foster (Ed.), *Therapeutic activities with the impaired elderly* (65–73). New York, NY: Haworth Press.

Fry, W. F. (1971). Laughter: Is it the best medicine? *Stanford, M. D., 10*, 16–20.

Greenblatt, F. S. (1988). *Therapeutic recreation for long-term care facilities.* New York, NY: Human Sciences.

Haight, B. (1992). The structured life-review process: A community approach to the aging client. In G. M. M. Jones & B. M. L. Miesen (Eds.), *Caregiving in dementia: Research and applications* (272–292). New York, NY: Routledge.

Harrison, C. L. (1980). Therapeutic art programs around the world - XIII: Creative arts for older people in the community. *American Journal of Art Therapy, 19,* 99–101.

Herrera, P. M. (1983). *Innovative programming for the aging and aged mentally retarded developmentally disabled adult.* Akron, OH: Exploration Series.

Holland, L. (1987). Life review and communication therapy for dementia patients. *Clinical Gerontologist, 6*(3), 62–65.

Hooyman, N. R. & Kiyak, H. A. (2008). *Social gerontology: A multidisciplinary perspective* (6th ed.). Boston, MA: Allyn and Bacon.

Jones, G. M. M. & Miesen, B. M. L. (1992). *Caregiving in dementia: Research and applications.* New York, NY: Routledge.

Kane, R. L. & Kane, R. A. (1989). Transitions in long-term care. In M. G. Ory & K. Bond (Eds.), *Aging and health care: Social science and policy perspectives* (217–243). New York, NY: Routledge.

Martin, R. A., Kuiper, N. A., Olinger, J. & Dance, K. A. (1993). Humor, coping with stress, self-concept, and psychological well-being. *Humor, 6*(1), 89–104.

McGuire, F. A. (1987). Recreation for the frail elderly. In M. J. Keller & N. J. Osgood (Eds.), *Dynamic leisure programming with older adults* (99–106). Alexandria, VA: National Recreation and Park Association.

McGuire, F. A. & Boyd, R. K. (1993). The role of humor in enhancing the quality of later life. In J. R. Kelly (Ed.), *Activity and aging: Staying involved in later life* (164–173). Newbury Park, CA: Sage Publications.

Morris, R. & Koppelman, M. (1986). Memory deficits in Alzheimer-type dementia: A review. *Quarterly Journal of Experimental Psychology, 38,* 575–603.

Patrick, G. D. (1987). The uses of recreation in geropsychiatry. In M. J. Keller & N. J. Osgood (Eds.), *Dynamic leisure programming with older adults* (85–97). Alexandria, VA: National Recreation and Park Association.

Salamon, M. J. (1986). A protocol for recreation and socialization programs for the aged. In P. M. Fos-ter (Ed.), *Therapeutic activities with the impaired elderly* (47–56). New York, NY: Haworth Press.

Stoukides, J., Holzer, C., Ritzau, J. & Burbank, P. (2006). Health issues of frail older adults. In P. M. Burbank (Ed.), *Vulnerable older adults: Health care needs and interventions* (3–24). New York, NY: Springer.

Stumbo, N. J. & Peterson, C. A. (2009). *Therapeutic recreation program design: principles and procedures* (5th ed.). San Francisco, CA: Pearson/Benjamin-Cummings.

Szekais, B. (1986). Therapeutic group activities. *Activities, Adaptation, and Aging, 8*(3–4), 11–20.

Taft, L. B., Delaney, K., Seman, D. & Stansell, J. (1993). Dementia care: Creating a therapeutic milieu. *Journal of Gerontological Nursing, 19,* 30–39.

Teaff, J. D. (1985). *Leisure services with the elderly.* St. Louis, MO: Times Mirror/Mosby.

Touhy, T. (2008). Chapter 27. Self-actualization, spirituality, and transcendence. In P. Ebersole, P. Hess, T. A. Touhy, K. Jett & A. S. Luggen (Eds.), *Toward health aging: Human needs & nursing response* (666–696). St. Louis, MO: Elsevier/Mosby.

Waxman, H. M., Carner, E. A. & Berkenstock, G. (1984). Job turnover and job satisfaction among nursing home aides. *Gerontologist, 24*(5), 503–509.

Williams, E. M. (1994). Reality orientation groups. In I. M. Burnside & M. G. Schmidt, *Working with older adults: Group processes and techniques* (3rd ed.)(139–152). Boston, MA: Jones and Bartlett.

Wlodkowski, R. J. (1978). *Motivation and teaching: A practical guide.* Washington, DC: National Education Association.

Woods, R. T., Portnoy, S., Head, D. & Jones, G. M. M. (1992). Reminiscence and life review with persons with dementia: Which way forward? In G. M. M. Jones & B. M. L. Miesen (Eds.), *Caregiving in dementia: Research and applications* (137–161). New York, NY: Routledge.

Young, G. & Dowling, W. (1987). Dimensions of religiosity in old age: Accounting for variation in types of participation. *Journal of Gerontology, 42*(4), 376–380.

• CHAPTER 14 •
Psychological Activities

Learning Objectives

1. To become familiar with the use of activities that meet the psychosocial needs of older adults.

2. To identify common activities that are appropriate to use in psychosocial therapeutic intervention with older clients.

3. To describe a sample psychosocial activity plan in therapeutic intervention with older clients.

4. To understand and apply therapeutic activity intervention in the following areas: intergenerational activities; socialization activities and special events; hobbies, crafts, and games; travel and outdoor activities; and other therapies (e.g., pet, horticulture, music, dance, art).

Key Terms

*   Adaptation
*   Adjustment
*   Creativity
*   Intergenerational
*   Psychosocial
*   Socialization
*   Social Network

Introduction

Socializing plays an important role in most peoples' lives. A broad range of activities may be used to address the psychosocial needs of older adults such as

(a) maintaining social relationships,

(b) expressing one's identity through appropriate and valued social roles,

(c) supporting self-esteem,

(d) communicating feelings with others and talking about things that are important,

(e) preserving a sense of autonomy and control over one's life, and

(f) generally maintaining a sense of connection with the social customs and aspects of everyday life in the community (Zgola, 1987).

Previously in this book the importance of activity in adjusting to later life changes in health, physical functioning, mental alertness, and social roles was stressed. This chapter focuses on changes in the psychosocial domain; that is, the use of activities in meeting psychosocial needs associated with older adulthood.

The first section of the chapter provides a brief review of the major psychosocial needs and adjustments experienced by older adults. Following this review is a discussion of the range of activities that can be used to promote successful aging in the psychosocial domain. Next a sample psychosocial activity plan is presented that blends a variety of activities to illustrate appropriate programming strategies. The sample plan also is intended to show the use of psychosocial activities as therapeutic intervention in the care and treatment of older persons. Completing the chapter is a list of additional resources and references for use in the psychosocial program development process.

Psychosocial Needs in Later Maturity

Individuals are challenged by developmental tasks that accompany different stages of life across the life course. Older adulthood, as in the other major periods of life, is no exception. The ability to adapt to changes that typically occur in later maturity varies from person to person with some individuals showing greater capability to handle the major challenges associated with growing older. Some of the major challenges that affect the psychosocial health of older adults include:

(a) adjusting to new life circumstances produced by the changes in social roles that often accompany retirement from one's lifelong occupation (e.g., job or childrearing);

(b) adjusting to changes in financial circumstances as one either retires or changes his or her level of employment;

(c) dealing with changes in residence and with whom one lives (e.g., alone, with non-relatives, or with relatives);

(d) coping with the loss of one's spouse, family members, and friends through death; and

(e) adapting to the loss of one's own youthful vitality, vigor, and physical reserves including dealing with possible chronic health conditions and one's own eventual mortality.

Adapting to changes in these areas and others can have a dramatic impact on the psychosocial functioning and well-being of older adults.

The ability of older persons to manage adjustments during a major challenge or life change is greatly influenced by individual personality, resilience, coping abilities, past experiences, health status, and a strong social network of family members and friends (Hooyman & Kiyak, 2008). While personality is relatively stable across the lifespan, it can either serve to help or to hinder in the process of handling challenging life events. Individual abilities in adapting to major change and coping with stress vary greatly from one individual to the next. Awareness of the aging process, personal coping style, and the importance of flexibility, re-evaluation, and acceptance in adapting to major change are factors that influence successful aging in the psychosocial domain.

Retirement from lifelong occupation to part-time employment or to full retirement constitutes a major change in daily life activity patterns as well as the social roles. For many individuals, their identity is tied closely with both the nature of their work and the people with whom they come into daily contact at work. At retirement, changes in role, social networks, daily rhythms, and social expectations may potentially impact the individual's psychosocial well-being. By taking time to recognize the needs that are fulfilled primarily through involvement in the workplace, the older individual can actively plan new involvements and environments that can satisfy these same needs. For example, many older persons retire from their lifelong career and begin new part-time jobs doing things that they always wanted to try; while other individuals put their energies into community leadership, volunteerism, and family-based activities (e.g., caring for grandchildren). Part-time work, volunteerism, and community leadership are some of the important ways in which older adults remain connected with society and their communities. Replacing the work role with other activities that serve to maintain one's involvement in the community represents one avenue for adjusting to the major life changes that accompany retirement. It should also be recognized that many older persons experience very little adjustment difficulty at retirement and look forward to increasing their involvement in favorite activities (e.g., travel, sport, social, educational, family caregiving) through which their identity needs are adequately expressed and fulfilled.

Dealing with the loss of one's lifelong partner, other family members (e.g., siblings and relatives), and close friends is a significant event that challenges older persons to adapt to dramatic change. The shrinking of one's primary social network can be a persistent theme in the daily lives of older people. The loss of persons on whom one has depended for daily social exchange and support is a potent force in the psychosocial adjustment of older persons. Maintaining an active life filled with opportunities to socialize with others, to expand one's social network to persons of all ages (thus buffering the persistent loss of age peers), and to celebrate the cultural heritage that holds together the social fabric of community are some of the ways in which older adults can cope with these losses. Leisure activities and recreation centers provide the structure through which social networks can be built and strengthened, especially through a focus on intergenerational programming.

A third major area of psychosocial adjustment in later life is learning to accept and adjust to the loss of one's own physical reserves and the eventuality of one's own demise. The accumulated effects of declines in physical functioning eventually affect all older persons. Some older adults continue to lead vigorous and active lifestyles while experiencing few limitations in their physical capabilities. Other persons, however, experience declines to such an extent that physical independence is impacted and eventually, these individuals may have impaired functioning. Physical functioning and independence are greatly influenced by several factors including: chronological age, physical fitness, health/disease status, and genetic endowment. While probably all older persons will eventually experience some reduction in their physical reserves, it is not until very late in life that many individuals will experience limitations in activity involvement due to declined physical status. Therefore, leisure activities that pro-

mote fitness and help to prevent decline are instrumental to the physical well-being of older adults.

The recognition of one's own mortality, coupled with declines in physical functioning, may pose a significant sense of personal loss. The preservation of one's social network can greatly help older persons to deal with these losses, as well as to maintain a sense of quality in their lives. Older persons' involvement in travel, group outings, special events, games, hobbies, holidays, celebrations, and low impact physical recreation activities can have direct psychosocial benefits when physical reserves have diminished and there is the need to preserve health status.

The maintenance of identity through meaningful role involvement and environmental supports is important in promoting continuity and activity involvement throughout life. Assisting older persons to adapt to the developmental tasks that are typical in later life becomes the focus and purpose of many psychosocial activity programs. These programs primarily support the following psychosocial needs: social role and identity, belongingness, self-esteem, adjustment, companionship and meaningful relationships, autonomy and independence, happiness, creativity, socialization, and pleasure. Psychosocial activity programs can be found in a variety of settings that provide care and treatment services to older persons, including senior centers, adult day care centers, assisted living facilities, nursing homes, rehabilitation centers, hospitals, and in the home. A discussion of how activities can help older persons manage the major developmental tasks associated with later life is the focus of the next section.

Meeting Psychosocial Needs Through Activities

Successful aging has been described as the ability to adapt to the major life events and challenges that typically present themselves in later maturity (Hooyman & Kiyak, 2008). In the previous section, we discussed three broad areas in which major challenges occur in older adulthood: (a) social role changes and identity, (b) loss of significant other(s), and (c) loss of one's own physical independence, as well as confronting one's own eventual death. Factors that influence how individuals cope with changes and challenges in these areas as well as how activities can be therapeutically used to support personal capabilities and adaption in later maturity are discussed in this section.

The ability of older persons to adapt to the major challenges that typically occur in older adulthood is greatly influenced by individual personality, physical health status, earlier life experiences and history, and the availability of a wide range of social supports (e.g., family, income stability, suitable housing, accessible recreation, valued social roles, etc.). As older persons confront late life events that threaten independence/autonomy, instigate emotional instability, remove valued social roles, alter living arrangements and standards, or dramatically affect lifestyle patterns, a series of reactions or defenses may result. Typical reactions include feelings of loneliness, fear, anger, depression, and anxiety. These reactions often produce negative behaviors or defense mechanisms such as repression, denial, withdrawal, projection, regression, fixation, manipulation, and displacement or rationalization. Older persons who are able to recognize their personal strengths and abilities will be more likely to cope positively with reactions and show fewer negative defense mechanisms. Many older people, however, may not deal well with these reactions and subsequently, they may present poor defense mechanisms and have poor coping skills. Personal coping style in late life typically mirrors the coping behaviors that were characteristic of earlier life adjustments. People who coped well earlier in life will be more likely to handle stressors in later life better than people who have struggled with coping throughout their adult life.

Successful coping is related to self-esteem, self-concept, health status, and one's ability to "think through" or cognitively process the events that are impacting one's life, as well as the stability of one's social network of friends and family members (Hooyman & Kiyak, 2008). Having constructive outlets through which to express one's self, a supportive environment, and others who are able to give emotional reassurance are helpful strategies for most persons who are experiencing the stresses associated with major life changes in older adulthood. Activities that build self-esteem (e.g., celebrating birthdays) and promote positive self-concept (e.g., developing a hobby into a special skill such as woodworking or a creative art) can be useful in providing a supportive, constructive environment through which successful coping may be promoted.

Activities to build self-esteem should address how the person feels about himself or herself. Personal feelings of worth can be promoted through recognition by others of having worth and importance. This acknowledgment can be promoted by providing individuals with opportunities to lead activities, honoring them for making contributions to a group or an activity, or appreciating the importance of a their existence through celebrating birthdays or other special occasions.

Self-concept, on the other hand, relates to the identity that each person constructs for himself or herself.

Identity can be built and reinforced through activities that produce outcomes that the individual values and are viewed as instrumental or valued by others. There are many activities that can promote a positive self-concept for individuals, especially when they feel valued and successful during engagement in these activities. Hobbies, sports and physical recreation activities, volunteering, community leadership service, continuing education, and many other activities can be effectively used in strengthening the self-concept of older persons.

Activities that promote fitness, health promotion, and a sense of well-being can be helpful in the process of successfully coping with the ongoing stress and challenges of older adulthood. By understanding that physical activities impact overall health and fitness, and also promote the inner strength needed to manage stress, the activity leader will be proactive in supporting positive coping. Physical recreation activities can include walking, low impact games, dancing, travel, and outdoor activities, to name just a few examples.

In regard to support the individual to cognitively process their personal stresses, socialization and group activities can be useful by setting the environment for sharing one's experiences and feelings with others. Some approaches that can be used to meet these purposes include: (a) self-help support groups; (b) club activities; (c) games, crafts, and hobby groups; and (d) horticulture, art, and music therapies. Several objectives associated with assisting older persons to experience successful coping are to

(a) maintain social engagement with others,
(b) promote the pursuit of meaningful activities,
(c) assist in setting new directions for personal growth and adaptation,
(d) promote feelings of self-worth, and
(e) prevent disablement due to deteriorating health.

The attainment of these objectives is enhanced through the implementation of a well-designed and skillfully led program of activities that meet psychosocial needs of older persons.

In summary, there are several major activity categories that can be used to enhance successful aging in the psychosocial domain. These include but are not limited to: intergenerational activities; socialization activities and special events; hobbies, arts, crafts, and games; travel and outdoor activities; and specific therapies (e.g., pet, horticulture, music, art). A wide range of specific activities are available under each of these main categories and the reader is encouraged to consult the resources at the end of the chapter for locating more information. Activities are selected from these categories to build a program that will (a) promote dignity and a sense of identity, (b) provide for meaning and connectedness within society and community, and (c) support personal resolve to one's eventual mortality. The sample program that follows is intended to demonstrate one approach to blending activities in meeting these psychosocial needs.

A Sample Program

The following sample program illustrates the kinds of activities that can be used to meet the psychosocial needs of older adults. The program can be adapted to a wide range of environments including community recreation centers, senior centers, adult day care, church-based organizations, retirement communities, assisted living facilities, nursing homes, and rehabilitation centers. The activity specialist will need to provide further program development details, such as facility arrangements, materials, costs, staffing, advertising, etc., in order to apply the outline as provided.

Program Purpose

The purpose of this program is to provide older adults with a diverse range of psychosocial activities that are instrumental in supporting identity, social roles, social network, positive coping, and optimal health and well-being. The program is developed and implemented based on the following principles:

1. Older persons desire a varied and diverse program of activities to meet their identified psychosocial needs and interests. Of particular relevance are the following activity objectives:
    (a) to maintain social relationships with others,
    (b) to promote the pursuit of meaningful activities,
    (c) to set new directions for personal growth and adaptation,
    (d) to promote feelings of self-worth, and
    (e) to prevent social isolation due to deteriorating health.
2. It is desirable to develop partnerships with local community-based organizations and agencies in meeting the psychosocial needs of older adults in the community.
3. Older persons prefer activities that promote self-development, independence/autonomy, and positive coping skills.

4. Older persons desire to participate in the planning, implementation, and evaluation of activities and programs that are designed to meet their specific psychosocial needs.

ACTIVITY AREA I— SOCIALIZATION ACTIVITIES AND SPECIAL EVENTS

Target Goal:

Participants will have a regular calendar of social events that provide for a diversity of interests, promote recognition of special dates both personal and cultural, and integrate activities with community events and happenings.

Enabling Objectives:

1. To assess the social activity interests of participants and select varying program formats to match these such as parties, celebrations, special performances, and special events (e.g., art fairs, white elephant sales, antique appraisal fairs, health fairs).
2. To assess community resources and the calendars of other community organizations for the purpose of identifying existing programs and activities in order to avoid duplication and to promote collaboration.
3. To develop a calendar of major religious, cultural, and community events, and to publish/disseminate the calendar to prospective participants in the community and in local long-term care facilities.

Activity Suggestions:

The social and special events calendar should includes both formal organized events as well as informal activities. For example, a monthly birthday party is scheduled for celebrating all birthdays that occur within each month. The social events calendar also includes the celebration of major holidays as a very popular way to promote social gatherings. In addition, regularly scheduled informal drop-in conversation times that are accompanied by refreshments should be included on the monthly calendar. These informal conversation hours are appreciated by many individuals who are either less inclined to large social gatherings or prefer to informally socialize on a regular basis. Less formal topical discussion times are also appropriate.

The monthly social calendar also reflects theme parties that include a half-hour special program and seasonal festivals as they are appropriate. Theme parties are developed around any topic of interest to prospective participants. The following can serve as possible themes for half-hour programs: favorite books or poems, favorite jokes, favorite movies, sharing holiday ornament and decoration ideas, the oldest thing I own, photograph sharing day, stories about my children and grandchildren, etc. By building upon themes generated by the participants themselves, half-hour socials are easily initiated and sustained as a regular aspect of the monthly social calendar.

Festivals serve as excellent opportunities to join with other community organizations in planning and conducting a schedule of annual festivals (e.g., Fall Foliage Festival, Festival of the Winter Solstice, Spring Blossom Festival, and Summer Music in the Park Festival). Festivals can be developed around cultural events, seasonal happenings, or historically significant dates to the community or state in which you live. Festivals typically involve socializing, special displays, events, and exhibits, and food—a real attraction to most adults. Festivals are excellent social events that serve to connect all generations and members of the community together in celebrating life and the culture that binds them together.

The social calendar is complete when an ample number of additional social events are scheduled such as dances, special parties (e.g., game parties, progressive lunches or dinners), special events (e.g., Health Fairs), and clubs (e.g., creative writing, hobbies, debate, politics, quilting, woodworking). The list is endless regarding ideas for a rich and varied social calendar; therefore, program staff will be wise to form a social committee of older persons to guide the ongoing development and implementation of the social program.

Implementation and Materials Suggestions:

Probably the single most important suggestion for social activity specialists is to remember that what is done *by* (as opposed to *for*) older adults is the key to successful programming. Involving the participants in all phases of social program planning, implementation, and evaluation will help to ensure that the program reflects this basic principle and therefore, that the participants' interests and needs will be attained. The second principle to ensure success is the importance of using other community resources. All the social needs and interests of older persons cannot be met in most communities by a single senior center, one club, or an individual organization. A professionally trained and skillful activity specialist will know what other resources, exper-

tise, facilities, programs, organizations, and services are available in the community for meeting the social needs of older adults.

There are other important ingredients to a successful social program. Some critical considerations are the (a) use of motivational techniques to attract and maintain the involvement of participants; (b) selection and preparation of good leaders; (c) skillful utilization of volunteers; (d) development of a sound program structure (e.g., selection of activity type, time allotment, materials and facilities, other environmental arrangements and supports); (e) consideration of all safety considerations and preparations; and (f) the need for transportation.

In regard to social events and special programs, the core considerations for program elements and implementation requisites will need to be addressed. These details include a list of materials, costs, adaptations, specified procedures for conducting the program, length of time needed for the activity/program, the goals/objectives of the program, maximum size of group, and any special concerns that will need to be addressed (such as risk management and safety). These considerations are specified as the written program plan is developed by the activity staff in collaboration with older adult advisory members.

ACTIVITY AREA II— INTERGENERATIONAL ACTIVITIES

Target Goal:

Participants will have access to a variety of activities that are designed to connect them with members from the younger generations in the community.

Enabling Objectives:

1. To assess the interests of older persons for activities and events that involve younger generations.
2. To evaluate community agencies and organizations for opportunities to develop intergenerational activities (e.g., schools, day care centers, churches, youth organizations, and family organizations).
3. To plan and conduct at least 4–6 intergenerational activities or programs on an annual basis.
4. To assess young people's organizations for the interest and willingness of younger people to interact with older people in specific activities and programs.

Activity Suggestions:

Intergenerational activities and programs are growing in importance and popularity as members from the different generations in the community continue to lead lifestyles that tend to isolate them from one another. Intergenerational activities and programs are those in which the primary goal is to bring older persons in interaction with younger persons, and vice versa, while engaging in an activity of mutual interest. A broad range of formats can be used to facilitate this goal. For example, older persons can develop a program of regular visits to child day care centers for the purpose of conducting a storytelling and/or reading hour. In this way, older persons can provide grandparenting to younger children whose natural grandparents may either live far away or may be deceased. In return, the younger children provide opportunities to the older adults to experience memories of when they were younger and rearing their own children. This type of intergenerational program also provides direct benefits to the child care center in that an expanded availability of adults to give more one-on-one attention to the children is possible.

Another intergenerational activity that can be successfully developed is extending invitations to young people from local schools or youth clubs to visit the older adult community center for the purpose of providing a special program such as a demonstration of a group project, the reading of short stories or poems written by the youth (or the older persons), or holding a joint musical/theatrical performance. By inviting young people to participate in center activities such as board games, cards, hobbies, and crafts, another opportunity for building intergenerational understanding and sharing can be created.

Community and civic organizations often join forces with older adult groups to plan special community-wide programs that target families and the younger generations. For example, after school tutoring and job mentoring activities are desperately needed by younger people. The wisdom and time that older persons have at their disposal can be effectively used to help meet this need through specifically developed intergenerational activities and programs.

Many families today have two working parents or reflect a single working parent home life. Children in these situations often need someone to talk with and someplace to go. Older adults can be effective advocates in meeting some of the needs of these youth. These activities involve taking the initiative to develop the idea for the joint program and then locating other community organizations to join forces in providing these needed services to young people. This approach can reduce the isolation that often develops when older citizens are viewed as "having their own center and programs." By opening up community centers at specific times to meet youth and older adult needs through intergenerational activities and programs, all citizens and community agencies may be enabled to join together to strengthen the community as a whole.

A final example of intergenerational activities that may appeal to younger people and older people alike are dance classes and dance events such as a local version of "Dancing with the Stars." Young people generally enjoy dancing and with an effective marketing approach, they may become interested in learning various new and old dance styles from older adults, especially when it is combined in a competition and special event format. Dancing is an activity that is of interest to people in all generations and it is an activity through which connections can be built across the generations.

Implementation and Materials Suggestions:

The development and implementation of intergenerational activities and programs depends upon several key ingredients: (a) interested and willing older adults, (b) enthusiastic leaders and facilitators who also understand child development and youth, (c) community support, (d) commitment of organizations and facility managers to provided the needed space and resources to support intergenerational events, and (e) young people of all ages who are interested in spending time with older adults. Beyond these basics, standard program development steps are pursued to establish and carry on intergenerational programs. These steps include assessing needs and interests, identifying program resources and leadership, planning the details of the program, conducting the program, and providing evaluation feedback about the program. Throughout the program planning process consideration is given to materials, program costs, time and space requirements, transportation, and other environmental supports (e.g., adequate lighting, heating/cooling, refreshments, safety). The success of intergenerational programs, however, rests largely on the motivation, involvement, and commitment of the participants to the overall program goals and outcomes.

Consideration is given to the interaction skills that will be needed by participants in order to enhance a successful program. Some aspects of social interaction that are addressed when planning an intergenerational activity or program include the following:

1. Does the program/activity emphasize cooperation or competition?
2. What size group is the activity/program best suited for?
3. Does the activity and environment serve to promote a high degree of interaction?
4. What degree of physical proximity does the activity entail and will it fit within a "comfort zone" for all participants?
5. How much initiative is required by both older and younger participants?
6. Is the activity structured so that it is appropriate for participants of all ages?

Group leadership skills that will help to ensure a successful program embrace both motivational aspects of the program as well as methods for maintaining interest (Leitner & Leitner, 1985). Some important leader skills are:

1. Be certain that the activity is within the interests and needs of prospective participants.
2. Design and implement the activity for varying ability levels; offer assistance as needed.
3. Use positive reinforcement. Motivate through encouragement to try the activity at least once, but do not force any one to participate who is not comfortable. In some cases, observing an activity is a form of passive participation and is within the comfort zone of more shy people.
4. Beware of boredom! Implementing new challenges within the program/activity is an important strategy for maintaining interest.
5. Be sure that the group meets on a regular schedule that neither leaves too much time between meetings nor meets so frequently that participants become bored or disinterested because novelty wears off.

It is very important in intergenerational programming to be attentive to both the younger and older participants. Considering both age groups requires that the leadership staff be aware of the needs, interests, and capabilities of each when planning and leading the program.

ACTIVITY AREA III— HOBBIES, ARTS, CRAFTS, AND GAMES

Target Goal:

Participants will have available to them hobby, art, and craft classes, materials, and facilities, as well as a calendar of regular times when popular games will

be played at various community-based locations (e.g., schools, community and senior centers, community organizations).

Enabling Objectives:

1. To assess the hobby, art, and craft skills and interests of the older adults in the community and local long-term care facilities.
2. To assess and evaluate the availability of community resources, facilities, and expertise in order to make optimal use of these in planning and implementing the hobby, art, and craft program.
3. To plan a regular calendar of board and table games.

Activity Suggestions:

Hobbies, arts, crafts, and games are immensely popular among most older adults. Items that older persons typically collect or pursue as hobbies include: photo and genealogy albums; scrapbooking; coin collecting; toy and doll collecting; old postcards, programs, and posters; rocks, flowers, birds, and plants specialty groups; taxidermy; fishing and hunting;, antiques and relics; Indian artifacts; stamps and seals; fine arts (e.g., sculpture, drawings, paintings, modeling, textile arts); crafts (e.g., needlework, rugs, quilts, weaving, woodwork, wood carving, textiles, beadwork, plastic, book binding, jewelry, puppets, pottery, stenciling, iron and metal work); enamel and glass; models (e.g., airplanes, cars, ships, buildings, trains, doll houses); and photography (Williams, 1962). The list of activities that people pursue as hobbies or collections is endless, and is generally bounded only by the interest of two or more people who wish to come together to share their passion. A wide variety of hobby and collecting clubs can be developed to meet the specific assessed interests of community members.

Clubs in other areas are also very popular. For example, creative writing and publishing has become a very exciting activity among older adults with several popular press books in print as a product of this kind of program. Educational and travel clubs (including the very popular Elderhostel programs) are a growth interest area among older persons. Other club types include literature clubs, bird club, silver striders walking club, golden age radio, catalog shopping club, community service clubs, optimist and public speaking clubs, computer-based specialty clubs, and game clubs (e.g., bridge, euchre, Scrabble).

A club format is not necessary in order to have informal hours available for games. Games that are popular with older adults include: recreational cards, checkers, chess, darts, horseshoes, billiards, bingo, board games, scrabble, etc. Open hours for games provide an important function in the availability of socialization opportunities for older adults who enjoy attending community centers, churches during nonservice times, or other community settings such as the library.

Arts and crafts provide an activity format that promotes socialization as well as meeting the need for regular use of fine motor skills and cognitive stimulation. Typical arts and crafts enjoyed by older adults include: painting, sculpting and ceramics, weaving, rug making, sewing, crocheting and knitting, photography, computer-based art, paper crafting, lamp making, stenciling, plastics, beadwork, woodwork, leather crafting, metal work, textile printing, braiding, knotting, wood carving, tatting, jewelry making, embroidery, stained glass, etc. It is not uncommon to find arts and crafts items for sale at community venues and centers, thus attesting to the popularity of this kind of activity. Arts and crafts classes, clubs, and one time activity sessions may be infused into the monthly social calendar with a fairly high success rate to be expected in terms of attendance and outcomes.

Implementation and Materials Suggestions:

The success of the hobbies, games, arts, and crafts components of an overall social recreation program rests largely on leadership. Leaders will provide a sound foundation for success if they remember a few important tips about programming in this area (Williams, 1962):

1. Declines in vision, fine motor control, muscle strength, and endurance can affect the older person's work at arts, crafts, and some hobbies, or participation in some games. Providing environmental supports (e.g., superior lighting, magnifying glasses, large print directions or audiotape directions, longer time allowance to complete a project but no individual work sessions that last more than two hours, assistance with heavy machinery) will be important in order to promote positive experience for all who participate in these activities.
2. Older people need encouragement, just as younger people do, that they have the ability to create beautiful objects. Help older people reach for high standards of workmanship and design.
3. Match skill levels in craft groups and hire skilled leaders. It can be discouraging to be involved in a group whose members' skills far exceed those of the beginner. Be sure that craft leaders also understand the needs and interests of older persons, as well as how to motivate and encourage older participants.
4. The quality of final products is enhanced by the materials, facilities, and tools that are available to the older artisan or craftsperson. Program leaders need to plan for adequate supplies, facilities, and tools through enlisting donations, sponsorship, and a having a budgetary planning process that provides adequately in this area. It is wise to plan in advance for the (a) rooms and equipment, (b) tools and supplies, and (c) leadership skills that will be needed.
5. Arts and crafts sales, hobby shows, art fairs, and game tournaments are excellent ways to showcase the work of older adults and for fund raising in order to support the program as well as providing another social event related to these activities. The organization and implementation of sales, shows, fairs, and tournaments can be completely managed by the older participants. By organizing themselves into various committees, they can have the opportunity to show off their talents. Essential committees for these events include: general overall program committee, finance and sponsorship, publicity, volunteers, location and equipment, exhibit or game space organization, decorations, hospitality and public relations, transportation, judging and prizes (optional), entertainment, and clean-up.

ACTIVITY AREA IV—
TRAVEL AND OUTDOOR ACTIVITIES

Target Goal:

Participants will have access to a travel and trip program that will include local and long distance trips, travel agency assistance, and staff assistance in planning and implementing an ongoing travel and outdoor activity calendar.

Enabling Objectives:

1. To plan and implement a varied program of local and distance travel and outdoor activity participation (e.g., bird watching, day hiking).
2. To develop a cooperative agreement with a local travel agency for the purpose of providing special packages for the travel program.
3. To train staff in leading trip and travel programs for older adults.

4. To annually survey older citizens in the community regarding their travel interests, requirements, and willingness to participate in a travel program.

Activity Suggestions:

Travel and outdoor activities are very popular with older adults, especially persons in the transition years (ages 65–80) who continue to enjoy good health and functional independence. Older adults comprise a large segment of the tourism market for both local and short day trips as well as extended travel tours. Activities in the out-of-doors also are increasingly popular among older adults.

Typical outdoor activities that are enjoyed include nature walks, bird watching, hiking, picnicking, gardening, fishing, walking for pleasure, boating, bicycling, park and nature preserve visiting, and camping. These activities can be enjoyed by most older adults with a few considerations (e.g., available restrooms, proper water and nutrition, proper clothing and shoes, and frequent benches for resting, preferably in the shade). Planning to include some kind of outdoor activity in the monthly social calendar helps to ensure a well-balanced program.

Outings, either local short day trips or long group tours to distant sights and locations, add a measure of excitement to the social calendar. A wide variety of settings can be used to develop a varied and stimulating travel program. Trips to the following destinations can be planned on a regular basis: concerts and theater productions, historic sites, specialty shows (e.g., antique, art, hobby), train excursions, tourist attractions and theme parks (e.g., Disneyland, Branson), shopping malls in large cities and local flea markets, festivals and fairs, camps and nature preserves, state and national parks, Elderhostel programs, zoological parks and botanical gardens, museums and galleries, sporting events, cruises, and special tours (Elliott & Sorg-Elliott, 1991). The list is practically endless based on the curiosity and creativity of the travel program planner and participants. Outings are successful when they are planned carefully with the needs and interests of the older participants in the forefront.

Implementation and Materials Suggestions:

The travel and outdoor program requires special planning to ensure its success including the enjoyment and safety of all participants (Elliott & Sorg-Elliott, 1991). Basic planning includes the following details:

1. Acquiring information about the (a) destination and/or event; (b) location layout and design; (c) date and travel times (e.g., departure, arrival at destination, return); (d) traveling information (e.g., route, directions); (e) kind of transportation and number of available seats; and (f) major objective(s) of the trip or outdoor activity.
2. Obtaining detailed information about participants including: (a) the number to attend; (b) participants with motor impairment and assistance needs (e.g., number of participants who need an attendant); (c) information about the health status and any health conditions of participants (with medical release if needed); (d) special dietary needs; and (e) a list of supplies and clothing that participants should bring with them on the outing.
3. Contracting or finalizing specific details and arrangements for the outing, including: (a) transportation arrangements (e.g., number and types of vehicles, routing, drivers, attendants, time); (b) dietary arrangements; (c) securing the necessary staffing, volunteers, and attendants; (d) budget and participant finances; (e) advertising the trip or outing; (f) evaluation plan; (g) safety plan (e.g., medical releases, emergency phone numbers, first aid); and (h) final enrollment figures.

Trip planning also requires that staff conduct a site assessment in order to safeguard accessibility, safety, and a good match between the objectives for the trip, the participants, and the destination choice. Elliott and Sorg-Elliott (1991) recommended that the trip leader/planner conduct a Trip Resources Assessment as presented in Figure 14.1. The information obtained from the assessment will help the trip planner to ensure that the safety, accessibility, and comfort needs of older participants are met at each destination included in the travel program.

ACTIVITY AREA V—
THERAPEUTIC ACTIVITIES
(e.g., EXERCISE, PET, DANCE, HUMOR/
LAUGHTER, HORTICULTURE, MUSIC, ART)

Target Goal:

Participants will have a variety of community, long-term care facility, and home therapeutic activities provided by trained therapeutic recreation specialists or associated professionals.

Assessment Date _____   Trip Date _____

Destination _____

Address _____
                Street, P.O. Box   City   State   Zip

Contact Person _____   Title _____

Phone Number _____

Size of Group _____   Cost _____ (group, individual)

Preferred Date & Times _____

Directions to Destination _____

_____

Emergency Information _____

_____

Program Title _____   Duration _____

Description _____

Attributes Assessment: Comments:

Type: unstructured |__|__|__|__|__|__| structured

Participation: entertainment |__|__|__|__|__|__| educational

Skill Level:

   Social: low |__|__|__|__|__|__| high

   Physical: low |__|__|__|__|__|__| high

   Cognitive: low |__|__|__|__|__|__| high

Physical Setting:

   Rest Rooms: none |__|__|__|__|__|__| wheelchair accessible

   Eating Area: none |__|__|__|__|__|__| wheelchair accessible

   Steps: many |__|__|__|__|__|__| wheelchair ramps
                              none

   Seating: none |__|__|__|__|__|__| seats with backs

   Walks/Trails: none |__|__|__|__|__|__| wheelchair accessible

   Terrain: hilly |__|__|__|__|__|__| flat

   Shelter: none |__|__|__|__|__|__| enclosed

   Water Fountains: none |__|__|__|__|__|__| wheelchair accessible

   Lighting: none |__|__|__|__|__|__| adequate

Source: Adapted from Elliott & Sorg-Elliott, 1991.

Figure 14.1 Trip Resources Assessment Form

Enabling Objectives:

1. To develop a resource list of trained therapists/ professionals who are willing to assist in the provision of a therapeutic activities program that is designed to meet prevention and rehabilitation goals in the psychosocial domain.
2. To train staff in therapeutic activity intervention.
3. To meet with older clients and plan a program of therapeutic activities including the provision of the program in various locations (e.g., home, nursing home, assisted living facility, rehabilitation center, community center).
4. To implement, on a regular basis, the offering of one or more therapeutic activities (e.g., pet therapy, horticultural therapy, modified exercise, art therapy, music or dance therapy, humor/laughter therapy, relaxation therapy).

Activity Suggestions:

Many activities can be planned and implemented as therapeutic intervention. Some of the more common therapeutic activities include pet therapy, horticultural therapy, modified exercise, art therapy, music and dance therapy, humor/laughter therapy, and relaxation therapy. Distinguishing attributes of activities that are used as therapy are (a) an identified impairment or disability is the target of intervention; (b) rehabilitation, prevention, or maintenance of social interaction skills constitute the goal of intervention; (c) a specified, individual treatment plan guides activity intervention; (d) therapeutic activity may be part of a larger patient treatment plan and thus, the activity specialist is a member of the treatment team; (e) activity intervention follows a clinical model; (f) activity services may be billable/ reimbursable; (g) treatment is provided by a qualified specialist (Certified Therapeutic Recreation Specialist); and (h) individual client outcomes are documented. The therapeutic benefits of interacting with pets, growing and caring for plants, engaging in modified exer-

cise, experiencing the creation of art, participating in dance or music, experiencing the physiological and psychological benefits from laughing, or engaging in relaxation are increasingly recognized as important by rehabilitation specialists who provide care and treatment to older persons.

Therapeutic recreation specialists either directly provide these therapeutic activity interventions or supervise specialists (e.g., art therapists) in the use of therapeutic activities with specific clients. Older adults who typically benefit from these activities are those whose social interactions have become impaired through illness (e.g., as in depression caused by medication use), disease (e.g., dementia of the Alzheimer's type), or injury (e.g., stroke). For these individuals, the road to recovery and independent functioning requires the specific application of activities for the purpose of regaining or expressing social interaction skills (e.g., communicating feelings to others as in the use of art therapy). Figure 14.2 provides contact information for activity professionals.

Implementation and Materials Suggestions:

Clinical practice of therapeutic activity intervention is based on the following process: client assessment, activity analysis, intervention planning and implementation, and documentation/evaluation. The participant or client will be assessed for their general functional status including degree of functional independence in the following areas: (a) physical (e.g., coordination, dexterity, endurance, vision and hearing, strength); (b) cognitive (e.g., orientation, alertness, perceptual, attention, comprehends and follows directions, safety awareness); (c) social (e.g., social interaction, helps others, participates, appropriate social behaviors, relates with others); (d) emotional (e.g., emotionally stable, confident, appropriate behavior); (e) initiative (e.g., shows motivation, independent judgment and decision making); (f) general (e.g., demonstrates interest, completes work, compliant to rules); and (g) special skills, interests, and capabilities are identified (Hamill & Oliver, 1980).

National Association of Activity Professionals—NAAP, PO Box 5530, Sevierville, TN 37864. NAAP is a national group that represents activity professionals in geriatric settings. NAAP serves as a catalyst for both professional and personal growth and has come to be recognized by government officials as the voice of the activity profession on national issues concerning long-term care facilities, retirement living, assisted living, adult day services, and senior citizen centers. NAAP is nationwide in scope with a growing membership in Canada and Bermuda.
Website: http://www.thenaap.com/
Phone: 865-429-0727; Fax: 865-453-9914

Figure 14.2 Resources for Activity Professionals

Activities are selected and analyzed for their specific match in meeting client needs and goals in the treatment process. Activity analysis entails systematically breaking down activities according to the skills and abilities that the client must have in order to engage in the activities. Activities are usually analyzed across three domains: physical, cognitive, and social/emotional. In the physical domain the activity is analyzed according to full or partial body involvement, the type of body movement required, mobility and physical fitness requirements, and the demands made by the activity on the senses (vision, hearing, hot/cold perception). In the cognitive domain the intellectual requirements of the activity are evaluated; for example, how many rules are involved in the activity and how complex are they, are reading and writing skills involved, what long- and short-term memory skills are required for participation, and what degree of attention is needed? In the social/emotional domain elements of the activity that are analyzed include: does the activity promote communication of feelings, release of tension or stress, the experience of fun or frustration, self-esteem, and creativity? Also of concern in the social domain are elements of cooperation, teamwork, what is the nature of social interaction and communication with others, does the activity promote motivation and initiative, and is the activity done with others or alone?

In planning and implementing the activity, clear client treatment-specified goals will guide the final selection of the therapeutic activity intervention. The treatment plan should contain treatment goals and enabling objectives as well as target outcomes to evaluate treatment effectiveness. In leading the therapeutic activity intervention, the specialist will pay specific attention to client/participant motivation, interest, and overall functional gains. Treatment documentation and evaluation evidence will be needed to assess whether the client treatment goals were met, to decide whether the activity was the appropriate treatment strategy, and to demonstrate the efficacy of the activity intervention in the overall care and treatment of the client.

Summary

This chapter covered the basic elements of activity programs that are designed to meet the psychosocial needs of older persons. These activities can be implemented in a variety of settings including community-based programs and centers, at home, or in long-term care or rehabilitation facilities. The sample program that was outlined can be used as a guide in the development of a more site/client/group specific psychosocial activity program. Readers are encouraged to consult the additional resources and references listed at the end of the chapter.

Comprehension Questions

The reader can check for comprehension of the material presented in this chapter by answering the following questions:

1. Discuss the importance of socialization and social activity involvement in older adulthood.

2. What late life developmental challenge and events are addressed through social programs and activities?

3. Describe appropriate psychosocial activities for older adults in five broad areas or categories.

References and Resources

Arrigo, S. (1998). *Beyond bingo 2: More innovative programs for the new senior.* State College, PA: Venture Publishing, Inc.

Cheshire, N. F. & Kenney, M. L. (1999. *Everything from A to Y: The zest is up to you! Older adult activities for every day of the year.* State College, PA: Venture Publishing, Inc.

Elliott, J. E. & Sorg-Elliott, J. A. (1991). *Recreation programming and activities for older adults.* State College, PA: Venture Publishing, Inc.

Flatten, K., Wilhite, B. & Reyes-Watson, E. (1988). *Recreation activities for the elderly.* NY: Springer.

Hamill, C. M. & Oliver, R. C. (1980). *Therapeutic activities for the handicapped elderly.* Rockville, MD: Aspen Publishers.

Hart, M., Primm, K. & Cranisky, K. (2003). *Beyond baskets and beads: Activities for older adults with functional impairments.* State College, PA: Venture Publishing, Inc.

Hooyman, N. R. & Kiyak, H. A. (2008). *Social gerontology: A multidisciplinary perspective* (8th ed.). Boston, MA: Allyn and Bacon.

Jones, L. (1987). *Activities for the older mentally retarded/developmentally disabled.* Akron, OH: Exploration Series Press.

Kindrachuk, K. (2006). *Recreation program planning manual for older adults.* State College, PA: Venture Publishing, Inc.

Leitner, M. J. & Leitner, S. F. (2004). *Leisure in later life* (3rd ed.). New York, NY: Haworth Press.

Messenger, B. (2004). *The melody lingers on: A complete music activities program for older adults.* State College, PA: Venture Publishing, Inc.

Powers, P. (1991). *The activity gourmet.* State College, PA: Venture Publishing, Inc.

Rice, W. & Yaconelli, M. (1986). *Play it!* Grand Rapids, MI: Zondervan Publishing House.

Tedford, J. (1958). *The giant book of family fun and games.* New York, NY: Franklin Watts, Inc.

Thews, V., Reaves, A. M. & Henry, R. S. (1993). *Now what? A handbook of activities for adult day programs.* Winston-Salem, NC: Bowman Gray School of Medicine, Wake Forest University.

Vickery, F. E. (1972). *Creative programming for older adults—A leadership training guide.* New York, NY: Association Press.

Williams, A. (1962). *Recreation in the senior years.* New York, NY: Association Press. [Available on microform from University of Michigan, digitized May 2, 2007.]

Zgola, J. M. (1987). *Doing things—A guide to programming activities for persons with Alzheimer's disease and related disorders.* Baltimore, MD: The Johns Hopkins University Press.

• CHAPTER 15 •

Documentation and Evalutation

Learning Objectives

1. State the purposes of documentation and evaluation in the care and treatment of older adults.

2. Discuss the process of evaluation.

3. Explain formative and summative evaluation in relation to therapeutic activity intervention.

4. Differentiate between qualitative and quantitative evaluation information.

5. Describe task analysis as a planning, documentation, and evaluation tool.

6. Discuss Goal Attainment Scaling as an evaluation tool.

7. Explain sociometry as an evaluation tool.

8. Conduct a case review and recommend a care plan based upon documentation and evaluation information presented in the case.

Key Terms

- Accountability
- Care Plan
- Documentation
- Evaluation
- Formative Evaluation
- Goal Attainment Scaling
- Interviews
- Merit
- Objectives-Oriented Evaluation
- Observations
- Qualitative Information
- Quantitative Information
- Questionnaires
- Sociometry
- Summative Evaluation
- Surveys
- Task Analysis
- Triangulation
- Worth

Introduction

Conscientious documentation and evaluation convey the message that caregivers and staff have a significant investment in intended outcomes associated with participation in a therapeutic activity program. Documentation and evaluation are instrumental to sustaining programmatic funding and reimbursement for treatment. Because documentation and evaluation are central to good professional practice in therapeutic activity intervention, we devote an entire chapter to reviewing these professional practice areas.

Evaluation refers to the consistent documentation, measurement, and analysis of client progress in attaining predetermined treatment goals, as well as the constant monitoring of outcomes associated with the overall activity program (Beddall & Kennedy, 1985; Stumbo & Peterson, 2009). Specific client goals and objectives provide standards for determining the merit and worth of both anticipated and unanticipated outcomes. Evaluation also is an ongoing process that enables the determination of the value of various aspects of the activity program in an effort to facilitate improvements in all areas. There is a close relationship between the evaluation of individual progress and the evaluation of the overall program that is designed to meet identified client needs (Greenblatt, 1988; Stumbo & Peterson; Wilhite & Keller, 2000). Therefore, the evaluation of overall activity programs, and the documentation and evaluation of individual client outcomes are considered in this chapter.

The chapter reviews the purposes of evaluation, as well as basic evaluation methods. Because there are a plethora of evaluation approaches and methods, a purposefully selected few are covered in this chapter. Formative and summative evaluation approaches as well as qualitative and quantitative techniques are presented. Various evaluation tools are discussed including interviews, observations, and surveys. Task analysis and Goal Attainment Scaling are described as they are applicable in program planning, documentation, and evaluation. The utilization of sociometry as an evaluation tool also is considered. Finally, a case review and recommended plan of care are described, based upon the information obtained from systematic documentation and evaluation efforts.

The Purposes of Documentation and Evaluation

The documentation of client progress coincides with the evaluation of specific activities as well as overall program content and process (Stumbo & Peterson, 2009). *Documentation* is at the heart of the evaluation process. The relevance of goals and activities, and the determination of progress are ascertained through the use of systematic documentation. The size and type of facility, nature of the participants, program budget, and number of staff members will determine the method of reporting that is necessary and practical (Hamill & Oliver, 1980).

Evaluation information is sought through documentation in order to appraise the *merit* of planned interventions in regard to specific client goals and objectives. Merit refers to the characteristics of the activity intervention or overall program that are valued by clients and staff. Does the program or specific activity produce the desired objectives that are important to the client?

Evaluation also is necessary to verify *accountability* (Bumagin & Hirn, 1990; Stumbo & Peterson, 2009; Wilhite & Keller, 2000). Accountability refers to determining whether clients have received what was approved or promised, and whether the treatment or services were cost-effective. Documentation and evaluation will confirm the efficacy of interventions, justify the program content, and provide evidence of the achievement of desired outcomes in an efficient and effective manner.

The attachment of values to facts is a basic component of program evaluation (Stumbo & Peterson, 2009; Teague, 1992). Evaluation results may be used to support funding needs and the apportionment of limited resources. Evaluation information provides evidence for program changes, as well as gives objective feedback to staff members regarding the effectiveness of care plans, specific interventions, and overall treatment programs. Finally, documentation and evaluation produce general information about the quality of care in relationship to established criteria and standards that are specified by external accrediting groups such as the Joint Commission on Accreditation of Healthcare Organizations (JCAHO) and the Commission for the Accreditation of Rehabilitation Facilities (CARF; Stumbo & Peterson, 2009; Theobald, 1979; Wilhite & Keller, 2000). Because of limited resources and increased accountability, systematic evaluation of clients' needs and expectations are of critical importance. Documentation and evaluation of individual activity interventions and overall programs offer explicit information regarding program improvement and the distribution of limited resources (Gillespie, Kennedy & Soble, 1988–89).

The Evaluation Process

Evaluation can be as simple as desired or as complex as necessary. The evaluation process will be staged or sequenced to serve both formative and summative evaluation goals. *Formative evaluation* is directed by processes that review the strengths and weaknesses of an activity intervention or program in order that improvements may be pursued *during* activity/program development and implementation. The intent of formative evaluation is to use information to modify or revise the activity intervention or program as it is taking place (McMillan & Schumacher, 2006). Typically, program staff is the user of formative evaluation information. As the data are compiled, information is produced that permits changes throughout the complete program planning process (Greenblatt, 1988; McMillan & Schumacher; Stumbo & Peterson, 2009).

Summative evaluation, on the other hand, appraises accomplishments at the completion of the activity intervention or overall program. The utilization of various procedures can substantiate conclusions regarding the effectiveness of the program. Actual outcomes are examined in order to determine if they correspond to the planned or sought outcomes. The identification of program strengths and weaknesses will facilitate changes and the future development of similar activities or programs (Greenblatt, 1988; McMillan & Schumacher, 2006; Stumbo & Peterson, 2009). The parties who will be most interested in summative evaluation findings are current participants, potential clients, funding sources, policymakers, and program administrators (McMillan & Schumacher).

While several approaches to evaluation are available to activity staff, we will review the objectives-oriented approach in this chapter (McMillan & Schumacher, 2006). The focus of an *objectives-oriented evaluation* is how well or to what degree the specific activity intervention or overall program objectives were attained. The first step in the process of an objectives-oriented evaluation is to formulate the measurable objectives that are associated with specified behavioral changes from the client's participation in the activity/program as well as specifying the criteria for measurement. Sources of data are identified and the methods for collecting the data are established. The timeframe for data collection is confirmed and the outcomes are measured according to the established criteria for measuring the successful attainment of the objectives. Methods for data analysis are selected during the planning phase of an objectives-oriented evaluation. Following the analysis of the data, recommendations are presented and results of the evaluation are integrated into the planning process (Gunn & Peterson, 1984; McMillan & Schumacher, 2006; Stumbo & Peterson, 2009; Teaff, 1985). The program planning process is cyclic and thus, an objectives-oriented approach can serve both formative and summative evaluation purposes (see Chapter 7 for a discussion of therapeutic intervention programming processes and evaluation).

The preparation of questions to evaluate the specified objectives provides a focus and direction to the objectives-oriented evaluation. Why and for whom is the evaluation being conducted? Audiences for the evaluation may include clients, relatives or guardians of the client, staff and/or treatment team members, accrediting organizations, and funding sources. According to Wilhite and Keller (1992), basic evaluation questions can include the following examples:

1. What were the outcomes of the program?
2. Were activities and interactions appropriate in regard to the stated objectives?
3. Were the objectives valid, realistic, and relevant?
4. Was the program implemented as designed?

Each evaluation question can evolve into several, more discrete sub-items that are used to answer the more comprehensive objectives posed in the first phase of the evaluation. Programs may be appraised with a variety of indicators such as calculations of attendance; however, attendance totals do not accurately describe the influence of the activity/program upon individual participants (Rossman, 2000). The identified sub-items will guide the selection of pertinent information sources such as attendance records, individual records, files, charts, test results, progress notes, and prior evaluation reports (Wilhite & Keller, 2000).

The evaluation methods that are used must be considered according to the costs required for implementation. The amount of time, money, specialized training, skills, and experience involved must be anticipated. Either or both *qualitative* and/or *quantitative* information can be obtained and analyzed (Riddick & Russell, 2008). Qualitative information is typically collected through anecdotal records, extensive case notes, interviews, and observations. Qualitative information or data are in the form of words or artifacts, and require specific skills and techniques to analyze and interpret their meaning in light of the overall goals and objectives of the activity/program. Basic descriptions, analytical accounts, and content appraisal may be included. A qualitative approach generally ensures increased understanding through more personal procedures and presentation such as the exploration of feelings, thoughts, insights, and descriptions in the familiar language of the clients (Reinharz & Rowles, 1988; Riddick & Russell; Wilhite & Keller, 2000).

Quantitative information or data are often derived from records, direct assessments, and surveys or questionnaires (Riddick & Russell, 2008). Quantitative data are analyzed and presented as numerical results or in the form of summary statistics such as averages, change measures, or frequency distributions. Both qualitative and quantitative evaluation data are useful in examining how well the activity intervention and program objectives are achieved (Greenblatt, 1988; Stumbo & Peterson, 2009; Wilhite & Keller, 2000). Certain evaluation techniques are inappropriate because of characteristics of the client (e.g., invasive or stressful measures taken on frail older adults) or the techniques themselves may impose unnecessary invasions into a client's affairs (e.g., probing sensitive interpersonal information; Wilhite & Keller, 2000).

The evaluation objectives and specified set of subitems will require distinct times for data collection. Attendance records should be compiled promptly and regularly. Characteristics of individual program participants will be gathered as needed and at regular cycles during the program. Data related to program outcomes will be generated at the end of an activity intervention and also sometimes at predetermined intervals (Wilhite & Keller, 2000).

Analysis and reporting of the evaluation data involves the determination of how the information will be used and by whom. Formats for the communication of evaluation results often include interim and final reports, case studies, graphs, tables, charts, videotapes, progress notes, care plans, or discharge plans. The formats and methods for relating evaluation information are determined by the purposes of the evaluation and by the intended audience (McMillan & Schumacher, 2006; Riddick & Russell, 2008; Stumbo & Peterson, 2009; Wilhite & Keller, 2000). Objectives-oriented evaluations typically are concerned with relating the final information to those parties who are directly concerned about the client who has received the activity intervention or participated in an ongoing activity program.

Methods of Evaluation

A variety of methods are available for documenting client progress, and for evaluating client and program outcomes (Austin, 2004; Stumbo & Peterson, 2009). *Documentation* plays a significant role in the delivery of activity programs. The format for individual client documentation varies within each facility. Regardless of the method used for client documentation, each individual must be reviewed regularly in order to determine if stated goals are being achieved and the plan of care is properly implemented (Austin; Greenblatt, 1988; Stumbo & Peterson, 2009).

Several methods used in evaluation are described in this chapter including *surveys, questionnaires, interviews, observations, task analysis, goal attainment scaling, sociometry,* and *triangulation.* Each method has its own particular advantages and disadvantages. For example, questionnaires and interviews assess variables more directly, while observation is less direct and can yield inaccurate interpretations. Observations are less intrusive and less inclined to prompt biased responses from participants than interviews and surveys (Leitner & Leitner, 2004). Task analysis and Goal Attainment Scaling are more formal techniques for planning and documenting client outcomes, and sociometry is useful when evaluating group performance and relationships. Triangulation is proposed as a method that blends several methods in order to gain a more complete view of program and activity intervention effectiveness.

Surveys, Questionnaires, and Interviews

Questionnaires and *surveys* completed by program participants can cover a wide variety of issues such as attitudes, beliefs, personal interests, perceived life satisfaction, former and present pursuits, and perceived health status. Written questionnaires or surveys are generally less costly, less time-consuming, and easier to administer to a large number of people. Written responses, however, often are not practical or possible with impaired older persons. Surveys and questionnaires should be as short, concrete (as opposed to abstract), and uncomplicated as possible in order to compensate for any deficiencies in cognitive functioning.

Interviews and *observations*, on the other hand, tend to be more effective with impaired older individuals. Interviews also may address beliefs, values, attitudes, needs and interests, perceived life satisfaction, perceived health status, and various other variables (e.g., family history patterns) (Leitner & Leitner, 2004).

The purposes of the interview are clearly stated to the participants. The interviewer will establish rapport with the interviewees. Interviews should be conducted in a quiet, private area that is free from sensory distractions or interruptions. Predetermined, standardized responses to requests for clarification of questions also can enhance the validity of the results. The interviewee may intermittently require reorientation to the topic of concern. Negative comments are not dwelled upon but they should be acknowledged and then the interviewee is redirected back to the interview questions. Other data collection methods can be used in tandem with interviews in order to enhance obtaining more valid results (Leitner & Leitner, 2004).

Observations of Behavior

Observations are one of the most common evaluation procedures used in treatment, and they can be completed with or without the client's awareness of the process. Typical observations might include the number of participants in an activity, the percentage of clients who chose to participate in the activity, the number of participants who arrived or left the activity early, clients who were active vs. passive participants in the activity, and the duration and frequency of the activity. Observations of behavior also may include documentation of participants' satisfaction with activities or other areas (Greenblatt, 1988; Leitner & Leitner, 2004).

Direct observation entails the use of specific procedures to record or evaluate various outcomes and behaviors such as tally sheets for target behaviors (e.g., display of social skills, use of motor skills, etc.), or observation logs (e.g., detailed descriptions of the participants and environment during the activity). Observations that are conducted by staff members who have been trained in observational techniques and associated tools or instruments (e.g., tally sheet or log) will increase the usefulness of the resulting information and help to control for unwanted bias.

The criteria used for evaluation of the effectiveness of a program or intervention will direct the observation of target behaviors. A behavior rating form can be used that lists the specific behaviors to be observed and recorded with added space to indicate the frequency of each behavior and any comments regarding the behaviors (Leitner & Leitner, 2004). Observers should be discreet and avoid staring at the persons under observation. Observational tools that might distract the attention of the activity participants should not be used (e.g., laptop computers for recording frequency of behaviors). The observer's status as a nonparticipant in the activities should be ensured. The use of observational techniques in evaluation should reflect a trained observer's objective perceptions of individual or group responses to an activity intervention (Leitner & Leitner, 2004).

Task Analysis

Task analysis is a preparatory phase that is used during planning, documentation, and evaluation of individual treatment plans within rehabilitation programs. Task analysis comprises a basis for the construction of evaluation instruments, as well as the design of instructional approaches, supports, and materials. It is a useful method for clarifying the step-by-step approach that is needed for teaching specific activity skills to impaired clients (Greenblatt, 1988; Stumbo & Peterson, 2009; Thiagarajan, Semmel & Semmel, 1974; see Chapter 7 for a discussion of activity analysis).

Task analysis is a process that examines the elements of an activity. It involves the study of behavior and the identification of its components. The procedures in task analysis include: (a) statement of task objectives, (b) identification of subtasks, (c) comparable treatment of each subtask by repetition of objective analysis, and (d) completion of analysis when the subtask results in a logical conclusion or behavior change (Stumbo & Peterson, 2009; Thiagarajan, Semmel & Semmel, 1974).

Initially, the primary task must have relevance to the client's needs. Task analysis should be complete including all the steps needed to fully engage in the activity. The inclusion of trivial tasks, however, is an error of excessive task analysis and should be avoided. Each subtask must be necessary for the performance of the primary task; subtasks should not be excessive or redundant (Thiagarajan, Semmel & Semmel, 1974).

An activity should be progressive in order to provide for differing physical and mental aptitudes, and sequential performance. The achievement of therapeutic goals requires that each functional task be analyzed. An analysis of each individual element provides a greater understanding of how a task may promote successful client participation. A task must permit modification either by simplification or by an extension to include additional challenge. The task also must allow for a conclusion with specified strategies for the verification of performance and competence (Hamill & Oliver, 1980).

Goal Attainment Scaling

Another method for the documentation and evaluation of progress toward established goals and objectives is *Goal Attainment Scaling* (Kiresuk & Sherman, 1968). The predominant aspects of the Goal Attainment Scale are: (a) establishment of goals; (b) specification of barriers to goal attainment; and (c) description of the most favorable, least favorable, and most likely outcomes of intervention (Bumagin & Hirn, 1990).

An advantage of Goal Attainment Scaling is that it provides recognition of partial success. The method is structured, yet flexible enough to be broad its applicability. Goals are established with the client, not in the absence of him or her. The design of Goal Attainment Scaling simplifies goals so that they are apportioned and explicitly defined. This process enables professionals to focus their efforts upon individual goals, and to adapt the evaluation to a variety of problems and situations (Bumagin & Hirn, 1990).

Sociometry

The process of *sociometry* can be used to identify relationships among group members. Sociometry is a technique that explores the organization of groups by determining the nature of structure that is operating within the group. Sociograms are graphic representations of group structure that identify persons who are accepted or popular and those individuals who may be rejected, disliked, or less accepted (Greenblatt, 1988).

Sociometric techniques are valuable for enhancing the social adjustment of the individual. The identification of acceptance or rejection through sociometric procedures can enable the activity leader to facilitate behavior change for those who require assistance in group formats. Leadership skills also may be fostered in individuals who possess leadership abilities (Danford, 1970).

Sociometric techniques can improve group relations by detecting problem areas within interpersonal relationships, thus allowing the activity leader an opportunity to facilitate more effective social situations. Sociometric approaches also may be used to improve the organization of groups. Sociometric methods identify individuals with similar personalities and preferences, and through the use of cooperative efforts, sociometry can increase the productivity of groups by the promotion of group cohesiveness (Danford, 1970).

Triangulation

Triangulation is a systematic approach that utilizes a variety of evaluation techniques and procedures to compile both qualitative and quantitative information. It encourages the use of a range of evaluative methods and resources to present a more comprehensive description of clients and programs (Howe, 1982; Riddick & Russell, 2008).

Triangulation is practical for the analysis of unanticipated outcomes with the emphasis placed upon clients' perspectives and developing a more complete understanding of their needs. The use of triangulation assists in the confirmation of results. Triangulation also yields a more accurate interpretation and application of the results of the activity intervention or program (Howe & Keller, 1988).

Case Review

The specified care plan, documentation process, and evaluation findings collectively play a significant role in the total care of the older client. The identification of problem areas and behaviors that determine level of activity participation, individual adjustment to the facility and the activity program, and the development of leisure pursuits will indicate the progress or lack of progress for each client. Awareness of these areas is essential for the generation of effective care plans, including plan evaluation and modification (Greenblatt, 1988; Stumbo & Peterson, 2009).

Documentation should include current care plans for clients whose status or classification has been modified. Any client who is reclassified to a different level of care requires a new treatment plan with revisions to the evaluation components as needed. A review of care plans also should be performed for those clients who come to the facility or program from another hospital or agency (Greenblatt, 1988; Stumbo & Peterson, 2009).

The basic considerations in all care plans include factors that relate the client's medical status, as well as physical and/or psychological limitations. Specific attention should be given to the following aspects: the client's response to the program, his or her level of participation in the program, social interactions and relationships with peers and staff members, staff or agency supports that are provided to the specific client, and any notable attitudes and patterns of behavior (Stumbo & Peterson, 2009).

A combination of these elements, as well as various external factors, appears to influence the thrust of the care plan and thus, will shape the documentation and evaluation process. Additional components may include standards established by the facility that are mandated by the various regulatory agencies (Greenblatt, 1988).

Case Review Example

The following case example highlights the use of Goal Attainment Scaling:

• • • • •

Upon discharge from the rehabilitation center, Mrs. W. and her family established a goal to hire a part-time caregiver/companion for Mrs. W. Mrs. W. is 76 years old and prefers to have a companion of her own ethic background. The companion is expected to assist in the care of Mrs. W. who is severely limited in her ability to perform daily routines of self-care. Her limitations are due to severe arthritis and muscular impairment.

After much searching the family could not locate an individual who fulfilled Mrs. W. and her family's main requirements. At that time, all members of the family agreed with Mrs. W. to interview potential caregivers/companions who did not share the same ethnicity.

By utilizing Goal Attainment Scaling as the evaluation measure, the most favorable, the least favorable, and the most probable outcomes were predicted in regard to locating an appropriate and satisfactory caregiver/companion for Mrs. W. The best possible outcome would be if the family was able to interview one potential part-time caregiver/companion and to be able to hire him/her. The worst outcome would be many candidates would be interviewed but none hired. The most likely result was that after interviewing several individuals, one would be hired on a trial basis. The result was that the family hired the first person who was interviewed; therefore, the most favorable outcome was achieved.

Subsequent goals considered different aspects of the arrangement between Mrs. W. and the caregiver/companion. For example, would Mrs. W., her family, and the caregiver/companion be satisfied? Would they be somewhat dissatisfied, but have the ability to resolve their difficulties? Would they be so dissatisfied that the caregiver/companion would be released within a short period of time? The efforts of the rehabilitation case coordination staff focused upon the identification of problems. This process provided assistance to Mrs. W., members of her family, and the caregiver/companion to resolve their differences.

If the relationship is eventually rejected, the formation of alternate goals will again be evaluated with Mrs. W. and her family. If the companion remains for a long enough period of time to enable the family members to obtain the needed release from daily caregiving responsibilities, partial success will be accomplished. Because of this initial experience, future attempts to hire a part-time caregiver/companion may reach a more satisfactory conclusion. Potential resolution of the dilemma also can involve the location of another part-time caregiver/companion or the consideration of an entirely different plan of care for Mrs. W.

• • • • •

Goal Attainment Scaling, utilized as the method of evaluation in the above case, fostered a team approach to meeting the client's needs (Mrs. W.). Members of her family and care coordination staff assumed different responsibilities in working toward the agreed upon goal. The structure of Goal Attainment Scaling assisted in reducing criticism and controversy by promoting cooperation and a more comprehensive realization of the overall purpose and goals of the client's program (Bumagin & Hirn, 1990). Goal Attainment Scaling proved to be an effective evaluation method for this particular client and her specific treatment goal(s).

Summary

Evaluation is fundamental to the planning process. It enables the determination of the value of various aspects of an activity and/or program in order to influence optimal outcomes in all areas. Evaluation methods frequently are selected based upon the costs required for implementation, as well as the intended outcome of the evaluation (e.g., client focused vs. program/agency focused).

Documentation is an essential component of evaluation. The significance of goals, objectives, activities, and inferences of progress may be determined through documentation. Documentation and evaluation of specific activity interventions and ongoing activity programs provide the necessary information for making immediate and long-range decisions.

The processes of formative and summative evaluation were discussed in this chapter, and the differences between qualitative and quantitative information were pointed out. Various evaluative methods were overviewed including surveys and questionnaires, interviews, observations, task analysis, Goal Attainment Scaling, sociometry, and triangulation.

Surveys, questionnaires, interviews, and observations collect client-specific information from individuals, as well as groups of participants. These techniques produce both quantitative and qualitative information that can be used in evaluating the effects of an activity intervention or overall activity program.

Task analysis was described as a basis for the development of instruments and approaches to evaluate client-program-activity fit. Task analysis concerns the analysis of a behavior or an activity through the identification of its components. Matching tasks to client needs helps to ensure attainment of behavioral objectives that are being sought through activity intervention.

Goal Attainment Scaling was emphasized as an additional method for documentation of progress toward affirmed goals and objectives, while sociometric techniques were articulated as a means to examine the structure within groups. Further, triangulation was defined as a systematic approach for achieving a more thorough description and characterization of clients and programs. Triangulation often will utilize multiple methods in concert to gain a better understanding of program impact on client progress.

Finally, care plans, documentation, and evaluation were conceived as integral to the comprehensive care of older clients. Insight into these areas was considered necessary for the development and implementation of effective care, treatment, and/or services. A case example was offered as an illustration of these points.

Comprehension Questions

The reader can check for comprehension of the material presented in this chapter by answering the following questions:

1. What is documentation and why is it important?

2. Describe three different methods that can be used in evaluating a specific activity intervention or overall program. Present the strengths and weaknesses associated with each method.

3. Describe the objectives-oriented evaluation approach.

4. Conduct a case review and provide a description of the evaluation approach and tools that could be used in the care plan.

References

Austin, D. R. (2004). *Therapeutic recreation: processes and techniques* (5th ed.). Champaign, IL: Sagamore Publishing.

Beddall, T. & Kennedy, D. W. (1985). Attitudes of therapeutic recreators toward evaluation and client assessment. *Therapeutic Recreation Journal, 19*(1), 62–70.

Biegel, D. E., Shore, B. K. & Gordon, E. (1984). *Building support networks for the elderly: Theory and applications*. Thousand Oaks, CA: Sage Publications.

Bumagin, V. E. & Hirn, K. F. (1990). *Helping the aging family: A guide for professionals*. New York, NY: Springer.

Danford, H. G. (1970). *Creative leadership in recreation* (2nd ed.). Boston, MA: Allyn and Bacon.

Gillespie, K. A., Kennedy, D. W. & Soble, K. (1988–89). Utilizing importance-performance analysis in the evaluation and marketing of activity programs in geriatric settings. *Activities, Adaptation, and Aging, 13*(1), 77–89.

Greenblatt, F. S. (1988). *Therapeutic recreation for long-term care facilities*. NY: Human Sciences.

Gunn, S. L. & Peterson, C. A. (1984). *Therapeutic recreation program design: Principles and procedures* (2nd ed.). Englewood Cliffs, NJ: Prentice-Hall.

Hamill, C. M. & Oliver, R. C. (1980). *Therapeutic activities for the handicapped elderly*. Rockville, MD: Aspen Publishers.

Howe, C. Z. (1982). Some uses of multi-modal curriculum evaluation in therapeutic recreation. In L. L. Neal & C. R. Edginton (Eds.), *Extra perspectives: Concepts in therapeutic recreation* (87–98). Eugene, OR: University of Oregon.

Howe, C. Z. & Keller, M. J. (1988). The use of triangulation as an evaluation technique: Illustrations from regional symposia in therapeutic recreation. *Therapeutic Recreation Journal, 22*(1), 36–45.

Kiresuk, T. J. & Sherman, R. E. (1968). Goal attainment scaling: A general method for evaluating comprehensive community mental health programs. *Community Mental Health Journal, 4*(6), 443–453.

Leitner, M. J. & Leitner, S. F. (2004). *Leisure in later life* (3rd ed.) New York, NY: Haworth Press.

McMillan, J. H. & Schumacher, S. (2006). *Research in education: Evidence-based inquiry* (6th ed.). Boston, MA: Pearson Education a division of Allyn and Bacon, Inc.

Reinharz, S. & Rowles, G. D. (Eds.). (1988). *Qualitative gerontology*. New York, NY: Springer.

Riddick, C. C. & Russell, R. V. (2008). *Research in recreation, park, sport, and tourism* (2nd ed.). Champaign, IL: Sagamore Publishing.

Rossman, B. (2000). *Recreation programming: Designing leisure experiences* (3rd ed.). Champaign, IL: Sagamore Publishing.

Stumbo, N. J. & Peterson, C. A. (2009). *Therapeutic recreation program design: principles and procedures* (5th ed.). San Francisco, CA: Pearson/Benjamin-Cummings.

Teaff, J. D. (1985). *Leisure services with the elderly*. St. Louis, MO: Times Mirror/Mosby.

Teague, M. L. (1992). *Health promotion: Achieving high-level wellness in the later years* (2nd ed.). Indianapolis, IN: Benchmark.

Theobald, W. F. (1979). *Evaluation of recreation and park programs*. NY: John Wiley & Sons.

Thiagarajan, S., Semmel, D. S. & Semmel, M. I. (1974). *Instructional development for training teachers of exceptional children: A sourcebook*. Bloomington, IN: Indiana University.

Wilhite, B. C. & Keller, M. J. (2000). *Therapeutic recreation: Cases and exercises* (2nd ed.). State College, PA: Venture Publishing, Inc.

• CHAPTER 16 •
Ethics and Standards of Care

Learning Objectives

1. Describe the relevance and importance of ethics and ethical decision making in activity intervention.

2. Discuss various situations that activity specialists may be confronted with that involve ethical decisions.

3. Identify basic concepts related to ethics and standards of care.

4. Discuss ways in which healthcare professions are dealing with these issues.

5. Describe standards of care in relationship to activity intervention and discuss why are they important to activity specialists working with older adults.

Key Terms

- Advocacy Model
- Autonomy
- Beneficence
- Competency
- Confidentiality
- Dilemma
- Ethical
- Ethics Dilemma
- Informed Consent
- Justice
- Living Will
- Nonmaleficence
- Power of Attorney
- Privacy
- Privileged Communication
- Standards of Care

Introduction

As the number of frail older adults in the population grows, the risk of ethical violations that affect older persons potentially increases. In order to prevent ethical violations, it is important for the practitioner or caregiver to have a basic grasp of ethical concepts, principles, and standards of care. Activity specialists, as well as other professionals in the healthcare industry, must be prepared to deal with ethical issues. Preparation is especially crucial for those who provide services to older adults. This chapter provides basic information related to ethics, standards of care, and working with older adults in therapeutic activity intervention.

Activity Specialists and Ethical Decisions

There are three important reasons why activity specialists working with older adults should be concerned about ethics and ethical decisions. First, older adults are vulnerable to ethical abuse because they have a greater risk of developing mental and/or physical impairments during the months or years preceding death. Mental impairments such as dementia may affect memory, concentration, and judgment. These impairments come at a stage in life when decision making concerning treatment may be critical. Physical impairments that may occur in later life, as well as mental impairments, may be responsible for the involvement of a variety of professionals in the delivery of healthcare services. Older adults may find that new faces and personalities suddenly become interested in very intimate aspects of their lives. In addition to these concerns, older adults with disabilities are at a high risk of being institutionalized and institutional living also may provide a setting in which ethical problems arise. Furthermore, professional ethics may be violated based on pervasive negative stereotypes that are commonly associated with older adults. These stereotypes typically portray older adults as not being competent to understand the particulars of their treatment (Chichin, 2004; Gilhooly, 1986; Kapp, 2004).

The second concern deals with the empowerment of older adults that has occurred in the past few decades. Older people requiring medical treatment have become better consumers and require professionals to be accountable for the decisions they make and the quality of care they provide. They now demand to have their views recognized and respected, and they expect members of the medical profession to be more sensitive and responsive to the needs and interests of the older adult (Gilhooly, 1986; Luttrell & Fisher, 1997).

Finally, the role of caretaker has dramatically changed to one of caregiver. There is a preference among many older adults to stay at or return to their home for care after a debilitating illness or accident. This tendency is the result of a current economic and political climate which discourages expensive nursing home care except for those who are most ill and/or impaired. As more family members become caregivers, they will be required to make more treatment decisions, as well as end-of-life decisions. Family members may require the assistance of healthcare providers to make ethical decisions that have legal ramifications. Professionals may face dilemmas when family decisions are based on their beliefs regarding the quality of life for their loved one and these decisions are not consistent with social norms codified in the law (Chichin, 2004; Hanks & Settles, 1988; Kapp, 2004).

Ethical Dilemmas and Patient Care

Ethics refers to the study of the appropriateness of human behavior based on what is good or bad, right or wrong, in relation to our moral duties and obligations to each other as human beings and within a societal context (Chichin, 2004). Our personal ethics are rooted in our character but they can be refined or developed (Gilhooly, 1986). Activity specialists also must be concerned with professional ethics. Members of professions explore ethical issues to determine a set of moral principles or behaviors that guide professional practice. Many professional organizations have developed Standards of Practice that serve as the code of conduct statement for their members (Loeffler & Henley, 1997; also see Appendix A for the Standards of Practice of National Association of Activity Professionals). These standards are meant to guide professional behavior in a general sense and may be open to different interpretations. As a result, it is important for professionals to conduct a thorough investigation of ethics throughout their professional careers. This section describes some important principles and concepts that are helpful in understanding ethical issues (for a copy of The Patient Care Partnership brochure in pdf format, go to http://www.aha.org/aha/issues/Communicating-With-Patients/pt-care-partnership.html—this brochure replaces the former Patient's Bill of Rights as formulated by the American Hospital Association).

Three fundamental ethical principles are *beneficence, autonomy,* and *justice* (Chichin, 2004). Each of these principles should guide professional decision making in the care and treatment of older adults. *Beneficence* means that our decisions and actions are always motivated by "doing good" for the older adult in our care. In spite of what the individual or his/her family wants, our actions must always be beneficial or good for the older adult. *Autonomy,* which is guided by the federal Patient Self-Determination Act legislated in 1991, primarily ensures that it is the older adult's right to accept or refuse treatment; that is, each individual is entitled to make decisions for his or her self. Finally, *justice* is concerned with how resources are distributed, especially when they are scarce. Justice is an ethical principle of particular importance for those individuals who are most vulnerable in society, such as the poor, very young, old, and those without food or home. These individuals usually have the greatest need and the least power in society to safeguard having their needs met. These three principles are crucial when confronted with an ethical dilemma in the care and treatment of older adults.

A *dilemma* is a situation that requires a decision between alternatives that appear to be equal. People face minor dilemmas every day, such as what movie to see, what telephone call to return first, and what to wear. Most of these dilemmas can be resolved fairly easily because the consequences of the decisions are not severe. It is not so easy to resolve ethical dilemmas. An *ethical dilemma* is a situation in which alternatives are defined by opposing ethical principles (Chichin, 2004; Howell, 1988). For example, a family is facing the decision of institutionalizing an 80-year-old man. He has Alzheimer's disease and the burden of caring for him at home is overwhelming his wife. One ethical dilemma that family confronts is how to resolve the care needs and living situation of their older member. Caregiving, staying in the home, and caregiving burden often present an ethical dilemma for families of older adults. In this case, the family may be considering the following two scenarios: (a) nursing home placement is a sign that the family is not able to adequately care for its member; and (b) if the man is not placed in a nursing home, his wife's health may fail because of the burden of everyday caregiving. The situation may be compounded by other factors such as a promise the couple made 20 years ago to never place each other in an institution. While sorting out and resolving this dilemma, the family will need to consider and balance issues of autonomy and beneficence. Clearly, resolving this issue will not be an easy task.

Howell (1988) suggested that most ethical dilemmas fall into one of the following categories:

1. Dilemmas arise with regard to the definition, discovery and defense of rights of individuals;

2. Dilemmas arise with regard to competence to make decisions, and consequent needs for protection through guardianship;
3. Dilemmas arise with regard to the process by which decisions can be made on behalf of the person who is deemed to be incompetent;
4. Dilemmas arise with regard to defining and measuring past wrongs or deprivations imposed by social policy, government action, and discrimination, and with regard to questions of restitution or recompense. (444–445)

In their jobs, activity specialists are most likely to deal with the first three categories of ethical dilemmas, which deal with patient autonomy. While all healthcare professionals should strive to protect patient autonomy, sometimes it is not possible to ensure autonomous decision making.

Remember, *autonomy* is an individual's natural right to be self-governing, which means it is the individual's right to determine his or her own destiny. The activity specialist is obliged to assist individuals come to this determination by providing appropriate information and helping them to understand that information so an informed decision can be made (Guccione, 1988). Once a decision has been made by the individual, it must be respected, even if it is not judged to be in the patient's best interest by the concerned healthcare professionals.

Autonomy can be an ambiguous concept. Although it is not appropriate to coerce a person into making a decision, autonomy does not prevent an individual from deferring decisions that must be made to another person. For example, a patient may not want to hear a detailed explanation of the medical treatment a physician has recommended. He or she may simply trust the physician to make the right decision. What is important, however, is that the physician provided the patient the opportunity to make an autonomous decision.

The key to maintaining patient autonomy is informed consent. *Informed consent* is the process by which information is provided to the individual regarding medical treatment and research so that he or she can make an informed decision (Tymchuk & Ouslander, 1990). Levine and Lawlor (1991) identified three components of the informed consent process:

1. The patient must be given information that is relevant and important to the service, procedure, or care that is being offered so that then the patient can knowingly refuse or give his or her consent.

2. The patient must demonstrate the capacity to understand and consent to the service, procedure or care that is being offered to him or her.
3. Voluntary consent must be obtained without any evidence of coercion.

A number of models for achieving informed consent exist. Gadow's (1981) Advocacy Model is useful in helping individuals to make their own decisions by promoting the following objectives:

*   Ensuring the possibility of self-determination;
*   Enabling the patient to select the information needed to make a decision;
*   Disclosing personal views;
*   Assisting the patients to determine their own values; and
*   Ascertaining how patients apprehend their own individuality.

Activity specialists may feel that informed consent is not as important for therapeutic activity because this kind of intervention is not invasive. The principle of informed consent applies to all types of treatments, services, and care that activity specialists provide; therefore, they must respect the decisions and right of some individuals to decline participation.

Patient *privacy* and *confidentiality* also must be respected in order to preserve individual autonomy. Privacy refers to the individual's right to have control over personal information and to be free of invasions into his or her life (Gilhooly, 1986; McLean & Yoder, 2006). In certain healthcare and program settings privacy may be difficult to achieve. Nonetheless, healthcare providers including activity professionals must take steps to ensure privacy. Activity specialists may help ensure privacy by providing older adults with the opportunity to socialize with family and friends in an environment where they will not be disturbed. Respect of the individual's possessions and living space is important. The public nature of a residential facilities for older adults (e.g., retirement communities, assisted living facilities, and nursing homes) may encourage staff to freely walk in and out of individuals' rooms or apartments. It is important to remember that the room or apartment is the individual's home and should be treated as such. Confidentiality is the ancient "ethical obligation not to reveal to others anything said by the patients or to acknowledge the existence of a relationship" (Gilhooly, p. 182). Confidentiality is the key to good communication between the older adult and practitioner, and provides the ethical foundation for this relationship (Gilhooly; Guccione, 1988; McLean & Yoder).

Ethical dilemmas often arise when there is concern that an individual is incompetent and no longer able to make decisions (McLean & Yoder, 2006). A person is believed to be *incompetent* when impairments limit his or her understanding and ability to make or communicate responsible decisions. Competency is not an all or none situation; an individual can be competent in one area, such as medical treatment, but not in another, such as finances (Guccione, 1988).

When discussing issues of informed consent, the activity specialist should keep in mind several factors that can influence consent such as age, values, level of education, physical functioning, cognitive capabilities, motivation, and other possible past experiences (e.g., recent death of a spouse). Different strategies to assess the person's capacity to make an informed decision can be used. For example, Tymchuk and Ouslander (1990) recommend using illustrations in a storybook format and the following seven step process:

1. Assess physical capacity, especially vision and hearing;
2. Assess mental status to help determine decision-making capacity and potential need for a proxy;
3. Assess reading comprehension;
4. Develop consent material (including how comprehension and application are to be assessed) in format and at difficulty level to match patient/subject abilities;
5. Present information;
6. Assess comprehension and if below criterion, provide some alternative intervention such as the use of repeated trials;
7. Follow up to determine whether comprehension of the information remains at criterion level, and whether they have changed their decision. (p. 250)

Professionals at a long-term care facility in New York City use a three-pronged approach to help resolve dilemmas such as informed consent, confidentiality, privacy, and end-of-life treatment issues. The approach includes education, direct practice, and research. A wide range of educational programs presenting cases involving ethical dilemmas are offered to all families, residents, paraprofessionals and professionals. Special attempts are made to include nurse's aides and orderlies, for they often know a great deal about the person in treatment, and can be greatly affected by treatment decisions. Monthly ethical meetings are extended that address ethical dilemmas dealing with end-of-life decision making such as tube feedings, restraints, and the impact of religious beliefs on medical decisions.

An ethics consultation team evaluates the mental and physical status of the individual including any records of the person's desires and whether or not family or friends would be available to help in the decision-making process. The primary treatment team and ethics team together implement decisions made by the person (Olson et al., 1993).

The appropriate legal procedure to pursue for the family of an incompetent individual is to obtain legal guardianship of that individual. Obtaining guardianship may entail a lengthy process for families as can be seen in recent "end-of-life" cases. In the situation where the individual is clearly incompetent but has not been declared incompetent in court and a guardian has not been appointed, it is important to involve the next of kin in the decision-making process. It is not clear whether or not family members can make legally binding decisions for individuals who have not been declared incompetent, however, involvement of the next of kin in making decisions for incompetent older adults is widely practiced throughout the health and adult care professions.

Problems regarding legal guardianship and incompetency can be avoided by appointing a durable power of attorney. This process involves the individual selecting one or more persons to make decisions for him or her when he or she is no longer able to (Levine et al., 1991). The person who is selected should know the desires of the individual and be trusted to carry them out. The duties of a durable power of attorney can be applied to general areas or specific areas, such as medical treatment. This legal procedure is fairly simple and allows the individual assurance that his or her wishes will be respected. It also saves the family the more lengthy legal process of declaring the individual as incompetent. Older adults who worry about retaining autonomy should not be frightened by durable power of attorney. It will be applied only in situations where the individual is clearly no longer competent.

An important related concept that ensures personal choice is the *living will*. A living will is a written legal document that establishes how a patient wants to be treated if he or she is terminally ill and can no longer make decisions concerning his or her health (Levine & Lawlor, 1991). Many older adults have living wills that indicate they do not want any extraordinary measures taken to prolong their lives such as the use of life support. Most states honor a living will at this time, however, there are still some controversies surrounding its use. The rights of family members to overturn the requests put forth in a living will, for example, have yet to be fully determined.

The ethical dilemmas related to competency arise when decisions made by caregivers or healthcare providers conflict with the wishes of the older adult. If the individual is deemed incompetent, a legal guardian or healthcare provider may initiate an action to which the individual is opposed if the action is deemed to be in the individual's best interest. For example, an older adult with Alzheimer's disease may wish to live alone in an apartment. If that older adult has started fires due to not remembering that the stove is on, legal action may be taken to remove that individual from an independent living situation. This type of action is called *beneficence*. Beneficence is the basis of doing good acts or deeds in an effort to promote the well-being of the individual. It is founded upon the principle that caregivers are committed to do as much good as they can (Guccione, 1988; Shank, 1985). In addition to acting in the individual's best interest, healthcare providers and other professionals also are obliged to do no harm to an individual. *Nonmaleficence* is the principle that care providers will do no harm (Guccione, 1988).

The process of determining the best decision for an incompetent individual should be consistent for each case. Hayes and Settles (1986) suggested a model for decision making to be used with individuals in a case management setting. Treatment and care planning would:

1. Explicitly state value premises that influence assessments;
2. Explicitly construct, based on available information, the individual's views of his or her situation and wishes;
3. Acknowledge data regarding the individual's past coping strategies and how these are likely to influence response to dependency and frailty;
4. Explicitly state beliefs and professional judgments regarding risks inherent in the current situation;
5. Explicitly state beliefs and judgments about risks inherent in available alternative options;
6. Elicit input from panel members regarding alternative value premises, ethical choices, and risk assessments;
7. Weigh risks and decide on the action which the professional, the team, and the agency will support on behalf of the individual. (Hayes & Settles, p. 47)

Decisions made on behalf of the individual can best be achieved with the assistance of family members who are most likely to know the individual's wishes, values, and beliefs.

Ethics and Aging Research

As the older population grows, more research is being conducted with older adults. While most research is positively viewed by older adults and their families, care should be taken to be sure that older adults know that their participation is voluntary and that their privacy is not invaded (Williams, 1993). When reviewing research proposals, the role of ethics committees should be:

1. To protect rights of all who are involved in the research (including older adult subjects and the staff who work with them), these protections include confidentiality and privacy as well as voluntary participation with appropriate informed consent.
2. To evaluate the scientific merit of the proposed research as well as the qualifications of the investigators in order to assure an appropriate risk-benefit balance. (Gilhooly, 1986)

Educators and trainers of all allied healthcare professionals need to ensure that their students develop ethical knowledge, skills, and sensitivities. The combination of a core curriculum based on the essential body of knowledge coupled within a case study method of learning provides a solid approach to teaching ethics (Gilhooly, 1986).

Standards of Care

Standards are established for two reasons. First, they guarantee that a minimum level of service is provided. Secondly, they protect the consumer. Activity specialists should be familiar with external standards set by agencies outside of the facility providing direct service (e.g., Joint Commission on the Accreditation of Healthcare Organizations and the Commission on the Accreditation of Rehabilitation Facilities; Loeffler & Henley, 1997). Activity specialists also need to be knowledgeable about internal standards set by professionals providing direct service (e.g., National Association of Activity Professionals and the National Therapeutic Recreation Society; Loeffler & Henley).

Standards of care for practitioners working with older adults provide the necessary framework for describing problems so that all professionals have a common understanding. Standards of care also suggest strategies to use when problems surface and recommend protocols to apply in care management (Janicki et al., 1995). Standards of care are based on the premise that the practitioner needs to understand the changes that take place during normal aging, what risk factors are involved for the older individual, and what changes may be indicative of an onset of physical or mental impairments. Standards suggest to the practitioner that assessments and evaluations should be conducted in order to confirm a suspicion of impairment. Finally, standards recommend the establishment of care management (Janicki et al., 1995).

Care management seeks to help the older adult to maintain and maximum his or her function, to seek appropriate treatment interventions, and to use the resources from many disciplines when planning care management. The level of care, support, attention, and sensitivity all may increase as the mental or physical impairment progresses (Janicki et al., 1995). The ongoing training of practitioners in standards of care is essential. Necessary elements of this training include learning about the normal aging process and changes that might indicate impairment. Training and educational materials also should be available to families and caregivers (Janicki et al., 1995).

Summary

Activity specialists working with older adults need to have an understanding of ethical concepts and standards of care because older adults are vulnerable to ethical abuse. In recent years, older adults have become better consumers of medical and allied healthcare and thus, they tend to be more informed about issues related to their care. In addition, the changing role of the caregiver has further underscored the importance of high standards of care and solid ethical practices. This chapter helps the activity specialist to recognize and resolve ethical dilemmas faced by older adults. Activity specialists should posses a basic understanding of privacy, confidentiality, incompetence, autonomy, beneficence, and nonmaleficence. The process of informed consent, the decision making required for creating a living will, and the responsibility needed when research is being conducted with older adults are also important considerations. Finally, standards of care used by activity specialists when working with older adults will help to ensure individual well-being. Activity therapists will apply these concepts as they develop sensitivity to the delicate ethical situations often faced by older people and their caregivers.

Comprehension Questions

The reader can check for comprehension of the material presented in this chapter by answering the following questions:

1. Identify four key concepts related to professional ethics. Define them and discuss why they are important to in the process of activity intervention.

2. Describe a situation in which the activity specialist may be confronted with an ethical dilemma. Discuss different strategies for dealing with the situation.

3. Discuss why standards are important in the delivery of professional services to older adults.

References

Chichin, E. R. (2004). Chapter 14. Ethics and the elderly. In L. M. Tepper & T. M. Cassidy (Eds.), *Multidisciplinary perspectives on aging* (229–244). New York, NY: Springer.

Gilhooly, M. L. M. (1986). Ethical and legal issues in therapy with the elderly. In I. Hanley & M. L. M. Gilhooly, *Psychological therapies for the elderly* (173–197). New York, NY: University Press.

Guccione, A. A. (1988). Compliance and patient autonomy: Ethical and legal limits to professional dominance. *Topics in Geriatric Rehabilitation, 3*(3), 62–73.

Gadow, S. (1981). A model for ethical decision-making. *Oncology Nursing Forum, 7*(4), 44–47.

Hanks, R. S. & Settles, B. H. (1988–1989). Theoretical questions and ethical issues in a family caregiving relations. *The Journal of Applied Social Sciences, 13*(1), 9–39.

Hayes, C. L., Soniat, B. & Burr, H. (1986). Value conflict and resolution in forcing services on "at risk" community-based older adults. *Clinical Gerontologist, 4*(3), 41–48.

Howell, M. C. (1988). Ethical dilemmas encountered in the care of those who are disabled and also old. *Educational Gerontology, 14,* 439–449.

Janicki, M. P., Heller, T., Seltzer, G. B. & Hoge, J. (1995). *Practice guidelines for the clinical assessment and care management of Alzheimer and other dementias among adults with mental retardation.* Washington, DC: American Association on Mental Retardation.

Kapp, M. B. (2004). Chapter 13. Issues in elder law. In L. M. Tepper & T. M. Cassidy (Eds.), *Multidisciplinary perspectives on aging* (217–228). New York, NY: Springer.

Loeffler, M. A. & Henley, S. (1997) Standards of practice: Are they relevant? In D. M. Compton (Ed.), *Issues in therapeutic recreation: toward the new millennium* (2nd ed.). Champaign, IL: Sagamore Publishing.

Levine, J. & Lawlor, B. A. (1991). Family counseling and legal issues in Alzheimer's disease. *The Psychiatric Clinics of North America, 14*(2), 385–396.

Luttrell, S. & Fisher, F. (1997). Ethical aspects of quality care. In P. P. Mayer, E. J. Dickinson & M. Sandler (Eds.), *Quality care for elderly people* (Chapter 2, pp. 17–35). London, UK: Chapman & Hall Medical.

McLean, D. J. & Yoder, D. G. (2005). *Issues in recreation and leisure: Ethical decision making.* Champaign, IL: Human Kinetics.

Olson, E., Chichin, E. R., Libow, L. S., Martico-Greenfield, T., Neufeld, R. R. & Mulvihill, M. (1993). A center on ethics in long-term care. *The Gerontologist, 33*(2), 269–274.

Shank, J. W. (1985). Bioethical principles and the practice of therapeutic recreation in clinical settings. *Therapeutic Recreation Journal, 19*(4), 31–40.

Tymchuk, A. J. & Ouslander, J. G. (1990). Optimizing the informed consent process with elderly people. *Educational Gerontology, 16,* 245–257.

Williams, S. G. (1993). How do the elderly and their families feel about research participation? *Geriatric Nursing, 14*(1), 11–14.

• CHAPTER 17 •

The Future: Trends and Issues

Learning Objectives

1. Identify national organizations that serve the professional needs of activity specialists.
2. Describe the general areas that comprise the body of knowledge for activity professionals.
3. Provide examples of current and future trends that influence the delivery of health-related services to older persons.
4. Describe trends and issues in public policy that are affecting activity services for older adults.
5. Describe the purposes of activity programs for different groups of Baby Boomers.

Key Terms

- Active Aging
- Activity Professional
- Ageism
- Aging in Place
- Aging Well
- Association for Gerontology in Higher Education (AGHE)
- Healthcare Reform
- Health Promotion
- Intergenerational
- Life Expectancy
- Long-Term Care (LTC)
- Maximum Lifespan
- Medicare
- Medicaid
- National Association of Activity Professionals (NAAP)
- National Certification Council for Activity Professionals (NCCAP)
- Omnibus Budget Reconciliation Act (OBRA)
- Population Aging
- Public Policy
- Retirement
- Selective Optimization with Compensation (SOC)
- Social Security
- Successful Aging

Introduction

This text introduces the reader to the older adult population from a variety of perspectives. The chapters in Unit I provide information about the population and discuss healthcare for older persons. Unit II provides an overview of normal aging processes including information about common illnesses, diseases, and disabilities experienced by older persons. Units III and IV give detailed information about the intervention process and activity strategies that are commonly utilized in the therapeutic care and treatment of older adults. Finally, in Unit V, the importance of documentation, evaluation, ethics, and standards of care is covered. In this final chapter of the text, trends and issues in the provision of care and services to older adults are addressed.

By now, most readers of this text recognize that the life course for most adults does not appear to follow a straight, linear pathway but rather weaves itself along a route that is affected by many factors including one's birth cohort, personal characteristics and genetics, and the time period in history in which one lives. The journey of life brings many events and personal circumstances. In older adulthood, most people must adjust to both gains and losses. With most losses, lifestyles will be affected, personal resources and social resources may be impacted and they may even dwindle. Maintaining a meaningful and active lifestyle is one way that older adults can keep in touch with each other, thus improving their health and quality of life. Conversely, cocooning in one's home and leading a sedentary, solitary life will more than likely undermine health and well-being.

The future quality of life for older persons and the role of professionals who provide services to them are influenced by many issues. Policy and service developments that are implemented or discontinued now will surely influence the future, just as the past has inspired the present. Public responsibility for services to an aging population is of vital concern. The need for service coordination, the acknowledgment of manpower shortages particularly in allied health fields, and the recognition of the limits of professionalism are critical factors affecting services to the older adult population—now and into the future (Schultz & Binstock, 2006). This chapter provides a discussion of two broad areas affecting the future of activity services for older adults: (a) information related to professionalism, and (b) discussion of current and future trends influencing services to an aging population.

Professional Qualifications for Activity Specialists

Federal and state agencies periodically review and improve the regulations that specify a level of professional qualifications for personnel who provide activity programs for older persons. Under the Omnibus Budget Reconciliation Act of 1987 (OBRA), federal law specified a checklist for nursing home facilities that provided the basis for advancing the profession for activity specialists. Under OBRA regulations, activity departments in nursing homes receiving Medicaid/ Medicare funding must be directed by a "qualified professional." An outgrowth of OBRA was the establishment of the National Certification Council for Activity Professionals (NCCAP), the only body that provides certification for activity specialists. Today, NCCAP is the recognized certifying body for activity professionals who work in a broad range of settings such as assisted-living facilities, adult day centers, and nursing homes.

The preparation of activity specialists has advanced to a level of professionalism that is supported by several organizations and different options for obtaining professional preparation. Some of the fields that are related with activity specialization are gerontology education, recreation, occupational therapy, physical therapy, specialized therapies (e.g., dance, art, music, horticulture), and other allied health professions. Typically, these fields are backed by degree programs from colleges and universities. Activity specialists have the added benefit of certification from the NCCAP. Activity specialists are also served by their own professional organization, the National Association of Activity Professionals.

New job opportunities in aging are expected to accompany the continued and rapid growth of the older adult population. It is widely acknowledged that one of the most stable employment areas in the country is in the healthcare industry, which is a growth industry. Healthcare jobs include nurses and doctors, the allied healthcare professions (e.g., occupational and physical therapy, pharmacology), and activity professionals. Jobs are available in nursing homes, clinics and healthcare centers, and companies and organizations that serve older adults (e.g., in-home care, assisted living).

While the availability of jobs is increasing, the growth in professionally prepared workers is not keeping pace. Individuals who are seeking jobs working with older adults will continue to need training and credentialing. At present, a number of organizations are addressing this problem as it relates to the activity specialist. In this final section of the book, three organizations that are concerned with professional preparation of the activity specialist are presented: (a) the Association for Gerontology in Higher Education (AGHE), (b) the National Association of Activity Professionals (NAAP), and (c) National Certification Council for Activity Professionals (NCCAP). These three organizations provide the foundation for education in gerontology and professionalism for the activity specialist.

Association for Gerontology in Higher Education (AGHE)

The Association for Gerontology Higher Education (AGHE) (www.aghe.org) is the leading national organization that is solely concerned with education in the field of gerontology. AGHE is devoted to sponsoring and developing initiatives in gerontological education that involve educators, students, officials, and researchers. AGHE is an association of member institutions of higher education and individuals. Member institutions are those that have aging studies programs. The purposes of AGHE are to:

1. prepare service delivery personnel who will work directly with elderly adults;
2. train educators who specialize in the physical and social attributes of aging;
3. educate society at large about the processes of aging and the implications of an aging society; and
4. instruct older adults seeking to maximize their options in a complex and challenging age.

AGHE offers a program of review for Educational Programs in Gerontology and recognizes programs that meet certain goals and objectives as "Programs of Merit." Programs of Merit are available at the Master's, Bachelor's, and Associate's degree levels. The POM initiative was initiated in 1998 by the Executive Committee of AGHE and is a voluntary program of evaluation that accomplishes the following objectives:

1. Verifies for students that the program is consistent with national practice and guidelines established by AGHE;
2. Assures the public of the quality of programs and their graduates;
3. Clarifies for employers the knowledge and skills imparted to students who graduate from individual gerontology programs;
4. Informs campus administrators of national guidelines, expectations, and practice in gerontology education; and

5. Indicates to interested students that the program is of appropriate quality.

AGHE provides consultation services and resources to institutions of higher education on topics related to the standards and guidelines for gerontology program development. The following volume contains recommended resource papers that address gerontology education:

Gerontology Program Development and Evaluation. Tom Hickey, Phyllis K. Stillman, and Elizabeth B. Douglass (Eds.). 1994. 150 pp. $50 AGHE members; $65 nonmembers. This resource book provides information about how higher education institutions should analyze their resources their resources and opportunities, define program objectives consistent with their academic missions, and plan new academic and service initiatives in aging-related areas. The collection of papers contained in the volume are:

- *AGHE Consultation Program: An Overview*
- *An Aging Society: Challenge and Response for Higher Education*
- *Promoting Gerontology Instruction: Institutional Perspectives and Administrative Issues*
- *Generating Resources for Gerontology Development in Higher Education*
- *Continuing Educational Opportunities for Gerontology Instruction*
- *Community Connections: A Key to Success for Gerontology Programs*
- *Teaching Gerontology: Developing a Course Syllabus*
- *Gerontology Program Self-Studies*
- *Guidelines for the Effective Use of a Consultant*
- *Selected References on Preparing for the Future of Higher Education*
- *Brief Bibliography: Developing Instructional Programs in Two- and Four-Year Academic Institutions*

AGHE also disseminates a set of standards and guidelines that are useful for any institution of higher education that is considering the development of a gerontology education program. The following publication outlines these standards and guidelines and the book can be purchased from AGHE:

Standards and Guidelines for Gerontology Programs. Fourth Edition. AGHE Standards Committee, J. Richard Connelly and Thomas A. Rich (First Edition Eds.). 2005. 87 pp. $20 AGHE members; $40 nonmembers.

This book includes a set of recommendations for gerontology program development that apply to any program regardless of academic level or type of credential awarded, as well as specific curriculum and policy recommendations for gerontology programs that offer an associate degree or certificate, a bachelor's degree, a bachelor's certificate or minor, a continuing education certificate at the undergraduate level, a master's degree, a graduate certificate, and a doctoral degree. A chapter on future issues in gerontological education and a glossary of terms are also included. Also included, is an expanded chapter on doctoral degree programs and a new chapter addressing on-line programs in gerontology.

The activity specialist who is interested in obtaining a college/university degree in gerontology (Associate, Bachelor, Master) is encouraged to consult the resources and website of the Association for Gerontology in Higher Education to learn more about institutions in the United States that offer programs in gerontology education.

National Association of Activity Professionals (NAAP)

The National Association of Activity Professionals (NAAP) (www.thenaap.com) is the primary national organization that was founded by activity professionals for the purpose of representing activity professionals who are practicing in geriatric settings. The mission of the NAAP is "To provide excellence in support services to activity professionals through education, advocacy, technical assistance, promotion of standards, fostering of research, and peer and industry relations" (quoted from NAAP website). NAAP provides assistance and growth opportunities to activity professionals. It is the recognized leader for the activity profession on national issues regarding activity settings and services to older adults. NAAP has grown in its membership to include members from the United States, Canada, and Bermuda. NAAP promotes the following ideals:

- The quality of life of the client/resident/participant/patient served is the primary reason for our services.
- The strength of NAAP lies in the diversity of its members. NAAP recognizes the rich cultural, and educational backgrounds of its members and values the variety of resources represented.
- The strength of NAAP also lies in the development and promotion of scientific research which further defines and supports the activity profession.
- NAAP values the development and maintenance of coalitions with organizations whose mission is similar to that of NAAP's for the purposes of

advocacy, research, education, and promotion of activity services and activity professionals.
- NAAP values members who become involved at the state and national level to promote professional standards as well as encourage employers to recognize them as professionals.
- NAAP affords Activity Professionals across the country the opportunity to speak with a common voice.

An important contribution made by NAAP was its work with the United States Congress regarding nursing home reform that now includes a mandatory activity program in all nursing homes receiving Medicaid/Medicare funding. Nursing home reform also specifies that this program is directed by a qualified activity professional (Omnibus Budget Reconciliation Act—OBRA). NAAP was instrumental in the Health Care Finance Administration's work that produced OBRA guidelines associated with nursing home reform. The NAAP continues its involvement with state and national efforts that promote standards of practice and certification of activity professionals. The next section describes the national certification program for activity professionals.

National Certification Council for Activity Professionals (NCCAP)

The National Certification Council for Activity Professionals (NCCAP) (www.nccap.org) is the leading national organization for the education and certification of activity professionals. It is recognized as *the only* national organization that specifically is devoted to certifying activity professionals. NCCAP certification is incorporated into the regulations governing professional practice in many states.

The NCCAP has established the standards, skills, and knowledge that must be attained in order to become a Certified Activity Professional. NCCAP provides three levels of certification:

- Activity Assistant Certified—AAC
- Activity Director Certified—ADC
- Activity Consultant Certified—ACC

For each level of certification, there are several tracks from which to choose in order to obtain credentialing. There are four qualifying components within each track:

- Academic Education—degree from an accredited institution and may be in social work, recreation, education, science, business, or related fields.

- Activity Experience—work experience (within past 5 years) with older adults (age 55 and older).
- Continuing Education—continuing education (within the past 5 years) including workshops, seminars, college courses, or equivalent educational experiences.
- Completion of the MEPAP (Modular Education Program for Activity Professionals), which includes 180 of educational instruction and 180 hours of experiential learning (practicum).
- Plus an additional component of Consulting Experience for the ACC level only, which includes activities such as conducting workshops, teaching a course, publishing professional articles, supervising students/activity staff.

The NCCAP has specified a body of knowledge that provides part of the foundation for certification. Among the topics included in the body of knowledge are:

- Working with Clients, which includes knowledge of human development, aging, and the older adult years; spirituality of aging; biology, sociology, and psychology of aging; leisure and aging; basic health; group instruction/leadership; therapy for the disabled; motivation; interpersonal relationships; skills for working with residents and staff; public speaking, public relations, and community relations; and regulations.
- Programming, which includes individual care planning, program management, computer skills, and the theory and practice of program types.
- Management/Personnel, Legal, and Ethical Issues, which includes personnel employment practices, management leadership, management writing skills, financial management, professional development, consulting, and resources.

In addition to basic NCCAP certification, specializations also are offered in several areas:

- Assisted Living
- Memory Care
- Adult Day Programs
- Education

The National Certification Council for Activity Professionals offers a comprehensive program of education and credentialing. The benefits for the activity specialist are many as noted by the NCCAP:

1. Federal Law, OBRA, states that an activity department must be directed by a qualified professional.

2. NCCAP certification is recognized by CMS (Formerly Health Care Financing Administration) as an organization that certifies activity professionals who work specifically with the elderly.
3. NCCAP certification assures administrators and surveyors that you have met certain professional standards to become certified.
4. Many administrators will only hire activity professionals who are certified.
5. Some administrators offer a higher salary to a certified professional.
6. Become NCCAP certified so others will know that you are nationally qualified and offering quality activity service to your residents/clients.

The future for the activity specialist is optimistic. The expectation is that employment will only grow as healthcare reform ensues and the older population enlarges to include the Baby Boomers. There is clearly a level of professionalism and professional growth that has evolved since the end of the 20th century, which has important consequences for the quality of care that is available to older adults. The activity specialist is an important part of ensuring quality care and quality of life for aging adults in the 21st century. See Appendix C for the NCCAP Code of Ethics, and contact the NCCAP National Office (P.O. Box 62589, Virginia Beach, VA 23466) for Certification Standards.

Prevailing Issues and Future Trends

As the 21st century completes its first decade, the United States is beginning to experience the "long Baby Boom," the era in which this generation enters their older adulthood (Goldsmith, 2008). Seventy-six million Baby Boomers are graying and they bring stark realities associated with inadequate public policies and systems to support the healthcare and retirement income security for the older population.

Population aging, or the steady increase in the size of the older population, is putting stress on the current healthcare system and is significantly exacerbating the costs for healthcare. It is predicted that healthcare expenditures at the current rate of escalation could reach 19% of the GDP (Gross Domestic Product) by 2014 (Kotlikoff & Burns, 2004). In 2006, Medicare alone accounted for more than 12% of federal budget (Hooyman & Kiyak, 2008). With the recent downturn in the economy coupled with increasing labor shortages, issues related to health services for an expanding older adult population require immediate policy reform and innovation. The need for a major overhaul of the healthcare system is evident.

The trends in demographic change are well-publicized on a daily basis in the media. Changes and reform in public policies affecting health services to older adults, however, are far too slow to evolve (Schultz & Binstock, 2006). Labor shortages, particularly in fields related to health services, coupled with economic shortages in meeting health expenditures will affect the quality and availability of care for a growing number of older citizens throughout the first half of the century.

In the sections that follow, selected areas that have implications for the provision of activity programs and services to older adults are discussed. The topics include: (a) aging in place, (b) life expectancy and retirement, (c) health status and health services utilization, (d) personnel shortages, (e) program and service proliferation, and (f) aging well through active living and successful aging.

Aging in Place

Aging in place is a term that is used to describe the ideal condition of not having to move from one's home when there is a change in the need for personal assistance and support services in older adulthood. *Aging in place* is the preferred alternative by the majority of older adults (Hooyman & Kiyak, 2008). To *age in place* requires the availability of and access to a range of in-home and community-based services that replace the need for placement into institutional care settings (assisted-living facilities or nursing homes). Approximately 90% of all adults over age 65 in the United States live in community-based, conventional housing and only about 5% live in nursing homes (Moody, 2009).

Aging in place has come to mean the idea of remaining within a familiar home and community that was established in preparation for or entry into later maturity. Typical residential options that support *aging in place* include continuing care retirement communities (CCRC) and planned senior communities (e.g., Sun City). In this regard, *aging in place* refers to any residential arrangement that has been planned for and chosen by the older person that will accommodate him or her throughout the remainder of life including any potential stages of disease or decline (Hooyman & Kiyak, 2008; Moody, 2009). *Aging in place* can become a process that results in older persons becoming concentrated in certain communities and neighborhoods over a period of time. This type of residential arrangement is call a Naturally Occurring Retirement Community or NORC (Moody, 2009).

Future aging Baby Boomers who choose to *age in place* will want the necessary assistance to meet their individual needs, and this preference will have significant implications for how services will be configured and delivered. It cannot be assumed that Baby Boomers will want the same kind of lifestyle that former cohorts of older adults have had, especially when it involves lifestyle factors such as leisure and recreational activity patterns. Even when and if long-term care is needed, the preference by the majority of older adults is to have this level of care provided in one's home and community rather than in an institutional setting (e.g., nursing homes). *Aging in place* presents a national challenge to health policy reform, especially as the United States enters the time of rapid expansion in the size of the older adult population.

A major deficiency in national healthcare policy is the lack of a structured and comprehensive system of long-term care (LTC) that uses various delivery approaches that can be interfaced with *aging in place*. Long-term care is defined as the "range of supportive services and assistance provided to persons who, as a result of chronic illness or disability, are unable to function autonomously on a daily basis" (Hooyman & Kiyak, 2008, p. 717). The need for LTC is typically related to assistance with activities of everyday life (ADLs and IADLs) rather than solely for medical care. Because LTC services are unlike hospital services, they are more difficult to fund directly through insurance, whether the insurance is government-based (Medicare, Medicaid) or private. Funding LTC is often difficult and is done on a patchwork basis, thus making the desire to *age in place* more challenging when additional LTC services are needed. The funding for LTC to accommodate an increasing number of frail elders who are Baby Boomers is a practical and urgent problem to address at the level of national and state policy development (Moody, 2009).

The "crisis in healthcare" that is widely discussed in the media refers to the growing number of people who are not insured, the growing cost associated with meeting healthcare needs, the enlarging size of the frail older adult segment of the population, and the increasing inability of federal programs to keep pace with expenditures. "Of all LTC expenditures in the United States (e.g., nursing home, home healthcare), nearly 70 percent are for people age 65 and over, or roughly $15,000 per person, with most costs paid out-of-pocket" (Hooyman & Kiyak, 2008). As the Baby Boomers enter the over age 65 age groups, these costs are expected to increase dramatically, which is why national health policy and programs are in immediate need of reform. National health policy and programs have a significant impact on the option to *age in place* for older adults.

Under the present social welfare system, program structures and requirements remain slanted toward the "medical model" of care with less attention being given to a wellness and health promotion perspective. To *age in place* under the medical model system means that increased healthcare spending and service delivery will be required. The medical model, institutionally-based perspective on health management is sustained partly because of the lack of a willingness to consider alternatives, especially options that are founded on principles of health promotion and wellness while *aging in place*. There is little agreement among policymakers about how to address this problem and consequently, the prospects for fundamental healthcare reform are precarious at best (Kotlikoff & Burns, 2004; Schultz & Binstock, 2006).

Individuals who age in conventional housing that is not designed to monitor needs or provide support services are at risk for either inappropriate transfer to institutional care or to neglect and decline. When these individuals are often inappropriately transferred to institutional care, the services that are provided are enormously expensive and result in noticeable functional loss, precipitous decline, or premature death. The more desirable situation would be one in which long-term care is provided in living arrangements that support *aging in place* and which promote healthcare cost containment for individuals, their families, and the government sponsored social welfare system.

Aging in place is a personal preference and social trend that holds multiple implications for the range of environments in which activity specialists may be delivering services and programs. Traditionally, activity specialists have considered the nursing home, assisted-living, rehabilitation hospital, and adult day activity center as the primary service delivery sites. With the trend toward supporting people to *age in place*, outreach service delivery is a growing service modality for the activity specialist.

Life Expectancy and Retirement

Life expectancy in the United States dramatically improved throughout the 20th century. As a result, the country is now in the throes of population aging; that is, the steady increase in the portion of the total population that is attributable to older adults. Consequently, increased life expectancy and population aging are creating significant policy challenges for the country. Issues related with healthcare, retirement, and income

security for the Baby Boomers are complex, which is causing great concern among policy analysts (Goldsmith, 2008).

There is very little disagreement on the fact that retirement as it has been experienced in the past will be likely to change dramatically with the aging of the Baby Boomers. There are many reasons that are affecting predicted changes in the work life and retirement of older adults.

- A very large population of potential retirees that will exert too great a demand on current social welfare programs for older citizens such that whole scale retirement may no longer be practical or possible.
- A downturn or shrinking of the economy, which is and will continue to affect national and state budgets for social services and individual retirement savings.
- The desire of many Baby Boomers to keep working because they are not ready to exit the work place, or they perceive that there is the necessity for them to maintain work engagement.
- A generally higher health status and increased life expectancy among Boomers, thus indicating the ability for continued participation in the workforce well into and potentially through the 7th decade of life.
- Labor shortages that will be likely to necessitate keeping Boomers in the workforce for their skills and experience as well as the need to continue to generate tax-related revenues necessary for maintaining Social Security for older adults who are unable to work.
- An outdated Social Security system that has significant problems in its structure and purpose, especially in light of fundamental changes in the size of the older adult population and changes in the nature of the society (e.g., a society based on information and technology rather than industry and farming).

From an individual perspective, increased life expectancy encourages people to think about taking a later retirement. Longer life expectancy generally means that retirement pensions, Social Security entitlement, and personal savings must be used to support income security over a significantly longer time period. From a societal standpoint, with a much larger older population, a smaller labor force must think about supporting a growing number of retirees, which may not be possible, practical, or realistic (Goldsmith, 2008; Kotlikoff & Burns, 2004; Schultz & Binstock, 2006).

The Social Security system, by itself, cannot sustain 76 million Baby Boomers all retiring around the traditional age of retirement and expecting to continue the lifestyle they have enjoyed. Currently, 64% of retirees depend upon Social Security for one-half or more of their income. Among those people who are receiving Social Security benefits, one-third depend upon Social Security for 90% of their income and one in five depend on it for 100% of their income (Villarreal, 2009). According to AARP surveys, around 80% of Boomers indicate that they expect and plan to work in retirement (RoperASW, 2004). Only 7% of Boomers see retirement as meaning "not working." Many will work full or part time; many more want to start second careers and new enterprises (Rogoff, 2008). According to all the current indicators, it is unlikely that the society can support a large number of fully retired Boomers.

One way to think about the Baby Boomers is to divide them into thirds: the *Set for Life* group, the *Might be OK* group, and the *Struggling and Anxious* group (Goldsmith, 2008). *Set for Life* Baby Boomers are generally financially well off and will probably continue to work. They are in good health and fully able to provide for their own activity needs. These Boomers most likely will continue to lead active lifestyles without the assistance of the healthcare system or activity professionals who provide therapeutic activities. With active lifestyles in store for most *Set for Lifers,* expansion in the non-healthcare activity market (e.g., tourism, specialty activities such as bike and sport-related clubs, and the like) can be expected.

According to Goldsmith, the *Might be OK* Baby Boomers represent a different picture in terms of income security and prospective health status. These Boomers may not have enough savings to fully retire and thus, maintaining work engagement will be important for having health insurance as well as the income to maintain an active lifestyle. If the health of Boomers in this group declines, they will be at risk of increasing their dependence on publicly-funded healthcare and health promotion activity programs. Some *Might be OK* Boomers could see their health deteriorate and their income become so inadequate that they become members of *Struggling and Anxious* group. *Might be OK* Boomers will need to maintain involvement in activity programs for health protection and health promotion purposes; some could be consumers of medically-oriented activity intervention programs.

Struggling and Anxious Baby Boomers tend to be less healthy and they are unable to independently take care of their health expenses and needs (Goldsmith, 2008). These Boomers have higher rates of obesity, poverty, alcoholism, depression, physical impairment, and chronic disease, thus they are prospective users of long-term care (LTC) as they move through the older adult years. Their capability for working is severely limited or nonexistent. *Struggling and Anxious* Boomers will be dependent upon the formal healthcare system and can be expected to be heavy users of Medicare and Medicaid. These Baby Boomers will be in the greatest need for activity interventions that respond to chronic conditions and they will have a very limited ability to pay for their services.

The utility of looking at the Baby Boomers using a three segments perspective is to underscore the point that they are a very diverse group with many able to independently meet their activity needs but also as many as one-third or more who will be entering the formal service system. Most Baby Boomers have not planned adequately for late life income security or healthcare assurance. According to a survey conducted by the Employee Benefit Research Institute, only 25% of current retirees are very confident about meeting their health expenses (Helman, Copeland & VanDerhei, 2009). This figure will be likely to increase among the Baby Boomers based on their characteristics as described above.

The trends that continue to affect and shape retirement practices will ultimately have an impact on activity programs and the activity specialist. Early Boomer retirees may need less direct activity intervention and more service delivery options, whereas Boomer retirees who are disabled may fit more closely with an *aging in place* model of outreach and in-home service delivery. Retiree income and health status, as well as projected life expectancy/longevity, are important trends to watch for the implications that they have on the need for and nature of activity services.

Trends in Health Status and Health Services Utilization

Our present knowledge about human aging may one day merge with scientific and technological advancements that can reshape the biology of aging to form a new picture for how we grow old in the future. The day is not far off when we will be able stave off the declines and diseases that are experienced by today's older adults. While it is still believed that the maximum lifespan of the human organism is about 120 years, with genetic engineering on the horizon new benchmarks for human health and longevity may be just around the corner. The future is uncertain regarding how long humans could actually live if chronic disease and disability were prevented or cured. Along with extended human lifespan and sustained improvements in life expectancy will come the expectation for a high quality of life throughout older adulthood.

Scientists predict that the 21st century will bring scientific advances that permit individuals to endure the expectations and the oddities of aging, and perhaps even control or alter them. For the present, however, longevity remains largely contingent upon health behavior and health interventions. It is still understood that a healthy older adulthood can be maximized by adhering to familiar risk-reduction strategies such as consuming a healthy diet, exercising regularly, and by avoiding smoking, alcohol abuse, and obesity (Hooyman & Kiyak, 2008). Extending healthy life, however, is not the most pressing health-related topic of concern to older adults. Assuring availability of and access to appropriate healthcare services and products, and containing healthcare expenditures are the most serious problems at present.

Getting control over current levels of healthcare spending far exceeds any problems associated with retirement income security and the Social Security system. Individual and governmental expenditures for healthcare in America are astonishingly high and continuing to rise on an annual basis. It is predicted that healthcare expenditures could reach 19% of GDP by 2014 (Schultz & Binstock, 2006). By 2030, roughly 20% of the population will be older adults and the nation's spending for healthcare could increase up to 25% in response to this demographic shift (CDCP and the Merck Company Foundation, 2007).

Even though the health status of older adults who are in their 60s and 70s is generally better than previous cohorts of older adults, the reality remains in place today that chronic disease and disability increases with age (Federal Interagency Forum on Aging-Related Statistics, 2008). In 2004-2006, 74% of adults over age 65 described their health as good or better, and this self-assessed health rating statistic has been fairly stable for decades. In general, older adults view their health status positively but the proportion who rate good to excellent decreases with age. Income is directly related to health. Poverty is a barrier to accessing adequate healthcare especially for those older adults who cannot purchase independent health insurance (National Center for Health Statistics, 2007). More than 40 million adults in 2005 were unable to meet their healthcare needs due to the inability to pay for them.

The link between health status and income is significant (National Center for Health Statistics, 2007). Even though the proportion of older adults living in poverty has steadily declined since the mid-1970s, the actual number remains troubling especially as it affects their ability to meet healthcare costs. In 2006, about 9% of older adults lived in poverty (Federal Interagency on Aging-Related Statistics, 2008). An additional 26% of older citizens lived with very low incomes. Older women (17%) were more likely to live in poverty compared with older men (7%). Racial and ethnic disparities also persisted with about 23% of older blacks and 19% of older Hispanics living in poverty.

Older people who are living with low incomes must rely upon social programs such as Medicare for their health insurance coverage. Living without adequate health insurance is a reality for the poor older adult. For the uninsured or underinsured older adult, out-of-pocket medical expenditures are an ongoing concern that is unlikely to ease when the Baby Boomers enter old age. Older people who are living in poverty struggle to have adequate housing, food, healthcare, and other essential services to promote health and well-being.

There is general agreement that the American healthcare system must be overhauled soon in order to be prepared to meet the needs of the Baby Boomers as they enter the older adult years. This is a complex problem and its solution is well beyond the scope of the present chapter. What is known, however, is that most Baby Boomers expect to live to very old ages (e.g., 80s, 90s, and 100s), which will pose additional demand on the healthcare dollar and system. *Struggling and Anxious* Boomers can be expected to be high healthcare consumers with little ability to pay for services and products on their own. How will these Boomers' needs be met when there is a shortage of geriatric health providers and an inadequate publicly supported funding system? What is the best approach for aiding *Struggling and Anxious* Boomers who are unlikely to be in the labor force and who are at high risk of increasing dependence due to very poor health status? These are aging adults who will need activity interventions to slow declines or prevent additional disability. Their ability to pay for services will be non-existent but the importance of slowing decline will be very high as they enter the older adult years.

Another concern is the capacity of *Might be OK* Boomers to continue to pay for their healthcare if and when they retire. Will Medicare coupled with individual supplemental health insurance be affordable for members of this group or will Medicare becomes narrowed to serve only the most poor and disabled Americans, thus excluding this group? How many *Might be OK* Boomers will be unable to afford individual health insurance? Will any of these Boomers become uninsured and at increased risk for slipping into the *Struggling and Anxious* group, particularly in terms of chronic disease and generally poorer health status? An older adulthood that comes with incentives to maintain labor force participation with healthcare insurance included as a benefit is likely to be very important for the *Might be OK* Boomers. In order to maintain high health status for *Might be OK* Boomers, sustaining an active, engaged lifestyle that reflects a health promotion of activity engagement will probably take on increased importance.

Aging Baby Boomers are anything but frail. An active lifestyle is important to containing healthcare costs and maintaining health throughout the older adult years. Health expenditures for older adults are three to five times more than people under age 65 (CDCP and the Merck Company Foundation, 2007). More than one-third of preventable disease and death is caused by smoking, poor diet, and a lack of a physically active lifestyle. Activity specialists who promote health through building a repertoire of activity choices offered in a broad range of service settings will be an instrumental component in any future comprehensive healthcare policy and system that is intended to reduce expenditure and promote well-being for aging Boomers.

It is readily understood that *Struggling and Anxious* Baby Boomers are likely to be consumed by their health concerns. While these Boomers will be more dependent upon the formal healthcare system, it is relevant to remember that health status is an individual responsibility. All older adults are ultimately responsible for the health choices that they make, including the choice to maintain an active, health conscious lifestyle. One thing is clear: unbridled consumption across of healthcare services and products is not a pattern of behavior that can be financially sustained when 76 million Baby Boomers move into their older adult years. Aging Boomers must maintain an active role in managing their own health status especially as healthcare reform struggles with increasing demand and shrinking resources with which to meet this demand.

Older adults with *functional impairment* often obtain long-term care services in the community. The trend in nursing home placement has reflected a steady decline over the past 20 years (Federal Interagency on Aging-Related Statistics, 2008). As nursing home placement declined, in-home care and assisted living have increased in prevalence. Using data from 2004, nursing home rates are lowest among adults ages 65–74 (less than 1%) increasing among people ages 75–84 (3.6%) and highest among adults age 85 and older (nearly 14%). Even though the percentage of the population living in nursing homes has declined the actual number of people has increased, which is a potential concern for a large cohort of Baby Boomers as

they enter older adulthood. Community-based health-related services include senior centers, adult day care, special transportation, meals provided at home or at community locations, and home visitations by nurses or health aides.

The majority of older people have little or no protection against the excessive costs of long-term care (LTC). Most long-term care is still provided in nursing homes or long-term care facilities (e.g., assisted-living). In recent years, there have been efforts to rebalance the delivery of long-term services and supports to people in their homes and communities (Kassner, Reinhard, Fox-Grage, Houser & Accius, 2008). This trend serves two purposes: (a) to provide older persons with the choice and control over their lives and care, and (b) to shift service delivery to more cost-effective models. Institutional care remains the most expensive approach to LTC and healthcare cost containment, by necessity, will need to embrace more cost-effective models in the future.

The funding of long-term care is derived principally from private individual or family payments and public payments by Medicaid. In 2006, nationally about 25% of all Medicaid long-term spending was for home and community-based services with the remaining 75% for institutional care (Kassner et al., 2008). Under rebalancing, Medicaid can provide LTC to almost three older people under the home and community-based services (HCBS) model for every one person in a nursing home. The amount spent for community and home-based LTC varied greatly across states with as high as 55% in Oregon and as low as 1% in Tennessee. Between 2001 and 2006, the nation made significant progress toward rebalancing Medicaid expenditures for LTC by increasing support to home and community-based care. During this time, Medicaid expenditures for HCBS increased 65% compared with 16% for nursing home care. While progress toward supporting home and community based long-term care is evident, only one in four Medicaid dollars are spent for the HCBS option. Looking toward the future, the pace of rebalancing the support for long-term care to non-nursing home alternatives must quicken in order to be prepared to meet the needs of aging Baby Boomers. It is also clear that individuals will be wise to exercise personal responsibility for LTC through the purchase of long-term care insurance, reverse mortgages, or arranging other financial mechanisms to safeguard their own care.

The current healthcare policy for the nation is ineffective and exceedingly expensive. With increasing needs and decreasing assets, the necessity to maximize the resources of both disability and aging policies for the benefit of everyone is essential. However, as long as there is a fragmented, public/private system that focuses upon acute medical intervention instead of prevention, the current problems will persist. Reform of healthcare policies and systems is unquestionably necessary in order for service sectors and professions to develop new strategies for ensuring adequate services to a growing older population. Such reform will assure access for all persons and establish a priority for quality care at a reasonable cost.

Personnel Shortages

In general, the United States is grappling with increasing rates of chronic conditions in the population as a whole. Along with this trend is a recognized shortage of the necessary number of healthcare workers to meet the growing demand for care (Bodenheimer, Chen & Bennett, 2009). In the area of healthcare workers who are trained to work specifically with older adults, there is a critical shortage (Kovner, Mezey & Harrington, 2002). In 2002, there were more than 35 million adults over age 65 and 76 million Baby Boomers moving rapidly toward their older adult years. Very few nursing and medical school programs have full-time faculty who specialize in geriatric medicine, fewer have stand alone geriatric education departments. The shortage of professionals in all health fields that work with older adults is a serious concern, especially when there is evidence that better health outcomes are more likely when care is given by workers who have gerontology/geriatric healthcare training. For example, "patients cared for by nurses prepared in geriatrics are less likely to be physically restrained, have fewer readmissions to the hospital, and are less likely to be transferred inappropriate from nursing facilities to the hospital" (Kovner, Mezey & Harrington, 2002, p. 79).

Older adults consume more than 25% of all office visits to physicians (Kovner, Mezey & Harrington, 2002). Compared with 6.5 visits by younger adults, the average older adult has about 10.5 visits to the doctor per year. In the United States, less than 1.3% of all licensed practicing doctors are qualified in geriatric medicine. This figure translates into about 2.5 geriatricians for every 10,000 older citizens (Kovner, Mezey & Harrington). Geriatric care attracts fewer specialists than other areas. Among professionals who provide direct care (certified nurse aids, personal care aids, and activity specialists) turnover is high. Overall, healthcare education programs that include some gerontology/geriatric care instruction are usually not comprehensive, so training is incomplete at best. Unless there

is a collective effort to increase the number of geriatricians and other healthcare professions that serve older persons, the severe shortage will worsen.

The severity of the shortage of healthcare providers with training to serve older adults, combined with the ongoing shift in the nation's demographic profile, make leadership critical by physicians, scientists, and faculty members to influence students to enter the fields of gerontology and geriatrics (Kovner, Mezey & Harrington, 2002). Activity specialists with specific preparation in gerontology can also be considered to be part of the allied healthcare workforce. More training programs are needed in order to ensure an adequate supply of activity specialists as the demand for health promotion and activity intervention services continue to rise.

Crucial to any solution to the manpower shortage problem is the recognition of the relative lack of teaching physicians trained in geriatric medicine and psychiatry, as well as other allied health professionals (e.g. social work, pharmacology, physical therapy, recreation therapy) with training in gerontology. Without such faculty members, the problem of manpower shortages will persist. The supply of general physicians, specialists, and allied healthcare professionals is a critical problem that must be addressed if the nation is enabled to meet the healthcare needs of a rapidly expanding older population (Kovner, Mezey & Harrington, 2002).

Program and Service Proliferation

Since the middle of the 20th century, remarkable growth has occurred in the service delivery structure, as well as a cadre of professions that provide support and care to the older. This growth has not happened without some serious side effects. The proliferation of organizational structures and bureaucratic procedures has created additional burdens and barriers for older persons, as well as the service providers who genuinely wish to meet their clients' needs. Elaborate systems for obtaining information and referral, gate-keeping systems like case management, and a never-ending process of rule changing and rule generation can make seeking assistance from government sponsored programs a formidable nightmare. These management elaborations (information, referral, and case management) add substantial expenditures to an already cost burdened system. While the functions of specialization, fragmentation, and organizational management might appear justifiable, the results have often not provided direct benefits to older consumers.

Service and program proliferation, while offering more options to meet varying needs, is very costly. Each agency or system requires its own infrastructure, documentation and evaluation systems, fundraising, etc. The growing industry of aging service providers, both public and private, adds to the cost of care for the older individual and also adds to class separation (e.g., near-poor, poor, well-to-do). Service and organization proliferation actually increases the volume of unmet needs, thus aggravating an already critical problem in the human services area.

As the 21st century unfolds, healthcare system and financing must be reformed. Inequities across different groups of older adults based on age, gender, race, ethnicity, and socioeconomic status will provide additional challenges as policy and system change occurs. The issues are complex but the need for change is unquestionable. Activity professionals will need to view themselves as part of an evolving system that needs to be both cost-effective as well as accessible by the older consumer. It can be expected that the training and preparation that activity specialists receive will probably grow in its importance as the service system engages in this change process.

Aging Well through Active Aging and Successful Aging

In recent years, old negative views toward growing older have begun to dissipate and be replaced by emerging perspectives on aging that are more positive and optimistic. Instead of thinking of aging as a medical problem that is reflective of decline, disease, and disability, gerontologist are engaged in thinking about active aging. *Active aging* is defined as "the process of optimizing opportunities for health, participation, and security in order to enhance quality of life" as one ages (World Health Organization, 2002, p. 2). This framework is one that promotes positive adaptation and choice as one grows older. The emphasis is on remaining active throughout one's older adult years, thus promoting a higher quality of life. Active aging also puts forth the idea that aging is a lifelong process, not just one that all of a sudden happens at age 60, 65, 75, or 100. Active aging has conceptual underpinnings in other contemporary concepts such as healthy aging, productive aging, successful aging, and aging well. All these concepts share the common theme of viewing aging as a positive process rather than something to fear and dread. Two of these concepts—successful aging and aging well—are highly related and are briefly discussed below because they exemplify positive outcomes of the WHO active aging perspective.

Early gerontology work focused on subjective well-being and quality of life. As the number of adult who are aging in good health has steadily increased,

more recent research interests embrace concepts of positive aging that reflect resilience, adaptation, productivity, health, and vitality (Hooyman & Kiyak, 2008). The majority of recent research has focused on defining what it means to age successfully, otherwise known as *successful aging* (George, 2006; Rowe & Kahn, 1997, 1998). Successful aging is the combination of positive physical health and functional status, high cognitive functioning, and active engagement in everyday live and society (Hooyman & Kiyak). Older people who are experiencing *successful aging* usually have low risk for disease, disability, and impairment. One of the ongoing criticisms of the *successful aging* concept is that it allows little room to include the individual who is not experiencing optimal conditions. The concept has also been criticized as promoting youthfulness rather than acknowledging the challenging personal and health circumstances that are not uncommon to aging. Thus, another related concept, *aging well*, may be better suited to understanding a positive perspective about aging and older adulthood.

The concept of *aging well* emerged from the literature on successful aging, healthy aging, and productive aging (Fontane & Soloman, 1996; Johnson, 1995; Krain, 1995). *Aging well* seeks to counterbalance negative images of older people as a burden to society. *Aging well* reflects a number of similarities with the concept of *successful aging* (Rowe & Kahn, 1987, 1997; Valliant, 2002). Both concepts reject one-sided negative opinions about older people (Scharf, van der Meer, Thissen & Melchiorre, 2003). A major difference is that the continuum for *aging well* anchors the lower end position to be *a difficult old age* and the upper end to be *aging well*. Further, the full continuum for *aging well* is contextualized by individual circumstances and the socio-cultural context in which one lives. Under this conceptual framework, *aging well* is relevant and relative to individuals, societies, and different cultures. It is contextually and situationally defined rather than being anchored to a singular, culture-bound viewpoint.

Successful aging and *aging well* both stress the importance of selective optimization with compensation (SOC), which is a process of adaptation originally proposed by Baltes and Baltes (1990). SOC also has been used as one definition for successful aging. SOC is a process of adapting to the changes that are frequently experienced by aging persons. The process involves making choices to maintain those activities and behaviors that are most useful to the individual as a compensation for competencies that are lost. In other words, when skills or capabilities are lost or diminished, the older adult will adapt by compensating through selection of the strengths that remain, thus optimizing individual potential and quality of life. Essentially, SOC reflects resilience and a process of adaptation for supporting *aging well*.

Aging well is more than just the individual practicing selective optimization with compensation. *Aging well* is understood as a blend of personal behavior in interaction with the social and physical environment, and also it embraces individual life circumstances. To achieve a quality of life that results in *aging well* requires an active vision of what you want for a desirable future and the ability to apply personal adaptation when circumstances are less than optimal (Hawkins, 2003; Vaillant, 2002). *Aging well* depends upon personal, social, and physical environments that provide supports and opportunities that enable individuals to practice active aging through healthy lifestyles. In a robust sense, *aging well* conveys a positive person-centered process in which the promotion and protection of physical, mental, social, economic, and daily lifestyles are paramount for achieving a sense of satisfaction, health, dignity, and well-being in old age.

Each of these contemporary concepts—*active aging*, *successful aging*, and *aging well*—provides a fresh view of the human aging experience. They are intended to remove the negative stereotypes associated with ageism and the dominance of a medical view of human aging with more positive perspectives. They will be instrumental in a society that is fully enmeshed in population aging and soon to be dealing with an older Baby Boomer generation. It is well-understood that Baby Boomers are unlikely to tolerate negative stereotypes about older adults, or to embrace a disease-based model to dominate their older adult years.

Prospects for the Future

The value placed on youth and appearance remains a pervasive theme in American life. Often, youth and appearance seem more important than productivity and usefulness. Also, Americans tend to focus upon individualism and independence, which are ideas that often work against mutual interdependence and community. As a consequence, the act of requesting assistance from others continues to be difficult for many older people. When assistance can be regarded as an instrument for autonomy rather than as an intrusion into personal control, society can concentrate upon the creation of community. One important strategy that has demonstrated the capacity to foster a greater sense of community is *intergenerational programming*. By bringing together people from different age groups to

work on common causes and issues, communities begin the process of breaking down age segregation and pervasive ageism. Through building intergenerational relationships and forging connections across the age groups, older persons may have more opportunities to function in positive roles such as mentors, teachers, counselors, and friends, which are much more customary in other cultures (Erikson, Erikson & Kivnick, 1986; Shimp, 1990).

The problems and prospects of older adults in the United States seem to point to the need to rethink our fundamental values and beliefs about people. When individualism is replaced by interdependence, self by a sense of community, and worth as measured by who we are and not what we look like, then there may be hope for an emerging society that is prepared for an aging population. In the preferred future, older adults are valued as an important resource based on their wisdom, experience, and characteristics that they bring to society. They are empowered because of who they are and no longer forgotten just because they have lived long enough to be conveniently excused from the mainstream of society.

Choices are created by restructuring society to embrace older adults as integral members of all aspects of community—as workers, teachers, friends, mentors, and colleagues. This is the new conceptualization of human aging. Choices in the aging process are not isolated variables; they are personal and situational, and individually experienced, not collectively defined. *Ageism* is rejected. Individual and societal choices that inspire higher levels of human consciousness are conceived within communities that are responsible to their older population. These are the hopes and desires of an aging nation and world.

Summary

Basic knowledge and practice skills are desired of all activity professionals in order to qualify them for providing high quality services to older adults. In addition to these basic qualifications, certification provides a credentialing process that advances the profession in important ways. One important way that certification advances the profession is through federal and state laws that recognize the profession through hiring policies and practices that give preference to certified activity professionals. Activity services that are provided by certified professionals are instrumental in promoting the health and quality of life for all older adults.

Current trends and issues that are affecting services to the aging population may be expected to provide new challenges to agencies in the future. Especially notable are the following trends: (a) the desire by older adults to *age in place*, (b) change in the nature of retirement and increased life expectancy, (c) issues and reform in healthcare, (d) labor shortages in the healthcare industry, (e) program and service proliferation, and (f) emerging concepts about the human aging experience (aging well, active living, successful aging). These trends and issues portend of dramatic changes that will come with the aging of the Baby Boomers. The future is uncertain but it is also exciting.

"Being human is being responsible—[truly] responsible for one's...existence" (Frankl, 1975, p. 26). Individuals cannot survive in an environment void of other responsive and caring beings. It is thus that activity professionals are entrusted with the task of creating humanistic programs and environments for all individuals, whether they be young or old, in the future society to which we all aspire.

Comprehension Questions

The reader can check for comprehension of the material presented in this chapter by answering the following questions:

1. Discuss three important national organizations that support activity professionals.
2. Identify the body of knowledge that underpins the National Certification Council on Activity Professional's certification program.
3. Discuss the importance of developing practice skills for working with older adults.
4. Why is it important to have established qualifications for working with older adults in activity programs?
5. What impact do current trends and issues have on activity specialists and what they do?

References

Association for Gerontology in Higher Education. (2005). *Standards and guidelines for gerontology programs* (4th ed.). Washington, DC: Author.

Association for Gerontology in Higher Education. (n.d.). *Programs of merit. The National Review of Educational Programs in Gerontology*. Washington, DC: Author.

Baltes, P. B. & Baltes, M. M. (Eds.). (1990). *Successful aging: Perspectives from the behavioral sciences*. New York, NY: Cambridge University Press.

Bodenheimer, T., Chen, E. & Bennett, H. D. (2009). Confronting the growing burden of chronic disease: Can the U.S. health care workforce do the job? *Health Affairs, 28*(1), 64–74.

Centers for Disease Control and Prevention (CDCP) and the Merck Company Foundation. (2007). *The state of aging and health in America 2007*. Whitehouse Station, NJ: The Merck Company Foundation.

Erikson, E. H., Erikson, J. M. & Kivnick, H. Q. (1986). *Vital involvement in old age*. NY: Norton.

Federal Interagency Forum on Aging-Related Statistics. (2008, March). *Older Americans 2008: Key Indicators of Well-Being*. Federal Interagency Forum on Aging-Related Statistics. Washington, DC: U.S. Government Printing Office.

Fontane, P. E. & Solomon, J. C. (1996). Editors' introduction—*Aging well* in contemporary society, part II—Choices and processes. *American Behavioral Scientist, 39*(3), 230.

Frankl, V. (1975). *The unconscious God*. New York, NY: Washington Square Press.

George, L. K. (2006). Perceived quality of life. In R. Binstock & L. K. George (Eds.), *Handbook of aging and the social sciences* (6th ed.). New York, NY: Academic Press.

Goldsmith, J. (2008). *The long baby boom: An optimistic vision for a graying generation*. Baltimore, MD: The Johns Hopkins University Press.

Hawkins, B. A. (2003). Aging well: Construct genesis and ideology. *Global Aging Initiative Newsletter*, Spring 2003. Bloomington, IN: Indiana University Center on Aging and Aged.

Helman, R., Copeland C. & VanDerhei, J. (2009). *The 2009 Retirement Confidence Economy Drives Confidence to Record Lows; Many Looking to Work Longer*. EBRI Issue Brief, no. 328. Washington, DC: Employee Benefit Research Institute, April 2009. Retrieved April 6, 2009, from EBRI.org.

Hooyman, N. R. & Kiyak, H. A. (2008). *Social gerontology: A multidisciplinary perspective* (8th ed.). Boston, MA: Allyn and Bacon.

Johnson, T. F. (1995). *Aging well* in contemporary society: Introduction. *American Behavioral Scientist, 39*(2), 120–130.

Kassner, E., Reinhard, S., Fox-Grage, W., Houser, A. & Accius, J. (2008). *A balancing act: State long-term care reform*. Washington, DC: Public Policy Institute, AARP.

Kotlikoff, L. J. & Burns, S. (2004). *The coming generational storm: What you need to know about America's economic future*. Cambridge, MA: The MIT Press.

Kovner, C. T., Mezey, M. & Harrington, C. (2002). Who cares for older adults? Workforce implications of an aging society. *Health Affairs, 21*(5), 78–89.

Krain, M. A. (1995). Policy implications for a society *aging well*: Employment, retirement, education, and leisure policies for the 21st century. *American Behavioral Scientist, 39*(2), 131–151.

Moody, H. R. (2009). *Aging – Concepts and controversies* (6th ed.). Thousand Oaks, CA: Pine Forge Press/ Sage Publications.

National Center for Health Statistics. (2007). Health, United States, 2007—With Chartbook on Trends in the Health of Americans. Library of Congress Catalog Number 76–641496. Washington, DC: U.S. Government Printing Office.

National Certification Council for Activity Professionals. (2009). *National Certification Council for Activity Professionals – Certification standards.* Virginia Beach, VA: Author.

Rogoff, E. G. (2008). *The Issues and Opportunities of Entrepreneurship After Age 50.* Occasional Papers, Number 5. Washington, DC: AARP, Office of Academic Affairs.

RoperASW. (May 2004). *Baby Boomers Envision Retirement II: Survey of Baby Boomers' Expectations for Retirement, Research Report-* Prepared for AARP by RoperASW. Retrieved April 13, 2009, from http://www.aarp.org/research/work/retirement/aresearch-import-865.html.

Rowe, J. W. & Kahn, R. L. (1997). The Forum - Successful aging. *The Gerontologist, 37*(4), 433–440.

Rowe, J. W. & Kahn, R. L. (1998). *Successful aging.* New York, NY: Pantheon Books.

Scharf, T., van der Meer, M., Thissen, F. & Melchiorre, M. G. (2003/4). *Contextualising adult well-being in Europe: Report on socio-cultural differences in ESAW nations.* University of Wales, Bangor, UK: ESAW Project Report.

Shimp, S. (1990). Debunking the myths of aging. *Occupational Therapy in Mental Health, 10*(3), 101–111.

Schultz, J. H. & Binstock, R. H. (2006). *Aging nation: The economics and politics of growing older in America.* Baltimore, MD: The Johns Hopkins University Press.

Vaillant, G. E. (2002). *Aging well: surprising guideposts to a happier life from the landmark study of adult development.* Boston, MA: Little, Brown, and Co.

Villarreal P. (March 2009). Ten ways to wreck your retirement. Policy Report No. 320. Washington, DC: National Center for Policy Analysis.

World Health Organization. (2002). *Active ageing: A policy framework.* Geneva, Switzerland: World Health Organization (WHO).

• APPENDIX A •

Standards of Practice of the National Association of Activity Professionals

Retrieved May 20, 2009, from http://www.thenaap.com/members/standards_general2.html

General Standards of Practice

PROVISION OF ACTIVITY SERVICES

1. **ACTIVITY ASSESSMENT/PROFILE:**
   The Activity Professional shall conduct an activity assessment/profile for each client/resident to determine his/her activity needs, interest, preferences, and abilities.

2. **ACTIVITY PLAN:**
   The Activity Professional shall develop an individual, interdisciplinary activity plan with each client/resident. The activity plan shall be based on the resident's/client's activity assessment/ profile and shall be designed to enable each resident/client to achieve and/or maintain his/her highest level of well-being.

3. **IMPLEMENTATION OF ACTIVITY PLAN:**
   The Activity Professional shall direct the activity plan and shall involve the interdisciplinary team in the implementation of the individualized interventions as stated in the interruptive guidelines for F-tag 28/249.

4. **EVALUATION OF THE ACTIVITY PLAN:**
   The Activity Professional shall continuously evaluate and document the resident's/client's response to each activity. The revision of the activity plan shall be based on the resident's/client's response to the interventions.

5. **ACTIVITY PROGRAM:**
   The Activity Professional shall be resident/client centered and enable the resident/client to maximize his/her potential in the activity program.

MANAGEMENT OF ACTIVITY SERVICES

6. **STAFF CREDENTIALS/EDUCATION:**
   The Activity Department shall establish a plan to ensure each activity employee is qualified to perform his/her assigned tasks, maintains appropriate credentials, and is provided with opportunities for professional development.

7. **PLAN OF OPERATION:**
   The Activity Department shall have written policies and procedures based on the National Association of Activity Professionals (NAAP) Standards of Practice and Scope of Practice; regulatory requirements; facility/corporate requirements, and the standards established by accrediting agencies.

8. **RESOURCE UTILIZATION:**
   The Activity Department shall develop and maintain a plan for identifying, acquiring, and utilizing resources to achieve the department's goals.

9. **QUALITY IMPROVEMENT/PROGRAM EVALUATION:**
   The Activity Department shall develop and implement a systematic and ongoing plan to evaluate the quality, effectiveness, and integrity of the activity services.

10. **ETHICAL CONDUCT:**
    The Activity Professional shall adhere to the NAAP *Code of Ethics.*

Source: The National Association of Activity Professionals. Used by permission.

• APPENDIX B •

Code of Ethics of the National Association of Activity Professionals

Retrieved May 20, 2009, from http:// www.thenaap. com/members/standards_code2.html

Preamble:

The National Association of Activity Professionals and its members are dedicated to providing activity services and programs, which meet the unique needs and interests of the individuals we serve. Principles:

I. Conduct

    The Activity Professional shall maintain high standards of personal conduct and professional integrity at all times. The Activity Professional shall treat colleagues with professional courtesy and ensure that credit is given to others for use of their ideas, materials, and programs. The Activity Professional shall obey the Bylaws and Code of Ethics governing all professional associations to which he/she belongs.

II. Dignity/Rights

    Dignity/Rights The Activity Professional shall treat the clients/residents, members of the interdisciplinary team, and professional peers with regard towards personal dignity at all times. The Activity Professional shall respect and protect the rights—civil, legal and human—of the clients/residents members of the interdisciplinary team, and professional peers at all times. The Activity Professional shall work through appropriate channels to protect the rights of clients/residents and report abuse and exploitation.

III. Confidentiality

    The Activity Professional shall treat any information about clients/residents, members of the interdisciplinary team, and profes-

sional peers as confidential. Information about clients/residents that must be shared with members of the interdisciplinary team and volunteers in the course of care shall be exchanged in a professional manner.

IV. Empowerment

    The Activity Professional shall enable clients/ residents to participate in the planning and implementation of their care, as well as making independent medical, legal, and financial decisions.

V. Participation

    The Activity Professional shall enable clients/ residents to maximize their potential in activity participation through adaptation, cues/ prompts, protection from undue interruption, and assistance in rescheduling of other events that may interfere with the client's/resident's ability to participate in activities of their choice.

VI. Record Keeping

    The Activity Professional shall maintain client/ resident records in an accurate, confidential, and timely manner. The Activity Professional shall follow facility policies and procedures in the formatting of such records. In the absence of facility policy the appropriate state and/or federal guidelines shall be followed.

VII. Professional

    The Activity Professional shall participate in continuing education opportunities, strive for professional competence and excellence in all matters, ensure accurate resumes, and differentiate between personal comments/actions and official NAAP positions.

VIII. Supervisory

    The Activity Professional shall treat persons he/she may supervise with dignity and respect, protect their rights, and provide accurate and fair evaluations.

IX. Communication

The Activity Professional shall strive to maintain open channels of communication with administration, other departments, families, clients/residents, and professional peers. The Activity Professional shall strive for accurate and truthful communication in all interactions.

X. Provision of Services

The Activity Professional shall provide programs—regardless of race, religion (or absence thereof), ethnic origin, social or marital status, sex or sexual orientation, age, health status, or payment source—which assist the client/resident in achieving and maintaining the highest practicable level of physical, intellectual, psychosocial, emotional, and spiritual well-being.

XI. Legal

The Activity Professional shall comply with all applicable federal, state and local laws regarding the provision of services. The Activity Professional shall comply with and uphold the Bylaws and Code of Ethics set forth by his/her professional associations.

XII. Professional Association(s)

The Activity Professional shall comply with the bylaws, policies and procedures, Standards, and Code of Ethics of the professional association(s) to which he/she belongs.

Source: The National Association of Activity Professionals. Used by permission.

• APPENDIX C •

Code of Ethics of the National Certification Council for Activity Professionals

Preamble

The National Certification Council for Activity Professionals (NCCAP) is a professional certification organization committed to promoting quality of life for persons receiving services from professionals certified with this organization.

All certified Activity Professionals are expected to adhere to the standards listed here in addition to general principles of ethical conduct endorsed by all health-related disciplines.

These ethical standards are intended to clarify to present and future certified members and to those served by them the nature of the ethical responsibilities held in common.

As the code of ethics of this organization, this document establishes principles that define the ethical behavior of certified members. All members of the National Certification Council for Activity Professionals are required to adhere to the Code of Ethics.

The following declaration establishes principles that define the ethical behavior of certified members and is called the Code of Ethics of the NCCAP.

The Code of Ethics will serve as the basis for processing ethical complaints initiated against members of the organization.

A. Professional Responsibility

All certified Professionals have a responsibility to read, understand and follow the Code of Ethics and Standards of Practice. They are expected to adhere to these standards in their professional practice and in order to maintain their certification.

B. General Standards

1. The certified member influences the development of the profession through continually endeavoring to improve professional practices, by teaching, through service, by advocacy and leadership.
2. The certified member recognizes that professional growth is continuous.

3. The certified member recognizes the need for continuing education to ensure competent services.
4. The certified member gathers data on the effectiveness of their practice and is guided by their findings.
5. The certified member neither claims nor implies professional qualifications exceeding those possessed.
6. The certified member recognizes the extent of their competence and provides only those services for which they are qualified by training or experience.
7. The certified member accepts employment only for positions for which they are qualified by education, training, and appropriate professional experience.

C. Resident/Client Relationship Standards

1. The certified member guards the rights and individual dignity of the resident/client and promotes their welfare whether in a group or individually.
2. The certified member does not condone or engage in discrimination based on age, color, culture, disability, ethnic group, gender, race, religion, sexual orientation, marital status, or socioeconomic status.
3. The certified member does not bring personal issues to the resident/client relationship.
4. The certified member shall advocate on behalf of the resident/client to receive accurate activity services.
5. The certified member must ensure that residents/clients of various functional ability levels have equal access to activity services and they are provided to them accurately in the context of the service setting.
6. The certified member must ensure that every resident/client in a given setting receive activity services if they desire them.
7. The certified member respects their resident/client's right to privacy and provides for the maintenance of client confidentially in discourse and in records. In group work, the certified member must set a standard of confidentially regarding group participants' disclosures.

D. Professional Relationship Standards

1. The certified member shall respect the agency offering quality of life by supporting administration and being an effective team member.

2. The certified member has a responsibility to the institution in which s/he performs service to maintain the highest standard of professional conduct and services to their clients. The acceptance of employment implies that the certified member is in agreement with their general policies and objectives, and therefore, provides services that are in accordance with them. If the certified member finds that the institutional policy and service systems hampers resident/client potential and/or prevents access to service, the certified member must seek to cause the employer to change such policy and/or systems. Failing to effectuate change after extensive efforts, the certified member should seriously consider terminating the affiliation.

3. Ethical behavior among professional associates, both certified and noncertified, is expected at all times.

4. The certified member must seek professional review and evaluation on a regular basis.

5. The certified member must establish interpersonal relations and working agreements with other department personnel and define relationships, responsibilities and accountability in regard to their common residents/clients.

6. The certified member who supervises activity staff must be responsible for in-service development of activity staff, must inform their staff of department ethics and core values and program goals, and provide staff with practices that guarantee the rights and welfare of each resident/client who receives their services.

7. The certified member who supervises activity staff must be just and fair with staff, give credit when it is due and give counsel when work performance is below standard.

E. Educational Standards

1. The certified member shall successfully complete academic and continuing education sessions in order to better understand the residents/clients and how activity services enhances their well being.

2. The certified member shall continue to complete educational sessions both academic and continuing education, in order to keep abreast of quality activity programming, as evidenced by appropriate and timely recertification through NCCAP.

3. The certified member shall report accurately and fairly the educational sessions attended and the credit received.

4. The certified member shall refuse to participate in falsification of any educational documents.

5. The certified member shall seek competency rather than to fulfill minimum requirements.

F. Experiential Standards

1. The certified member shall learn activity programming through supervised experience in conducting activities in the various gerontological settings.

2. The certified member shall meet federal and state regulations regarding standards to be a certified and qualified director of an activity program before marketing oneself as a professional in the provision of activities programming.

3. The certified member shall be a high quality provider of activities that enhances the lives of residents/clients.

4. The certified member will avoid any falsification or misrepresentation of one's employment record.

5. The certified member shall function at the highest practical level of one's ability and skills to the benefit of the residents/clients.

G. Professional Preparation Standards

The certified member who trains has particular ethical responsibilities that go beyond that of the certified member who does not train other activity professionals.

1. The certified member who is responsible for training other Activity Professionals must be guided by the Standards for Professional Preparation of Activity Professionals.

2. The certified member who trains must emphasize and support the uniqueness of activity profession, rather than teach the orientation of other professions whose members may give services in the activity realm, regardless of the certified member's personal college work.

3. The certified member responsible for education programs must be skilled as a teacher and practitioner.

4. The certified member who has been approved as a MEPAP trainer must follow the Program Administration Guidelines in all aspects, or ensure that their sponsoring agency follows them.

5. The certified member who has been approved as a MEPAP trainer and who conducts the MEPAP training must be in compliance with the current Teacher Manual.

6. The certified member who is the primary instructor of the MEPAP must assure that academic study and supervised practice (practicum) are integrated, and have clearly stated policies regarding the responsibilities of the supervisor and the student for the field work and their responsibilities to the institution where the supervised work is taking place.

7. The certified member who has been approved as a MEPAP trainer must orient students to Program expectations and requirements for successful completion.

8. The certified member who has been approved as a MEPAP trainer must evaluate students informally and formally through testing.

9. The certified member who has been Approved as a MEPAP trainer must encourage students to value the ideals of service through leadership and advocacy for their residents/clients in their places of employment.

10. The certified member who has been approved as a MEPAP trainer must persuade students of the need for continuous education to ensure competent service and professional growth throughout their career. They must ensure students learn that to influence the development of the profession they must make continuous efforts to improve their own professional practices.

11. The certified member who has been approved as a MEPAP trainer must make students aware of their ethical responsibilities and of the standards of the profession.

12. The certified member who has been approved as a MEPAP trainer must make students aware of their responsibilities to advocate for their residents/clients in the local, state and national arenas.

H. Consulting Standards

The certified member who provides consulting services to define and solve work-related problems or potential work-related problems with an activity professional or their work system has unique ethical responsibilities that go beyond that of the certified member who does not consult with other activity professionals.

1. The certified member, acting as a consultant, must have a high degree of self-awareness of their own values, knowledge, skills, limitations, and personal needs when entering a relationship that involves human and/or organizational change.

2. The focus of the consulting relationship must be on issues to be resolved and not on the person or persons presenting the issues.

3. The certified member in the consulting relationship and the person(s) consulted with must agree upon the problem definition, ensuring goals and the predicted results of interventions.

4. The certified member in the consulting relationship must encourage growth, coping, and self direction in the person consulted with. The certified member-consultant must not become a decision maker for the person consulted with or create a dependency on the consultant.

I. Resolving Ethical Issues

Certified Professionals are responsible for understanding and following this Code of Ethics. Lack of knowledge or misunderstanding of an ethical responsibility is not a defense against a charge of unethical conduct.

If it is found that a Certified Activity Professional is not adhering to the NCCAP Code of Ethics—through written reports, through "doctored" documents, etc.—the certification will be rescinded or denied. The mechanism for review in such instances will be through the Certification Review Committee, the Executive Director, and finally the Appeals Committee.

Adopted by the NCCAP Board of Directors—September 22, 1990.

Revised by the NCCAP Board of Directors—April 29, 2003.

Other Books by Venture Publishing, Inc.

Facilitation Techniques in Therapeutic Recreation
    by John Dattilo
File o' Fun: A Recreation Planner for Games & Activities, Third Edition
    by Jane Harris Ericson and Diane Ruth Albright
Functional Interdisciplinary-Transdisciplinary Therapy (FITT) Manual
    by Deborah M. Schott, Judy D. Burdett, Beverly J. Cook, Karren S. Ford, and Kathleen M. Orban
The Game and Play Leader's Handbook: Facilitating Fun and Positive Interaction, Revised Edition
    by Bill Michaelis and John M. O'Connell
The Game Finder—A Leader's Guide to Great Activities
    by Annette C. Moore
Getting People Involved in Life and Activities: Effective Motivating Techniques
    by Jeanne Adams
Group Games & Activity Leadership
    by Kenneth J. Bulik
Growing With Care: Using Greenery, Gardens, and Nature With Aging and Special Populations
    by Betsy Kreidler
Hands On! Children's Activities for Fairs, Festivals, and Special Events
    by Karen L. Ramey
Health Promotion for Mind, Body, and Spirit
    by Suzanne Fitzsimmons and Linda L. Buettner
In Search of the Starfish: Creating a Caring Environment
    by Mary Hart, Karen Primm, and Kathy Cranisky
Inclusion: Including People With Disabilities in Parks and Recreation Opportunities
    by Lynn Anderson and Carla Brown Kress
Inclusive Leisure Services: Responding to the Rights of People with Disabilities, Second Edition
    by John Dattilo
Innovations: A Recreation Therapy Approach to Restorative Programs
    by Dawn R. De Vries and Julie M. Lake
Internships in Recreation and Leisure Services: A Practical Guide for Students, Fourth Edition
    by Edward E. Seagle, Jr. and Ralph W. Smith
Interpretation of Cultural and Natural Resources, Second Edition
    by Douglas M. Knudson, Ted T. Cable, and Larry Beck
Intervention Activities for At-Risk Youth
    by Norma J. Stumbo
Introduction to Outdoor Recreation: Providing and Managing Resource Based Opportunities
    by Roger L. Moore and B.L. Driver

Introduction to Recreation and Leisure Services, Eighth Edition
    by Karla A. Henderson, M. Deborah Bialeschki, John L. Hemingway, Jan S. Hodges, Beth D. Kivel, and
    H. Douglas Sessoms
Introduction to Therapeutic Recreation: U.S. and Canadian Perspectives
    by Kenneth Mobily and Lisa Ostiguy
Introduction to Writing Goals and Objectives: A Manual for Recreation Therapy Students and Entry-Level Professionals
    by Suzanne Melcher
Leadership and Administration of Outdoor Pursuits, Third Edition
    by James Blanchard, Michael Strong, and Phyllis Ford
Leadership in Leisure Services: Making a Difference, Third Edition
    by Debra J. Jordan
Leisure and Leisure Services in the 21st Century: Toward Mid Century
    by Geoffrey Godbey
The Leisure Diagnostic Battery Computer Software (CD)
    by Peter A. Witt, Gary Ellis, and Mark A. Widmer
Leisure Education I: A Manual of Activities and Resources, Second Edition
    by Norma J. Stumbo
Leisure Education II: More Activities and Resources, Second Edition
    by Norma J. Stumbo
Leisure Education III: More Goal-Oriented Activities
    by Norma J. Stumbo

Leisure Education IV: Activities for Individuals with Substance Addictions
by Norma J. Stumbo
Leisure Education Program Planning: A Systematic Approach, Third Edition
by John Dattilo
Leisure for Canadians
edited by Ron McCarville and Kelly MacKay
Leisure Education Specific Programs
by John Dattilo
Leisure Studies: Prospects for the Twenty-First Century
edited by Edgar L. Jackson and Thomas L. Burton
Leisure in Your Life: New Perspectives
by Geoffrey Godbey
The Lifestory Re-Play Circle: A Manual of Activities and Techniques
by Rosilyn Wilder
Making a Difference in Academic Life: A Handbook for Park, Recreation, and Tourism Educators and Graduate Students
edited by Dan Dustin and Tom Goodale
Managing to Optimize the Beneficial Outcomes of Leisure
edited by B. L. Driver
Marketing in Leisure and Tourism: Reaching New Heights
by Patricia Click Janes
The Melody Lingers On: A Complete Music Activities Program for Older Adults
by Bill Messenger
Models of Change in Municipal Parks and Recreation: A Book of Innovative Case Studies
edited by Mark E. Havitz
More Than a Game: A New Focus on Senior Activity Services
by Brenda Corbett
The Multiple Values of Wilderness
by H. Ken Cordell, John C. Bergstrom, and J.M. Bowker
Nature and the Human Spirit: Toward an Expanded Land Management Ethic
edited by B.L. Driver, Daniel Dustin, Tony Baltic, Gary Elsner, and George Peterson
The Organizational Basis of Leisure Participation: A Motivational Exploration
by Robert A. Stebbins
Outdoor Recreation for 21st Century America
by H. Ken Cordell
Outdoor Recreation Management: Theory and Application, Third Edition
by Alan Jubenville and Ben Twight
Parks for Life: Moving the Goal Posts, Changing the Rules, and Expanding the Field
by Will LaPage
The Pivotal Role of Leisure Education: Finding Personal Fulfillment in This Century
edited by Elie Cohen-Gewerc and Robert A. Stebbins
Planning and Organizing Group Activities in Social Recreation
by John V. Valentine
Planning Areas and Facilities for Sport and Recreation: Predesign Process, Principles, and Strategies
by Jack A. Harper
Planning Parks for People, Second Edition
by John Hultsman, Richard L. Cottrell, and Wendy Z. Hultsman
The Process of Recreation Programming Theory and Technique, Third Edition
by Patricia Farrell and Herberta M. Lundegren
Programming for Parks, Recreation, and Leisure Services: A Servant Leadership Approach, Third Edition
by Donald G. DeGraaf, Debra J. Jordan, and Kathy H. DeGraaf
Protocols for Recreation Therapy Programs
edited by Jill Kelland, along with the Recreation Therapy Staff at Alberta Hospital Edmonton
Puttin' on the Skits: Plays for Adults in Managed Care
by Jean Vetter
Quality Management: Applications for Therapeutic Recreation
edited by Bob Riley
Recreation and Leisure: Issues in an Era of Change, Third Edition
edited by Thomas Goodale and Peter A. Witt

Recreation and Youth Development
    by Peter A. Witt and Linda L. Caldwell
Recreation Economic Decisions: Comparing Benefits and Costs, Second Edition
    by John B. Loomis and Richard G. Walsh
Recreation for Older Adults: Individual and Group Activities
    by Judith A. Elliott and Jerold E. Elliott
Recreation Program Planning Manual for Older Adults
    by Karen Kindrachuk
Recreation Programming and Activities for Older Adults
    by Jerold E. Elliott and Judith A. Sorg-Elliott
Reference Manual for Writing Rehabilitation Therapy Treatment Plans
    by Penny Hogberg and Mary Johnson
Research in Therapeutic Recreation: Concepts and Methods
    edited by Marjorie J. Malkin and Christine Z. Howe
Service Living: Building Community through Public Parks and Recreation
    by Doug Wellman, Dan Dustin, Karla Henderson, and Roger Moore
Simple Expressions: Creative and Therapeutic Arts for the Elderly in Long-Term Care Facilities
    by Vicki Parsons
A Social History of Leisure Since 1600
    by Gary Cross
A Social Psychology of Leisure
    by Roger C. Mannell and Douglas A. Kleiber
Special Events and Festivals: How to Organize, Plan, and Implement
    by Angie Prosser and Ashli Rutledge
Stretch Your Mind and Body: Tai Chi as an Adaptive Activity
    by Duane A. Crider and William R. Klinger
Survey Research and Analysis: Applications in Parks, Recreation, and Human Dimensions
    by Jerry Vaske
Taking the Initiative: Activities to Enhance Effectiveness and Promote Fun
    by J. P. Witman
Therapeutic Activity Intervention with the Elderly: Foundations and Practices
    by Barbara A. Hawkins, Marti E. May, and Nancy Brattain Rogers
Therapeutic Recreation and the Nature of Disabilities
    by Kenneth E. Mobily and Richard D. MacNeil
Therapeutic Recreation: Cases and Exercises, Second Edition
    by Barbara C. Wilhite and M. Jean Keller
Therapeutic Recreation in Health Promotion and Rehabilitation
    by John Shank and Catherine Coyle
Therapeutic Recreation in the Nursing Home
    by Linda Buettner and Shelley L. Martin
Therapeutic Recreation Programming: Theory and Practice
    by Charles Sylvester, Judith E. Voelkl, and Gary D. Ellis
Therapeutic Recreation Protocol for Treatment of Substance Addictions
    by Rozanne W. Faulkner
The Therapeutic Recreation Stress Management Primer
    by Cynthia Mascott
The Therapeutic Value of Creative Writing
    by Paul M. Spicer
Traditions: Improving Quality of Life in Caregiving
    by Janelle Sellick
Trivia by the Dozen: Encouraging Interaction and Reminiscence in Managed Care
    by Jean Vetter